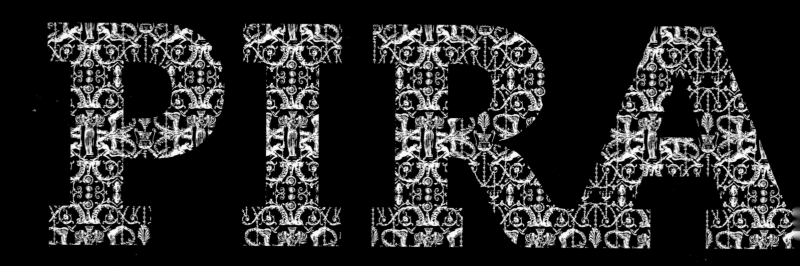

Smithsonian
Cooper-Hewitt, National Design Museum
NEW YORK

EDITED BY

SARAH E. LAWRENCE

WITH

JOHN WILTON-ELY

PETER EISENMAN

ALVAR GONZÁLEZ-PALACIOS

MICHAEL GRAVES

ALICE JARRARD

PETER N. MILLER

RONALD DE LEEUW

DAVID ROSAND

BENT SØRENSEN

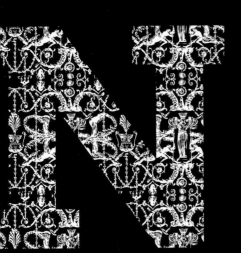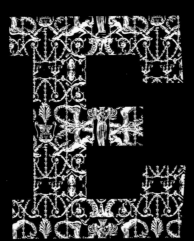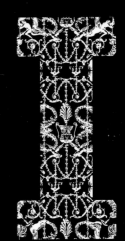

...NESI

AS DESIGNER

The *Piranesi as Designer* exhibition is mounted in association with the Rijksmuseum, Amsterdam, and the Teylers Museum, Haarlem, the Netherlands.

CONTENTS

07 FOREWORD
PAUL WARWICK THOMPSON
DIRECTOR, COOPER-HEWITT,
NATIONAL DESIGN MUSEUM

**11 DESIGN THROUGH FANTASY:
PIRANESI AS DESIGNER**
JOHN WILTON-ELY

**93 PIRANESI'S AESTHETIC
OF ECLECTICISM**
SARAH E. LAWRENCE

**123 PIRANESI AND THE
ANTIQUARIAN IMAGINATION**
PETER N. MILLER

**139 COL SPORCAR SI TROVA:
PIRANESI DRAWS**
DAVID ROSAND

171 THE PROJECTS FOR THE
RECONSTRUCTION OF THE
LATERAN BASILICA IN ROME
BENT SØRENSEN

203 PERSPECTIVES ON
PIRANESI AND THEATER
ALICE JARRARD

221 PIRANESI AND FURNISHINGS
ALVAR GONZÁLEZ-PALACIOS

241 DEALER AND CICERONE:
PIRANESI'S INFLUENCE
ON THE NORTH
RONALD DE LEEUW
DIRECTOR, RIJKSMUSEUM,
AMSTERDAM, THE NETHERLANDS

269 DRAWING FROM PIRANESI
MICHAEL GRAVES

301 PIRANESI AND THE CITY
PETER EISENMAN

306 SELECTED EXHIBITION OBJECTS

318 ARCHITECTS' STATEMENTS
MICHAEL GRAVES, ROBERT VENTURI
AND DENISE SCOTT BROWN,
ROBERT A. M. STERN, DANIEL LIBESKIND,
PETER EISENMAN

328 TIMELINE

331 LIST OF ILLUSTRATIONS

340 NOTES

351 SELECTED BIBLIOGRAPHY

354 SELECTED INDEX

358 ACKNOWLEDGMENTS

359 PHOTOGRAPHIC CREDITS

PAUL WARWICK THOMPSON

FOREWORD

Pietro Labruzzi
PORTRAIT OF GIOVANNI
BATTISTA PIRANESI, 1779
Oil on canvas

PIRANESI AS DESIGNER IS THE FIRST MUSEUM EXHIBITION TO PRESENT PIRANESI'S FULL RANGE AND INFLUENCE AS A *DESIGNER*, BY MEANS OF ETCHINGS, ORIGINAL DRAWINGS, AND AN IMPRESSIVE SELECTION OF OBJECTS. FOR WELL OVER A CENTURY, PIRANESI STUDIES HAVE BEEN LARGELY dominated by the artist's undoubted reputation as a major graphic artist. To a wide audience, as much as to the scholarly world, he is still best known for his etched views of Rome and its antiquities, as well as for the highly important suite of "Imaginary Prisons"—the *Carceri d'invenzione.* Yet Piranesi, who trained as an architect, consciously set out from his earliest years to reform architecture and design by means of his graphic art, polemical writings, and completed projects. The impact he had on several generations of leading architects and designers in Neoclassicism was profound. His particular influence continued in a variety of ways throughout the nineteenth century, involving both stage design as well as work by the more idiosyncratic architects of the classical tradition, and reemerged in twentieth-century film-set design. Most significant, Piranesi's ideas have surfaced in the work of leading architects such as the Postmodernists Michael Graves, Robert A. M. Stern, and Robert Venturi and Denise Scott Brown, as well as in the Deconstructivist work of Peter Eisenman and Daniel Libeskind, whose videotaped interviews and own architectural projects are included at the end of the exhibition.

One of the most exciting aspects of realizing this exhibition has been the enthusiasm it has generated among so many of the most significant architect-designers working today, who cite Piranesi as a great source of inspiration in their work. A self-fashioned visionary of design reform, Piranesi promoted the creative recombination of Etruscan, Egyptian, Greek, and Roman ornamental vocabulary as the underlying principle of modern design. His writings and images, through which he developed these ideas, have had profound resonance for contemporary architects and designers. When we see styles collide in unexpected ways in the buildings of Michael Graves and Robert Venturi and Denise Scott Brown, surprising juxtapositions that prompt us to respond to familiar forms in new ways, we can appreciate the evident repercussions of Piranesi's innovation of thought and design. Robert A. M. Stern's adaptation of historic style to a contemporary context is undertaken in the very spirit of Piranesi's transformation of the classical past into a modern idiom. The fragmentation of rational space and the dialectic of solid and void essential to the works of Peter Eisenman and Daniel Libeskind unavoidably conjure the emotional intensity of the confined, menacing world of Piranesi's *Carceri*. This ongoing dialogue between Piranesi and these twenty-first-century architects eloquently conveys the impact of historic design on the present. It is this sense of a design continuum which most fascinates us at Cooper-Hewitt.

The core of this exhibition has been drawn from the riches of the Smithsonian Institution and from New York City public collections, most notably from the Cooper-Hewitt, Morgan and Avery Libraries. We are extremely fortunate to have in New York the largest concentration of Piranesi's original designs for architecture and the decorative arts in the world. Featured alongside these drawings is an unprecedented display of objects gathered from prestigious collections around the world, especially the magnificent mantelpiece and pier table from the Rijksmuseum in Amsterdam. Our collaboration with the Rijksmuseum has greatly enhanced our conception and realization of this exhibition and facilitated its continuation across the Atlantic at the Teylers Museum in Haarlem, the Netherlands. Rijksmuseum Director Ronald de Leeuw's passionate interest in and vast knowledge of Piranesi have been an unexpected benefit of our joint involvement, and the Board of Trustees at Cooper-Hewitt and I thank him for the alacrity with which he agreed to collaborate with us on this project.

We also had in our midst the curatorial team for this project, Professor Sarah E. Lawrence, Director of the Graduate Program in the History of Decorative Arts and Design, housed in Cooper-Hewitt and offered jointly with Parsons The New School for Design. She first began work on this exhibition upon her arrival in 2001 as part of her research on the history and theory of ornament. John Wilton-Ely, undoubtedly the preeminent scholar on Piranesi, has been on the faculty of the graduate program for many years, and was a natural partner in the endeavor. His longstanding commitment to the study of Piranesi has proved invaluable in elucidating the complex and varied material brought together here. Floramae McCarron-Cates, Associate Curator in the Department of Drawings, Prints, and Graphic Design, brings to bear her expertise and has contributed significantly to the formulation of the exhibition.

The authors in *Piranesi as Designer* were invited intentionally because they are scholars who normally do not work on Piranesi, but who are illuminating new ground by turning their searchlights on him. To this powerful team have been joined some of the most interesting contemporary architects, who have revered Piranesi for their whole careers. Their contributions not only make the catalogue a book of lasting interest, but will also captivate those interested in contemporary design.

Thanks are also due to Jocelyn Groom, Head of Exhibitions; Chul R. Kim, Head of Publications; Steven Langehough, Registrar; exhibition designers Leven Betts Studio; and our graphic designers Tsang Seymour Design.

Lastly, the *Piranesi as Designer* exhibition would not have been possible without the generosity of The Polonsky Foundation, the Arthur Ross Foundation, Elise Jaffe + Jeffrey Brown, The Italian Cultural Institute, and Mr. and Mrs. Frederic A. Sharf. Additional support has been provided by Furthermore: a program of the J. M. Kaplan Fund, The Felicia Fund, and The Cowles Charitable Trust. This publication has benefited from the assistance of The Andrew W. Mellon Foundation. We are grateful to them all.

JOHN WILTON-ELY

DESIGN THROUGH FANTASY
PIRANESI AS DESIGNER

DETAIL
DESIGN FOR A CHIMNEYPIECE
AND CHAIR, n.d.
Pen and brown ink over black
chalk on off-white laid paper

PIRANESI'S CHOSEN PROFESSION AS AN ARCHITECT WAS A CONSTANT AND DOMINATING FACTOR THROUGHOUT HIS HIGHLY PRODUCTIVE CAREER OF NEARLY FORTY YEARS—A CAREER THAT INVOLVED THE GRAPHIC ARTS, ARCHAEOLOGY, POLEMICAL DEBATE, INTERIOR DESIGN, DECORATIVE ARTS, and the restoration of classical antiquities. The unique combination of his early Venetian training and his long and passionate association with Rome produced in him a highly original approach to design that was shaped and, ultimately, transformed by the controversy of the Graeco-Roman debate. As a product of the European Enlightenment, he was profoundly influenced by the major reassessment of antiquity under Neoclassicism, which opened up fresh inspiration from the creative diversity of past cultures such as ancient Egypt and Greece, as well as the Etruscans and the Late Roman Empire. However, the resulting awareness of the need to create a radical contemporary style in design was to place him at variance with more conventional practitioners of his time. The experimental freedom that originated from his origins in the world of rococo Venice provided him with the capacity to employ a highly imaginative and idiosyncratic use of the past, involving the exercise of fantasy through the medium of the *capriccio*. This intensely speculative cast of mind placed him in the tradition of the more experimental artists, architects, and designers of the late Renaissance and high Baroque, whose work was largely out of favor during his lifetime. Other

JO. BA... PIRANESI
VENET. ARCHITECTUS

aspects of his work, which involved deeply emotional responses to visual forms, looked forward to the world of Romanticism. The power of his perennial appeal across the centuries to our own era is rooted in the fact that his images and ideas continue to stimulate creative experiment in so many fields of study. That he continues to speak through the potency of his graphic images to not only artists and architects but also writers and, more recently, film directors and even musicians is an exceptional aspect of his legacy. Indeed, his chosen self-portrait of 1750 (etched by his friend Polanzani) (fig. 1)—which portrays him in the guise of a living classical fragment, a Janus figure creatively interpreting the past for the present—remains as true today as it was for his own time.

THE FORMATIVE YEARS: VENICE, 1720–CA. 1745

While Piranesi is best known as an ingenious graphic artist, his origins in the architectural world of Venice laid the foundations for his future achievements.[1] He was born on October 4, 1720, in Mogliano, near Mestre on the Venetian terra firma, and was baptized in Venice the following November. His father, Angelo, although recorded as a *tagliapetra*, or stonemason, appears to have been a master builder. His family originated from Piran in Istria, the source of the fine white limestone of which monumental Venice is constructed. Giambattista was clearly destined for an architectural career from the outset, being apprenticed to his maternal uncle, Matteo Lucchesi, a leading architect and hydraulics engineer in the Magistrato delle Acque.[2] Following disagreements with his uncle, Piranesi left to continue his training in the deeply rooted idiom of Palladian design in Venice under Giovanni Scalfurotto, Lucchesi's senior colleague in the Magistrato. The young architect may have assisted in the final stages of his new master's chief building, the church of SS. Simeone e Giuda on the Grand Canal, constructed between 1718 and 1738. During this time, he may have assisted Scalfurotto's nephew, the radical architect and theorist Tommaso Temanza, whose survey and restoration of the Roman arch and bridge at Rimini in 1735 could have initiated Giambattista's interest in the study of antiquity. A taste for controversy and archaeological inquiry would also have been gained from the Lucchesi circle, with its heated discussions about the Etruscans as the originators of Greek architecture.[3]

Piranesi's outstanding imaginative faculties were developed in a variety of ways, in particular through stage design. By the early eighteenth century, Italian designers, notably members of the prolific Bibiena family, had perfected a science of illusion that exploited linear perspective to create a world of almost limitless possibilities. Inevitably, most imaginative architects from Bernini to Juvarra had resorted to this discipline, which offered a rich experimental field for evolving new ideas and concepts. Venice, with its many opera houses and theaters, provided a particularly sympathetic environment for this activity. It appears that the Valeriani brothers provided Piranesi with formal training in stage design, and the engraver Carlo Zucchi taught him the elaborate systems of perspective composition.[4]

In a very real way, the urban intensity of Venice itself provided a theater of architectural experiences that Piranesi later successfully developed into the topographical view, or *veduta*, an art form perfected by Canaletto during the mid-1720s. Venice, as the leading center of engraving and fine book production, hosted the subsequent development of engraved *vedute* (souvenir prints marketed to the grand tourists).

Among the most potent of these Venetian influences on Piranesi was the combination of the baroque stage set and the topographical view as presented in architectural fantasies, or *capricci*. Those glimpses of a lapsed arcadia, which originated from the antiquarian reveries of Andrea Mantegna and Francesco Colonna, eventually reached their mature expression in Marco Ricci's etched fantasies published in 1730, and developed stylistically from Canaletto's etched imaginary compositions, or *vedute ideate*, in the following decade. The stimulus of the Venetian capriccio, amplified by stories of ancient Rome told to Piranesi by his elder brother Angelo, was to find its full impact in 1740 when he entered the Eternal City as a draughtsman in the retinue of Marco Foscarini, the Venetian ambassador.[5]

THE FORMATIVE YEARS: ROME, 1740–55

Piranesi's arrival in Rome in 1740 inaugurated a critical period in his career. The city, already the thriving center of the Grand Tour, was becoming the intellectual capital of Europe. There he encountered the ferment of new ideas and the radical questioning of the past that characterized the Enlightenment. By the close of the decade, Piranesi's architectural visions, transformation of the *veduta*, and growing involvement in archaeology began to make their impression on the European view of antiquity.[6]

The initial impact of Rome on Piranesi was both exhilarating and frustrating. On the one hand, there was the unlimited visual drama of a city. The huge monuments of antiquity like the Pantheon and Colosseum or great ceremonial spaces such as Piazza di S. Pietro and Piazza Navona created violent contrasts in scale. On the other hand, opportunities for an ambitious young architect were scarce. Rome was nearing the end of a considerable building boom that included such structures as the Spanish Steps, the Lateran façade, and the initial construction of Salvi's Trevi Fountain.[7] Apart from these major works, the general character of contemporary Roman architecture was distinctly uninspiring to someone like Piranesi.

A natural means of livelihood for an architect manqué in Rome was the production of *vedute*—a prosperous souvenir trade that was served by the outstanding view painter Giovanni Paolo Panini and the Sicilian engraver Giuseppe Vasi. Within a short time, Piranesi appears to have entered the latter's studio, where he acquired the rudiments of etching and likely contributed to some of the views in Vasi's compendium *Le Magnificenze di Roma*.[8] However, after considerable disagreements with Vasi, Piranesi soon struck out on his own. Some of his earliest independent plates were produced for guidebooks in collaboration with young French artists studying at the French Academy in Rome; these associations laid the foundations for Piranesi's highly significant relationship with that institution.[9]

Piranesi's main productive energy, however, was increasingly concentrated on devising a variety of architectural fantasies through which his creative visions could be given free expression. Panini's ambitious painted vedute ideate now supplemented the early influence of the Venetian capriccio. Unlike Panini, however, Piranesi was far less interested in the theatrical possibilities of combining familiar monuments in imaginary settings. Instead, the ruins around him inspired his creation of new visions in design. He was aided in this process through a long-established tradition of fanciful reconstructions pioneered by Renaissance mannerist architects like Pirro Ligorio and continued into the eighteenth century by Johann Bernhard Fischer von Erlach (see Lawrence, fig. 2).[10]

In 1743, Piranesi published a selection of his imaginary architectural compositions in the twelve plates of his first independent publication entitled *Prima Parte di Architetture e Prospettive*.[11] It was dedicated to his early patron, the Venetian builder Nicola Giobbe, whose library appears to have provided Piranesi with works by a wide range of graphic pioneers such as Giovanni Castiglione and Salvator Rosa.[12] From his prefatory text it is clear that Piranesi's etched plates of ideal structures and dramatic ruin scenes—such as that of an imperial mausoleum (fig. 2)— were intended to reprove the mediocrity, as he saw it, of the contemporary architectural profession. To any receptive designer or architect, the "speaking ruins," as he expressed it, revealed visions of the creative potential offered by these heroic remnants from antiquity. In this respect the *Prima Parte* was a remarkably prophetic book, since the rest of

Mausoleo antico eretto per le ceneri d'un Imperadore Romano. All'intorno di questo vi sono dè Sepolcri piramidali per altri Imperadori. Vi sono pure dell'Urne dè Famigliari dette anche Olle Sepolcrali in cui si poneuano le loro Ceneri. Ve ne sono pure dell'altre pè Servi, e Liberti. Questo Mausoleo, è attorniato di magnifiche Scale, ai cui piedi si vedono ornamenti Sepolcrali secondo il costume degli antichi Romani. 3.

Piranesi's career, in all its diversity, involved developing the imaginative range provided by the past for the inspiration of his own time.

This experimental activity, represented throughout the 1740s by a wide range of drawings and etchings, as well as a his growing success as a *vedutista* brought Piranesi into the circle of art and architectural students at the French Academy, then the liveliest center of research in Rome. Piranesi's visions began to stimulate the imaginations of the *pensionnaires*, as evident in the festival designs of Louis-Joseph Le Lorrain and the fantasies of Charles Michel-Ange Challe, among others.[13] As these designers subsequently accepted significant professional posts, Piranesi's ideas gradually entered the mainstream of French neoclassical architecture during the 1750s.

At this time, Piranesi went south to Naples, where he was struck by the exciting possibilities resulting from the discoveries at Herculaneum, which were beginning to add fresh dimensions to the knowledge and interpretation of antiquity. Moreover, Camillo Paderni, future director of the excavation museum at Portici, encouraged Piranesi to explore ways of effectively presenting archaeological discoveries in visual terms.[14]

It still remained for Venice to exercise its final impression on Piranesi's imagination. Severe financial problems brought him back to his native city on at least two occasions, around 1744–45, where he encountered the works of its greatest artist, Giambattista Tiepolo.[15] Whether or not Piranesi actually worked in this master's studio as early sources suggest is unclear; however, his style of drawing and the tightly organized mode of his etching underwent a dramatic transformation within a few years. This unprecedented breadth of imagination and fluent technique are reflected in his first activities as a decorative designer, which were recorded at this time. While no trace thus far has been found of the palace interiors he is said to have produced, a unique group of some half a dozen designs in New York's Morgan Library include scintillating rococo studies for wall decoration, furniture, and book design. The finest of these works is the red chalk design for a *bissona*, or ceremonial gondola, in which, as Hylton Thomas observed, "the motifs incorporated into the design are extraordinarily abundant in number and variety, and each echoes or balances another with the exquisite precision and buoyant harmony of a Mozart quartet."[16] (fig. 3)

However, Venice could no longer hold Piranesi with the first impressions of heroic antiquity still fresh in his mind. Around 1745, with promised financial support from the printseller Joseph Wagner, Piranesi returned to Rome, taking with him a fully mature language of expression and a highly charged imagination that would continue to be a

3. DESIGN FOR A "BISSONA"
(FESTIVAL GONDOLA)
Pen and brown ink over black
chalk, on paper; (verso) graphite

source of creative vigor throughout his remaining thirty years. This transformation of Piranesi's style is reflected in the four mysterious plates of the *Grotteschi*.[17] (fig. 4) These arcane compositions, evoking the living inspiration of antiquity amid the process of decay, symbolize the inherent property of rejuvenation that Piranesi found in Roman civilization. They also reflect the recondite literary allusions characteristic of the Academy of the Arcadians in Rome, to which Piranesi had been elected.[18] The fusion of Venice and Rome, however, reached its most striking expression in fourteen plates of Prison interiors, entitled *Invenzioni capric di Carceri*, a complex fusion of the Venetian capriccio and the awesome masonry structures of Roman engineering.

In acts of creative archaeology, Piranesi continued to experiment with new forms of architectural composition in his drawings of the later 1740s, returning obsessively to certain themes of the *Prima Parte*—particularly the monumental forum and the lofty columnar hall (fig. 5). In so doing, he swiftly transformed the architectural fantasy into a means of exploring architectural ideas and, ultimately, a vehicle for communicating those ideas to other designers.[19] In a closely associated evolution of drawing technique, he replaced his early pen and wash studies with a bolder use of mixed media. Rapid chalk sketches were resolved with fluent penwork or boldly hatched with a broad reed pen. By 1750, he reissued most of the *Prima Parte* with additional fantasies of an unprecedented originality in a compendium of his fantasies, the *Opere Varie*. Among these etched plates is a highly complex plan for a massive college: a brilliant synthesis of Baldassare Longhena's Venetian church of S. Maria della Salute with the planning of ancient Roman baths, together with concepts derived from Francesco Borromini, whose works continued to act as a major source of stimulus in his later career. More

4. THE TRIUMPHAL ARCH from
the series GROTTESCHI, 1750
Etching on off-white laid paper

Gio. Batta Piranesi Arch.i inv. ed incis. in Roma

Sala all' uso degli antichi Romani con Colonne, e nicchie ornate di Statue. Evvi nella facciata il luogo oue potean vedersi le Feste. Al piano poi sotto i Piedestalli vi sono dè Sedilli secondo il costume d'allora.

9.

5. HALL IN THE CORINTHIAN
ORDER (SALA ALL'USO
DEGLI ANTICHI ROMANI CON
COLONNE…), plate VI from
PRIMA PORTE DI ARCHITETTURE
E PROSPETTIVE, 1743
Etching on off-white laid paper

arresting still is his *Monumental Roman Harbour*, an extremely adventurous combination of motifs from ancient Roman ornamental vocabulary, which anticipates by a decade his revolutionary eclectic style of the 1760s.[20] The Morgan Library possesses a meticulous drawing for a similar monumental composition which was never engraved (fig. 6).

THE ARCHITECT AS VEDUTISTA

This new breadth of expression also enriched Piranesi's continuing work as a vedutista, in which his radical transformation of the genre through the evolution of exceptional compositional and graphic skills provided a critical influence on all his other activities. Piranesi is universally known today as one of the greatest interpreters of Rome thanks to a lifetime's production of several hundred engraved views of the Eternal City and its surrounding sites and monuments. He would have hardly achieved this stature, however, if he had simply restricted himself to this limited field. The powerful appeal of his images depended on

the unique interaction of his varied activities as an architect and de-signer as well as an archaeologist and polemicist. His vedute, conse-quently, not only reflected the course of his stylistic development, but also provided insights into his changing preoccupations. Moreover, his powerful command of the etching process, achieved through ceaseless experiments in this particular art form, would have a significant impact on generations of architects and designers.

As early as the 1740s, there were already signs in his plates of a new ap-proach toward defining the specific character of architecture while con-veying its dramatic emotional impact on the spectator. At the same time, these early plates also revealed the beginnings of a much freer approach to the medium itself. Piranesi's early plates showed a new preoccupation not only with properties of light, but also with the potential of etching to register an architect's understanding of structure and materials.[21]

Around 1748, he moved from modest plates to the monumental scale of his celebrated series, the *Vedute di Roma*, a formidable sequence of 135 images that appeared individually or in groups over his remaining thirty years of activity. With the larger format these copperplates provided, Piranesi was able to accommodate his rapidly accumulating knowledge and to challenge the painted veduta on its own terms. His intense archaeological researches of the 1750s gradually absorbed the larger part of his creative energies, and his topographical skills were transferred to the illustrations of specialist publications where his pictorial innovations served didactic functions. The veduta, accordingly, became a descriptive aid to the archaeologist as well as a source of inspiration for the designer. It was invested with new powers for portraying sentiment as well as recording fact, as expressed in his plates of Hadrian's villa at Tivoli, where Piranesi was undertaking a significant survey.[22]

By the early 1760s, the veduta was no longer a mere souvenir; it was also a serious scholarly vehicle of communication, often accompanied by extensive captions emphasizing the durability of vast structures like the Pantheon, which was undiminished by the ravages of time and human despoliation. This expression was to continue in the vedute of the late 1770s, including some of his most heroic images as he returned to certain subjects of the *Magnificenza*, such as Piazza Navona and the Colosseum, the latter summed up in a breathtaking aerial view. In the course of thirty-five years, Piranesi had transformed the veduta from a subtle rococo vision of elusive melancholy into an uncompromising statement of the sublime that left an indelible impression on European romantic sensibilities.

THE INSPIRATION OF ARCHAEOLOGY

In Piranesi's lifetime, the Enlightenment, through its concern with the phenomenon of historical change and the social context of antiquities, gave birth to cultural history. The wave of discoveries in the eastern Mediterranean during the middle of the century led to a polarization between the respective claims to originality of Greece and Rome. Archaeology became a live issue in the formation of architectural principles, and the ensuing controversy, for all its polemical distortion of facts, had extremely productive side effects for contemporary design. Despite the expanding range of these new discoveries, archaeological illustrations continued to concentrate on the surface appearance of monuments and on such literary evidence as inscriptions, with a marked indifference to the environment of individual finds and the physical character of the structures containing them. There was a growing need for a new system of images that would reflect the widening concerns of archaeological discovery and communicate them effectively. Since these discoveries closely influenced contemporary architecture, the role of such images was of critical importance beyond the academic field. Although, he produced vedute of the most prominent monuments of the city, Piranesi's architectural training led him toward less familiar material through which his powers of reconstruction could be exercised, especially the large quantity of funerary monuments in and around Rome. While he produced a folio volume on the tomb of the household of Augustus around 1752, it soon became clear that a more ambitious publication was needed; he thus began a four-volume work that would provide a comprehensive survey of the remains of the Eternal City.[23]

When they appeared in 1756, the volumes of *Le Antichità Romane* represented a landmark in the history of classical archaeology, not merely in terms of their illustrative techniques, but also in the application of a fresh and highly original mind to a hitherto restricted field of study—a mind capable of combining a specialized understanding of engineering and architecture with imaginative faculties of the highest order. Besides representing a major advance in the communication of archaeological discoveries, the *Antichità* directed attention in a visually original way to largely neglected aspects of antiquity.[24] Among them were the techniques of Roman building science and aspects of unorthodox decoration and planning that lay outside the conventional canons of the ancient theorist Vitruvius. Piranesi, fully conscious of its unique character, addressed his work to an unusually wide audience, including antiquarians and practicing architects who, inevitably, suffered some abrasive criticism.

Unlike past antiquarian works, the 250 plates of the *Antichità* play a dominant and carefully coordinated role in conveying information through sequences of specialized illustrations. The first volume describes the urban structure of ancient Rome in terms of its walls, defenses, and aqueducts as well as its principal civic and religious monuments. The second and third volumes, which were developed out of the earlier publication, *Camere sepolcrali*, are devoted to funerary architecture, sculpture, and decoration. Apart from the sheer extent of its survival largely underground, this area of Roman achievement provided Piranesi with evidence of ornamental invention and complex forms that he wished to impart to fellow designers (fig. 7). Volume four, which celebrates Roman structural genius in works such as bridges, theaters, and porticoes, stands apart with its tendency to exaggerate feats of engineering and highly ingenious planning.

During the 1750s, Piranesi began to move away from the circle of the French Academy and soon developed contacts with visiting British artists and architects such as William Chambers and Robert Adam, who

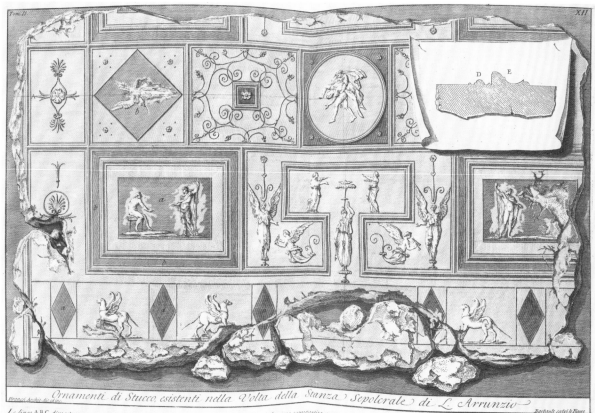

7. ORNEMENTI DI STUCCO,
ESISTENTI NELLA VOLTA
DELLS STANZE SEPOLCRALE
DI L. ARRUNZIO (STUCCO
DECORATIONS ON THE VAULT
OF THE TOMB CHAMBER
OF L. ARRUNTIUS), Plate XII,
Vol. 2, LE ANTICHITÀ ROMANE,
1756–57
Etching on off-white laid paper

hailed from a more pragmatic tradition in design. While Chambers learned striking methods of presentation from Piranesi, his period of training in the French system under Blondel in Paris led him to regard the Venetian's more extreme fantasies with skepticism.[25] (fig. 8) Robert Adam, however, swiftly recognized their stimulating value, and Piranesi in return found in the Scottish architect a kindred spirit with the same understanding of the revitalizing uses of antiquity in the creation of novel systems of design, aided by the former *pensionnaire*, Charles-Louis Clérisseau.[26] These experiences, augmented by the catalytic effects of Piranesi's visionary drawings on the Scottish architect's imagination, ultimately proved to be the greatest single influence on the evolution of the Adam style.

CONTROVERSY IN DESIGN

Polemics were to occupy an increasing amount of Piranesi's energies during the 1760s, since his position as the leading authority on Rome placed him in the front line of a growing controversy about artistic originality. Despite its somewhat tedious and involved nature, however, this archaeological debate bore extremely fruitful results for Piranesi's creative development, as he created through its heated exchanges a novel

and highly influential system of contemporary design. An inclination for controversy was endemic to Piranesi's character. His irascible and volatile temperament was closely bound to his sturdy independence as a Venetian, as well as his developed self-reliance as an autodidact in scholarly matters. His last thirty years were punctuated by conflicts and quarrels that gave rise to some of his most original images, either by way of satire or self-justification. Images rather than words were his stronger weapons, and he was ready to go to extraordinary lengths to defend himself with their aid.

His first polemical work was a vigorously admonitory publication addressed to the young Irishman Lord Charlemont, who had not only failed to honor his promised financial support for the costly plates of the *Antichità* but, in Piranesi's opinion, also lacked respect for the importance of the artist and his achievements.[27] In the abrasive pamphlet, the *Lettere di Giustificazione...a Milord Charlemont*, issued in 1757—which de-

fended his decision to delete the dedication of the *Antichità* to this unworthy patron from the title page and related plates—his ingenious use of defamatory and satirical images demonstrated his capacity to conduct an argument in visual terms. The intensity with which Piranesi threw himself into the vendetta against Lord Charlemont and his agents indicates the extent to which he had begun to identify himself with the material of his archaeological studies by the late 1750s. An attack on Rome became, in effect, a personal affront to the artistic genius of the Romans reborn in himself, and certain aspects of the *Antichità* revealed his early responses to the developing Graeco-Roman debate.

The new interest in Greece, which emerged during the middle of the century, grew out of current architectural theory. It rapidly became a live issue rather than a narrow academic quarrel, with claims of artistic originality and aesthetic ideals as the subjects of fierce dispute.[28] One of the most influential texts in defending the superiority of Greek over Roman design was the *Essai sur L'Architecture*, published in Paris by the Jesuit Marc-Antoine Laugier in 1753.[29] Appealing to the principles of nature, as exemplified by the mythical "rustic hut" of primitive mankind first mentioned by Vitruvius, he considered that the Romans had corrupted this functional ideal found in Greek architecture. Moreover, it had been further debased by the architects of the Renaissance and in more recent times by Italian designers like Borromini. These rationalist criteria of function and formal simplicity struck at the baroque principles of creative fantasy and unlimited invention at the heart of Piranesi's beliefs. As the decade advanced, the Hellenists' claims encroached increasingly on Piranesi's world, and, in 1755, Winckelmann, the greatest protagonist of all, arrived in Rome to serve as librarian to the major patron Cardinal Alessandro Albani, shortly after publishing his seminal essay *Gedanken über die Nachahmung der griechischen Werke (On the imitation of Greek works)*.[30] This book defended Greece with a literary expression as emotionally powerful as Piranesi's visual rhetoric in the *Vedute* and the *Antichità*. Shortly after, the first specific evidence in support of Greek claims to architectural superiority appeared in 1758 with the plates of the Parthenon and buildings of the Athenian acropolis found in Julien-David Le Roy's *Les Ruines des Plus Beaux Monuments de la Grèce*.[31] Meanwhile, Piranesi began to prepare his first salvo in the engagement, which was issued in 1761 with a folio volume grandiloquently entitled *Della Magnificenza ed Architettura de' Romani*.[32]

In reply to the rationalism of the French, Piranesi based his defense on the Etruscans as the sole founders of Roman civilization, using the extensive research by scholars like Antonio Gori and Mario Guarnacci.[33]

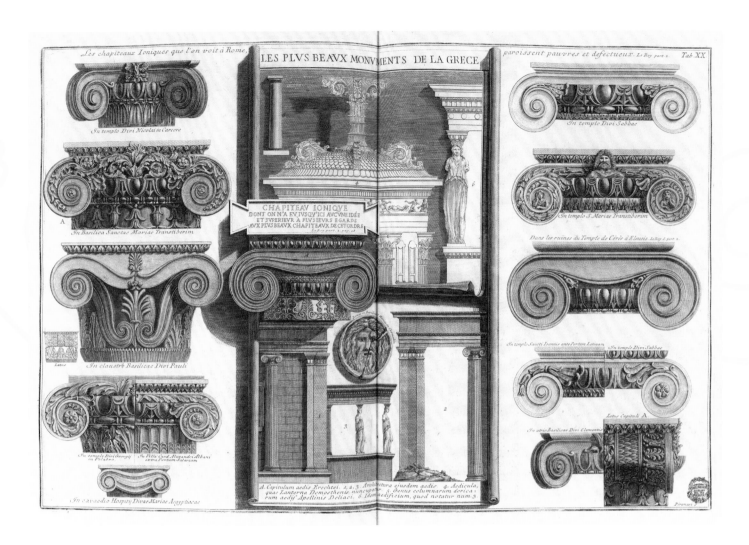

He praised the severity of Etruscan architecture, continued in the utilitarian engineering of Rome, which he contrasted with the "vain prettiness of the Greeks." He also challenged the logic of Laugier's thesis on the evolution of wood to stone architecture and, by means of a substantial series of particularly striking plates, emphasized the greater richness and variety in fragments of Roman ornament. In some of these plates, Le Roy's austere line engravings of Attic detail were pinned illusionistically onto ambitious folding plates of Roman fragments, often accompanied by satirical comments (fig. 9).

Della Magnificenza was circulated widely, and, through the active patronage of the new Venetian pope, Clement XIII, to whom the work was dedicated, Piranesi developed his arguments in a series of impressive archaeological folios during the early 1760s.[34] Most significant of all was *Il Campo Marzio dell'Antica Roma*, published in 1762 and dedicated to Robert Adam, with whom Piranesi had undertaken certain physical researches during its preparation.[35] (fig. 10) Despite its introduction of some thirty-three pages of learned text, the sequence of plates provided the main argument. Supported by a series of vedute, which strikingly isolated the original structures from their medieval surroundings, a group of maps traced the evolution of the site from primitive beginnings to a densely monumental townscape under Augustus and his successors. The virtual fantasy of the master plan, or *Ichnographia*, represented the climax (fig. 11). This tour de force was not only an apotheosis of the Roman genius for planning, but also a vigorous exhortation and encouragement to Adam and his fellow designers. In addition, it offered a polemical rejoinder to Winckelmann, who equated the richness and complexity of Roman design with a decline in taste.

By the mid-1760s, Piranesi abandoned his exclusive attitude toward non-Roman styles and cultures, including Greece, and through the experimental medium of the capriccio, had begun to combine a variety of foreign sources with Roman ones. The highly enlightened patronage of Clement XIII and leading members of the Rezzonico family gave Piranesi the opportunity and financial backing to try out his ideas on two architectural commissions: a projected tribune for S. Giovanni in Laterano, and the reconstruction of the modest church of S. Maria del Priorato. During the same years, he was also applying these ideas to suites of furniture, schemes of interior decoration, and elaborate chimneypieces. By the time the critic J. P. Mariette initiated a new phase in the controversy in 1764, through a published letter criticizing the arguments of *Della Magnificenza*, Piranesi had moved on to an inclusive theory advocating eclectic design.

When Piranesi eventually replied to his French adversary with the three-part publication *Osservazioni sopra la lettre de M. Mariette* in 1765, his intellectual position was fully adjusted to his artistic inclinations and development.[36] The principal part of this work, *Parere su l'architettura*, is a debate between two architects: Protopiro, a rigorist designer following the ideals of Laugier and Winckelmann, and Didascolo, who supported Piranesi's beliefs in the creative license of the designer. Instead of referring to specific monuments from antiquity, Piranesi illustrated his thesis with a series of highly original, if bizarre, compositions, in which the last traces of conventional classical composition disappeared (see Lawrence, fig. 6).[37] Bold juxtapositions of Greek, Egyptian, Etruscan, and Roman motifs were used with deliberate exaggeration for polemical effects.

By the close of the decade, Piranesi's activities as a designer absorbed his polemical ardor, and his final statement in the controversy took the form of an illustrated demonstration of his new aesthetic in action in the *Diverse maniere d'adornare i cammini* of 1769 (see Lawrence, fig. 12). The prefatory essay—which introduced a collection of his own designs for chimneypieces, furniture, and portions of complete interior schemes—

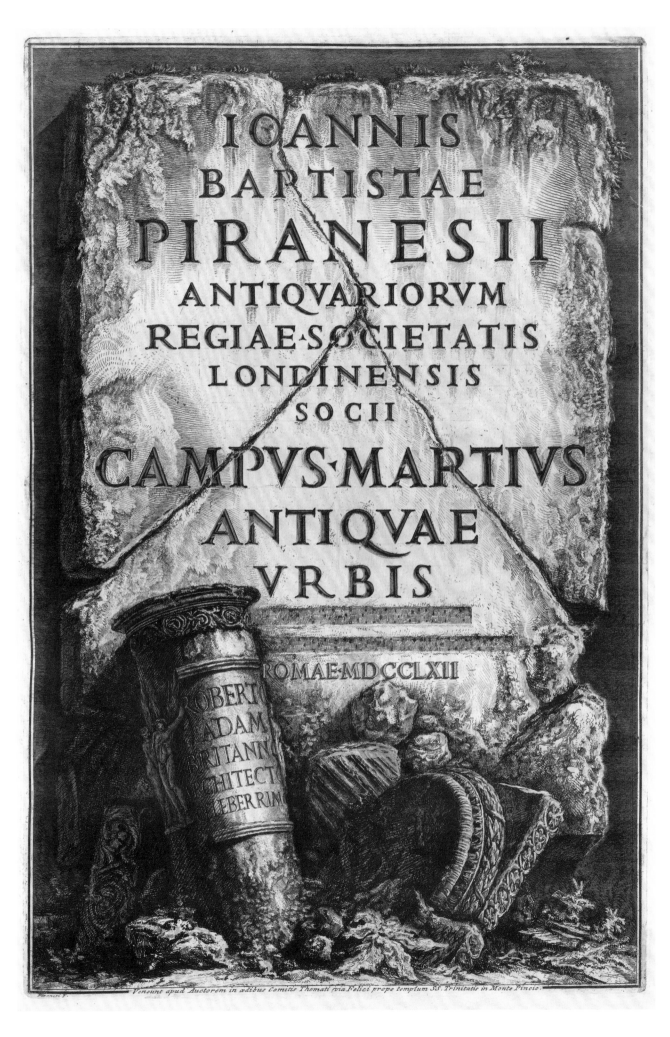

IOANNIS
BARTISTAE
PIRANESII
ANTIQVARIORVM
REGIAE·SOCIETATIS
LONDINENSIS
SOCII
CAMPVS·MARTIVS
ANTIQVAE
VRBIS

ROMAE·MDCCLXII

ROBERTO
ADAM
BRITANN
CHITECT
EBERRIM

Piranesi F.   Veneunt apud Auctorem in ædibus Comitis Thomati via Felici prope templum SS. Trinitatis in Monte Pincio.

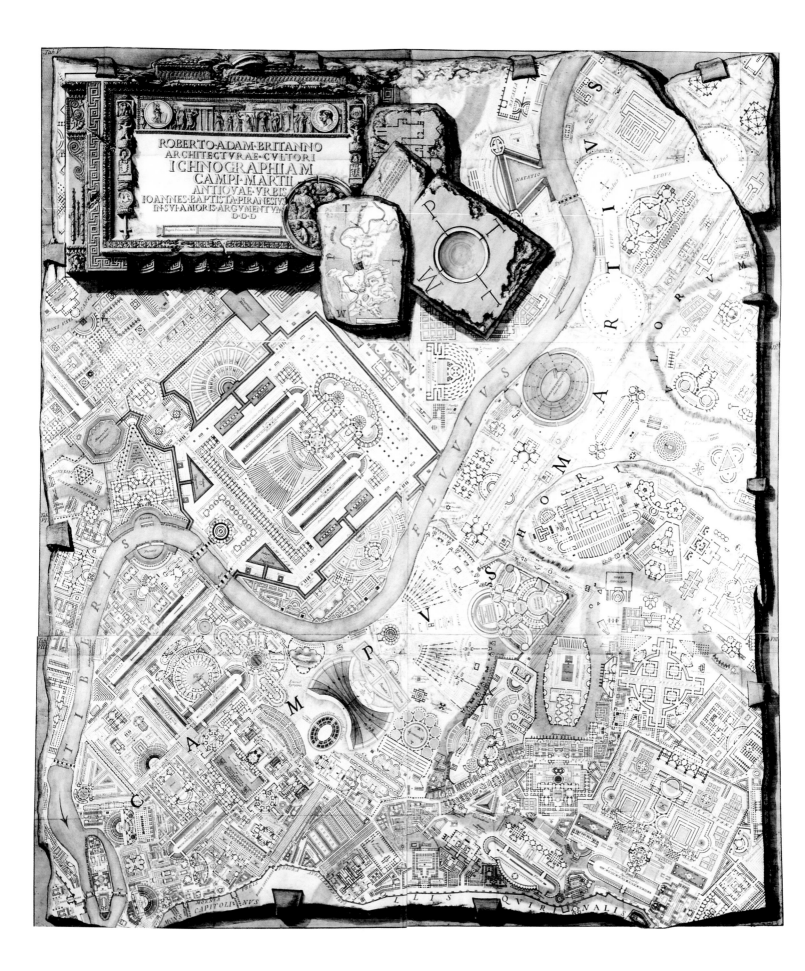

contained the most considered defense of his innovatory system of design, born through controversy.[38] Although the Etruscans' inventive genius was summarized in a chart as well as in the text, the narrow issues of scholarly debate were abandoned for an impassioned defense of imaginative eclecticism. Nature, to whom Laugier had appealed in the name of functional simplicity, was also shown to be the perpetual source for the complex forms of the past and present. The lack of imagination by contemporary architects, which Piranesi had lamented in the preface of the *Prima Parte* nearly thirty years earlier, was answered with a new and challenging philosophy of design.

THE *CARCERI*

In the heat of controversy, Piranesi reissued a powerfully refashioned version of the remarkable set of plates produced in Rome after the last of his brief returns to Venice. Next to the *Vedute di Roma*, the *Carceri* are his most celebrated works, exerting an influence and a fascination disproportionate to their modest position within the artist's immense œuvre of more than one thousand plates.[39] The first appearance of the *Carceri*, around 1745, and their reissue in a more dramatic form in 1761 occurred during two highly significant periods in Piranesi's intellectual and creative development as a designer. This series reinforced the central role of the architectural fantasy in his creative process.

The initial version of fourteen plates was an intensely private work of limited production that clearly proved too advanced in expression for contemporary tastes. Piranesi's name, in fact, does not appear on the frontispiece or on many of the plates. Moreover, their low price compared with the *Vedute* in the 1750s suggests the artist's diffidence in offering them to the public. As their original title indicates, the *Invenzioni capric di carceri* were essentially *scherzi* in the manner of Tiepolo's etched fantasies, swiftly sketched onto the copperplate with a certain elusive imagery similar to that of the four *Grotteschi*. These works, part Venetian, part Roman, represented an experimental field of composition involving brilliant improvisations on a limited set of themes. Careful study of surviving drawings reveals a highly controlled imagination at work (fig. 12). Piranesi exploits the mechanics of baroque illusionism through perspective and lighting to explore new dimensions of architectural expression. Bearing in mind Piranesi's recent criticism in the *Prima parte* of the lack of vision in modern Rome, these compositions similarly represented an act of defiance to the mediocre patrons and architects whom Piranesi deemed unworthy of their inheritance.

12. PREPARATORY DRAWING
for plate IV of the series
CARCERI D'INVENZIONE,
ca. 1749
Pen and light brown ink, brush
and brown wash over black
chalk on off-white laid paper

Significantly, the origins of these visions were rooted in Piranesi's training in stage design, where the prison scene was a common theme, as seen in the engraved compositions of precursors such as Ferdinando Bibiena, Marco Ricci, and Filippo Juvarra. It provided Piranesi with a useful stripped system of stone construction that allowed the maximum freedom in manipulating plain surfaces and voids. The *Carceri* compositions evolved from two basic formulas: the grandiose staircase hall, and the vista framed in the arch of a monumental bridge. In fact, a preparatory drawing in the British Museum for an ornamental interior, related to *Carceri* plate XI, provides the missing link between the palatial and penal fantasy.

The potent appeal of the early *Carceri* comes from the manner in which the eye of the spectator is forced on a restless journey through the plate (fig. 13). This is achieved through a series of conflicting illusions and pictorial techniques involving a mesh of interweaving lines and contradictory hatching. Expectations are aroused then abruptly thwarted by visual paradoxes and teasing spatial ambiguities. Largely contributing to this mood are muffled figures, huddled together in groups or disturbingly isolated. In this situation, each plate represents a powerful architectural experience in itself, whereby the entire Renaissance system of pictorial space is questioned with a degree of daring almost unparalleled before Cubism.[40]

Early in the 1760s, on the threshold of major commissions for architecture, Piranesi reissued the fourteen plates, with two additional compositions under his name, as the *Carceri d'invenzone*, which can be understood to mean *Imaginary Prisons* or, more significantly, *Prisons of the*

Imagination. These arresting images not only reflected his new preoccupations, but were also meant to stimulate the imagination of a new generation. The fresh version contained a major degree of intensive reworking with heightened tonal contrasts and more specific definition of form (fig. 14). The addition of further staircases, galleries, and roof structures receding into infinity amplified the structural immensity and spatial ambiguity. The inclusion of chains, gallows, and instruments of torture emphasized the macabre and sinister. The original collection of *scherzi* became a sequence of melodramas. Two new plates were added, their subject matter reflecting the architect's obsession with the Graeco-Roman debate as well as his efforts to formulate an innovatory mode of architectural composition, later justified in the *Parere su l'Architettura.* Research into the imagery of these two plates and the ex-

14. THE DRAWBRIDGE, plate VII
from CARCERI D'INVENZIONE
(late state), ca. 1760s
Etching on off-white laid paper

tensively refashioned Plate XVI suggests that these three works in particular conform to a specific iconographic program. Among Piranesi's
principal arguments against the Greek side of the controversy were the
superior nature of the *Lex Romana,* or Roman system of justice, which
was founded on civic virtue and equity in primitive times, and the way
in which moral law was expressed through Roman architecture.[41]

The new imagery of the *Carceri* spoke to a generation educated by the
philosopher Edmund Burke's influential aesthetic treatise of 1757, *An
Enquiry into the Sublime and the Beautiful,* in which themes of obscurity, pri-
vation, vastness, infinity, and magnitude in building were related to the
fear aroused by the infinite and by "greatness of dimension."[42] Quite
apart from the symbolism of penal retribution reflected in contemporary prison designs, the revised *Carceri* impressed themselves on the romantic imaginations of artists such as Turner. By the opening of the
new century, the fortune of these seminal images came full circle when
they re-entered the world of stage design, as shown in Simeone Quaglio's
set for *Fidelio* (1820), in which the heroic vision of Piranesi found its true
expression through the music of Beethoven.[43]

ARCHITECTURE: THE TRIBUNE OF SAN GIOVANNI IN LATERANO

The early 1760s represented a climactic point in Piranesi's career as a designer. Worldly success had come swiftly to him as the leading topographical engraver in Rome, with a prosperous new printmaking business
established at Palazzo Tomati in Via Sistina, close to the English quarter
of the Piazza di Spagna. His extensive contributions to Roman archaeology had earned him international recognition with an honorary fellowship from the Society of Antiquaries of London in 1757, followed by his
election to the Accademia di San Luca of Rome in 1761. However, his greatest wish to become a practicing architect of consequence eluded him.

The pontificate of Clement XIII, from 1758 to 1769, marked a new phase
of patronage in Rome after a relative lull under Benedict XIV. The new
pope, while not politically astute, had a highly developed sense of his
cultural responsibilities and the remarkable discernment, shared by
leading members of his family, to give practical support to Piranesi as a
designer.[44] While the pope and his nephews, Monsignor Giambattista
and Senator Don Abbondio Rezzonico, commissioned domestic interiors
and furnishings from the artist for Castelgandolfo, the Quirinal, and
the Campidoglio, respectively, two ecclesiastical commissions marked
their greatest confidence in Piranesi's exceptional design abilities.

Since its founding under Constantine in the early fourth century, S.
Giovanni in Laterano had been closely associated with the papacy. It not

only housed the pope's throne as the mother church of Rome, but also featured, in the middle of the transepts, the papal altar (with a four-teenth-century canopy made for Urban V), where only the pope could say mass. Rebuilt many times during its history, very little of the Lateran's original structure had survived when the modernization of the nave took place under Borromini beginning in 1646.[45] While the west end of the church (liturgically the east end since, like St Peter's, the Lateran is oriented in reverse direction to customary usage) and pontifical altar remained largely unaffected, the east end had been given a new facade based on Alessando Galilei's design during the 1730s.

Until 1972, the main evidence for Piranesi's designs was a group of drawings in the Pierpont Morgan Library, on which Manfred Fischer based his pioneering study of the commission.[46] That year, the Avery Art and Architectural Library of Columbia University announced the dramatic discovery of a set of magnificent presentation designs for Piranesi's tribune, which was a gift to the library from the late Arthur M. Sackler.[47] The twenty-three designs (others are missing from the set, which Piranesi ordered and numbered himself) are exceptional in quality and size among the several hundred surviving drawings by the artist. According to an inscription on the first sheet, they were prepared for the pope by Piranesi (with considerable studio assistance in the subordinate parts) in 1764. Largely executed in pen and brown ink over pencil with brown and gray washes, they were subsequently adapted by the designer, with characteristically ingenious embellishments involving illusionist effects and vignettes, for presentation to his other principal patron, Monsignor Giambattista Rezzonico, in 1767 when the commission was abandoned. It is possible that Clement XIII's conferment of the knighthood of the *Sperone d'Oro* the same year was intended to compensate the architect for this considerable disappointment.

Borromini's scheme of renewal, carried out at the Lateran under Innocent X between 1646 and 1649, was clearly a major inspiration for Piranesi, especially in the challenge of applying a highly original contemporary system of design to the venerable structure. Piranesi was virtually alone among the designers of his time in his complete sympathy with the ideas and spirit of the *seicento* master, since the latter's reputation was increasingly in decline and the austere tastes of Laugier and Winckelmann prevailed in Rome.

Among the five solutions proposed in the presentation drawings, two schemes presented a relatively modest solution. However, given such an unparalleled opportunity for ornamental display, Piranesi's imagination took full flight in a third, more ambitious solution, represented by seven drawings in the Avery Library's set. More visually arresting than the earlier proposals, it offered a fitting climax to the end of Borromini's dynamic and polychromatic nave, with considerable debts to Piranesi's Venetian roots. This scheme proposed an ambitious plan with an ambulatory defined by a monumental columnar screen, leaving the pontifical altar in the transepts as before. The elevational treatment in Tavola 8 shows the apsidal screen enclosing the high altar, with light directed onto it from a clerestory hidden above the arch between antechoir and sanctuary (see Sorensen, fig. 10). Further light filters laterally through side windows in the walls of the ambulatory itself. Here Piranesi was drawing again on the scenic tradition of Venetian church design, developed from Palladio and given vivid expression by Longhena in S. Maria della Salute—a building of equal significance to that of the former's church of the Redentore in Piranesi's formative years.[48] While the repertoire of ornamental detail shows a neoclassical fidelity to antique sources, the total cohesion of this highly decorated interior is undeniably baroque, and Piranesi can be seen as the conscious heir to Borromini's intentions.

Piranesi's predilection for richness of ornament—far closer to northern Italian designers than to any contemporary source in Rome—was emphasized by a group of four specialized decorative studies. Two of these featured the rear space of the ambulatory looking west and east respectively (Tavole 9 and 10; see fig. 15 and Sørensen, fig. 10) and the others included an exceptionally free rendering of the apse coffering (Tavola 19; see Sørensen, frontispiece) as well as a detailed study of the central portico to the rear of the columnar screen (Tavola 25). With this sumptuous design providing an appropriate finale to Borromini's nave, Piranesi explored the possibility of bringing the papal altar with its baldacchino from the transept crossing into the forechoir (Tavola 11 and 12; see Sørensen, figs. 11, 12). In Tavola 12, the baldacchino, with its explicit Borrominian motifs—winged seraphs, palms, and swags—also recalls the fluency of Piranesi's early rococo Venetian designs and emphasizes the artist's heroic resistance to the increasing restraints of Winckelmann's theories.

The Avery set also contains a group of four separate designs for the papal altar with its baldacchino, certain of them incorporating the reliquary containing the heads of Saints Peter and Paul, a major possession of the Lateran discovered by Urban V in 1368. Three studies, largely rendered in a somewhat mechanical manner by a studio assistant with evidence of brilliant interventions by Piranesi, pursued this Borrominian idiom such that the architect inscribed them "inventato su lo stile (or

"lo gusto") del Borromini." However, a fourth study for the altar (Tavola 20), which is unmistakably in Piranesi's own hand, represented a distinct break from the seicento fluency of the other three drawings (see Sorensen, fig. 20). This particular design—executed in a vigorous disjunctive mode of composition characterized by one of Piranesi's fantasy drawings now in Bologna (fig. 16)—comes extremely close in style to the additional plates of strange architectural designs produced around 1767 to reinforce the polemical arguments of the contemporary *Parere su l'Architettura* (see Lawrence, fig. 11).

As if aware of the overambitious nature of his ideal design, Piranesi decided to unite the extreme richness of the third scheme with the greater practicality of his initial two proposals. This compromise resulted in two schemes represented by the remaining five drawings, in which the columnar apse with ambulatory is implied without the extensive structure required by the third and ideal solution.

In addition to the abundance of information illustrating Piranesi's response to the greatest challenge of his architectural career, a few sheets of decorative studies connected with the Lateran commission have also survived. These include a design in the Morgan Library for a projected reliquary for the heads of St. Peter and St. Paul in the baldacchino, which is striking in its vigorous pen and wash (fig. 17). In contrasting this study with the simple, classicizing nature of the funerary monument for Piranesi's major patron, Monsignor Giambattista Rezzonico in S. Nicola in Carcere, executed by the British sculptor Christopher Hewetson in 1783, the question arises as to whether the Lateran scheme was shelved in 1767 for reasons of taste as much as of finance.[49] Clement XIII himself, whose own monument in St Peter's was eventually carried out by Canova much later in 1787 with an even greater neoclassical severity, had been swift to recognize the significance of Winckelmann's scholarship, while promoting the extremely diverse genius of Piranesi in more private and personal commissions.[50] What was still officially acceptable in Rome during the early 1760s was to appear increasingly behind the times by the close of the decade. Moreover, in final analysis, it might be added that the sheer brilliance of Piranesi's visionary Lateran survives more effectively in the virtuosity of his pen and ink drawings than in the reality of an executed building.

ARCHITECTURE: THE REMODELING OF S. MARIA DEL PRIORATO

In 1764, while Piranesi was involved in the early stages of the Lateran project, Monsignor Giambattista Rezzonico, as Grand Prior of the Knights of Malta, commissioned him to renovate and enhance his priory church.[51] This had been established on the Aventine hill toward the end of the fourteenth century when the order, abandoning its headquarters in the forum of Augustus, took over the remains of the Augustinian convent of S. Maria de Aventina. After various vicissitudes the church had been rebuilt in 1568 and the adjoining building enlarged to become the Villa di Malta. During the seventeenth century, the villa was enlarged and fine gardens were laid out, featuring the avenue of laurel with its celebrated vista of St. Peter's cupola. When Piranesi took over, the church badly needed reconstructing, and an unusually full documentation of the work covering the period from November 1764 to October 1766 is provided in a detailed book, now in the Avery Library, prepared by the *capomastro muratore* Giuseppe Pelosini.[52]

Owing to the undistinguished nature of the entrance to the priory from the ancient Vicus Armilusti (the modern Via di S. Sabina), Piranesi created a rectangular piazza outside the priory grounds (the present Piazzale de' Cavalieri di Malta; fig. 18). This was fronted on the priory side by a handsome screen building with its door aligned with the laurel avenue. (An early sketch for this is in the Kunstbibliothek, Berlin; fig. 19). As elsewhere in the commission, the screen was ornamented with

rich relief passages in the spirit of the mannerist designers Ligorio and Peruzzi, featuring symbols of the order and the Rezzonico family. On the opposite wall he set three imposing stelae, or monumental tablets, bearing relief decorations, the outer ones flanked by obelisks, and the shorter end wall was given another stela recording the circumstances of the commission. Today, the subsequent growth of the cypresses behind these enriched walls and the later buildings of S. Anselmo nearby have considerably dwarfed the composition. In Piranesi's time, these heroic monuments, set against the sky on their high podium, would have evoked an atmosphere of awesome solemnity.

Among the nine surviving drawings by Piranesi associated with the Aventine commission (six of which are in the collection of the Morgan Library) are two meticulous working drawings for reliefs connected with the stelae (figs. 20, 21). In the complex iconography involved, Piranesi the archaeologist combined Rezzonico heraldry (such as the castle and twin-headed eagle; fig. 22) and antique symbols representing the order's military achievements with "Etruscan" motifs relating to the Aventine's early associations with Roman history. Influenced by current polemical concerns, he organized these varied images within a

compositional system that consciously emulated the eclectic character of Roman art then being justified in the text of the *Parere su l'Architettura*.

The Aventine reliefs and the ornamental themes throughout the commission developed certain learned ideas and artistic concepts introduced by Piranesi's archaeological researches and controversial claims over the previous decade and later worked out in his book of designs, *Diverse Maniere*, which was dedicated to the Grand Prior in 1769. Toward the end of the prefatory essay, which draws attention to the creative eclecticism of the Romans, Piranesi inserted a diagram indicating 114 separate items that he claimed were derived from Etruscan civilization. From among this tendentious anthology appear more than twenty images used on the various reliefs ornamenting the Aventine buildings, such as the lyre, cameo, cornucopia, serpent, bird's wing, and shepherd's pipes. Moreover, the fact of their appearance in this particular area of the city had specific relevance, since Piranesi was well aware that the Aventine had possessed a special significance in the early history of Rome.[53] Among the Seven Hills, it alone was set outside the *Pomerium*, or sacred area of Rome, due to the association of the hill with foreign cults and colonies, notably from Etruria.

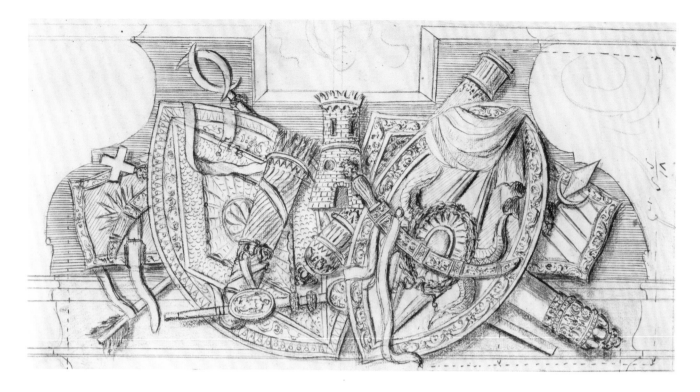

20. DESIGN FOR DECORATIVE
RELIEF PANEL BELOW CENTRAL
STELA OF SOUTH WALL,
PIAZZALE DE' CAVALIERI
DI MALTA, ROME, 1765–66
Pen and brown ink over black
chalk, additional work in black
chalk on off-white laid paper

21. DESIGN OF A VERTICAL
WALL PANEL WITH MALTESE
CROSS AND INSIGNIA OF THE
REZZONICO FAMILY FOR S.
MARIA DEL PRIORATO, 1765–66
Black chalk, pen and brown ink
on off-white laid paper

23. DETAIL OF SPHINX CAPITAL
from Plate XIII, DELLA
MAGNIFICENZA ED ARCHITET-
TURA DE'ROMANI, 1761
Etching on off-white laid paper

22. DETAIL OF FAÇADE,
S. MARIA DEL PRIORATO

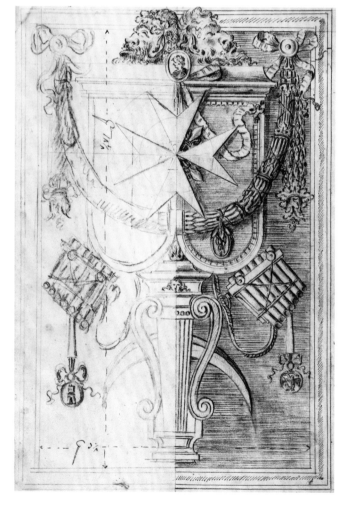

In the text dedicating the *Diverse Maniere* to Monsignor Rezzonico, Piranesi recalled various works of architecture and design undertaken for this patron, Clement XIII, and other members of the papal family. Owing to the abandonment of the Lateran tribune only a few years earlier, pride of place was given to the Aventine priory, which had been "rinovato, anziche ristorato" ("renewed rather than restored"). Considering the extremely modest character of the original church, as recorded in earlier views, this was no understatement. The church was erected in the sixteenth century at the southwest angle of the hill as a simple rectangular structure comprising a nave of four bays with rudimentary transepts and a shallow apse. Its only external embellishment was a pedimented west front, articulated by pairs of pilasters at the outer edge to either side of the doorway with a circular window above it. Since the ground fell away sharply in two directions, access was possible only laterally through the garden or via a steep road from the north side of the hill. Since the most prominent part of the façade was viewed from the banks of the Tiber below and from the ancient Via Marmorata skirting the southern foot of the Aventine, Piranesi added another story, which French artillery subsequently destroyed during the Risorgimento (it was never replaced).[54]

According to the neomannerist aesthetic advocated in the *Parere*, Piranesi transformed the existing architectural elements by means of finely balanced encrustations of highly diverse ornaments. Military, Rezzonico, and "Etruscan" motifs are repeated from the piazza reliefs, intricately combining his archaeological and aesthetic principles. Apart from the stole and insignia of the order in the pediment, the Rezzonico tower is dexterously set within the six Ionic capitals (two on the returns of the façade) with confronted sphinxes following an antique version at Villa Borghese, illustrated in plate XIII of *Della Magnificenza* (fig. 23). Even the fret serving as a frieze has a topical relevance derived from Piranesi's investigations of Etruscan tomb decorations at Tarquinia.[55] Unfortunately, the only surviving studies for this façade are of ceremonial swords imposed on the pilasters (now in the collections of the Morgan Library and the British Museum, respectively). A completely new motif is introduced at the center of the façade, later to be featured conspicuously within the church: namely, the reeded sarcophagus with a circular panel (ingeniously incorporating the existing window), accompanied by flanking console brackets entwined with serpents. This denotes the funerary nature of the church, which contains the tombs of the illustrious dead of the order and immortalizes their martial achievements. The antique standards flanking the entrance and bearing

the initials F.E.R.T. (*Fortitudo eius Rhodum tenuit*) refer to the knights' heroic defense of Rhodes against the Ottoman forces through four desperate sieges during the fifteenth and sixteenth centuries.

On entering the nave, the brittle flatness of the façade reliefs is replaced by an impressive sense of space in the cool, white interior that culminates in the intensified drama of the high altar (fig. 24). Here Piranesi amplified the modest interior by means of theatrical devices characteristic of Venetian church design. Significantly, it was probably at this time that the architect was formulating the particularly elaborate third version of the Lateran tribune, in which he set a highly sculptural altar against an apsidal screen of columns, amplified by the sensuous effects of concealed lighting.

Understandably, the Aventine altar exercised Piranesi's greatest imaginative faculties both in terms of theme and visual impact. In a rapid pen sketch from the Morgan Library, he introduced the basic concept from which the final result evolved—a sarcophagus supporting a *mensa*, or altar slab, behind which a superstructure, fronted by a relief of *The Madonna and Child*, supports a highly expressive tableau featuring *The*

Apotheosis of St. Basil of Cappodocia (the latter being the dedication of the original priory church in the forum; the definitive form of the altar emerges in a chalk and pen drawing, now in the Kunstbibliothek, Berlin).[56] (figs. 25, 26) This consists of two precisely defined sarcophagi, the upper one supporting a sculptural group in which the saint is borne heavenward by angels and putti. A highly finished working drawing in pen and ink with wash from the Morgan Library—possibly among the set presented to the patron—represents the lower part of the altar (fig. 27). This is extremely close to the executed work undertaken by the *stuccatore*,

Tommaso Righi, who likely produced the detailed design for the upper portion, which is absent from the drawing. This highly baroque apotheosis comes close to the figure style of Righi's Balestra monument in SS. Martina e Luca. In Piranesi's definitive version for the altar, he blends, as before, a considerable variety of decorative sources in the "Etruscan" chart of the *Diverse Maniere*. A minor but significant addition at this stage was the application of a triple ram of swords to each end of the upper sarcophagus, ingeniously transforming a funerary into a maritime image.

From the altar, the saint's gesture directs the eye upward to a small lantern set in the vault, which is lit by an oblique light source to indicate the dove traced on its roof. Surrounding the oculus of the lantern is

a four-lobed molding enclosing four exquisitely rendered scenes from the *Life of St John the Baptist*, patron of the prior and the order. Meanwhile, further west along the Borrominesque vault, a large relief panel extends the length of the two central bays of the nave, its composition closely following the detailed drawing in pen and brown ink with wash, in the Morgan Library, which was probably intended for presentation (fig. 28). This celebrates the order within the conventional framework of baroque ceiling design, but with a new archaeological exactitude, controlled to the smallest detail by the architect's direction. Beyond the traditional iconography, a predominantly maritime theme is emphasized by a large rudder, providing the axis for the entire composition of the panel. This is supported at its lower end by juxtaposed prows with the triple ram of swords, introduced in the ornaments of the entrance screen in the piazza and repeated on the altar below. Maritime symbols are equally prominent in the decoration of the transepts, as well as throughout Piranesi's iconographic program on the Aventine. This can be explained by reference to the historic role played by successive leaders of the Italian division of the order. The "bailiff" of the

Italian knights was responsible as grand admiral for naval operations, and Piranesi paid specific tribute to an outstanding protagonist within the church. During the restoration of the priory in 1617, four early tombs from the order's initial building on the Aventine had been reinstated in the nave bays. Piranesi, following the example of Borromini at the Lateran, skillfully incorporated these monuments into his scheme of modernization. The tomb of the distinguished admiral Frà Sergio Seripando, who died in Rome during an embassy from Rhodes in 1465, had been placed in the westernmost bay, immediately inside the entrance. Above his monument the architect placed an elaborate trophy that includes prows with triple swords and twin *aplustres* (fanlike terminals on the stern of an ancient warship), as appropriate to one who, according to the original epitaph, had brought terror into the hearts of the enemy: *quem tremuit Maurus et tremuere Phryges* (fig. 29).

Finally, returning to the Piazzale de' Cavalieri di Malta, the total conception and particular location of Piranesi's monumental forecourt, with its stelae and military symbols, suggests that Piranesi may have also been aware of the Aventine's association with the ancient ceremony of the *Armilustrium*. According to ancient sources, this ceremony, which was enacted in a special sanctuary on the hill and close to the site of the church, was performed by the priests of Mars, who ritually purified Roman weapons and equipment deposited there at the end of the army's summer campaign. It is singularly appropriate that, by the late eighteenth century, when the heroic phase of the Knights of Malta was over, their arms were deposited in true fashion in the military motifs that appear extensively in Piranesi's reliefs throughout both piazza and buildings.

THE *DIVERSE MANIERE:* CHIMNEYPIECE AND INTERIOR DESIGN

Piranesi's achievements as a highly imaginative designer of interiors, featuring chimneypieces and a wide range of furniture, were compressed into a period of barely a decade and a half. His principal publication concerning design, *Diverse maniere d'adornare i cammini ed ogni altra parte degli edifizi* (1769), serves both as a manifesto and a demonstration of his new aesthetic in action. Its sixty-five etched plates not only illustrated a number of significant works already produced, but also offered a wide variety of designs that vary from compositions of polemical exaggeration to more practicable compositions containing ideas and motifs for selective use. The prime subject of the book is the chimneypiece—the architectural element of a decorative interior that offered the greatest scope for applying his aesthetic to strictly modern needs—but the

wide application of the system is also demonstrated by more than one hundred separate items of furniture and decorative design. The author was very conscious of the significant role of clients as well as creators; the folio was appropriately dedicated to Monsignor Giambattista Rezzonico as the model of a sympathetic and enlightened patron of contemporary art.

Like many of his earlier polemical works, the relation of the thirty-five-page introductory text, *An Apologetical Essay in Defence of the Egyptian and Tuscan Architecture* (using Piranesi's own words), to the plates that followed was complex and often uncoordinated, but it nevertheless represented a considered summing-up of his theories of creative license based on the twin sources of inspiration—antiquity and nature.[57] No longer like *Della Magnificenza*, which was directed toward the critics and antiquaries of the earlier phase in the debate, its parallel texts in Italian,

French, and English were addressed to an international audience of patrons and practicing designers. Despite its title, the essay was much more than a continuation of his defense of the Etruscans, although they featured prominently; in addition to the chart of their supposed inventions, he added two diagrams ingeniously suggesting the possible influence of shell forms on their vase designs (see Lawrence, fig. 13). His prime objective, however, was to emphasize the creative eclecticism of the ancient Romans, who had first utilized Etruscan ideas and then absorbed Greek and Egyptian material into their living system of design. The creation of a personal style of expression was the dominant theme of the essay, and he justified the complexity and multiplicity of forms in his designs that followed on the basis of aesthetic judgment rather than on academic orthodoxy. He also sought to explain the boldness as well as a certain stiffness, especially in Egyptian art, with a remarkably advanced defense of stylistic abstraction in architectural forms. He also pointed to the considerable delicacy and intricacy in small-scale Egyptian art, which, although it had largely vanished, was reflected in the details of natural observation that could still be seen on monumental works such as the obelisks in Rome.

Because the chimneypiece is the dominant theme of the etched designs, the *Diverse Maniere* can be considered a rejoinder to the considerable body of publications produced in France in which this dominant feature of interior design was discussed and illustrated at length, all the more so given that French designers had largely embraced the Greek side of the debate.[58] This subject was also enterprisingly directed toward the British, who had a far greater interest in this interior feature, as Piranesi stated in the caption to one of his chimneypieces. In fact, due to the increasing papal control of the export of significant antiquities in the 1760s, Piranesi began to create chimneypieces from antique fragments with the assistance of dealers and skilled restorers, and it is significant that the first two plates of the book show outstanding executed examples that were already in situ. The chimneypiece in the state bedroom of Burghley House, Lincolnshire, was probably commissioned during the ninth Earl of Exeter's second visit to Rome in 1769.[59] In a detailed comment on the inadequacy of the plate to record the full visual effect, Piranesi stressed the chromatic qualities of the antique elements, such as the satyr heads on the jambs, or vertical members, and three reliefs in *rosso antico* on the lintel (the central one being framed in gilt bronze), which contrast with the white marble (fig. 30). Equally striking is the exquisite Carrara marble chimneypiece (now in the Rijksmuseum) that embellished the cabinet of the Amsterdam house owned by the

Cammino che si vede nel Palazzo di Sua Eccza Milord Conte D'Exeter a Burghley in Inghilterra.
Le Cariatidi e li tre Camei di pietra rossa d'Egitto con fondo lattato sono antichi, tutto il resto de'
suoi finissimi intagli sono di marmo bianco, le cornici de'Camei e l'orlo della tavola di pietra rossa sopra la cornice sono di metallo dorato. Fatto in Roma con la direzzione e disegno del Cav. Gio. Batta Piranesi Architetto.

31. CHIMNEYPIECE DESIGNED
FOR JOHN HOPE, from DIVERSE
MANIERE D'ADORNARE
I CAMMINI..., 1769
Etching on off-white laid paper

Scottish merchant John Hope (see de Leeuw, fig. 9).[60] According to the caption, part of it was also composed of original fragments, including the caryatids. Other such composite chimneypieces were produced, including two at Gorhambury House in Bedfordshire, one at Wedderburn Castle, Scotland, and another (now in Portugal) at Stowe, Buckinghamshire.[61] From this enterprise a whole industry of chimneypiece production subsequently developed in Rome to satisfy the resulting demand from the Grand Tour market.

Since, according to the essay, Piranesi had found little evidence for the use of chimneypieces in antiquity, he was at liberty to show the way in which his eclectic system of design, even without incorporating original antique elements, could be applied to modern commissions. Some sixty-one designs, including one produced for the pope's nephew, Senator Abbondio Rezzonico, ranged from comparatively simple compositions to wildly complex ones that were exaggerated for polemical effect. Taking his fundamental design concept of the fragment as an inspirational starting point, the rectangular chimneypiece format composed of vertical members and the horizontal lintel was encrusted with motifs taken from antique ornaments and motifs as well as plaques in relief (fig. 31). The more elaborate versions of these compositions provided enterprising designers with an anthology of motifs to select and develop, as seen in a sheet of Adam's preliminary sketches made from the *Diverse Maniere* that ultimately led to his innovative chimneypiece designs of the 1770s.[62] Alternatively, a classical ornamental form, such as the monopod—the Roman chair or table support in the form of an animal's head with a single leg and foot—was applied on an inflated scale to the jambs of a chimneypiece. Such a concept might also be extracted from this composition for the enrichment of a desk, as illustrated in Percier and Fontaine's *Recueil des décorations intérieures* (1801) (fig. 32). Similarly, the presence of elaborate andirons within this and several other Piranesi chimneypiece designs provided designers with further material for use, as shown by Bélanger's use of the griffin motif for an andiron design possibly associated with Marie Antoinette, now in Cooper-Hewitt's collection.[63] (fig. 33) Behind these ingenious variations was Piranesi's belief in the inexhaustible inspiration of nature for antiquity, as represented by dolphins, rams, oxen, dogs, serpents, eagles, and all manner of mythical beasts such as sphinxes, griffins, chimeras, and hippocamps. This is demonstrated in a vigorous pen and ink study for an unpublished chimneypiece with confronted elephant heads (fig. 34).

While virtually all these etched chimneypieces indicate the presence of a room setting, it is tantalizing that so little evidence has survived to

2.

enable reconstructions of the interiors Piranesi is known to have carried out for Clement XIII's summer residence at Castelgandolfo, Monsignor Giambattista Rezzonico's Palazzo Quirinale, and Senator Abbondio Rezzonico's Palazzo Senatorio on the Campidoglio, or Capitoline Hill.[64] Several pen studies in the Berlin Kunstbibliothek provide evidence of wall systems, especially one that features perhaps the most extreme of the *Diverse Maniere* chimneypiece designs (fig. 35). This preparatory study indicates not only a mirror flanked by sconces with a full-length portrait above, but also a chair and fragments of a richly dense wall system. Another such study in the Morgan Library also depicts one of the flanking chairs with a shield-back design, and, again, hints of a possible mirror over the mantle. Meanwhile, other etched chimneypieces incorporate flanking vases and even candelabra as prominent adjuncts that suggest a continuation of interior decoration beyond the plate margin.

The etched plates for the fabricated chimneypieces for Lord Exeter and John Hope, together with two other plates, all provide a surrounding wall decoration that is closely inspired by the painted trellislike compositions of Fourth Style painted schemes of Pompeian decoration as well as the grotesque style of Raphael's Vatican decorative schemes.

33. Jean-Démosthène Dugourc
after François-Joseph Bélanger
DESIGN FOR TWO ANDIRONS
AND A SCONCE OF GILT
BRONZE FOR THE PAVILION
DE BAGATELLE, PARIS, 1777
Pen and ink, brush and
yellow, green, blue, and brown
watercolor on white laid
paper, lined and mounted

While it is quite possible that a certain degree of license was exercised in presenting the executed chimneypieces in this fashion, according to the essay, Abbondio Rezzonico was provided with such a painted room. Indeed, such ephemeral schemes were to lead to one of the most remarkable instances of an attempt to create a consciously contemporary style of expression advocated by Piranesi. In a series of at least eight so-called "Etruscan" rooms from the 1770s and early 1780s, Adam pushed the boundaries of his innovatory style to new degrees of ingenuity, epitomized by the dressing room at Osterley Park, near London, of 1775.[65] (fig. 36) In the *Diverse Maniere* essay, Piranesi recognized the possibilities of using vase motifs for decorative purposes, following the widespread misconception that many examples published in Sir William Hamilton's celebrated publication were of Etruscan origin. Adam, combining the color and decoration of vases with Pompeian forms allied to the grotesque, created a striking unity of expression, including walls, ceiling, carpet (unexecuted), door, furniture, chimneyboard, and even the curtain cornice, to achieve the complete coherence of the modern style advocated by Piranesi.

34. SKETCH DESIGN FOR
CHIMNEYPIECE WITH
CONFRONTED ELEPHANT
HEADS, before 1769
Pen and brown ink over black
chalk on off-white laid paper

THE EGYPTIAN STYLE

Undoubtedly, the boldest flights of Piranesi's imagination in pursuit of a new expression in design in the *Diverse Maniere* were the designs for eleven chimneypieces in the Egyptian taste and the plates that recorded two walls of his painted interior for the Caffè degli Inglesi, or English coffee house, in Piazza di Spagna.[66] With these designs Piranesi pioneered the Egyptian style as a coherent visual taste and, at the same time, provided other designers with a whole repertoire of motifs and concepts.[67] It is significant that these are among his boldest excursions into fashioning a new compositional system that had virtually no precedents in Western interior design. His interest in the stylistic potential of this civilization went back to his early years in Rome, when he was gathering inspiration from the reconstructions of Fischer von Erlach. Frequent references to Egyptian monuments occur in his architectural fantasies, in which he was clearly impressed by the play of abstract forms conveyed by obelisks and pyramids as well as the stylization of natural forms and animals. Research into engraved sources, such as the Tabula Bembi and the compendiums of Bernard de Montfaucon and the Comte de Caylus, as well as material in the Vatican collections and sur-

viving monuments of the Romans' own Egyptian Revival reinforced his
theories in favor of imaginative eclecticism.[68] As he became increasingly
engaged in the Graeco-Roman controversy, Egyptian art provided an exceptional field of visual experiment unconstrained by traditional conventions. Egyptian elements notably played a significant role in the
vigorous disjunctive compositions illustrating his eclectic theories in
the *Parere su l'Architettura*. They also inspired some particularly macabre
compositions among his contemporaries, such as Desprez's designs for
tomb fantasies, now in Cooper-Hewitt's collection.[69] (fig. 37) As a consequence, the chimneypiece designs in the Egyptian style are among the
most experimental of the series, showing considerably more of the sur-

rounding wall compositions with adjacent furniture as well as figures and animals of monumental scale. Unconstrained by practicable solutions, Piranesi used conventional chimneypiece formulas to put into operation a series of what are essentially monumental capricci. Aware of his originality in applying the decorative range of this remote culture to the intimacy of domestic settings, Piranesi wrote in 1768 to the English antiquarian Thomas Hollis, when sending him proof plates of the *Diverse Maniere*, "Egyptian architecture appears here for the first time; I want to stress that people always believed that there was nothing more than pyramids, obelisks, and giants, neglecting the parts that would be adequate to adorn and support this architectural style."[70] While the extremes in his compositions were far too bold for contemporary taste, the role of these compositions as a fertile quarry for exotic motifs can be seen, for example, in one of Bélanger's books of chimneypiece designs around 1770–80 in the Bibliothèque Nationale.[71]

During the mid-1760s, Piranesi created the first comprehensive Egyptian revival interior in the Caffè degli Inglesi, which was already among the most popular meeting places for the travelers, dealers, and artists of the Grand Tour. Surprisingly, no trace or record survives of this highly significant scheme except the plates in the *Diverse Maniere*, which show what were presumably two adjacent walls (fig. 38). Applying the concept of Pompeian illusionistic wall decorations to enhance this narrow space, Piranesi used the traditional Western type of wall system to frame views of Egyptian monuments in a desert setting. The screening structures are composed of a rich collage of human figures and beasts, both three-dimensional and in relief, which are enriched with hieroglyphics and selected from a wide range of publications and monuments. It is possible that an appropriate chimneypiece was placed on the window wall opposite to the longer composition (fig. 39). Reactions at

Spaccato della bottega ad uso di caffè detta degl'Inglesi situata in piazza di Spagna. Le pareti dipinte di questa bottega rap=
presentano un Vestibulo adornato di Simboli Geroglifici, e di altre cose allusive alla Religione e politica degli antichi Egiziani.
In lontananza vi si vedono le fertili campagne, il Nilo e quelli maestosi sepolcri della medesima nazione.

Disegno ed invenzione del Cavalier Piranesi.   *Piranesi inc.*

the time appear to have been unfavorable: In 1776, the painter Thomas Jones described it as "a filthy vaulted room the walls of which were painted with sphinxes, obelisks and pyramids from capricious designs by Piranesi, and fitter to adorn the inside of an Egyptian sepulchre, than a room of social conversation."[72] Earlier in 1769, another painter, James Barry, wrote to the philosopher Edmund Burke that Piranesi would go down to posterity with a deserved reputation "in spite of his Egyptian and other whimsies, and his gusto of architecture flowing out of the same cloacus as Borromini's and other hairbrained moderns."[73] But for all this negative response, the idea of a coherent style was launched well before the later Egyptian revivial inspired by the

Altro spaccato per longo della stessa bottega, ove si vedono frà le aperture del vestibolo le immense piramidi, ed altri edifizj sepolcrali ne' deserti dell' Egitto.

Disegno ed invenzione del Cavalier Piranesi   *Cav.' Piranesi F.*

39. EGYPTIAN DECORATION
OF THE CAFFÈ DEGLI INGLESI,
ANIMALS ON THE CORNICE,
INCLUDING A BULL AT
THE CENTER, from DIVERSE
MANIERE D'ADORNARE
I CAMMINI…, 1769
Etching on off-white laid paper

Napoleonic publications of Denon in the early nineteenth century. Although clearly deriving inspiration from the latter, among the most original responses to Piranesi's stylistic concept was the exceptional Egyptian or "Black Room" designed by the Regency connoisseur Thomas Hope in a sequence of stylistic interiors for his London house, which were published in 1807.[74] (fig. 40) Although the house has since been destroyed, some of its striking furniture survives.[75] In one of the two couches (fig. 41) the complex blend of inspiration from Egypt with Greek ornamental vocabulary owes far more to the impact of Piranesi's visionary eclecticism than to the effects of Denon's publications.

40. Thomas Hope
EGYPTIAN OR BLACK ROOM,
DUCHESS STREET, from
HOUSEHOLD FURNITURE AND
INTERIOR DECORATION, 1807

FURNITURE DESIGN

In the aesthetic climate of the 1760s, with the increasing taste for classical restraint inspired by the reactions in France toward rococo style and the impact of Winckelmann's Greek revival writings, Piranesi's furniture designs in the *Diverse Maniere* represented a unique polemical response. Like the chimneypieces and interior designs, his furniture compositions also provided a comprehensive alternative approach to a system of design that drew widely and fancifully from a range of cultures—Greek and Roman as well as Etruscan and Egyptian.[76] While the archaeological sources, where they existed, merely provided points of departure, they supported the central theory of Piranesi's treatise that to emulate the inclusive culture of ancient Roman civilization is to give the widest possible scope to the creative imagination, unfettered from rigid and restrictive doctrines of taste. Style is the personal expression of the designer, and it is not surprising that Piranesi's sympathies lay with

41. Thomas Hope
SETTEE IN THE EGYPTIAN
TASTE FROM THE EGYPTIAN
ROOM, DUCHESS STREET,
LONDON, 1800–04
Mahogany, painted black
and gold with bronze mounts

movements such as the Mannerism of the late Renaissance, the baroque imagination of seicento masters such as Borromini and Bernini, and the rococo idiom of his early Venetian years (fig 43). While his designs owed little to other contemporary designers, he was clearly aware of current neoclassical tastes such as the *goût grec* in France, with its complex inspiration from antique furniture forms and the *Grand Siècle*. The application of style across the range of the decorative arts was remarkable, and, in addition to the furniture and wall fittings that appear around the chimneypieces, he included six commodes, ten tables, three tripod stands, four chairs, two pairs of shutters, two candelabra, two candlestands, twelve candlesticks, three sconces, twenty-three clocks, twelve vases or urns, twelve tea or coffee pots, various portions of beading and moldings, and the woodwork of six coaches and twelve sedan chairs. Surviving preparatory sketches, notably in the Morgan Library and Berlin Kunstbibliothek, indicate many further ideas in gestation.

42. DESIGN FOR SCONCES
Red chalk over black on
off-white laid paper

**43. DESIGN FOR A WALL PANEL
IN THE FORM OF A ROCOCO
SHIELD WITH SCONCES**
Pen and brown ink, brush and
brown wash, over black chalk
on off-white laid paper

44. SIDE TABLE, CA. 1768
Oak, limewood, marble, gilt

45. SKETCH DESIGNS FOR PART
OF A TABLE, n.d.
Pen and brown ink over red
chalk on off-white laid paper

Clement XIII and members of the Rezzonico family during the 1760s gave Piranesi a unique opportunity to carry out some of these ideas in decorative schemes. In these commissions a comprehensive approach could be achieved at the highest level, and it is fortunate that at least two surviving pieces of furniture confirm not only the accuracy of the *Diverse Maniere* plates concerned, but also the outstanding quality of execution. The gilt and wood side table in the Rijksmseum (and its match in the Minneapolis Institute of Arts) is an exceptional fusion of rococo vitality and complexity with the use of antique ornamental features, such as bucranea, husks, pinecones, and acanthus as well as the supporting chimera monopods that reflect the possible influence of antique furniture then being excavated at Herculaneum and Pompeii.[77] (fig. 44) Yet the inspiration of nature as the designer's other key source is never far away, as illustrated in a freely sketched pen study (in the Victoria and Albert Museum) of the natural form of an animal's leg as the basis for the monopods.[78] (fig. 45) In the same plate of the *Diverse Maniere*, the cap-

53

Questo tavolino ed alcuni altri ornamenti che sono sparsi in quest'opera, si
vedono nell'appartamento di Sua Eccza Monsigr D. Gio: Batta Rezzonico
Nipote e Maggiorduomo di N. S. PP. Clemente XIII.

Cavalier Piranesi inv. e inc.

In the same plate of the *Diverse Maniere*, the caption mentions that other unspecified items feature in the same scheme, and some rare insights into this process of stylization are provided by a sheet of chalk studies in the Morgan Library for the two sconces at the top of the same plate as the table (fig. 42). Here the designer's predilection for the sinuous curves of rococo found a response in the natural patterns of a tree branch.[79] In another plate, featuring a particularly lavish wall clock according to the caption produced for Don Abbondio's palace on the Campidoglio, a study in red and black chalk precedes another bizarre clock in the form of a pineapple, also in the Morgan Library (fig. 47).

In a seminal article on the *Diverse Maniere* relating to three preparatory drawings in the Gahlin Collection, William Rieder discusses the complex nature of Piranesi's etched designs for furniture and chimneypieces in terms of their ambiguity as well as their sources of inspiration and impact on contemporary designers.[80] While the furniture types, such as commodes, tables, and chairs, are not dissimilar from late baroque and

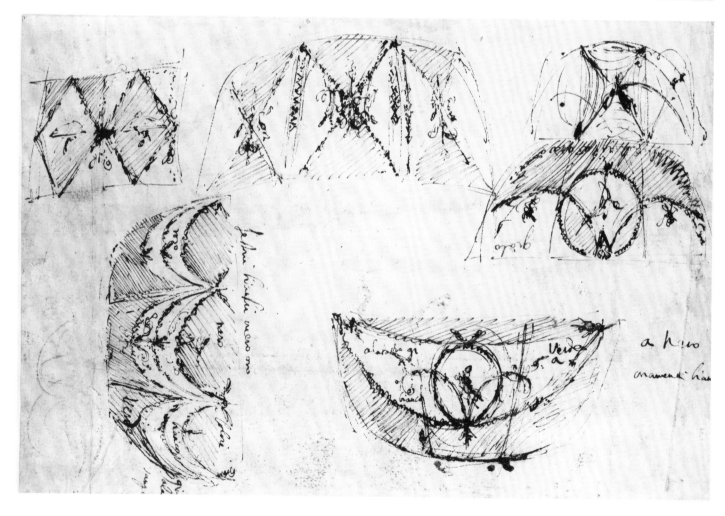

neoclassical works in Italy and France, it is the sheer diversity and original application of ornament that distinguishes them from contemporary expression. The preparatory ink studies from the Gahlin Collection (figs. 48, 49) provide a rare opportunity to see Piranesi's idiosyncratic working procedure, in which the basic structure was outlined, along with some of the main decorative features, before he evolved and elaborated the design in the actual process of etching—a skill in extemporization for which he was famous. There was little consistency in indicating practical considerations of function or spatial relationships as found in conventional furniture pattern books. The role of ornament, in all its complexity and richness, is so reminiscent of a Venetian *horror vacui* and remains the prime consideration, as illustrated throughout the *Diverse Maniere* compositions. As with the chimneypieces, the overwhelmingly embellished surfaces of the furniture, as well as the occasional painted wall decorations, offer the selective designer a positive arsenal of imaginative concepts.

Although the range of Piranesi's decorative applications is exceptionally comprehensive, his basic predilection for the sinuosity of Rococo, with its license for extravagant display, is particularly found in designs for coaches and sedan chairs in which highly ephemeral ornament was particularly acceptable (fig. 50). At least one such commission was recorded in a letter of 1768 from the fifth Earl of Carlisle in Rome to George Selwyn: "Do you think you shall come to Paris? I have just got the drawing for the coach with antique ornaments by Piranesi which I intend executing there if I can afford it."[81] Similarly, at the other end of the spectrum of ephemera, Piranesi's designs for clocks are some of the most ornate and ingenious of his creations, some of them almost vying with Surrealism in their bizarre and improbable casework. While the monumental clock for Abbondio Rezzonico has vanished, the impact of his imaginative fertility extends from lavish timepieces in Adam's *Works in Architecture* to the British Regency age with Thomas Hope's clock for his Flaxman or star room in the Duchess Street house, now at the Royal Pavilion at Brighton.[82] (fig. 51) The theme of this densely iconographic room was the passage of the hours connected with the story of Cephalus and Aurora, Roman goddess of the dawn, as displayed in a sculpture group by Flaxman.[83] Hope, taking his starting point from Piranesi's designs for clocks embodying deities and mythical figures, designed one borne by a black basalt figure of the horned Isis, symbolic of the moon, framed by two hieroglyphic blocks of ormolu, topped by bull divinities. It is this originality of transposition from one culture to another and the strange ornamental language applied to conventional furniture and

51. Thomas Hope
CLOCK IN THE EGYPTIAN
STYLE, n.d.
Bronze, ormolu, and Rosso
Antico marble

interiors through the exercise of fantasy that fulfilled Piranesi's central objective in his unique publication.

RECREATING ANTIQUITY

Piranesi's fabrication of chimneypieces in the 1760s, closely associated with the antiquarian market of the Grand Tour, was given fresh financial incentives with the decline of Rezzonico patronage after Clement XIII's death in 1769.[84] Toward the end of the essay in the *Diverse Maniere*, he referred to his extensive collection of architectural and decorative fragments as an immediate source of stimulus for his novel designs. In this process of transposing random survivals from the past, it was natural for Piranesi to apply his baroque imagination in the recreation of decorative antiquities.[85] In this work, as well as in his thriving printmaking business, he was helped by a team of specialized assistants during the early 1770s, along with his son Francesco, who was born in 1758. He also collaborated with other dealers and entrepreneurs and took advantage of the skilled services of leading restorers like Bartolomeo Cavaceppi and Vincenzo Pacetti and the sculptors Jospeph Nollekens and Giuseppe Angelini. This prolific output was documented and advertised with the issue of 119 individual etched plates that were subsequently collected together in two volumes and issued, just before he died in 1778, as the *Vasi, Canderabri, Cippi, Sarcafagi*—a work that was as influential as the *Diverse Maniere*. While largely produced with studio assistance and lacking the nervous vitality of Piranesi's line, these etchings depicted many works in Piranesi's *museo*, or showroom, in Palazzo Tomati, in other Roman collections, or in those of his colleagues. In a characteristic combination of business flair and erudition, the captions to many images provided detailed information about the circumstances and location of their original discovery; some thirty-five works were in twenty-five separate British collections, where many still remain.

Owing to the contemporary taste for complete objects, Piranesi frequently included in the same plate suitable ornamental bases and supports, and indicated the fact in the caption. However, this skill in decorative synthesis prompted him to take increasing liberties with the actual restoration, especially when an object was substantially incomplete. His capacity for enhancement and imaginative transposition were particularly expressed in monumental vases and ornamental candelabra, their virtuosity recognized by leading connoisseurs such as Charles Townley and Thomas Hope as objects that merited inclusion along with more "authentic" antiquities in sculpture collections and galleries of antiquities.[86] Prime among these magnificent vases was the

Si è dimostrata la Pianta della stessa grandezza del manico per far vedere l'architettura delle scanalature.

Dimostrazione in piana superficie delle foglie, che adornano il gran corpo del Vaso.

HOC·PRISTINAE·ARTIS
ROMANAEQ·MAGNIFICENTIAE·MONVMENTVM
RVDERIBVS·VILLAE·TIBVRTINAE
HADRIANO·AVG·IN·DELICIIS·HABITAE·EFFOSSVM
RESTITVI·CVRAVIT
EQVES·GVLIELMVS·HAMILTON
A·GEORGIO·III·MAG·BRIT·REGE
AD·SICIL·REGEM·FERDINANDVM·IV·LEGATVS
ET·IN·PATRIAM·TRANSMISSVM
PATRIO·BONARVM·ARTIVM·GENIO·DICAVIT

A Sua Eccellenza il Sig. Cav. Hamilton Ministro Plenipotenziario della Mtà di
Giorgio III. Re della Gran Brettagna presso alla Mtà di Ferdinando IV. Re delle due Sicilie.
Amatore delle Belle Arti

In atto d'ossequio il Cav. Gio. Batta Piranesi D.D.D.

Veduta in Prospettiva di un antico Vaso di marmo di gran mole, ritrovato l'anno 1770. nell' escavare, e diseccare il Lago detto Pantanello, Luogo anticamente situato nel Recinto della Villa Adriana presso a Tivoli due miglia. Sì l'Invenzione di esso, che le sue ben'intese Sculture dimostrano la perfezione delle Arti del Secolo di Adriano. L'Iscrizione, che si legge nel suo moderno Piedestallo parimente di marmo, indica il Personaggio, che si è preso la cura di far ristaurare questo antico Monumento.

Cav. Piranesi F.

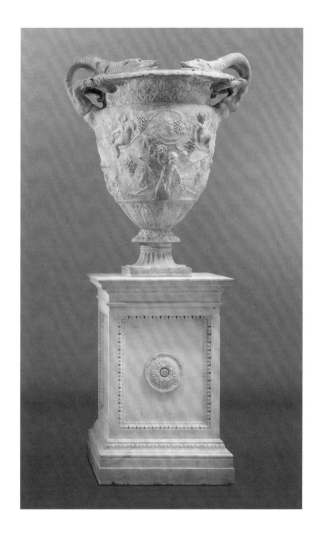

one created for Sir William Hamilton from fragments that Gaven Hamilton excavated from the Pantanello area of Hadrian's villa in 1771.[87] (fig. 52) Later known as the Warwick Vase after it entered the collection of Hamilton's nephew, George Greville, Earl of Warwick, it has been in the Burrell Collection in Glasgow since 1978. Less than a third of the vase is original, but, after its restoration based on Piranesi's design, probably by Cavaceppi, it became one of the most celebrated decorative pieces in Europe (Charles Townley, in his reply to a letter from Piranesi [fig. 53], likened its restoration to a "phoenix").[88] Its innumerable copies ranged from full-scale replicas in bronze to reductions in silver gilt wine coolers, especially during the Regency era, when the exact plates of the *Vasi* served as working drawings for designers and silversmiths.[89] Such was the case of the more modest marble vase with *putti* and fruiting vines (now in Los Angeles), excavated at Hadrian's villa in 1769 and acquired by Lord Temple, later marquis of Buckingham, for Stowe in 1774.[90] (fig. 54) This not only provided the model for the silver-gilt Doncaster racing cup by Rebecca Emes and Edward Barnard of 1828 (fig. 55), but also sets of silver-gilt wine coolers by Barnard in 1828, four of which are now at the Minneapolis Institute of Arts (fig. 56).[91]

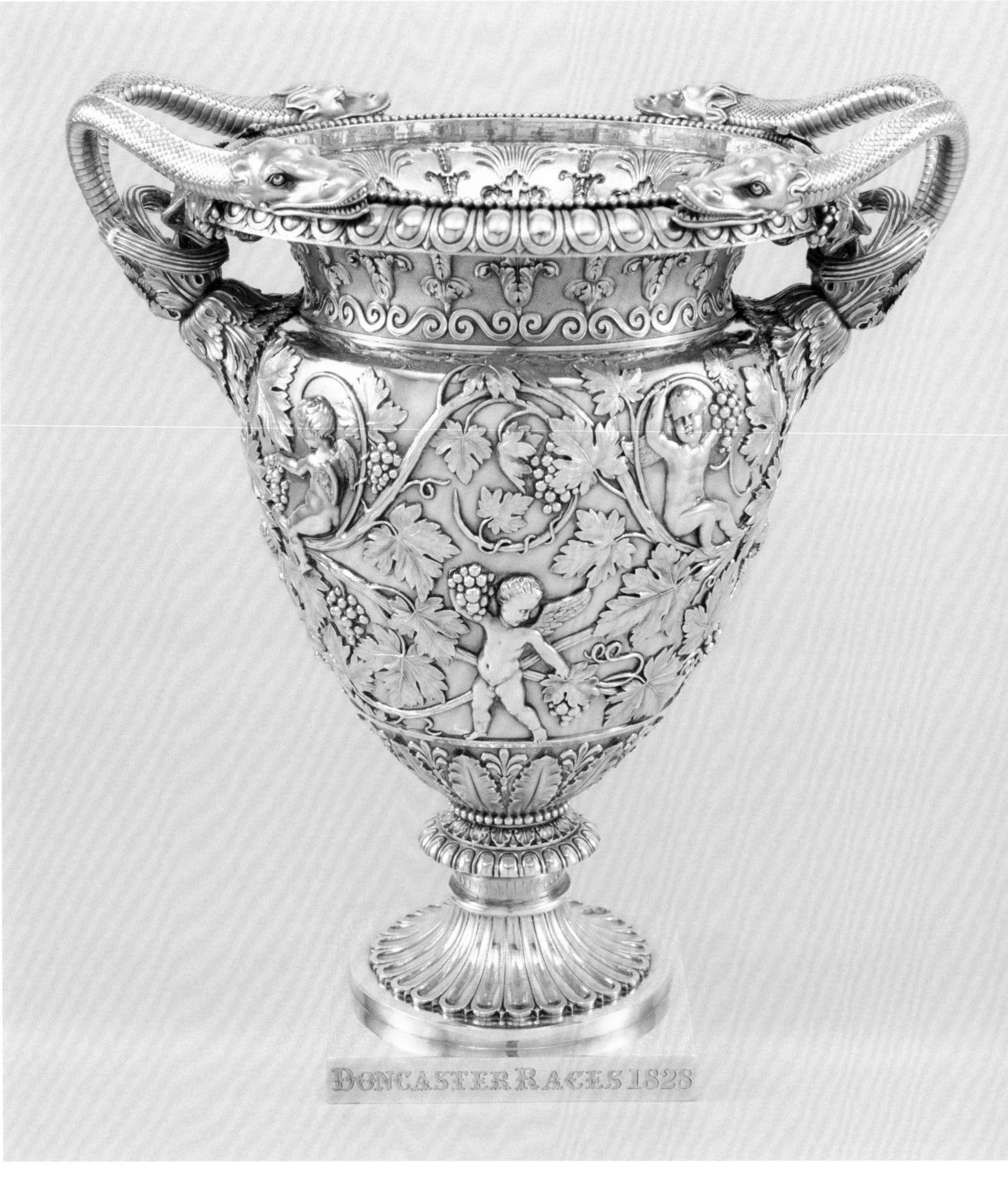
DONCASTER RACES 1828

55. Rebecca Emes
and Edward Barnard
THE DONCASTER RACE CUP
OF 1828
Silver gilt

56. Joseph Barnard
After Giovanni Battista Piranesi
(Italian, 1720–1778)
WINE COOLER, 1828
Silver gilt

Monumental candelabra possessed a special appeal for Piranesi, and during the 1760s they had already featured as church furnishings in projected designs both for the Lateran and S. Maria del Priorato. This ornamental feature developed to heroic proportions and complexity in his visionary recreation of more than a dozen examples in marble. In 1775, the British connoisseur Sir Roger Newdigate acquired from Piranesi two particularly important examples derived from fragments uncovered at the Villa Adriana, both of which were etched in the *Vasi* (fig. 57). One features cranes, and the other has elephants among the ornaments; each was presented to the University of Oxford.[92] Now in the Ashmolean Museum, they were described in 1777 as exciting "the admiration of all who see them, being indeed a perfect school in themselves, of Sculpture and Architecture." The fact that Piranesi intended a giant candelabrum to serve as his own funerary monument indicates the importance he at-

57. PERSPECTIVE OF NEWDIGATE
CANDELABRUM WITH CRANES,
from VASI, CANDELABRI.
CIPPI, SARCOFAGI..., 1778
Etching on off-white laid paper

58. ELEVATION OF
PIRANESI'S OWN FUNERARY
CANDELABRUM WITH PUTTI,
from VASI, CANDELABRI.
CIPPI, SARCOFAGI..., 1778
Etching on off-white laid paper

*Al suo Carissimo Amico il Sig.r Giacomo Byres Architetto Scozzese
Il Cavalier Piranesi.*

Cav.r Piranesi F.

Al Signor Carlo Morris Cavaliere Inglese

Un tal Lume perpetuo antico di mirabil lavoro, dovrà collocarsi sopra
magnifico piedestallo rotondo, dinanzi la Tomba dell'Autore nella
Chiesa della Certosa. L'tre Geny, che a piedi gli si veggono stanno
in atto di lutto, con l'ali dimesse, e con in mano le rovesciate faci.
Il basamento triangolare sostenuto da zampe di Leone, circondato
da sfingi alate, e vestite a strie, con le code spirali, ovvero serpegg-
gianti, che racchiudono canestri di fiori, e conchiglie; le tre teste
d'arieti sporgono ad esse sfingi e dimostrano di regger l'ara rotonda.
La sua base circolare, è intagliata sopra a strie, à fittece intrec-
ciate, frondi, e squame. Le quattro teste di Fauni, e siano maschere
sceniche alludenti ai quattro generi della Poesia sostenute da

soreggimento scorniciate, rappresentano anche le quattro Età
dell'Uomo, ovvero le quattro stagioni simboliche alla vita umana.
La siringa a lato de la maschera, e il Pedo appartengono alle due
teste di Fauni, figurati per l'Estate, e l'Autunno: all'opposto si vedono le figure di Fauni accanto alla Maschera dell'inverno in atto
di raccoglier pigne, ultimo frutto della stagione, simbolo del termine
della vita umana. Il rimanente dell'Opera è un complesso d'Ornamenti di frondi, festoni, e teste di Leoni che circondano il fusto
che regge la patera cose tutte allusive alle produzioni della
terra, necessarie per la vita dell'Uomo. Quarto Lume o Signore si ve-
deva una volta a pezzi divisi nel Palaz° del Duca Salviati alla Longara.
In segno d'Ossequio Il Cavaliere Gio: Batta Piranesi

Cavalier Piranesi del e inc.   Palmi Romani numero sei.

tached to this decorative feature. This impressive work, now in the Louvre (fig. 58), and featured in the background of Labruzzi's posthumous portrait of the artist as designer, is composed from a substantial amount of antique fragments with modern additions.[93] According to one of two etchings in the *Vasi*, the complex iconographic program involved references to poetry and the arts as well as the passage of the seasons and the transitory nature of human life. The importance of this work in the early nineteenth century, before archaeological purism demoted these confections from museum displays to storerooms, is emphasized by the fact that Piranesi's candelabrum was originally the centerpiece of an entire room in the Louvre.

Given Piranesi's ceaseless dialogue with the fragmentary past, it was but a short step from substantial restorations to almost new compositions. For Cardinal Alessandro Albani he contributed an ornamental lunette relief of trophies (fig. 59) in the famous Galleria del Parnaso at his celebrated villa on the Via Salaria as well as a fountain in the gardens that partially survives.[94] According to a drawing in the Morgan Library (fig. 60), it was ingeniously composed of ornamental fragments that resulted in a bowl fed by spouting dolphins and surmounted by a tripod of winged harpies supporting a basin, worthy of a mannerist designer such as Buontalenti. This process of creative synthesis was particularly stimulating to designers such as Robert Adam in their quest for novelty and variety. Among the most eloquent examples of these artistic experiments are Adam's various candlestands and torchères, which were necessary for illuminating a classical interior while retaining antique decorative forms. The pair surviving from the dining room in the London house of the connoisseur and collector Sir Watkin Williams Wynn, designed in 1777 (now in the Victoria and Albert Museum), combine the antique forms of a tripod incense burner with a sacrificial altar.[95] (fig. 61) Predictably, some of Piranesi's more extreme productions were well in advance of contemporary taste, and several of them remained in his *museo* after his death when Gustav III of Sweden acquired them from the artist's son, Francesco, during a visit to Rome in 1783.[96] Among the most ambitious works, now in the Royal Museum, Stockholm, are two candelabra, a giant urn on an elaborate pedestal, and a funerary monument featuring a colossal cornucopia terminating in a boar's head. Typical of the impact of such bizarre designs, especially on early nineteenth-century designers, the two *Vasi* plates depicting the latter creation were imaginatively used to transpose the concept into the modest form of an ornamental colza lamp in ormolu made by Thomas Messenger and Sons of Birmingham in 1838.[97] This transposition

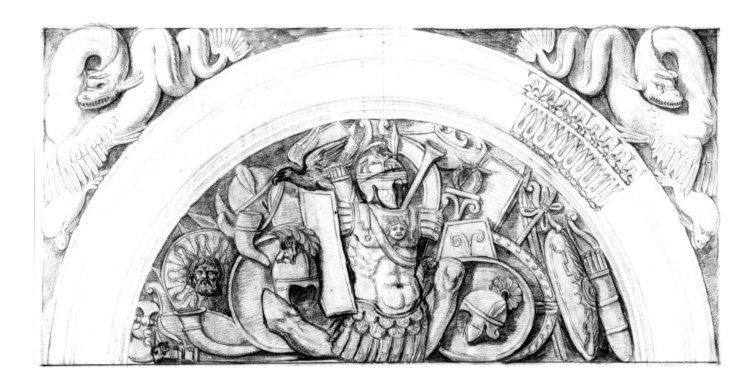

59. DESIGN FOR AN OVER-DOOR
DECORATION WITH TROPHIES
IN THE LUNETTE AND WINGED
SERPENTS AND DOLPHINS IN
SPANDRELS FOR MAIN SALON
OF VILLA ALBANI, ROME
Red and black chalk
on off-white laid paper

of an antique motif from the graphic image, rather than initiating a mode of speculative thinking, is indicative of the change of attitude toward Piranesi in an age increasingly concerned with archaeological fact. It was in other areas of creative activity that the impact of Piranesi's vision was transmitted to our own time.

PIRANESI'S LEGACY

At his death in 1778, Piranesi left behind a formidable body of graphic inspiration. Already, in his lifetime, his influence as a designer had waned with the advance of the archaeological rectitude of Neoclassicsm as promoted by the successors of Winckelmann; yet the impact of his original mode of architectural thinking was absorbed by architects who had no direct contact with him except through his widely disseminated etchings. Such was the case with Claude-Nicolas Ledoux and Etienne-Louis Boullée (fig. 62), two of the most original architects working in France at the end of the eighteenth century. Sharing Piranesi's belief in the prerogative of the designer's imagination to create revolutionary forms by pictorial means, some of the most unusual concepts of Ledoux's *barrières*, or tollhouses, in Paris took their starting point from the etched fantasies of the 1760s.[98] (fig. 63) But as a new academic orthodoxy replaced

60. FOUNTAIN WITH UPPER
BASIN TOPPED BY A PINE CONE
SUPPORTED BY WINGED
HARPIES, DOLPHIN SPOUTS
EMPTYING INTO LOWER BASIN,
n.d.
Black chalk on paper

61. Robert Adam
CANDLE STAND FROM THE
EATING ROOM, 20 ST. JAMES'S
SQUARE, n.d.
Pine and mahogany with
carved decoration applied

Pl. 29

Fragments des Propylées.

Vue Perspective.

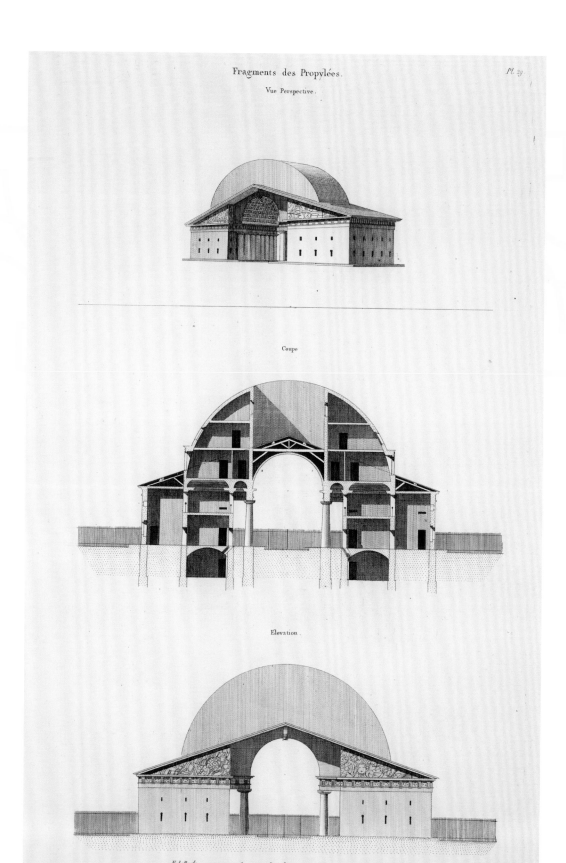

Coupe

Elevation.

Echelle de 1 2 3 4 5 6   10 toises

Le Doux Architecte du Roi   Gravé par Van Maelle

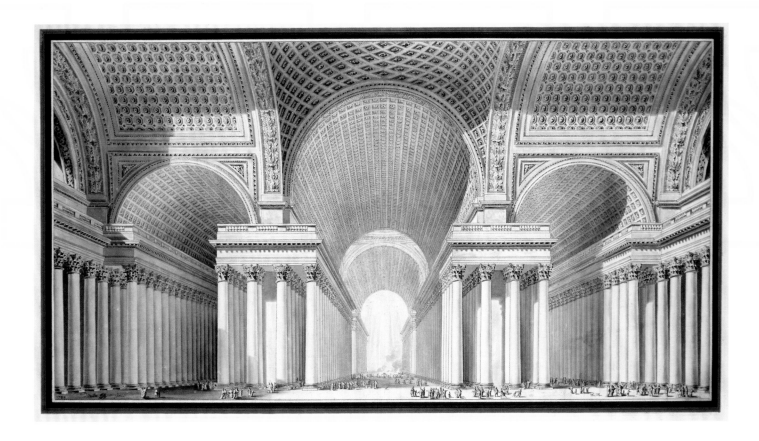

flights of the imagination as the basis of architectural education, a race of fresh theorists was swift to condemn Piranesi's visionary language, both in his etchings and executed designs. Francesco Bianconi, a devoted follower of Winckelmann, criticized the Aventine buildings when composing Piranesi's obituary in 1779 as "overloaded with ornaments which, even though taken from antiquity, were not in harmony with one another"; and Francesco Milizia, some nine years later in his survey *Roma nelle belle arti del disegno*, could not bring himself to mention the creator of S. Maria del Priorato by name.[99] It is predictable that the idiosyncratic theories of Piranesi would be equally unacceptable to one of the high priests of French classicism, Quatremère de Quincy, who makes no reference to him as a designer in his architectural dictionary that appeared from 1788 onward, even though he recognized the value of Piranesi's archaeological publications in providing evidence of license in antiquity.[100] This selective appreciation was also evident with the major Regency designer, Sir John Soane. In his lectures as professor of architecture at the Royal Academy, he had to confront the achievements of Piranesi, who had been such a catalytic force in his early development and whose publications continued to provide him with such rich visual resources.[101] While Soane's bold and radical forms of classicism in the ornamental details, expressive sequences of spaces, and interior vaulting of his masterpiece, the Bank of England, London (1788–1833), were deeply indebted to the Venetian (fig. 64), he warned his students that "novelty, although a bewitching siren, has bounds; variety, with all her charms, has limits. In both the artist must show moderation and sound judgement, not overstepping the modesty of nature lest he should fall into the excesses of Borromini and those of his school . . . like Piranesi."[102]

Throughout the nineteenth century and for most of the twentieth, Piranesi's theoretical ideas and imaginative forms were largely neglected in favor of the romantic evocations of a ruined past in the *Vedute di Roma*. The same can be said of the emotional intensity of a confined and menacing world in the *Carceri d'invenzione*, which inspired stage designers as well as a long line of writers and poets, from Samuel Taylor Coleridge and Victor Hugo to Aldous Huxley and Marguerite Yourcenar, providing them with literary inspiration or psychological metaphor.[103] Significantly, it was during the 1970s—when scholars and theorists such as Maurizio Calvesi, Manfredo Tafuri, and Joseph Rykwert began to develop new inquiries into the nature of architectural language—that Piranesi's importance to the exploration of profound issues of meaning in design was recognized.[104] In this intellectual climate, a close examination of the full range of his remarkable technical and formal expression in design resulted in a fresh awareness of its integral relationship to his theoretical and polemical writings. It is a sure indication of Piranesi's protean genius that the profound issues raised by his ceaseless visual experiments will continue to be relevant as long as the complexity and contradictions inherent in architecture and design (to paraphrase Robert Venturi's book title) continue to provoke a wider debate on the creative processes of the imagination.[105]

SEPULCHRVM

SERVILIORVM

VIA
APPIA

SARAH E. LAWRENCE

PIRANESI'S
AESTHETIC
OF ECLECTICISM

GIOVANNI BATTISTA PIRANESI BELONGS TO AN EXCEPTIONAL TRADITION OF ARTISTS WHO ARTICULATED THEIR VISIONS SIMULTANEOUSLY THROUGH GRAPHIC EXPRESSION AND VERBAL EXPOSITION.[1] IT HAS BEEN RIGHTLY ASSERTED THAT PIRANESI IS, FIRST AND FOREMOST, A VISUAL ARTIST, MORE eloquent through image than through word. The writings that accompany his published folios of etchings play an important role, nonetheless, in elucidating the motivations and meaning that inform his formal innovations. Scholarly attention to Piranesi's writings, scant in comparison to the consideration given to his artwork, has notably reproached Piranesi for contradicting himself or questioned his authorship of the ideas expressed there.[2] Recently, a more sympathetic and purposeful reading of these texts has recognized the coherence and significance of his ideas as demonstrated through a concise summary of Piranesi's remarks.[3] The intention of this essay is to allow Piranesi to speak to us through his writings in a sustained discourse over the length of his career.

Piranesi's writings interacted with his images as if in dialogue.[4] Occasionally, subsidiary plates were interspersed to illustrate his text, but in every instance a prefatory essay preceded the folio of etchings. He maintained a rhetorical pause between his verbal and graphic arguments. Piranesi's writings touched on many things, but he sought to articulate a system for the practice of design, rather than point to a specific stylistic solution. He underscored the absolute primacy of artistic license

93

in the creative process, and advocated the innovative recombination of ornamental motifs drawn from diverse cultures without the impediment of rigid theoretical requirements. The images that followed his writings demonstrated the visual richness that resulted from following this system of eclectic design, the wonders that had been achieved by the artists of ancient Rome, and a prospect of what could be achieved in the fantasies of Piranesi.

––––––––––

The *Prima parte di Architetture e Prospettive* was Piranesi's first published work, produced in 1743 when he was only twenty-three years of age. He had been in Rome just three years, and this suite of thirteen etchings of imagined architectural compositions constituted the artist's initial effort in the reform of contemporary architectural design through the didactic power of his prints.[5] The publication was dedicated to Nicola Giobbe, a Venetian architectural entrepreneur who was one of Piranesi's first significant patrons in Rome.[6] Piranesi's dedication letter spoke of the formative impact of his experiences in Rome, his circle of acquaintances, and his careful study of Giobbe's "rich and choice collection of paintings, drawings, and engravings, of which there is not one larger, or at least one formed with more exquisite taste and knowledge."[7] He began his dedication by describing the powerful impression of studying the ruins of ancient Rome firsthand:

I will tell you only that these speaking ruins have filled my spirit with images that accurate drawings, even such as those of the immortal Palladio, could never have succeeded in conveying, though I always kept them before my eyes. Therefore, having the idea of presenting to the world some of these images, but not hoping for an architect of these times who could effectively execute some of them . . . there seems to be no recourse than for me or some other modern architect to explain his ideas through drawing.[8]

While he kept a precise image of actual sculptural and architectural remains in his mind's eye, Piranesi emphasized that the designs of the *Prima parte* were not faithful copies of them. Rather, his etchings were architectural inventions whose forms were inspired by the experience of the ancient ruins, and conceived in the spirit of their example. Piranesi credited his patron with teaching him this model of creative emulation:

Most of all however, I recognize that I am indebted to your teaching, since you not only showed me piece by piece all the most singular beauties of this kind, ancient and modern that can be found in Rome; but you have shown with the example of your excellent drawings how one can make praiseworthy use of the discoveries of our great predecessors in new forms.[9]

From the very start, then, Piranesi identified the creative act as a process of appropriation and transformation that moves necessarily and significantly beyond mere imitation of ancient example.[10]

Piranesi's production and publication of his etchings were astonishingly prolific over the next decades. The *Prima parte* was followed shortly by the *Invenzioni capric di Carceri* (1749), *Varie Vedute di Roma Antica, e Moderna* (1745), *Opere varie* (1750), *Le Magnificenze di Roma* (1751), the *Trofei di Ottaviano Augusto* (1753), and *Le Antichità Romane*, which was published in 1756. With the appearance of this last publication, a major four-volume undertaking, Piranesi established himself throughout Europe as one of the foremost experts on ancient Rome, and whose authority was predicated on nearly a decade of archaeological excavation and topographical study.

It is not surprising, then, that Piranesi would be provoked by the assertions made for Greek supremacy over the allegedly inferior adaptations made by the Romans. The sweeping claim made by Marc-Antoine Laugier in his *Essai sur l'architecture* of 1753 that "architecture owes all that is perfect to the Greeks, a nation privileged . . . to have invented everything with the arts," was taken as a personal affront by Piranesi.[11] Two other publications to which he felt compelled to respond were a pamphlet published anonymously (by the painter Allan Ramsey) in *The Investigator* in 1755 and Julien-David Le Roy's *Les ruines des plus beaux monuments de la Grèce* in 1758.[12] During this same period, J. J. Winckelmann arrived in Rome, following the publication of his *Gedanken über die Nachahmung der griechischen Wercke in der Mahlerey und Bildhauer-Kunst* (1755) in Frankfurt, to become librarian to Cardinal Alessandro Albani.[13] In his polemical response, *Della Magnificenza ed Architettura de' Romani* (1761), Piranesi created a rhetorical tour de force that asserted the supremacy of ancient Roman architecture and ornament, using impassioned text, witty graphic devices, and, above all, his extraordinary etchings of Roman ruins. A central argument of his thesis was that Roman art developed out of an indigenous Etruscan culture, one even older than the Greek, which had already achieved excellence in the fine and mechanical arts. Drawing on current archaeological study of the Etruscan civilization, Piranesi was able to give Roman art the authority of a more ancient cultural heritage.[14]

Della Magnificenza was the culmination of two decades of work during which Piranesi dedicated himself to the study and imaginative reconstruction of ancient Rome. He presented his publications for the instruction of artists, scholars, and patrons alike, to guide them in the potential inspiration to be found there. While Piranesi genuinely delighted in the beauty of Roman architecture and celebrated its feats of ingenious engineering, the most significant achievement, in his estimation, was the abundant variety and richness of architectural design and decorative vocabulary. Each of Piranesi's publications is a celebration—in word and image—of ornamental invention and creative license. The texts that accompany his etchings are alternately antiquarian, archaeological, historical, and mechanical in their concerns. They are not, properly speaking, elaborations of an aesthetic theory. It is possible, nonetheless, to tease out the threads of recurrent themes that subsequently are woven together into the fabric of a coherent system of design in Piranesi's later works.

In both his selection of architectural subjects and his analysis of their design, Piranesi held up as exemplary those buildings that deviated from expectations and challenge established rules. His position was in direct opposition to the basic premise of Greek example as set forth by Laugier, who insisted that architecture should be based on a strict adherence to the fundamental principles of nature, as demonstrated by Vitruvius in his account of the rustic hut. This absolute, functionalist criterion for architectural design precluded any opportunity for variations in structural proportions and inventive ornament. In contrast, Piranesi persistently featured the very structures which did exactly that. He gave scant attention to those standards of Vitruvian rule, and instead focused on more complex, problematic instances of creative adaptation, for herein lay the lesson of the ancients for the moderns to follow.

In *Le Antichità Romane*, to give but one example from his discussion of the Theater of Marcellus, Piranesi offered the following advice:

One must not always rely upon Vitruvian rule as on some invariable law. Because when one examines the ancient monuments, one finds a large variety of proportions, the actual regularity of which—when speaking of the most significant architectural monuments—may be recognized from the circumstances of the specific place and from the constructions themselves, as I intend to explain in my book on architecture.[15]

The transgression of rules was not the result of an architect's error, but rather testament to the architect's sensitivity to the particular requirements of the building's function and situation. Piranesi was hardly the first to recognize significant divergences from Vitruvius in ancient Roman building—he followed quite consciously in a tradition from Sebastiano Serlio's *I Quattro libri dell'architettura* (1570) to Claude Perrault's *Ordonnance des cinq espèces de colonnes* (1683)—but he was surely out of sync with his eighteenth-century contemporaries.[16]

Piranesi's attention to the preponderance of anti-Vitruvian design in Roman building is evident in *Il Campo Marzio dell' Antica Roma*, published just one year after *Della Magnificenza*, in 1762.[17] In the preface to the *Campo Marzio*, Piranesi addressed his colleague and friend Robert Adam, to whom this volume was dedicated:

I am rather afraid that some parts of the Campus which I describe should seem figments of my imagination and not based on any evidence: certainly if anyone compares them with the architectural theory of the ancients he will see that they differ greatly from it and are actually closer to the usage of our own times. But before anyone accuses me of falsehood, he should, I beg, examine the ancient [marble] plan of the city . . . he should examine the villas of Latium and that of Hadrian at Tivoli, the baths, the tombs, and other ruins, especially those beyond the Porta Capena, and he will find that the ancients transgressed those strict rules of architecture just as much as the moderns. Perhaps it is inevitable and a general rule that the arts on reaching a peak should then decline, or perhaps it is part of man's nature to demand some license in creative expression as in other things, but we should not be surprised to see that the ancient architects have done the very things which we criticize in buildings of our own times.[18]

Here Piranesi was making reference to the sharp criticism given to work in the baroque style, epitomized in the work of Borromini, who was an important precedent in Piranesi's own practice.

In this context, one can appreciate Piranesi's persistent demonstration of what he called, in the *Trofei di Ottaviano Augusto*, the "capricious inventions" of architectural ornament seen in the ruins of ancient Rome because they, in particular, were "useful for painters, sculptors, and architects."[19] The frontispiece to the second volume of *Le Antichità Romane* is an extraordinary fantasy of the Appian Way.[20] (fig. 1) In the first of his letters to his intended patron Lord Charlemont, Piranesi explained in a note, "The second plate in the beginning of the second volume, that treats of the ancient sepulchers, represents the Appian Way near Rome . . . Cicero states that here the Romans' magnificence and their wish to transfer their names to the future made them erect these giant sepulchers, and that some of them recalled temples or palaces, rather than places consecrated to death. The author [Piranesi] wanted to give an idea of this con-

fusion that, as Cicero tells us, became universal."[21] This aesthetic principle of "confusion," of which Cicero did not approve any more than did Piranesi's contemporaries, was for Piranesi the very directive modern design should follow: the imagined combination of discrete architectural fragments whose fictive coherence creates a new modern vision.[22]

———

Piranesi's essential aesthetic principles of ornamental invention and creative license were derived from his sustained study of the ruins of ancient Rome. He sought to do as the Romans did. This did not mean, however, that Roman art was his only source of inspiration. A sheet of sketches by Piranesi after illustrations in Fischer von Erlach's *Entwurff einer historischen Architektur* of 1721 attests to his very early attention given to Egyptian building and ornament as another rich stylistic source (fig. 2). Greek architecture and sculpture were often seamlessly integrated into his capricci. It was not until the early 1760s, however, that he began to explore the decorative permutations possible in a truly eclectic system of design, a possibility implied but not yet fully realized in his written and graphic explorations. Piranesi added a group of ten small capricci to the *Opere Varie*, which are remarkable in their unexpected juxtaposition of Egyptian, Greek, and Roman architectural elements.

3. ANCIENT SCHOOL BUILT
IN THE EGYPTIAN AND GREEK
MANNER, from OPERE VARIE
DI ARCHITETTURE, PROSPETTIVE,
GROTTESCHI, ANTICHITÀ, 1761
Etching on off-white laid paper

In one of these, entitled *Ancient School Built in the Egyptian and Greek Manner*, Piranesi created a fantasy that combined contrasting architectural structure and ornament from these different ancient civilizations (fig. 3). Through the doorway of an entirely fanciful Egyptian post-and-lintel building in the foreground, richly decorated with hieroglyphs, one can see a classical Greek portico beyond. Although the Roman manner is unmentioned in the title, Piranesi incorporated the recognizably Roman form of a vaulted, coffered ceiling in the Egyptian-style building. In the etching entitled *Architectural Elements of Ancient Baths with Stairs that Lead to the Gymnasium and Theatre*, Piranesi created an architectural pastiche of interpenetrating, opposing architectural systems (fig. 4). Archaic Doric colonnades intersect a vaulted Roman interior, while the piers of the

4. ARCHITECTURAL ELEMENTS
OF ANCIENT BATHS WITH
STAIRS THAT LEAD TO THE
GYMNASIUM AND THEATRE,
from OPERE VARIE DI
ARCHITETTURE, PROSPETTIVE,
GROTTESCHI, ANTICHITIA, 1761
Etching on off-white laid paper

arches are curiously ornamented with applied entablatures and pediments. These fantasies convey Piranesi's earliest explorations of eclectic design, in which he followed the model of ancient Roman example: "This is what the Romans did," he was to write just five years later, "having relied for centuries on Etruscan architecture, they subsequently incorporated the Greek and little by little fully integrated the two."[23]

In 1764, the French critic, collector, and connoisseur Pierre-Jean Mariette published a letter critical of the arguments in Piranesi's *Della Magnificenza*. Piranesi responded swiftly in three different modes, bound together in a single publication that appeared the following year. The first component, entitled *Osservazioni sopra la lettre de Monsieur Mariette*, was a detailed refutation of Mariette's text, alternately critiqued and ridiculed line by line. The third, *Della introduzione e del pro-*

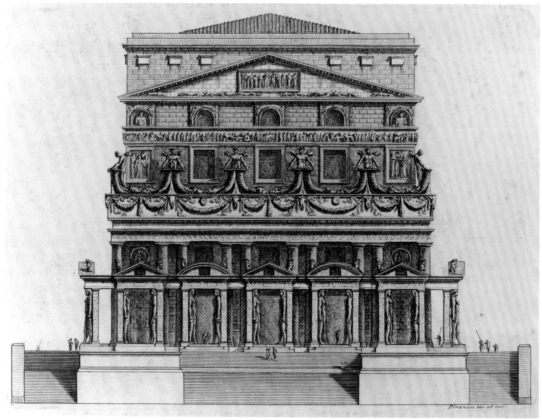

gresso delle belle arti in Europa ne' tempi antichi, essentially rehearsed his argument that the Romans were taught not by the Greeks, but by the Etruscans, in all matters of the arts as well as in politics, mathematics, and philosophy. The second essay, *Parere su l'architettura*, stood apart from the other two both in form and in substance. Piranesi finally liberated himself from the stultifying terms of the Graeco-Roman debate, and addressed the deeper issues of artistic originality and creative license that, for Piranesi, lay at the heart of the matter.

Opinions on Architecture was written in the form of a Socratic dialogue in which two architects debate the role of ornament in architecture, but the two adversaries turn quickly to the problem of imitation as a creative act. It is immediately evident from their very names that Didascalo is the teacher (διδάσκαλος) who is going to enlighten the nascent intellect of the young Protopiro (πρῶτος). Protopiro defends the ideal of a "beautiful and noble simplicity" in architecture, based on the example of the ancient Greeks; whereas Didascalo is both an admirer and an acquaintance of his colleague Piranesi, and shares his enthusiasm for the richness of ornament found in Roman architecture. The exchange was framed in response to new designs published by Piranesi, included as vignettes of fanciful porticoes that illustrated the opening and closing pages of the dialogue (figs. 5, 6). These two architectural fantasies displayed a degree of ornamental extravagance that was extreme even for Piranesi, but, intentionally provocative, they were perfectly suited to the pedagogic needs of the debate. As Didascalo remarks, "Piranesi . . . in these designs of his, has taken the crazy liberty of following his own caprice."[24] And that, of course, was exactly the issue.

Protopiro is predictably dismissive of the designs, and starts with a paraphrase of Montesquieu that "a building laden with ornament is an enigma to the eye, as a confused poem is an enigma to the mind."[25] Didascalo compels Protopiro to lay out his position in full and to articulate the functionalist criterion for architectural ornament. True to his creed, Protopiro proclaims, "Let the triglyphs show that they derive from a well-set beam, and the modillions from a regular arrangement of joists in the roof of a building." Didascalo incites him further, aiding Protopiro's argument only to drive him to the extreme conclusion that the only pure and proper architecture is an exact replication of the Vitruvian primitive hut. Didascalo, of course, holds the opposing position that all ornament should be recognized as independent of function: "What will you say, if I prove to you that austerity, reason, and imitation of huts are all incompatible with architecture? That architecture, far from requiring decorative features derived from the parts necessary for constructing and holding up buildings, consists of ornaments that are all extraneous?"[26]

Not only is the functional criterion for architectural ornament a logical impossibility for Didascalo, but also any such slavish adherence to a set of rules will prove the downfall of architecture. He challenges Protopiro:

Show me designs by any of the rigorists, anyone who thinks he has conceived a wonderful design for a building; and I warrant he will look more foolish than the man who works to please himself—yes, more foolish—because the only way he could imagine a building without irregularities is when four upright poles with a roof— the very prototype of architecture—can remain entire and unified at the very moment of being halved, varied, and rearranged in a thousand ways; in short, when the simple becomes composite, and one becomes as many as you like.[27]

The rationalist doctrine of architecture, taken to its extreme, cannot in fact even produce a building. And more significant, any architectural design that is wholly dictated by a strict adherence to theory, rather than driven by an artist's personal vision, is doomed to failure.

Didascalo then turns to another line of argument: the very human desire for variety that generates innovation. He asks, "When your simple manners of building were first established, why did the successors of those who established them soon begin to find different ways of decorating their buildings?"[28] When Protopiro denigrates the capricious ornament of Bernini and Borromini, Didascalo retorts: "You criticize the very spirit that first invented the architecture that you praise; the spirit that, seeing the world still unsatisfied, has found itself obliged to seek variety in the same ways and means that you dislike."[29] Innovation in architecture not only satisfies the demands of the public, but it constitutes the very act of creative design.

Didascalo asks that Protopiro consider what would happen if there were no innate human desire for variety. He proposes:

Let us imagine the impossible: let us imagine the world—sickened though it is by everything that does not change day to day—were gracefully to accept your monotony; what would architecture become? A low trade, in which one would do nothing but copy, as a certain gentleman has said. So that not only would you and your colleagues become extremely ordinary architects, as I said before, but further you would be something less than masons. By constant repetition, they learn to work by rote; and they have the advantage over you, because they have the mechanical skill. You would ultimately cease to be architects at all, because clients would be foolish to use an architect to carry out work that could be done far more cheaply by a mason."[30]

7. Plate IV from PARERE SU
L'ARCHITETTURA, 1765
Etching on off-white laid paper

Didascalo concludes, "And so, to set matters straight, I ask only this: by all means treasure the rationality that you proclaim, but at the same time respect the freedom of architectural creation that sustains it."[31]

As eloquent as Didascalo is made to be, the fullest expression of this "freedom of architectural creation" is found in the images therein. When the tripartite text was originally published, each essay was illustrated with small vignettes at the start and finish of each section. Three of these are assemblages of antique fragments, in which Piranesi identified the source of the central fragments as if to ensure their authenticity.[32] The other three illustrations, ostensibly the initial subject of the exchange, are absurdly gigantic temples, whose scale is indicated by the minute figures clustered in the entryways and stairs. All three buildings are characterized by their profusion of applied ornament. The temple façade on the opening page of the *Parere* bears an inscription to the Society of Antiquaries of London, an organization that had recently named Piranesi an honorary fellow.[33] Carefully suited to the pedagogic concerns of the dialogue, these architectural fantasies display anti-Vitruvian constructions that employ an ornamental system wholly independent of the structural character of its support.

A subsequent edition of the *Parere*, issued shortly after 1767, included six additional full-page plates, which are unique in their direct involvement in the polemic of Piranesi's text.[34] Their addition undoubtedly was intended to strengthen his rhetoric. The first of these is a plan and elevation for an unadorned Etruscan portico that apparently constitutes the underlying structure of the building to which the subsequent designs pertain (fig. 7). There follows a series of elaborately constructed façades, shown complete and in partial sections, that are so complex in their decorative composition that it is difficult to resolve their constituent parts. In addition to the intricate layering of ornament, Piranesi incorporated meaningful inscriptions taken from classical texts and a plethora of enigmatic iconography.

In Plate V (the first etching to follow the Etruscan portico), the upper right section of a temple façade combines components of Egyptian, Greek, and Roman ornament (fig. 8). Elaborately varied foliate decoration is conjoined with disparate motifs such as Egyptian winged ankh, a triton enlarged from an ancient cameo, and other curious motifs such as the statuary feet and a prostrate dog.[35] An inscription on the frieze is taken from Terence's *Eunuchus*: "You should know this and make allowances if the moderns do what the ancients used to do."[36] In its original context, "this" refers to copying another's prose, rather than providing one's own translation. In Plate VII, an inscription from Ovid's *Metamorphoses* reads, "Nature, the great renewer, makes up forms from other forms."[37] (fig. 9) This structure resembles a funerary monument in that it combines a sarcophagus with strigilated decoration that is topped by oversized profiles in bas relief, symmetrically arranged on either side of paired pan pipes. The inscription itself is incorporated into the upper frieze, which shows a more conventional arrangement of robed female figures hanging a garland on herms. The next plate, numbered VIII, turns to a contemporary source for its quotation from the philhellenic Julien-David Le Roy, "So as not to make this sublime art into a vile profession where one would only copy without choice."[38] In this amazing façade, recognizable classical elements are juxtaposed with incongruous inventions of Piranesi's own, such as a ram's head set into shells (fig. 10). This composition is particularly challenging to read, as shifts in scale and deceptive overlay create the trompe l'oeil effects exploited by Piranesi's innovative graphic design.

With the exception of the very first of these illustrations, the final composition is the only one to present a complete façade and extends to fill a double-width plate (fig. 11). Here, a particularly pointed inscription is taken from Sallust's *Bellum Igurthinum*, which reads, "They despise my novelty, I their timidity."[39] This plate is the proper culmination of the series in which shifting planes of ornamental reliefs—plaques, foliate borders, heraldic shields, and tablets—are suspended in ambiguous relation to one another. Their correspondence to the underlying structure is tenuous, yet the ornamental components recognize the essential elements of architectural forms by emphasizing the vertical accents of the columnar façade and the horizontal axis of the pediment. The components are Egyptian, Greek, and Roman, with other elements entirely of Piranesi's own imagination. All of the quotations that Piranesi inscribed here were quite clearly pointed references to his central thesis that slavish imitation undermines architecture—even in the case of Le Roy, who ostensibly was an advocate of such exact replication.

These astonishing images were a vivid realization of Piranesi's enthusiasm for unrestrained ornamental elaboration. It is perhaps challenging, though, to recognize these plates as meeting Piranesi's requirements of ornamentation:

Let [the architect] single out the main subject from the accompaniment; spectators should not be faced with a multitude of objects, all or most of them competing to be the main attraction. The decorations should be graded as they are in nature, some being more imposing and dignified than others. In such art, as in nature, the eyes will not see confusion but a pleasing arrangement of things. And, in truth, if the ornaments used in architecture are beautiful in themselves, then the architecture will also be beautiful.[40]

Piranesi demanded a perceptible hierarchy of ornament, one that allowed the viewer to readily discern primary motives from peripheral elaborations. Furthermore, ornament should not conceal the underlying structure of the building, but delineate it. The legibility of decorative order is achieved in these designs by the responsible correspondence of the ornamental components to the essential, prominent horizontal and vertical divisions of architectural form.

Tav.VI

Cavaliere Piranesi inv.

8. Plate v from PARERE
SU L'ARCHITETTURA, 1765
Etching on off-white laid paper

9. Plate VII from PARERE
SU L'ARCHITETTURA, 1765
Etching on off-white laid paper

In his last publication, with the unwieldy and rather mundane title *Divers Manners of Ornamenting Chimneys and All Other Parts of Houses, Taken from the Egyptian, Tuscan, and Grecian Architecture, with an Apologetic Essay in Defence of the Egyptian and Tuscan Architecture* (1769), Piranesi shifted his rhetorical mode from the *Parere*'s highly stylized Socratic dialogue, in defense of the architect's "crazy liberty of following his own caprice," to a systematic and practical application of his aesthetic of eclecticism to interior decoration.[41] The *Diverse maniere*, as it is commonly known, was dedicated to Cardinal Giambattista Rezzonico, the nephew of the Venetian Pope Clement XIII and one of Piranesi's most significant patrons during this period. In the dedication, he complimented Cardinal Rezzonico on his judicious taste:

*Dissatisfied with contemporary fashion in architectural decoration, you would like
our architects in their work to use not only the Greek style, but also the Egyptian and
the Etruscan styles, with discernment and sensitivity, taking from those monuments
whatever is subtle and beautiful.*[42]

The frontispiece to the *Diverse maniere* provides the reader with an immediate and dramatic manifestation of Piranesi's proposition (fig. 12). A
richly ornamented façade, reminiscent of the plates illustrating the
Parere, is a bold combination of Egyptian figures and hieroglyphs that
support Greek and Roman ornament. More staid than the *Parere* illustra-

11. Plate IX from PARERE
SU L'ARCHITETTURA, 1765
Etching on off-white laid paper

tions, the relief decoration is coherently applied to the architectural support behind it and designates a chronological progression from Egyptian sources at its base, rising upward toward the culmination of Roman triumphal imagery at the top.

In the 1760s, largely due to Rezzonico patronage, Piranesi undertook several significant commissions that allowed him to apply his newly articulated aesthetic theory to architectural ornament and interior furnishings. This included schemes for the new tribune for the west end of S. Giovanni in Laterano; the refurbishment of the priory church for the Order of Malta on the Aventine; and the private apartments of the Rezzonico family at Castel Gandolfo, the Quirinal, and the Palazzo Senatorio, complete with furnishings. Many of his designs for these decorative interiors were illustrated in the *Diverse Maniere* along with an extensive series of designs for mantelpieces, some of which were completed commissions for other private patrons, as well as his program for the painted decoration of the Caffè degli Inglesi, a coffee-house at the foot of the Spanish Steps. The remaining designs in its sixty-six engraved plates were proposed schemes designed to instruct practitioners and solicit business.

The prefatory essay of the *Diverse maniere* was presented in three parallel texts in Italian, French, and English, an indication of the international scope of his intended audience. At the very start, Piranesi explained his purpose: "What I pretend by the present designs is to show what an able architect may make of the ancient monuments by properly adapting them to our own manners and customs."[43] In addition to architectural remains, he listed ancient medals, cameos, bas reliefs, and statuary, all of which provide a repertoire of ornamentation, that could be "united in an artful and masterly manner" to create a new modern idiom. He boasted of his particular authority in recommending this novel method of design: "I flatter myself that the great and serious study I have made upon all the happy remains of ancient monuments has enabled me to execute this useful and . . . even necessary project."[44] He also underscored the considerable significance of this endeavor: "Whoever has the least introduction to the study of antiquity may plainly see how large a field I have thus laid open for the industry of our artists to work upon."[45] It was an industry, however, that had to be undertaken with care. The successful designer appropriated ancient motifs with discretion and transformed them with artistic imagination into innovative design.

The decline of eighteenth-century architectural design, and of its ornamentation in particular, Piranesi attributed as much to the patron as to the architect: "One would think that ornaments are used in architecture not to embellish them, but to render them ugly. I know indeed that in this the caprice of those for whom the buildings are made has often more part than the architect who makes the design."[46] Piranesi appreciated the importance of suiting decoration to the character of the situation, whether this was the function of the building or the particular interests of the client.

A military man will have arms and instruments of war everywhere, whether they be proper or not. A seafaring man will have ships, tritons, dolphins, and shells. An antiquarian will have nothing but ruins of ancient temples, broken columns, statues of gods, and emperors. Let them have their will, for no curb ought to be put on the caprices of men, but then let them be executed according to rules of art. Let tritons and fish be placed on chimneys, if it be so required, but let them not so cover the frame as entirely to hide it, or take away its character. Let the architect be as extravagant as he pleases, so he destroys no architecture, but gives every member its proper character.[47]

Both the architect and the patron may indulge their decorative whims, he cautioned, as long as the integrity of the architectural support remained firmly intact. In doing so, one emulated the excellent example of

DIVERSE MANIERE
D'ADORNARE I CAMMINI
ED OGNI ALTRA PARTE DEGLI EDIFIZI DESVNTE
DALL'ARCHITETTVRA EGIZIA ETRVSCA GRECA E ROMANA

PRESENTATE
A
MONSIG D GIOVAMBATISTA
REZZONICO
NIPOTE E MAGGIORDVOMO
DELLA SANTITA DI N S
PP CLEMENTE XIII
E GRAN PRIORE IN ROMA
DELLA SAC RELIGIONE
GEROSOLIMITANA

DAL CAV GIOVAMBATISTA PIRANESI
SVO ARCHITETTO

the ancients: "This the ancients had in view: we ought to follow their manner and observe the kind of ornaments used by them, the manner in which they disposed them to make them harmonious with the whole."

Following the general tenor of his previous writings, Piranesi constructed his essay as a rebuttal against criticism that he anticipated in response to his program of eclectic design: "It will be said, for instance, that I have loaded my designs with too many ornaments; others again will find fault that in ornamenting cabinets, where the agreeable, the delicate, and the tender ought only to have place, I have employed the Egyptian and Tuscan manners which are, according to the common opinion, bold, hard and stiff."[48] In answer to this first concern, Piranesi reiterated his position given in the *Parere*: "If the artist knows how to order them in such a manner that those above make no confusion with those which are under, and to give to the reliefs that just projection which is proper to each, the whole will appear graceful, and in no wise offend the eye."[49]

The second and more substantive issue that Piranesi sought to redress was that elaborate ornamentation may be poorly suited to certain decorative modes: "Each nation has its own [character and manner], from which it is not lawful to deviate."[50] Both the Egyptian and Etruscan styles were associated with spare and monumental forms that might not readily serve as a source of ornamental motifs. Piranesi was quick to challenge this characterization of either Egyptian or Etruscan art, and insisted that a more careful study would reveal how rich their ornamentation in fact was. It is curious, in advocating an eclectic system of design, that Piranesi would suggest that decorative motifs—extracted from their original context and recombined with another's ornamental vocabulary—should remain beholden to their indigenous stylistic character. This may well have been a rhetorical ruse, the real purpose of which was to emphasize the ornamental richness of Egyptian and Etruscan art and hence their significance as a suitable resource for Piranesi's eclectic decorative vocabulary. The remainder of his essay was a sustained consideration of the decorative values to be found in these cultures.

In Rome, at the start of the eighteenth century, there was a keen interest in things Egyptian following the discovery of five Egyptian statues from what came to be recognized as a pavilion built by the emperor Hadrian.[51] Piranesi played an important role in the cultivation of a taste for the Egyptian style at this time, particularly in its application to ornament. In 1768, he sent a set of proof plates for the *Diverse maniere* to Thomas Hollis, a colleague at the Society of Antiquaries, with a letter that emphasized the originality of his ideas: "You will see in this work something that has been hitherto unknown. For the first time

Egyptian architecture makes an appearance, for the first time I stress, because until now the world has thought it consisted of nothing but pyramids, obelisks, and cast statues, and concluded that these were insufficient to form a basis for architectural ornament and design."[52] In his introductory essay to the *Diverse maniere*, he cited examples of rich ornamentation to be found in statuary, obelisks, capitals, and urns. One decorative scheme that he described in detail featured "a head of a character between the human and that of a lion, covered with a horned cap, a stiff statue with four faces under the banner with a kind of obelisk on each side, on the top of which sits a bird on a festoon, a dypteric ovolo, with two birds expanded under the festoon, and lastly the *Tao*, or something resembling that letter, adorned with two horizontal triglyphs, which descend from the transverses. Now from whence could such a disposition of things on a goal take its rise? From the artist's intention of representing a mystery, or of delighting the eye with ornament?"[53] Piranesi perceived a kindred spirit in the artist who had created this inscrutable and extravagant imagery. He rejected the customary characterization of Egypt as a mysterious and distant culture, whose pictographic language and highly stylized forms were part of a hermetically obscure civilization. "These are not mysteries," Piranesi insisted, "but caprices of Egyptian artists."[54]

Furthermore, in his estimation, this decorative ornamentation showed a high degree of naturalism. Egyptian artists were commonly criticized for the lack of grace and expressiveness so perfectly achieved by the figural arts of the Greeks. Piranesi defended the artistic ability of the Egyptians: "If we reflect a little, we find that we accuse of hardness what is only a solidity required by the quality of architecture." The deliberate archaizing, he maintained, was necessitated by a profound veneration for the sacred in Egyptian culture, and thus affirmed the architect's sensitivity to the particular requirements of the building's function. Piranesi concluded with the specific example of the sphinx on the famous obelisk in the Campus Martius: "I am certain that an understanding eye will see in it not only the grand and the majestic, which no one denies the Egyptians, but likewise that delicacy, that fleshiness, and that palpableness, which are supposed to have been known only to the Greeks and never to the Egyptians. But far from being ignorant of them, they knew them even long before the Greeks."[55]

Turning to the Etruscans, Piranesi insisted that Etruscan art originated in the abstraction of natural forms, particularly seashells.[56] Inserted in the text were several plates that demonstrated the close imitation of the form and patterning of shells evident in Etruscan vase decoration and architectural ornament, most notably the Ionic capital (fig. 13). The juxtaposition of this plate with one of the fragmentary motifs from antiquity is meaningful: the lesson of eclectic design manifest in the history of art is but a reflection of the same lesson found first in nature's variety within species.[57] Not only did Etruscan art emerge independently of Greek influence, but it evolved autonomously out of nature itself and thus can lay claim to the most ancient and authentic origins possible.

In closing, Piranesi claimed to have vindicated Egyptian and Etruscan art from the unfair criticism they had received, and he justified his recommendation to combine Egyptian and Etruscan decorative motifs with the Greek:

But let us at last shake off this shameful yoke [of the exclusive imitation of Grecian manners], and if the Egyptians and Tuscans present to us in their monuments beauty, grace, and elegance, let us borrow from their stock, not servilely copying from others, for this would reduce architecture and the noble arts to a pitiful mechanism, and would deserve blame instead of praise from the public, who seek novelty. . . . No, an artist who would do himself honor, and acquire a name, must not content himself with copying faithfully from the ancients, but studying their works he ought to show himself of an inventive and I had almost said of a creating genius; and by prudently combining the Grecian, the Tuscan, and the Egyptian together, he ought to open himself to the finding of new ornaments and new manners.[58]

Piranesi made no mention, here or in the title, of Roman architecture; only Egyptian, Greek, and Etruscan. But, as Piranesi stated in his dedicatory remarks, this was because the Romans exemplified the successful practice of assimilating and recombining the ornamental vocabulary of these three cultures into a distinct and original decorative language. Roman art provided the practical model of eclectic design that Piranesi admonished his contemporary architects to follow.

Much like the Etruscan portico of the *Parere*, the mantelpiece served as the structural support for Piranesi's eclectic design. In choosing this feature of domestic interiors, Piranesi knowingly contributed to an established literature of pattern books in vogue that were concerned specifically with the decoration of the mantelpiece. It has been suggested that Piranesi's selection was motivated by a continuing preoccupation with the Graeco-Roman controversy, for he offered up a Roman improvement on what is usually thought of as a French (Philhellenic) concern.[59] More significant, perhaps, the mantelpiece was a ubiquitous feature of the modern home, one that lacked ancient precedent. Piranesi was able to

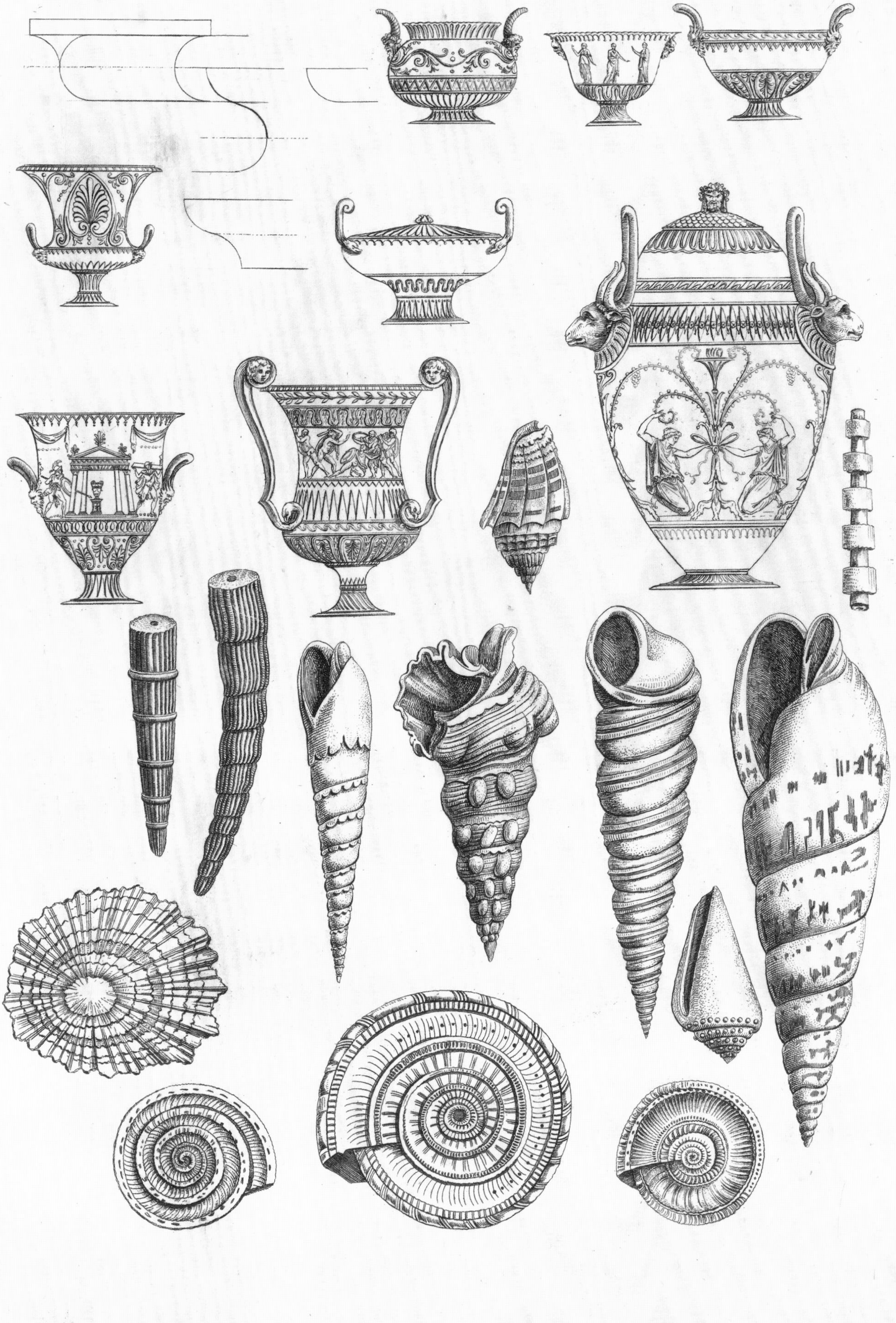

Cavaliere Piranesi incise

give currency to his system of eclectic design, unfettered by ancient precedent, in a way that pertained directly to the domestic circumstance of his readership. This strategy underscored the viability of his method, and also had the pragmatic potential to encourage commissions for himself and be most immediately useful to other practicing designers.

These mantel designs have less of the astonishingly peculiarity of Piranesi's plates in the *Parere*. In the *Diverse maniere*, the introductory essay accompanies the plates; the plates do not illustrate the essay. There are others interspersed with the text that do—specifically the plates juxtaposing the morphology of shells with Etruscan ornamental form. These mantelpiece designs effectively demonstrate the rich variety of manners in which Piranesi's method of eclectic design could be realized. The designer may choose to work in a single mode, or combine ornament from diverse sources in a single work. Piranesi summarized the design process himself:

The Roman and Tuscan were at first one and the same, the Romans learned architecture from the Tuscans, and made use of no other for many ages; they afterwards adopted the Grecian, not on account that the Tuscan was deficient either in parts, ornaments, or beauty; but because novelty and merit rendered agreeable certain elegances and graces peculiar to the Greeks, as each nation has its own; the Tuscan and Grecian were mixed together, the graces and beauty of the one became common to the other, and the Romans found means to unite them both in one and the same work. That is what I likewise have pretended to do in these chimneys, which are not after the Egyptian manner, to unite the Tuscan or what is the same, the Roman with the Grecian, and to make the beautiful and elegant of both of them united subservient to my design. The connoisseurs will easily distinguish what belongs to the Greeks and what to the Tuscans.[60]

There were mantelpieces that are executed "in the Egyptian Style," in which Piranesi imaginatively combined motifs from diverse Egyptian sources of varying scale—scarabs, sphinxes, obelisks—to fabricate a coherent and entirely original design (fig. 14). In only rare instances did Piranesi combine elements from Egyptian, Etruscan, Greek, and Roman art, fully integrated in a single design. In one example, the central decorative element over the fireplace opening combines a Pompeian motif of winged victories above a garland of masks entwined by a snake, a motif that Piranesi identified elsewhere as Etruscan. The pilasters of this mantelpiece feature Egyptian figures in profile, flanking a vertical post decorated with hieroglyphs.[61] (fig. 15)

119

15. MANTELPIECE IN THE
EGYPTIAN STYLE, from DIVERSE
MANIERE D'ADORNARE..., 1769
Etching on off-white laid paper

In the *Diverse maniere*, Piranesi set out a flexible system of design, applied here to interior decoration, but arising—as we have seen—from a concern for architectural design in the broadest sense. This was made plain in his concluding statement:

Some one will perhaps accuse my works of extravagance, but whoever he might be, I desire he will show me where they are wanting with regard to laws and rules of good design, of proportion, of character, and of form. If he be not able to show me these defects, I shall be very easy by what names my works shall be characterized by such as think every thing extravagant which deviates from the monotonous style. I hope the public will do justice to my labors, and will discover in these designs, and in those which I shall hereafter publish, an ardent zeal for the fine arts, but chiefly for architecture.[62]

Piranesi found in the magnificent ruins of ancient Rome a model for the creative practice of the architect. More significant even than the vast repertoire of architectural structure and ornament displayed in their work, the Roman architects enacted a process of appropriation and transformation from diverse sources—first of Etruscan and then of Greek influences—to produce a consciously original Roman style. Piranesi embraced this method, and encouraged the inclusion of the Egyptian style as yet another potent source of inspiration in the creation of his own innovative design. This model can be endlessly extended: the history of human creativity provides the artist with a vast repertoire of decorative motifs that can be explored in ever new combinations. Piranesi effectively broke the boundaries of the previously closed system of creative license within a specifically classical tradition. His writings and art demonstrate a historical sensibility that situates Piranesi firmly within the intellectual mindset of the European Enlightenment. He consciously sought out a modern system of design, not a style to be followed. He demonstrated complete confidence in the highly original results of such a process, which transforms the future of architectural design and alters our conception of its past.

PETER N. MILLER

PIRANESI
AND THE ANTIQUARIAN
IMAGINATION

1. Jean-Baptiste-Siméon Chardin
THE ANTIQUARIAN MONKEY
(LE SINGE ANTIQUAIRE), 1743
Oil on canvas

NO SINGLE IMAGE HAS BEEN MORE DEVASTATING TO THE REPUTATION OF ANTIQUARIAN SCHOLARSHIP THAN JEAN-BAPTISTE-SIMÉON CHARDIN'S *LE SINGE ANTIQUAIRE* (FIG. 1). IT MOCKS THE DILIGENCE—PRESENTED HERE AS MYOPIA— OF THE ANTIQUARIAN. SEDULOUSNESS, IF NOT DOWNRIGHT
credulousness, is the byword. But as Jean Seznec taught us long ago, Chardin belonged to Denis Diderot's bid for cultural authority against learned mandarins like the Comte de Caylus.[1] The caricaturing of "erudition" in the *Encyclopédie* was, perhaps, the final blow in a century-long campaign, the earlier high points of which included Shackerly Mermion's *The Antiquary* (1640), which left the image of the antiquary itself in ruin.

But Edison was right: while invention might be ninety-nine percent perspiration, one percent of inspiration always remains. If we think about the great erudite labors, and laborers, of the early modern age, we find Herculean feats of scholarship, but also, always, that flash of inspiration. Whether it is Joseph Scaliger's feats of textual emendation; Peiresc's leaping, comparative conjectures; or Caylus's own deeply emotional feeling for objects, we will always find that irreducibly human, even "romantic," one percent. Indeed, any kind of restoration, of a painting or poem or pot, implies an ability to imagine a wholeness that once preceded fragmentation. Of course, this imagination is based on almost endless study—but that was precisely Edison's point.

123

Now, if a single term could describe antiquarian scholarship in Europe, it would have to be "reconstruction." Antiquity could not be revived before it was reconstructed, and that labor—philological, archaeological, and, yes, even psychological—was the burden of the antiquarian. The bewildering style of antiquarian scholarship, always ready to veer off into yet another minor side point, and rarely prepared to explain its importance, is actually a function of how distant we are from that very practice of reconstruction. Scholars interested in putting the remaining, and often fragmentary, pieces of that old Humpty Dumpty back together again took the past as their last. They fit the pieces within the categories their learning had taught them were the past's own categories, whether calendars, legal codes, weights and measures, lists of consuls, or children's games. The articulation of monographic theses and the marshaling of evidence to serve single arguments were not the realm of antiquarians. That work was for later generations who could make use of their spadework and for whom the past loomed less large, less awesome.

Chardin's monkey presented the act of reconstruction in its dimmest, waning light. It was, alas, by this light that subsequent generations saw the antiquarians of the sixteenth, seventeenth, and eighteenth centuries. But perhaps there are other ways of understanding the practice of the antiquary at that moment in the mid-eighteenth century, when the tide was supposedly already turning? And perhaps these ways can not only help make better sense of the prior history of antiquarianism, but also pierce the darkness of the *later*, modern history of that antiquarian urge to reconstruct? For this enterprise, Giovanni Battista Piranesi, architect, artist, and antiquarian, is the crucial figure.

———

If we reapproach the history of antiquarian scholarship—that wide lost sea that was partially, but ever so provocatively, charted by the great Arnaldo Momigliano—we find that, from the beginning of the revival of letters, erudition and imagination were intertwined.[2]

A popular humanist trope was the walk through Rome. It was inaugurated by Petrarch, made famous by Poggio, canonized by Vasari—of Brunelleschi he wrote that "such was this study that he became completely capable of seeing Rome in his mind's eye, just as it was before it was ruined"—and then, as usual, cribbed from him by Burckhardt. The account of the young Peiresc's walk through Rome around 1600 was, therefore, already a cliché—and therefore all the more valuable as evidence for the commonplace connection between imagination and erudition. As Peiresc walked through Rome, his biographer wrote:

He would fain know, as much as might be, where stood the Temples of the Ancients, their Chap-Schooles, Libraries, Amphitheaters, Theaters, Wrastling-places, Horse-race-places, Places to represent Seafights, Fields, Musick-Rooms, Markets, Faires, Granaries, Armories, Baths, Hotbaths, Waters, Bridges, Collosuses, Spires, Columns, Statues and a thousand other things which in his reading of Authors he had observed, and noted into Books which he carried around with him.[3]

All these learned strollers looked out upon the malarial ruins of the modern city and saw instead the splendors of ancient Rome, *caput mundi*. What made this possible was imagination. It was precisely this faculty that was implied in Cyriac of Ancona's legendary boast that his epigraphic and archaeological research could wake the dead.[4] In fact, only through imagination can the past be brought back to life. When Freud recurred to the humanist's imagined Rome in *Civilization and Its Discontents*, he showed a perfect grasp of the intertwining of past and present implied in the work of imagination and reconstruction.[5]

As early as the end of the fifteenth century, however, one could already discern what a shift in the balance of erudition and imagination might look like. Francesco Colonna's erotic archaeological novel *Hypnerotomachia Poliphilii* is imbued with passion for learning, and learned passion, as Anthony Grafton has observed.[6] With woodcuts gently paraphrasing Cyriac's careful drawings into a vernacularized antiquity, Colonna's masterpiece tapped the imagination latent in any encounter with the past.[7] Nothing like its wondrous, innocent vision would be produced again, but the idea of the antiquarian novel would find imitators.

In the world of the antiquaries, Cyriac, with his prayers to Mercury and invocations to the dead, was followed by Pomponio Leto (1425–1498), who not only wrapped himself in Roman learning and clothing, but also, along with his friends, marked the ancient Roman festivals. After him, the outstanding figure of the next generation was Pirro Ligorio (1510–1583), an architect and learned advisor to popes and cardinals, who was at the heart of antiquarian life in Rome in the middle of the sixteenth century. Central to his legacy—and a subject of much dispute amongst his contemporaries—was his reconstruction of ancient monuments. His detailed drawings of existing structures, coins, and inscriptions were infused with his own "completion" of surviving fragments. Should they be considered forgeries or restorations?[8] Howard Burns's judgment seems worth recalling:

Ligorio's knowledge, concern with authenticity, and constant reference to his sources should never be underestimated: to accuse him of forgery, as was once done, is a com-

plete misunderstanding of his methods, and of the ways in which his aims departed from those of the modern archaeologist. His concern was to make broken antiquities, ruined Rome, whole again. To do so meant continual reference to analogous examples, continual restoration of individual works by reference to types.... Attention to sources, and dedication to historical authenticity however is no less central to his project than it is to that of modern scholars.[9]

———————

The "case" of Ligorio offers the best introduction to the problematics of Piranesi: Is a visual intelligence inherently less scholarly than a textual one? Is the use of learned imagination to "complete" or "perfect" the broken remains of antiquity a skill or a sin? And if it is a skill, then what does it teach us about the relationship between imagination and erudition, a relationship which goes back to the beginning of antiquarian scholarship and sensibility in the era of Petrarch and Cola di Rienzo?[10] If Piranesi's work on ruins was all too often treated as a kind of "black" sequel to the *Hypnerotomachia*, what followed placed him instead in a line that began with Cyriac of Ancona and passed by way of Ligorio into the eighteenth century. In the final part of this essay, I will try to sketch the arc of this line as it passes beyond Piranesi and suggest how this approach to the study of antiquarian work reveals new connections to nineteenth- and twentieth-century literature.

The landmark works of twentieth-century Piranesi scholarship, such as Focillon's biography, shifted attention away from the romantic Piranesi of the *Carceri* and *Prima Parte di Architettura* and back to the historical context of Piranesi's Italy.[11] Other work, like John Wilton-Ely's *Mind and Art of Piranesi*, focused on Piranesi as a theorist of neoclassicism battling with the French and Germans over the value of Roman style.[12] All these works helped to put the focus on the *content* of Piranesi's work. Along with this shift came much closer scrutiny of Piranesi's writings, especially the polemical texts, but also the more methodological prefaces. Collections such as *Piranesi e la cultura antiquaria* (1985), Norbert Wolf's essay *Der Römische Circus* (1977), and Lola Kantor-Kazovsky's monograph on Piranesi's intellectual context (2006) in turn not only attached Piranesi to the debates of his own time, but also delved deeper still into the background of some of Piranesi's writings.[13]

How Piranesi compared to other antiquaries can be debated, but there can be no doubting the erudite impression his images were designed to produce. Augusta Monfereini suggested that Piranesi's novelty was in uniting all the strands of the archaeological culture of his time: text-based erudition, an architect's graphic style, an engineer's interest in models, and a dilettante's passion for the past. For her, it was Piranesi's "empiricism" that marked his approach.[14] For Susan Dixon, by contrast, the key to Piranesi's visual culture rested in his entrenchment in an eighteenth-century Italian antiquarianism that relied on the power of images for reconstruction. Serious antiquaries such as Francesco Bianchini (1662–1729), in particular, have emerged as crucial models for Piranesi's archaeological work of the early 1760s.[15]

Antiquarianism, yes, and images, yes, but not imagination. And yet what distinguishes Piranesi's reconstructions from those of his predecessors was the extent to which the traditional antiquarian activity of reconstructing the past was actually given content by the work of his imagination. If all reconstruction requires imaginative leaps, then, in the case of Piranesi, the pursuit of what the past was like led him to envision structures and processes that could not be reconstructed because they either did not survive (things) or could not survive (processes). In his *Entwurf einer Historischen Architekur* (1721), Fischer von Erlach explained that one may "in historical imagination not rely on knowledge drawn from narratives alone, for the eyes themselves can draw conclusions from plans."[16] But what Piranesi added to this belief was the serious learning of an antiquarian in the Italian tradition.

Yet no matter how learned the scholar, this sort of imagining could easily look like invention. Reactions to Ligorio, both in his own lifetime and later, reflected this. He was appreciated for his erudition and scorned as a forger. Much the same was said about Piranesi. But these judgments were based on a notion of reconstruction that in some sense was anachronistic and misleading. The past, according to nineteenth-century archaeologists, did not exist "out there," or, in this case, "under there," just waiting to be disinterred. Pre-modern antiquaries understood this truth long before it became "postmodern" to invoke it. Waking the dead, as Cyriac hoped, and as those who follow him hope, is not about dusting off the thing outside of oneself, but about training oneself to better perceive those fragments outside of oneself that do survive. The essence of modern archaeology is precisely this ability to imagine from a few rows of stones the elevation of a building; from scattered tools, their use; and from broken bones, the lives and deaths of our ancestors. None of the high-tech tools of modern science could achieve their end without an imagination capable of integrating information into something living. In the end, waking the dead is a function of the living inquirer's own imagination.

So, rather than looking at instances of Piranesi's imagination in action—whether in inspired fantasies like the *Carceri* or more archaeologically informed examples such as the "Via Appia Antica" or "Arena" that served as frontispieces to volumes two and three of *Le Antichità Romane*—I prefer to turn to examples of Piranesi using his imagination as a tool of the most concrete reconstruction.

In his "Preface to Students of Roman Antiquities," Piranesi began by noting that "simple exterior observation of the remains of the ancient magnificence of Rome" provided enough material for those concerned with the question of good taste in architecture. But what he proposed to do was something else entirely: not only looking at the external appearance of things, "but also at plans and at the interior; distinguishing the parts by way of sections and profiles and indicating the materials and sometimes the manner of their construction, according to what I have been able to depict in the passage of many years of tireless, most exact observation, excavations and researches; things that were never tried in the past."[17]

How did Piranesi propose to "see into the life of things?"[18] By "many years of tireless, most exact observation." Only by doing the scholarship could he have reached the position of being able to complete the transformation of fragments into an accessible whole. Whether he was cutting away the side of a hill or peeling back the skin of a building, Piranesi was constantly looking into things with his mind's eye. Some of this can be attributed to archaeology—to knowledge derived from excavation, as in Piranesi's dissection of a Roman road (in this case the Via Appia) in figure VII of volume three (fig. 2) of the *Antichità*. But most of the time, Piranesi's cross sections were extrapolated from reality, as in his depiction of the tomb of Alexander Severus (vol. 2, fig. XXXII) (fig. 3). A comparison to some of the archaeological images in the Comte de Caylus's *Recueil d'antiquités égyptiennes, étrusques, grecques, romaines, et gauloises* (7 vol., 1752–67) reveals just how much richer Piranesi's picture of the past was as a whole.

Perhaps nowhere, though, is Piranesi's use of imagination to completely realize his erudition so obvious as in the two plates that conclude volume three of the *Antichità Romane*. Having launched into a treatment of the tomb of C. Metella on the Via Appia, these two final plates departed from depictions of the tomb itself in order to analyze just how it was made. The first, figure LIII, was an examination of Roman building tools in action. The second, figure LIV, was of the tools themselves. What is striking is that, in both cases, Piranesi had no evidence to work from—and he acknowledged as much in the captions to these two engravings.[19]

Introducing figure LIII (fig. 4), Piranesi explained that "visiting the ancient monuments of Rome every day and examining all of their most

Tab. VII

Veduta dell'antica Via Appia, che passa sotto le mura già descritte nelle passate tavole dell'Ustrino, oggi ricoperta nelle rovine del medesimo. A. Letto del terreno ben sodato, e battuto con pali, prima di stendere la grossa riempitura alta palmo uno a simiglianza di lastrico composto di calce pozzolana, e scaglie di selci, sopra di esso piantati a forza i selci B. tagliati nel roverscio a punta di diamante C. Altri selci posti a guisa di cunei, i quali stringono e gagliardamente rinserrano i selci sudetti, che lastricano la Via già detta, fra quali ogni 30 palmi ewene uno D. più emimente, e superiore degli altri di tal fatta, quale dovea servire forse a quelli, che montavano, e smontavano da cavallo, e di riposo a Viandanti. Questo e gli altri inferiori sono piantati sopra un grosso muro di riempitura di simili scaglie di selci, ma più grandi delle mentovate di sopra

Piranesi Archit. del. inc.

*Spaccato del Sepolcro di Aleſſandro Severo. A Contorno del Maſſo, oggi detto il Monte del grano. B Ingreſſo, il quale porta al Centro, ove poſava l'Urna di marmo colle ceneri . C Cen-
tro del Sepolcro. D Altr Ingreſſi riempiuti dalle rovine . E Volta inferiore, la quale era ſoſtenuta da Colonne, è nel mezzo roſtava aperta . F Pozzo antico. G Fineſtre le quali portavano il lume. H Laſtrico compoſto di minute scaglie, tavolozza, e calce, il quale è coperto da un altro Laſtrico più liſcio compoſto della ſteſſa materia molto più fina . I Scala, la quale porta al piano del
Centro del Sepolcro. Al tempo di Flaminio Vacca, ſiccome egli laſciò scritto nelle ſue memorie, un Cavatore ebbe l'animo di forare sì enorme ſoda mole ſino al centro, donde fu eſtratta l'
Urna, la quale vedraſsi qui appreſſo.*

Piranesi Archit. diſ ed inc.

3. SPACCATO DEL SEPOLCRO DI
ALESSANDRO SEVERO (SECTION
OF THE TOMB OF ALEXANDER
SEVERUS), fig. XXXII, vol. 1, LE
ANTICHITÀ ROMANE, 1756–57
Etching on off-white laid paper

4. MODO, QUALE FURONO
ALZZATI I GROSSI TRAVERTINI…
(MEANS BY WHICH THE LARGE
BLOCKS OF TRAVERTINE AND
MARBLE…), fig. LIII, vol. 2, LE
ANTICHITÀ ROMANE, 1756–57
Etching on off-white laid paper

minute parts, I saw, in those great blocks out of which they were built, squared openings, intentionally hollowed out." He explained that these holes must have been used for inserting the tool that lifted the stone, described by Vitruvius as a *Forfice* or *Ulivella*. The purpose of the other hole, on the side of the stone, remained "unknown and obscure; nor do I know whether it has been truly penetrated by anyone to this day."

Piranesi continued, inside the caption, with his narrative: "Amidst the ruins of the tomb of Cecilia Metella, called the Ox's Head, my eye chanced upon some fragments of giant travertine [F,G] in which I would discover what, for such a long time—ever since I found myself in Rome—I could never understand." Piranesi then went on to describe these pieces and their shapes and indentations, and made certain sup-

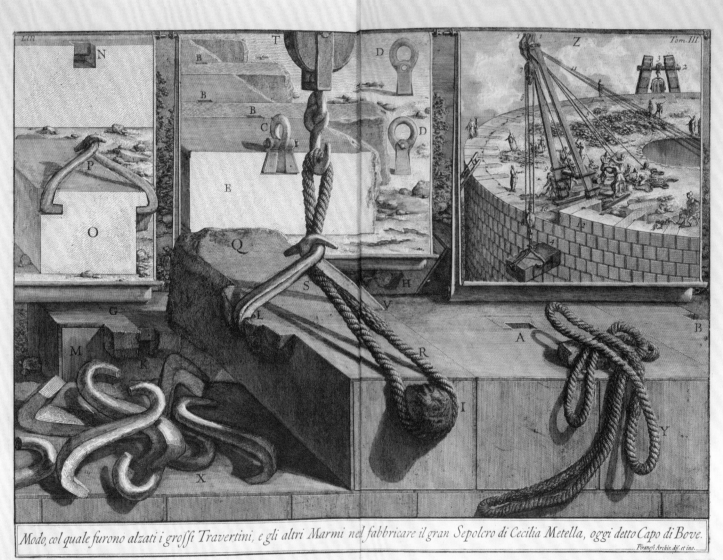

Modo, col quale furono alzati i grossi Travertini, e gli altri Marmi nel fabbricare il gran Sepolcro di Cecilia Metella, oggi detto Capo di Bove.

Piranesi Archit. dif. et inc.

Visitando io tutte giorno i Monumenti antichi di Roma, ed investigando ogni loro benche minuta parte, sopra in que grossi macigni, de quali sono costruiti, dei Buchi quadrati, scavati a bella posta: in alcuni d'essi nel mezzo del piano di sopra, come A: in altri nel lato e destro, e sinistre, come B. Quanto al buco scavato nel mezzo del piano di sopra, è cosa manifesta, che serviva per alzare il sasso sin, dove avvasta a porre in opera, mediante uno Stromento di ferro C, (eccone ancora i suoi Profili D) chiamato da Vitr. Forfice, da altri l'Uvella, ricondotte, ed incontrato nel buco stesso, come nello Spaccato E quale Stromento in oggi pur si mette in pratica. Ma qualuso potesse avere l'altro buco, scavato nel lato, a cui non vedasi corrispondere altre buce nel lato opposto, ove aggrappar si potesse il macigno per sollevarle, riuscivami affatto ignoto, ed oscuro; ne si sia stato a quest'ora da veruno penetrato. Tralle rovine del Sepolcro di Cecilia Metella, detto Capo di bove, mi venere sotto gli occhi alcuni Framm.ti di grossi Travertini, F, G, i quali mi scopersero ciò, che per si lungo tempo, da che ni trovo in Roma non mi venne fatte di comprendere. Il Framm.to F ha un rialto a guisa di Bozza, nella stessa pietra lasciato ad arte, segnato H, et simile ad I. Il Framm.to G ha una bozza, e d'un buco scavato in mezzo alla stessa, marcato K, et simile ad L; il qual buce è fondo sine alla superficie del Lato M, e corrisponde direttam.te al buco del Lato opposto N. E verisimile, che questi due Travertini non sieno stati posti in opera, e per le meno in que corpi, ond'è formata la superficie esterna del Mausoleo; e ciò puo essere accaduta, o per natural difetto della Pietra, scoperto dopo laverata, o per mancanza delle Scarpellino: in fatti l'uno di essi appare spezzato d'un capo. Per tanto, siccome si pensa, ecco brevem.te l'Uso di predetti Buchi, e delle Bozze. Osserviamo nello Spaccato O la piegatura, e profondità di Buchi, et il modo, con cui sono intredetti in essi gli Uncini P, i quali equilibrando il Macigno Q per mezzo della Fune R congiunta a cappio, raccomandata alla Bozza I, indi passata sotto gli Uncini, e ripassara ancora sotto medesima in S, qualora il peso dalla parte della bozza le costringesse a trascorrere, mottono in pronto il detto Macigno, per esser tirato su, poscia sul cappio al rampino della Taglia T, al suo destinare. Quivi nello stesso modo si può facilm.te muovere e rimuovere quante volte richiede il bisogno, sinche egregiam.te connettesi cogli altri marmi: indi lasciato posare tanto disgiunto, quanto: si possa levare dall'Uncino V, colle Leve, e Pali diferse: spignesi acceso. Depo di che le Scarpelline taglia le bozze, e pareggia la superficie. X, Uncini di ferro di varia grandezza. Y, Funi, o Cappi di varia lunghezza. Z, Dimostrasi la Macchina, mediante la quale alzavansi li grossi Macigni. 1 Due Travi proporzionate ai più, che doveansi alzare, piantate a piramide, e mobili sopra un Piano di grossi tavoloni di legno, concatenati insieme a foggia d'telaro: legate da capo da un Perno di ferro segn.to 2, al quale raccomandavasi la Taglia 3. Fermato il Piano di sud.i tavoloni, o sia Piede della Macchina ad alcuni Travertini, piantati qua, e la nel maggior legare i corpi delle Scaglie, e data alle Travi sufficiente pendenza, e sporte fuori del Muro, sicche possano ricevere comodam.te il Sasso 4, colle Funi 5 assi curavansi. Alzato il Sasso col mezzo della Fune 6, delle Taglie 7, 8, e del Mulinello 9, sino al piano 10, tiravasi mediante le Funi 11, le Travi per il capo indietre tanto, quanto il Sasso potesse posare sul detto Piano, ove usate le predette diligenze di farlo ben connettere univasi agli altri Sassi del Corso 12. Da ciò può dedursi, che gli Antichi sopra ogni cosa, studiassero la facilità d'innalzare simili enormi Macigni, per costruire Fabb.e corrispond.ti alle loro grandi idee, e di perpetua durabilità. Lasciandole tal volta rozze, e senza Ornam.ti. In vere molte se ne veggono di tal fatta, ma si maggiore, si che, che sembrano fatte più dalla Natura, che dall'Arte.

positions about their possible location in the monument.

This brought him to the central issue: the use of Roman tools. The tools were inanimate; it was the caption that provided the animation:

We observe, in the section [O], the profile and depth of the holes and the way the grappling hooks are inserted into them [P], which balance the block of stone [Q] by means of a rope [R] knotted into a loop, which is wrapped around the boss [I] and from there passed under the grappling hooks and twisted around itself [S], conducting the weight from the boss-end of the block to the hook of the pulley [T], and allowing the block to be pulled into place in the intended location.[20]

Framed in the background, Piranesi depicted the tools in use, including a large crane lifting stones to be placed in a circular structure resembling the tomb of C. Metella. After a detailed commentary on the process shown in the engraving, Piranesi concluded "that the ancients, above all things, studied how to raise similar enormous blocks in order to construct structures corresponding to their grand ideas and lasting forever, leaving them sometimes rough and unornamented." But no amount of description can obscure the fact that Piranesi could never have seen the Romans using their tools to build their buildings. In this engraving, then, Piranesi reconstructed a process by imagining how tools probably would have been used. In the plate that follows, Piranesi imagined the tools themselves.

He began by noting, in the caption to figure LIV (fig. 5), that the *Ulivella* "found" by Brunelleschi and still in use was commonly believed to be that identified by Vitruvius as *Forfice* or *Tanaglia*. Brunelleschi's tool was very useful; Vitruvius's "was certainly different, and perhaps even easier to put to use." Relying "simply" upon the passage in Vitruvius and on his observations about those holes in the stones, Piranesi remarked, "I wanted here to give some Idea (*delineare una qualche Idea*) of the Tanaglie of Vitruvius." Then he proceeded to describe the shape and workings of the imagined Vitruvian tool, based on, but also improving upon—especially in scale—Brunelleschi's version. How Brunelleschi hit upon the very same design—whether by a chance encounter with a Roman example, or because the Roman tool remained in use among artisans, or because building practices conservatively maintained enough of the old Roman practice to make it possible for someone like Brunelleschi to himself to imagine the kind of tool that could be required—is a question that Piranesi left hanging. He told us only, by shunting Brunelleschi's tool to the side of the plate and dwarfing it next to the imagined implements of the Romans, that the moderns were Lilliputians by comparison.

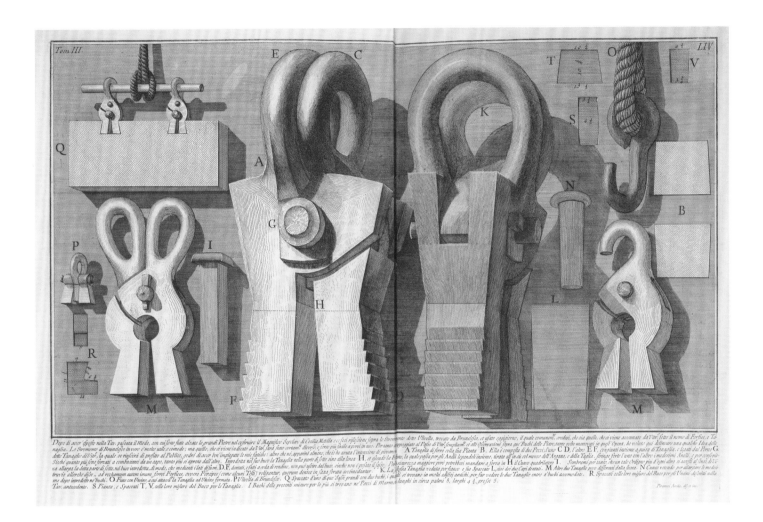

5. DOPO DI AVER'ESPOSTO
NELLA TAV. PASSATA IL MODO…
(AFTER HAVING SHOWN
IN THE PREVIOUS PLATE THE
MEANS…), fig. LIV, vol. 2, LE
ANTICHITÀ ROMANE, 1756–57
Etching on off-white laid paper

In his later archaeological books, as Dixon describes them, Piranesi often replaced captions with a more detailed table of contents at the front of the book. But here, too, though stripped of the narrative, we can on occasion gain some insight into Piranesi's self-conscious vision of the complementary functions of imagination and reconstruction. In the *Rovine del Castello dell'Acqua Giulia* (1762), two plates illustrated the inner workings of the sluice gates and conduits, which diverted the flow of water deep inside the castle. One of these images showed a variety of valves and plates "that are frequently found, and found in other underground places in Rome." (figure XV, illustration VII) (fig. 6) But in referring to some of the material depicted in figure XIV—more of the innards of the hydraulic system—Piranesi noted, "The stone covers are a pure imagination" ("sono una pura immaginazione") and the sluice gates "are mere supposition" ("una mera supposizione") (fig. 7).

Is it a coincidence that depicting some of the most detailed Roman remains—both building tools and hydraulic mechanicals—elicited from Piranesi an explicit reliance on the role of imagination? These instances of reconstruction, Piranesi seemed to be saying, would have been impossible without imagination. The result was not intended as fantasy, however, but as a serious contribution to our understanding of the reality of life in the Roman world—the common goal of all antiquaries.

———

But if Piranesi shared reconstruction as a goal with those who preceded him, his willingness and ability to use imagination were qualitatively different. To understand this better, we should perhaps place Piranesi alongside one of the usual suspects—Winckelmann—and some unlikely ones—Edward Gibbon and Jean-Jacques Barthélémy.

Each shared with the others, first and foremost, a deep respect for antiquity; second, a passionate relationship to that past; and third, an ability to convey that respect and passion in a narrative form that could hold the attention of nonscholarly readers—indeed, that seemed *designed* for nonscholarly readers. It is almost a watchword to identify Winckelmann with passion and with narrative; and Gibbon, according to Momigliano, owed his place in the history of historiography to his ability to reconcile his love for antiquarian scholarship with an ability to cast it in a beautiful *and* philosophical story. In all this, Piranesi was their colleague. Indeed, Lola Kantor-Kazovsky has suggested that one of his distinguishing features was his ability to present the fruits of antiquarian scholarship in an easily accessed narrative form. According to her, Piranesi effectively transformed the visual culture of Italian antiquarianism into something "painterly." The inquiring figures depicted amidst his ancient structures are emotionally engaged, as are those who view the scenes.[21] Indeed, like Gibbon, Piranesi's achievement was no less than taking synchronic antiquarian research and transforming it into something diachronic, into a story. The depiction of those building tools, for example, was presented as a narrative in the captions.

But by far the most arresting and informative parallel is with the Abbé Jean-Jacques Barthélémy (1716–1795). An antiquarian from Provence and keeper of the Cabinet des Medailles from 1753, he published extensively on ancient numismatics and iconography. But he is best known for his novel *Voyage of the Young Anacharsis* (1788), a fictional account of a young Scythian prince's visit to Athens during the fourth century BC. The plot, however, was merely the vehicle for a dazzling display of antiquarian learning, now marshaled directly to bring that past to

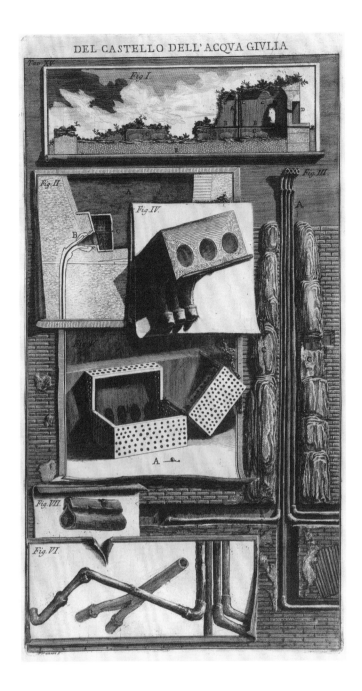

life—and to an audience of young boys and older ladies. Indeed, Barthélémy intended his work to catch the changing tastes of a society that the philosophers had successfully inoculated against the pleasures of erudition. In Barthélémy's view, inscriptions could only be saved for the future if they were converted into belle-lettres. As a measure of his success in this, Flaubert introduced us to the young Charles Bovary reading *Anacharsis* before bedtime in his boarding school in Rouen.[22] For nearly one hundred years, it served as a primer for the encounter with antiquity, only surpassed, eventually, by those German *Handbücher* that made lovers (amateurs) into experts by the time the nineteenth century gave way to the twentieth.

But, in the longer perspective, Barthélémy represented the recogni-tion that in the world of the "Moderns," or, alternatively, "commercial society," knowledge only mattered if it could reach beyond the narrow society of scholars. With literacy expanding down the social ladder and across the gender divide, the relative importance of the erudite reader declined drastically. Mark Phillips has written persuasively about how the development of parahistorical genres like memoir and historical fiction in late eighteenth-century England represented an intellectual response to this set of social trends.[23] Similarly, those who cared about the past, like Barthélémy and Piranesi, had to adjust or resign them-selves to respectable obscurity. The key to reaching this new market or audience was, precisely, imagination.

Imagination may seem too idiosyncratic and unreliable a tool for those seeking truth—a dark truth and, at best, a guilty pleasure for the philologist at heart. But it reflects an essential and inescapable truth about the close encounter with the past: it is an affective relationship as much as an intellectual one. The painters and poets of the Roman Campagna understood this.

So did Nietzsche. In his lectures on the antiquaries' scholarship of 1871, he spoke of their "longing" (*Sehnsucht*) for reconstruction. But there was no place for this kind of affective relationship to the past in the bold new world of German history—aside, perhaps, from his Swiss colleague and friend Jacob Burckhardt, who was himself marginalized by many German academics for his reliance on imagery, anecdote, and biography.

One of the amazing facts of contemporary scholarly life is the way in which antiquaries and professors have swapped roles. The antiquaries were once accused of narrow, dry-as-dust scholarship—*quisquillia* in Nietzsche's own terms. The professors, in turn, narrated the great tales of political, national, and religious revival. But anyone who reads reviews of academic books in publications like *The New York Times* knows very well that the readiest tag is to disparage their dry, narrow, pedantic character. Today, "academic" does all the work that "antiquarian" used to do.

At the very same time, however, without anyone noticing it, the passionate desire to reconstruct the past has survived. Like water that always finds its level, the need to reconstruct—back to Nietzsche's *Sehnsucht* again—has found other avenues. Literature and art in the nineteenth and twentieth centuries carried forward the project of the early modern antiquaries. Readers of W. G. Sebald's *Rings of Saturn* or *Austerlitz*—with its Warburg & Courtauld-trained protagonist—have already met the modern antiquarian. In many ways, he is us.

The extent of the entwining of imagination with erudition marks Piranesi's fundamental modernity. With him the role of feeling beccame a tool in the hands of the self-conscious investigator. The older antiquarianism aimed to reconstruct the past, but was driven by curiosity; in some sense, commercial society has contributed to diminishing the value of curiosity—it has, after all, little obvious commodity value—but has elevated that of imagination. And with imagination, passion emerges as the avenue down which most of us are led to encounter the past: "what it was really like."

DAVID ROSAND

COL SPORCAR SI TROVA
PIRANESI DRAWS

DETAIL
TOMB OF NERO, from the
series GROTTESCHI, 1750
Etching on off-white laid paper

IN STYLE AND IN FUNCTION, THE RANGE OF PIRANESI'S DRAWING CORRESPONDED TO THAT OF HIS ARTISTIC AMBITION AND ACHIEVEMENT.[1] FROM RAPID SKETCHES SET DOWN WITH IMPULSIVE ENERGY TO THE MOST DELIBERATELY FINISHED ARCHITECTURAL RENDERINGS, HE DEMONSTRATED a control of graphic media that was confident and exploratory, precise and yet open, and always suggestive. Piranesi's was a fundamentally graphic imagination. He thought with pen, chalk, or etching needle in hand, considering his activity on the grounded copperplate to be the same as drawing on paper.

Piranesi's earliest drawings reflected his youthful training and professional ambition, and they established a basic visual vocabulary that served him throughout his career. The son of a stonemason and builder, he turned naturally to the study of architecture, and architectural form became the foundation of his subsequent graphic invention. At the core of an architectural curriculum was the mastery of perspective, the applied geometry of linear representation, its rules assuring representational conviction and, if at times only by implication, commensurability. Those principles, which enabled an artist to project three-dimensional space onto a flat surface, had been especially exploited by the art of scenography, the make-believe constructions that were the marvels of baroque stagecraft. Particularly in the publications of the Bibienas, Ferdinando and his son Giuseppe, one could readily study the guidelines

1. DIAGONAL VIEW OF TWO
COLONNADED COURTYARDS
Pen and brown ink and gray
wash over ruled black chalk
sketch on off-white laid paper

of such complex projection, and Piranesi evidently did so, learning the rules that made fantasy appear as reality—making *quello che non è sia*, in the terms of older Renaissance artistic discourse (fig. 1).[2] Perspective construction provided the seductive structural logic for the fantastic worlds imagined by the artist, the tectonic scaffolding on which he could hang the individual pieces of organic form, whether natural growth or archaeological fragment, that constituted the formal palette of his imagination.

In addition to the lessons in perspective rendering learned from the Bibienas' publications, Piranesi developed his penmanship through the study of other graphic models: etchings and engravings by masters of the previous century, such as Jacques Callot, Stefano della Bella, Giovanni Benedetto Castiglione, and Salvator Rosa, as well as by contemporary Venetian artists, specifically Marco Ricci, Michele Marieschi, Antonio

2. TOMB OF THEODORIC
AT RAVENNA
Pen and brown ink on off-white
laid paper

Canaletto, and Giambattista Tiepolo.[3] Ever since artists of the Renaissance looked to the work of Albrecht Dürer for lessons in graphic structure, prints have played an important role in drawing instruction, teaching draftsmen the expressive as well as representational potential of line and its combinatorial possibilities in creating chiaroscuro values.[4] From Canaletto in particular, Piranesi learned a grammar of linear systems: tonal structures comprised of sensitively wavering strokes and large-scale tectonic patterns of individual inflected units (fig. 2). Such regular patterns of vertical hatching have a long history in drawing practice; in Venice, they date back to the drawings of Giulio and Domenico Campagnola, which provided models for later draftsmen like Marco Ricci. Such patterns lend a sense of structure in the rendering of architecture in particular, and Piranesi applied them especially in his drawings of actual monuments, as seen in his late views of archaeological sites, where the use of the stiffer reed pen adds to such structure.

3. ARCHITECTURAL SKETCHES,
N.D.
Pen and deep brown ink on
off-white laid paper

Piranesi's early concern with tonal values was verbally attested on the verso of the elaborately rendered exercise in two-point perspective, in which rapid sketches of vaulted halls and courtyards offer a formal alternative to the linear structures of the recto (fig. 3). The artist annotated these rough designs with directions for their eventual graphic completion, anticipating their fuller tonal rendering in chiaroscuro: "*prima scuro e poi chiaro*," "*scuro/chiaro/scuro*," "*chiaro*."

His Venetian elders and contemporaries also introduced Piranesi to the possibilities of the architectural *fantasia*, or *capriccio*. An imaginative extension of the architectural *veduta*, or view of an actual site, the capriccio consisted of impossible visions, the fantastic juxtaposition of real—or, at least, apparently real—architectural monuments in totally imagined settings. If his initial introduction to the genre came from

Venetian models, the possibilities of such capricious imaginings expanded significantly with his first Roman sojourn in 1740 in the entourage of the Venetian ambassador, Marco Foscarini. Already instructed in ancient history by his brother, a Carthusian monk, Piranesi discovered in the ruins of Rome a new source of significant monuments and resonant fragments of antiquity, figural and ornamental motifs that enriched his formal vocabulary as they enlarged his imaginative potential—"these speaking ruins" ("*queste parlanti ruine*"), as he called them.[5] And it was in Rome that this self-proclaimed *architetto veneziano*, his architectural ambitions frustrated, first turned to printmaking. He learned the techniques of etching from Giuseppe Vasi, with whom he collaborated in the production of *vedute*, views of Rome that were increasingly in demand by grand tourists.

Very quickly, however, he was developing his own project, the *Prima Parte di Architetture e Prospettive inventate ed incise da Gio. Battā Piranesi architetto veneziano*, which he published in 1743 (fig. 4). On the title page, the "Venetian architect" announced his double achievement as inventor and engraver, responsible for both idea and execution. He stressed that dual accomplishment in his dedicatory letter to his host and patron, the builder and antiquarian Nicola Giobbe; praising perspective and its importance to the architect, and vaunting his own mastery of it, he declared that, with the knowledge of architecture he had gained in Rome, he had acquired the art of drawing his own inventions and the ability to engrave them.[6] The two operations, invention and execution, remained inseparable throughout his career.

Following the publication of the *Prima Parte*, due to a lack of financial support, Piranesi returned to Venice briefly in 1744; he was back in Rome the following year and then again in Venice, where he remained until August 1747.[7] It was during these years in the lagoon city that Piranesi became particularly responsive to Giambattista Tiepolo's drawings and prints. His knowledge of the drawings is indicated by chalk studies like the ones in a small sketchbook, in which the red chalk medium was handled with a broken touch resembling that of Tiepolo.[8] Piranesi's response to the older master is especially evident in a group of ambitiously conceived figure compositions executed in pen and wash, which seem to have been removed from the same relatively large sketchbook. Although hardly typical of the artist, these drawings attest to an interest in *istorie*, or full-scale narrative painting. Most of them represent scenes of violence, a generic iconography relating to the martyrdoms of altarpiece painting.[9] The broadly brushed wash, which defined both form and space, established its pictorial completeness; although Piranesi did not pursue

PRIMA PARTE
DI ARCHITETTURE
E PROSPETTIVE
INVENTATE ED INCISE
DA GIAMBATISTA PIRANESI
ARCHITETTO VENEZIANO
FRA GLI ARCADI
SALCINDIO TISEIO

this interest in figure painting, the technique he explored in these exercises became a preferred means for his architectural imaginings.

In Venice, Piranesi also turned to interior decoration, adding a further dimension to the architecture and perspective that had been the guiding elements of his imagination and production. In Rome, Vasi, disapproving or jealous of Piranesi's spirited technique, is said to have advised him that he was too much of a painter to be an engraver.[10] It is indeed a pictorial or painterly quality that emerged as the draftsman engaged the natural forms of rococo ornament. A design for a wall panel epitomizes the tense dialectic between the tectonic and the organic that was critical to Piranesi's art, as the measured rectangle of the bounding frame fails to contain the expansive proliferation of the irregular cartouche (fig. 5).

As Piranesi discovered the brush through the example of Tiepolo's draftsmanship—its luminosity of washes applied to pen drawing—he

6. DECORATIVE SHELL
Pen and brown ink and wash
over black chalk on off-white
laid paper

7. DESIGN FOR A
FESTIVAL GONDOLA
Pen and brown ink and wash
over black chalk on off-white
laid paper

extended that discovery from the figural to the ornamental or the purely inventive, bringing it under more precise control (fig. 6). Following the meandering patterns of rococo arabesque and foliation, he explored the suggestive markings of the drawing implement itself. From shadowed breadth to linear accentuation, the brush offered new possibilities of expression and representation. The metamorphic impulse and momentum of the forms themselves—scallops, curls, and spirals, sudden bursts of radiance—seem to inspire and guide the draftsman's hand as the energies of execution become one with the energies of ornament; touches of the brush become both form and shadow (fig. 7). Scribbling, the rapid back-and-forth motion that sets down a hatched shorthand of shadow or modeling, asserts itself as more than a servant of representation; insisting on a certain expressive independence, it becomes a form of its own, at once a source and declaration of graphic energy that animates the object and the surface of the drawing. Rococo ornament became a graphic playground for the draftsman (figs. 8, 9).

8. DECORATIVE DESIGN
Pen and brown ink and wash
on off-white laid paper

9. DECORATIVE DESIGNS
AND RECLINING FIGURE
Pen and brown ink and wash
on off-white laid paper

In addition to inviting exploration of drawing media, Tiepolo presented Piranesi with new possibilities of figural invention, particularly through the two series of etchings that have come to be known as *Vari Capricci* and *Scherzi di Fantasia*.[11] (fig. 10) The enigmatic iconography of these images presents exotic figures in pantomimic dialogue; they act within minimally described landscape settings marked by a dominant tree or architectural monument—obelisk, column, tomb, altar—and further punctuated with vases or sculptural fragments and animated by serpents or owls. An ominous inflection of the *locus amoenus* of pastoral convention, this is a world of romanticized antiquity, suggesting sorcery and myth, part of the popular diffusion and romantic transformation of a classical tradition handed down especially in the graphic arts—in seventeenth-century prints by Castiglione and Rosa, among others. Such imagery opened new and darker possibilities to an imagination already inspired by the "speaking ruins" of antiquity.[12]

Being forced to be an architect only on paper may well have freed Piranesi's imagining hand, as architectural forms absolved of functional responsibility could serve as independent, liberated elements of design—as they effectively were in the surviving fragments of those speaking ruins. Purely graphic invention became a combinatorial art, and in the title plate for the *Prima Parte* the young Piranesi had already demonstrated his mastery of that art. Back in Venice, Tiepolo would have offered a model for further consideration of the title page as a formal field that invited such iconographic assembly.[13] (fig. 11) Piranesi explored the possibilities of this model in a number of independent drawings, in which he confirmed the status of the title page as a compositional and iconographic genre of its own (fig. 12). Like the design for a wall panel, these drawings combined tectonic and organic forms, with the added spatial dimension of perspective and foreshortening. The generic requirement of a title page calls for a field to accommodate text, usually a tablet, scroll, or cartouche. When such text is scribbled illegibly, it invites a projected reading, a participatory interpretation on the part of the viewer; the invitation becomes even more insistent when the field is left totally uninscribed and blank, an open whiteness of paper (fig. 13). In its conventional function, as the introduction to a volume, the title page serves as a portal, an invitation to the reader. As an independent design, it exploits such conventional expectation, but, without an informing text to guide, the design leaves even more to the imagination.

In the group of four etchings he published shortly after his definitive return to Rome in 1747, which he subsequently called *Grotteschi*, Piranesi built upon the format of the title page.[14] (fig. 14) Evidently conceived as

11. Giovanni Battista Tiepolo
SCHERZI DI FANTASIA:
TITLE PAGE, UNLETTERED
Etching on off-white laid paper

12. DESIGN FOR A
FRONTISPIECE WITH SCROLL,
CROWN, AND SARCOPHAGUS
Pen and brown ink with
brown wash over black chalk
on off-white laid paper

**13. DESIGN FOR A TITLE
PAGE WITH SCROLL, CHAIN
OF MEDALLIONS, AND PULPIT**
Pen and brown ink with brown
wash and pink water color
over black chalk on off-white
laid paper

14. *THE MONUMENTAL*
TABLET—STATE 1 from the series
GROTTESCHI, 1750
Etching, engraving, drypoint,
and scratching on off-white
laid paper

Ara antica sopra la quale si facevano anticamente i sagrifizi, con altre ruine all' intorno.

Gio Batta Piranesi Architetto inventò, ed incise in Roma.   7.

such, the plate known as *The Monumental Tablet* presents itself as an illusion within an illusion, a tapestry hanging from a winged bull's head and curling away from the paper upon which it casts its shadow. Piranesi had already developed the horizontal format in plate VII of the *Prima Parte*, an intimate landscape of an "ancient altar on which sacrifices were made, surrounded by other ruins" ("*Ara antica sopra la quale si facevano anticamente sagrifizi, con altre ruine all' intorno*").[15] (fig. 15) An apparently irrational juxtaposition of ruins, architectural and sculptural fragments, and human skeletal remains, the *Ara antica* still offers a coherent spatial representation. The space of the *Grotteschi* is more complicated, the juxtaposition of elements more fantastic; in an apparent but inconsistent landscape setting, fragments of stone and human skeleton merge with, and are joined by, serpentine ties and actual serpents, all merging with

16. TOMB OF NERO from the
series GROTTESCHI, 1750
Etching on off-white laid paper

and emerging from the paper itself (fig. 16). Piranesi would have discovered serpents and serpentine forms in Tiepolo's *Scherzi* as well as among the vases he noted in Fischer von Erlach's *Entwurff einer historischen Architecture* (1721), book five of which, devoted to "Divers Vases Antiques, Ægyptiens, Grecs, Romains, & Modernes: avec Quelques uns de l'invention de l'Auteur," must have held a particular attraction for Piranesi the draftsman (see Lawrence, fig. 2).[16] The serpentine line, an essential aspect of rococo aesthetic in general, became dynamically charged in Piranesi's art, conceitfully shifting between meandering ornament and actual snake. The spiral itself came to stand for the linear principles governing his graphic inventions, an epitome of "what there is in nature which could furnish . . . such a variety of ideas and forms," as he later wrote of shells.[17] And shells, with their expansive undulation of surface and contour, play a central role in the compositional form of the *Grotteschi*—whether as monumental mollusk or more modest rocaille with inverted Ionic volutes.[18]

INVENZIONI
CAPRIC DI CARCERI
ALL ACQVA FORTE
DATTE IN LVCE
GIOVANI
BOUCHARD IN
ROMA MERCAN
AL CORSO

In the *Grotteschi*, the lessons of the draftsman, the consciousness of paper not merely as supporting ground but as participating medium, become part of the printmaker's art. Creating and following sequences of serpentine forms, the drawing needle finally dissipates its own momentum in scribbles that extend its energies out into the space of the surrounding paper. Vasi's comment that Piranesi was more painter than printmaker is understandable in light of Piranesi's own development. Piranesi revealed the inspiration of the great *peintres-graveurs*, from Tiepolo back to Rembrandt, not only in the internal contradictions and tensions of composition, in which representational logic is sacrificed to a purely pictorial rationale, but also in his handling of the etching needle like a pen. Responding to the challenge of that graphic tradition, he claimed his position as its culminating master. Describing Piranesi's deliberate intention to transform the art of etching, his first biographer concluded that he must be celebrated as *"il Rembrand delle antiche rovine."*[19]

The architectural fantasy that informed certain plates in the *Prima Parte* and the capriciousness of the *Grotteschi* climaxed in the most celebrated and influential product of Piranesi's imagination: the suite of the *Carceri*, first issued about 1749–50.[20] (fig. 17) These images of monumental masonry vaults, heavy piers, catwalks, bars, and chains—ominous instruments, all of which dwarf the human inhabitants—related to the traditions of architectural fantasy and the scenographic conventions of the theater, the prison scene being a standard element in Italian baroque opera. The title Piranesi chose for the first edition alerts us to the twin aspects of genre and technique: *"Invenzioni capric[ciose] di Carceri all'acqua forte"* ("Capricious inventions of Prisons in etching"). As capricci, the images claim the privilege of the genre itself, freedom from rules and laws—including rules of perspective, verisimilitude, and history. They are presented as variations on a theme, exercises in invention but also in drawing—*disegno* in the full Renaissance sense.[21] The *Carceri* are, in the first instance, a demonstration of the art of their maker—of his technical skill in invention, drawing, and etching, his mastery of line.

Although a number of drawings apparently were preliminary to the project (fig. 18), it seems evident that much of the invention took place directly on the plate, in the course of the needlework on the grounded copper.[22] While sharing such practice with the *Grotteschi*, these compositions are more complete; their architectural theme seems to demand a more finished, less suggestive execution. They do not float as sketched vignettes suspended within the field, but rather extend to secure themselves at the limits of the plate, where insistent framing lines or scribbles deliberately enclose them. From the very beginning of the series, in

the title plate, Piranesi established a dynamic structural motif that would remain crucial to the subsequent inventions: the spiral, here on a truly monumental scale. Opening to fill the entire field, this form controls the spatial energies of the composition, initially by establishing the shadowed proscenium arch that frames the scene beyond. Winding centripetally to focus on the central core, this spiral implies its own spatial intrusion. Entering from the repoussoir of the proscenium shadows at top, its circling fragment pretends to follow the flight of the steps behind; and yet, playing its flat masonry against that flight, insisting on the unforeshortened purity of its own curve, this encircling line finally denies access to that background space. The cast of arbitrary shadow, flattening three-dimensional forms and collapsing distant planes, further frustrates perspective impulse. And the parallel thrust of foreshortened timber confirms the pictorial game being played, in which spatial contradiction finds resolution only at the pictorial surface. The composition itself seems to instruct us in the process of its own invention, generated by the circling, imagining hand of the artist sweeping broadly across the surface, laying out the basic controlling structure. The resulting large, curving articulation of the field is then further refined and complicated by straight architectural lines.[23]

These basic designing motions are those of Piranesi's drawings: circling movement leading to spiral form, patterns of shadow imposing linear continuities upon spatially differentiated surfaces. To varying degrees, they are the motions that determine all the other images in the printed suite. The energy of the drawing hand informs the *Carceri* of the first edition. Freely executed, they bear the character of monumental sketches, and they claim the privileges of that category: an openness and suggestiveness of form, a sweeping line that is at once exploratory and secure in its own trajectory, an indulgence of the scribble, of the shifting patterns of smaller motions, as surrogate for the mimetic information of representation. It was natural for Piranesi's admirers to compare his etchings to those of Rembrandt, for both were "like original drawings, in which the feeling of the artist is conveyed immediately on the copper plate."[24] And Piranesi himself, when asked why he did not make more finished preparatory drawings, responded that he did not want his etchings to be mere copies: "When I create the effect on copper, I make of it an original."[25] Generated by the drawing hand, Piranesi's *Carceri*, in their first edition, testify to the operations of the hand as an agent of invention.

This sense of etching as drawing was underscored as it was modified when the plates were subsequently reworked for the second edition, is-

19. CARCERI: TITLE PLATE,
STATE III, SECOND EDITION
Etching and engraving on off-
white laid paper

sued in 1761. If in the first edition he credited the publisher, Giovanni Buzard (de-Venetianized as Bouchard in a second state), in the modified title page to the second edition he was his own publisher—profession: Venetian architect (fig. 19). The transformation was emphasized in the changed title of the series. No longer called capricci (*invenzioni capricciose*), they were now primarily prisons of invention: *Carceri d'invenzione*.[26] The lettering of the title, originally only roughly sketched in, was now chiseled with a new lapidary crispness and monumentality. The images were subjected to new weight and deepening chiaroscuro, rendering them more ominous. They were also subjected (or resubjected) to the ostensible regimen of perspective, as ruled lines traversed vaulted spaces and beam and truss link distances—although space thereby became only more ambiguous. And, with the addition of two new plates evoking events of Roman antiquity, the *Carceri* seemed destined to acknowledge the laws of history as well. They did indeed appear to insist upon more serious, less capricious interpretation. The compositions were denser, weightier. Formally, the governing curves were controlled (at least apparently) by tectonic orthogonals; the texture of the flowing lines of the sketch were thickened, their movement slowed, their character more deliberately varied, as mimetic responsibility became more insistent. The inventing impulses of the hand were disciplined. A similar shift marked Piranesi's later drawing style—a move away from the sweeping gestures of arches and spirals toward a more structured system of coordinates, a more insistent sense of measure.

In their second edition, the *Carceri* carried different meaning—or meanings. A decade after their initial conception, the artist reconsidered his freely rendered work and saw new possibilities in it. This is indeed the function of the sketch, at least since Leonardo da Vinci articulated it as a challenge to its maker. Deliberately open and unfinished, the sketch invites its creator to discover new prospects in its linear chaos. In the case of the *Carceri*, only very generally prepared with preliminary drawings, the plates of the first edition stood effectively as sketches in their rapid execution; as such, they did indeed invite further contemplation by the artist, and Piranesi responded to that invitation.

Again, the biographer Legrand proved sensitive to this creative situation, during which, from the graphic chaos of his rapid sketches, Piranesi arrived at a fully satisfying form through his work on the plate. Legrand observed that Piranesi did not make highly finished drawings, but instead drew broadly, first in sanguine, then with pen or brush, but only enough to set down his ideas in a drawing that was almost illegible; it was nearly impossible to discern just what he was trying to fix on the

Ex collectione Bartholomæi Cavaceppi
Statuarii · Romani ·

DISEGNI
RACCOLTA DI ALCUNI DEL BARBERI DA CENTO DETTO IL GUERCINO
Incisi in rame, e presentati al singolar merito del Sig. Tommaso
Jenkins Pittore, ed Accademico di S. Luca, in atto di rispetto, e
d'amicizia dall' Architetto, e suo Coaccademico
Gio. Battista Piranesi.

Si vendono presso il medesimo Piranesi nel Palazzo del Sigr. Conte Tomati, a
Strada Felice vicino alla Trinità de' monti.

paper. The drawing was merely "a chaos, the elements of which he mixed on the copper with an admirable art." Legrand described how the painter Hubert Robert—with whom Piranesi would venture out to draw from nature—while appreciating his colleague's talent, could not understand how he could draw so rapidly. To such astonishment Piranesi explained, "The drawing is not on the paper, but entirely in my head, and you will see it on the plate." And, Legrand added, the plate was indeed a finished image.[27]

That Piranesi did indeed make drawing a public act is documented in a large architectural fantasy, signed and, unusually, dated "I. B. Piranesi. fecit. dec.ᵐ: 31. 1765." On the verso, the English patron recorded his audience on the occasion: "Piranesi / Drawn at Rome in the presence of Joseph Wyndham Esq." As Andrew Robison has observed, the drawing must have been completed on an easel, for in accenting the vault to the left, the artist allowed the dark ink to run down the page. Having been present at the kind of impulsive rendering described by Legrand, Mr. Wyndham presumably fully appreciated such permanent evidence of the fire of inspiration, which he was privileged to witness personally.[28]

Since the Renaissance, the sketch has been considered the product of the artist's inspired mind; the first thoughts produced *dal furor dello artefice*.[29] Piranesi's own declaration of the aesthetic of the sketch appeared in 1764, on the frontispiece to an album of reproductive etchings after drawings by Guercino and others—mostly the work of other printmakers (fig. 20). Printed in a combination of black and reddish-brown inks—a chromatic combination he often exploited in his own drawings in ink over chalk—the design features a sheet with a drawing from the collection of the sculptor Bartolomeo Cavaceppi. At the bottom of the page, before the dedicatory field and just below the name of Giovanni Battista Piranesi, the severed head of John the Baptist figures the artist's name. The larger, formal conceit of the frontispiece features an animated frame of studio trophies with a heraldic palette at its core, set upon an open drawing manual. On that palette, Piranesi inscribed the motto that affirmed his belief in Leonardo's aesthetic of the sketch as a source of new inventions: *COL SPORCAR SI TROVA*, which can loosely be translated as "messing about, one finds."[30]

With this motto, Piranesi reaffirmed the idea and practice enunciated centuries earlier by Leonardo da Vinci, who first applied the word "sketch" (from the Italian *schizzare*, to spurt) to the compositional and figural notations set down rapidly by the draftsman. Leonardo encouraged the artist to study those products of his drawing hand, to look into those roughly executed designs as a spur to further invention, for in

21. TWO FIGURES, N.D.
Black and red chalk
on off-white laid paper

22. TWO MEN
(DRAWN OVER FOOT), N.D.
Pen and brown ink; foot in red
chalk on off-white laid paper

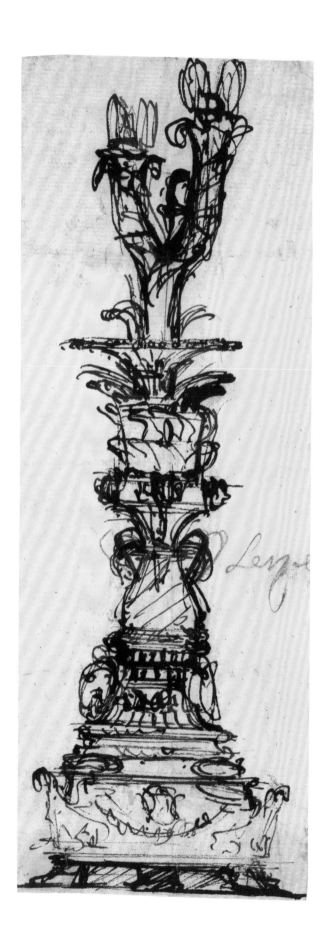

23. SKETCH DESIGN FOR A
MONUMENTAL CANDELABRUM,
N.D. Pen and brown ink on off-
white laid paper

those *componimenti inculti* (Leonardo's term)—as in the chaotic patterns of ashes, clouds, mud, stained walls—he could discover new pictorial ideas: in such *macchie*, one finds.[31]

Unlike the purely fantastic realm of the early *Grotteschi*, the world of Piranesi's archaeological sites and *vedute* of Rome was inhabited by human beings, their small size enhancing the scale of the monuments.[32] Functioning simultaneously as participants and observers, actors and audience, they respond actively to the great works before them; looking and pointing, they arouse and direct the curiosity of the viewer. Such staffage was an essential and traditional iconographic component of the capriccio of Rosa and Tiepolo: the figure who indicates, a vectoring action that engages and directs the attention of the viewer to some part of the enigmatic scene. The varieties of movement and gesture to be found in Piranesi's actors were studied in the streets of Rome, where the artist found his models. He carried paper and chalk with him, recording the human body in action, the energies of the chalk transferred to the figure that it represented.[33] (fig. 21) Such drawings have in the past been attributed, understandably perhaps, to Watteau. The majority of the figure studies that have come down to us, however, are in pen and ink (fig. 22). Rapidly and energetically set down, they were informed by systems of hatching that Piranesi had initially developed within the context of architectural rendering. Such hatching patterns define broad tonal relationships that may model form or be form itself, as with an extended limb or shadow; very rarely is wash added. The animation of these figures, the economy with which they are registered, led to past attributions to Francesco Guardi, with whose *macchiette* they indeed share a certain vitality; however, the sheer variety of their actions and posturing distinguishes them from the somatic anonymity of Guardi's caped figures.[34]

That animation, the vitality and variety of touch and stroke, distinguished every aspect of the draftsmanship of Piranesi, from his designs for carriages, furniture, and candelabra (fig. 23) to his studies of trees. Moving rapidly, his pen slowed at moments to leave a heavier deposit of ink, an accentuated mark that assumed a foliate character—ornamental or natural. The designing pen was Piranesi's means of inventing as well as of seeing.

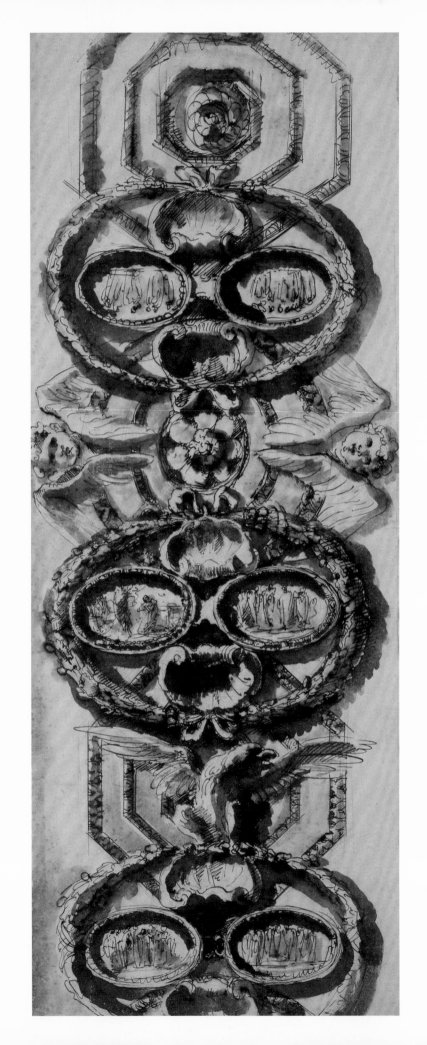

BENT SØRENSEN

THE PROJECTS FOR THE RECONSTRUCTION OF THE LATERAN BASILICA IN ROME

DETAILED DESIGN FOR
PANEL OF VAULTING COFFERS
IN APSE, CORRESPONDING
TO NUMBER 9 (TAVOLA 19)
Pen and brown ink, brush
and brown wash over graphite
on off-white laid paper

ALTHOUGH LACKING PREVIOUS ARCHITECTURAL PRACTICE, PIRANESI'S FIRST ATTEMPT TO WORK AS AN ARCHITECT IN-VOLVED NOTHING LESS THAN THE RECONSTRUCTION OF A SUBSTANTIAL PORTION OF ONE OF THE MOST IMPORTANT CHURCHES IN CHRISTIANITY, THE BASILICA SAN GIOVANNI in Laterano, the cathedral of Rome.[1] (See Eisenman, fig. 5; San Giovanni is at lower right, next to the compass.)

The basilica was founded in AD 313 by Constantine. It was almost totally destroyed by an earthquake in 896 and was rebuilt from 904 to 911. Nicholas IV added a huge transept and a new apse in 1291. The basilica was damaged by fire in 1361, whereupon Urban V embarked on essential restorations and built the Gothic ciborium with the papal altar below designed by Giovanni di Stefano in 1367. Martin V commissioned the pavement of the nave and completed further restoration between 1417 and 1431. In the sixteenth century, Pius IV began construction of the great gilt coffered ceiling of the nave designed by Daniele da Volterra. In 1586, Sixtus V added the benediction loggia by Domenico Fontana. In preparation for the Holy Year of 1600, Clement VIII undertook the redecoration of the transept; a gilt coffered ceiling designed by Taddeo Landini was installed, while below, Cavaliere d'Arpino directed a team of artists to paint a fresco cycle. Scenes from the life of Constantine decorated the walls of the transept, and a fresco of the Ascension was added to the transept's south wall above the new altar of the Blessed

Sacrament. Giovanni Battista Montano designed a monumental organ that was installed on the transept's north wall. The most remarkable restoration was undoubtedly Borromini's transformation of the nave between 1646 and 1650 for Innocent X. Despite Borromini's hope that he might have the opportunity to vault the nave, rebuild the choir, and build the basilica's east façade, work was abandoned thereafter. The east façade was not built until nearly a century later, between 1733 and 1735, by Alessandro Galilei. In 1763–64, when a new restoration project was considered, the Lateran basilica displayed many disparate elements that had grown from the accumulation or restoration of successive building blocks, each of which revealed the fashion of its time.

Our knowledge of Piranesi's undertaking is unfortunately very deficient, as nothing specific is known of the circumstances leading to this project. Even information about the number of architects asked to submit proposals or the particular conditions of the commission can only be partly deduced.[2] The earliest reference occurs in the manuscript chronicle *Diario di Roma*, published recently by Susanna Pasquali; on December 5, 1762, the pope was contemplating having the basilica renovated "through the construction of an apse according to the celebrated architect Borromini's design." Piranesi's name appears in *Diario di Roma* for the first time on September 18, 1763: "Given Our Lord's keen interest in embellishing the Lateran Basilica with a new apse—and because of the multitude of drawings presented, his choice has yet to be made—the pope has recently received a number of them by the celebrated and well-known architect and engraver, Sig. Piranesi, which were rather highly praised by His Holiness, who will be able to choose from the different versions the one most in keeping with his generous intentions." Two days later, Charles Natoire, director of the French Academy in Rome, informed the marquis de Marigny that Clement XIII had asked Piranesi to make a drawing for a new papal altar.[3] A few days later, on October 1, the architect Luigi Vanvitelli mentioned another aspect of the project when he wrote to his brother Urbano: "In truth, if they were to get Piranesi to carry out some building, one could see what would come out of a madman's head, without any sound basis. Nor should a lunatic complete the tribune at San Giovanni in Laterano, even though Borromini, who restored the church, was not particularly level-headed, and if it is to be Panini, it would be equivalent to Piranesi."[4] Piranesi was not chosen; the *Diario di Roma* entry dated February 7, 1764, informs us that the chosen designs were those of Carlo Marchionni. The whole project, however, was soon suspended and then abandoned.

As can be seen from Piranesi's drawings, the various schemes entailed the transformation of the west end of the basilica and the design for the new papal altar and baldacchino. The schemes are fairly well known thanks to the survival of several autograph preparatory drawings now in the Mogan Library & Museum in New York,[5] and an incomplete set of large finished presentation drawings that Piranesi subsequently offered to the pope's nephew, later cardinal, Giovanni Battista Rezzonico, in 1767. Of the twenty-six drawings in the presentation set related to San Giovanni in Laterano, twenty-three are in the Avery Architectural Library, Columbia University, New York, and one drawing is in the State Hermitage Museum, St. Petersburg.[6] The whereabouts of two presentation drawings, numbered 24 and 26, are so far unknown. Two fragments of an unfinished drawing—which must initially have been destined for the same set of presentation drawings, but was for some reason abandoned and later covered with figure studies—are in the École nationale supérieure des Beaux-Arts, Paris, and a private collection in Paris.[7]

We would know much more about the intentions if the competing projects survived. Apart from Piranesi's drawings, however, we unfortunately only know of a single drawing by Melchiorre Passalacqua, which Antonio Foscari found in the Rezzonico archive, and was most likely also given to the pope's nephew, Giovanni Battista Rezzonico.[8] The drawing, a ground plan approximately the same size as Piranesi's presentation drawings, shows the entire western section of the Lateran basilica, from the cloister to the south to the benedictional loggia to the north as well as the last bay of Borromini's nave, the transept, the western section, the medieval apse, the ambulatory, and his proposed reconstruction. For the present purpose, the most important indication is that there were no Borrominian elements recycled by Passalacqua, nor any particular regard for Borromini's nave. To ensure that his decoration in the transept was identical on both sides, Passalacqua did not hesitate to insert columns inside Borronini's arches between the aisles and the transept.

Some have thought that there were only two options open for any potential architect of a Lateran choir: either be faithful to Borromini's nave, or follow the transept; but there are other possibilities.[9] He could, like Passalacqua, propose his own solution without regard for the nave or the transept; or he could, like Piranesi, propose his own solutions, but nevertheless relate this design beyond the separating polychrome transept to Borromini's nave through a continuity of horizontal accents, recycling some decorative elements from the nave and making it essentially white. Perhaps it is only in this sense that one should understand the inscriptions—"*immaginati con architettura corrispondente a quella*

1. LONGITUDINAL SECTION
BEGINNING AT TRANSEPT
OF THE PROPOSED TRIBUNE
OF S. GIOVANNI IN LATERANO
Pen and brown ink, brush
and brown wash with traces
of graphite on off-white
laid paper

della gran Nave"—found on many of the drawings. In all of Piranesi's projects the three-dimensional structures were of his own invention, without any serious attempt to relate them to Borromini's nave. Only in the decoration do we find his eclectic mixture of elements of his own invention and recycled decorative elements from Borromini's nave, fused into what he must have considered a convincing whole.

Among the determining factors was the need to adapt the designs to the particularly constraining conditions of the site. From the basilica's western end toward the baptistery, the terrain fell off sharply, and any extension westward entailed escalating costs due to the increasingly important foundations required. Also, there was the obligation to ensure a convenient passage from the church to the courtyard behind the apse and beyond it to the baptistery, as well as another passage to the sacristy and beyond it to the cloisters.[10]

Piranesi created no fewer than seven different plans, nine if the variant options are counted, most of which are more or less developed in the finished presentation drawings. Although interconnected, they are clearly distinct from one another in their objectives. The different schemes are, in terms of the plan, essentially variations on the medieval apse and ambulatory. They can be organized into three groups that correspond to the three distinct treatments of the elevation.

In all the schemes, Piranesi took care to distinguish the new building block as a separate construction, with its outer limits clearly established by the framing arch with the papal escutcheon of Clement XIII. A spectator looking at the presbytery from the transept would see, in the first three plans, Piranesi's extensive remodeling of recycled decorative elements from Borromini's nave; in the next two schemes, he would stand in front of Piranesi's semicircular columnar screen; and in the remaining two designs, he would see Piranesi's decoration around the altarpiece. With the exception of the first three schemes, nearly all of the elements reused from Borromini's nave are found on walls out of sight for a spectator looking at the presbytery from the transept.

The first group consists of three projects in which the height of the coffered ceilings over the forechoir and the semidome over the presbytery is the same as that of the ceiling of the nave. The first scheme is only known by an autograph drawing (fig. 1) in the Morgan Library and involves a simple apsidal presbytery with a narrow "exedra," or forechoir, occupying the same space as the medieval apse and ambulatory, but extended farther westward with a complete ambulatory.

The second scheme, illustrated by drawings 1, 2, and 3 (a plan, a section, and a transverse section; figs. 2–4), involves the same simple apsidal presbytery with a narrow forechoir. To limit the extension westward, however, the ambulatory is not complete, but runs only its innermost sections in the form of a corridor on the south side and a small vestibule on the north side.

The third scheme is illustrated by drawings 4 and 5 (a plan, a section, and a transverse section; figs. 5, 6). Compared with the second design, Piranesi pushed the apse wall farther back, thereby allowing room for a larger presbytery and forechoir. It is, as in the second scheme, not surrounded by a complete ambulatory, but one that runs along only its innermost sections.

In the first and second schemes, the presbytery is seen through a framing arch with the papal escutcheon of Clement XIII above, surrounded by garlands and a large banderole of Piranesi's own invention. In the presbytery, the decoration is a reduced adaptation of the tripartite elements on the pillars in the nave, and is set six steps above the nave, creating a discontinuous floor level. This meant that he had to operate a reduction in height in order to ensure a continuity of horizontal accents from the nave. The oval frame for a painting is inserted into the semidome and changes into windows or purely decorative panels. On the wall, the rectangular stucco relief is retained, but the tabernacle niches are replaced with smaller decorative panels of Piranesi's own in-

2. TITLE PAGE OF PRESENTATION
DRAWINGS EMBODYING
PROPOSALS FOR A NEW
SANCTUARY (TAVOLA 1)
Pen and gray and brown ink
on off-white laid paper

3. CROSS SECTION SHOWING
WEST WALL OF TRANSEPT
AND VIEW INTO SANCTUARY
(TAVOLA 2)
Pen and gray and brown ink on
off-white laid paper

4. LONGITUDINAL SECTION
SHOWING SOUTH WALL OF
SANCTUARY, WITH TRANSEPT
AND BEGINNING OF NAVE
(TAVOLA 3)
Pen and gray and brown ink on
off-white laid paper

Tavola Sec^{da}.

Elevazione ortografica, o sia Fronte della Tribuna e degl' ingressi deretani della Basilica Lateranense.

I numeri dall'uno al dodici circoscrivono l'opere da farsi per gl' ingressi deretani, e per la Tribuna.

Scala di Palmi Romani CXX.

Cav. G.B. Piranesi fece.

Tavola Terza.

Sezione ortografica di fian... ...la Tribuna del Presbiterio, e dell' Esedra della Basilica Lateranense... ...inati con architettura corrispondente a quella della gran Nave.

Cav. G.B. Piranesi fec.

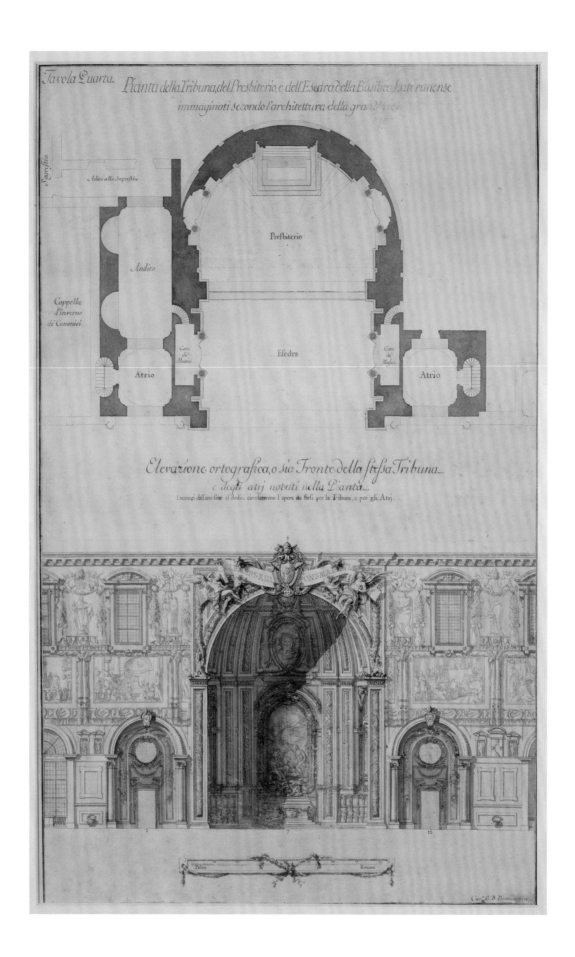

THE PROJECTS FOR THE RECONSTRUCTION OF THE LATERAN BASILICA IN ROME

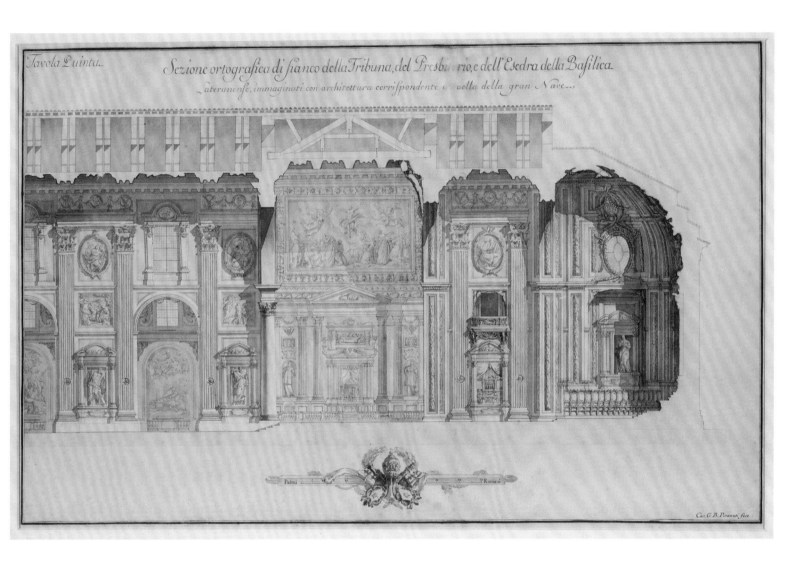

Tavola Quinta.   *Sezione ortografica di fianco della Tribuna, del Presbiterio, e dell'Esedra della Basilica. Lateranense, immaginati con architettura corrispondente a quella della gran Nave.*

Palmi   Romani

Cav. G. B. Piranesi fece.

5. PLAN AND VIEW OF
SANCTUARY FROM THE
TRANSEPT (TAVOLA 4)
Pen and gray and brown ink
on off-white laid paper

6. LONGITUDINAL SECTION
SHOWING SOUTH WALL OF
SANCTUARY, WITH TRANSEPT
AND BEGINNING OF NAVE
(TAVOLA 5)
Pen and gray and brown ink on
off-white laid paper

7. PLAN OF SANCTUARY WITH
SCREEN OF COLUMNS AND
AMBULATORY (TAVOLA 6)
Pen and gray and brown ink
on off-white laid paper

vention. The fluted Corinthian pilasters, which in the nave are separating these elements, are replaced with slender naturalistic laurel leaves in sunken panels copied from Borromini's pilasters of the aisles. In the forechoir, a pillar framed with pilasters, a decorative motif from the nave, is reused, but some elements are given another use. The upper section with an oval frame for a painting is retained, whereas the rectangular stucco relief is turned into a balcony and the tabernacle niche for statuary is turned into a structure enclosing organs.

In the third scheme, the presbytery is again seen through a framing arch, with another variant above the papal escutcheon of Clement XIII surrounded by angels, garlands, and a large banderole. The fifth-century mosaic head of the Savior, which was incorporated into the main mosaic in the apse in the thirteenth century, is inserted into the semidome above the altarpiece showing the preaching of the Baptist. According to ancient tradition, this head of the Savior was manifest to the eyes of the worshippers on the occasion of the dedication of the church. Double laurel leaves in sunken panels of the pilasters, a motif continued in the semidome, are on both sides of the altar. Because Piranesi had to again achieve a reduction in height, a section that is a reduced adaptation of the tripartite pillar from the nave follows the pilasters to ensure a continuity of horizontal accents. The oval frame is again inserted into the semidome, and a decorative frame created by Piranesi surrounds the windows. This time, he suppresses the rectangular stucco relief and reworks the tabernacles, which are inserted into a huge recess in the wall and become purely decorative. The dynamic tension of Borromini's tabernacles is lost, as they concurrently cut into the mass of the piers and force the columns outward into the nave. In the forechoir, a pillar framed with pilasters from the nave is again reused. As in the second scheme, it is clear that Piranesi decided first on the proportions in his plan and only subsequently tried to arrange for the decoration of the walls, as the pillar does not fit into the available space. In the second design, the capitals are truncated, whereas in the third, the wall space is too large.

The second group consists of two projects. The fourth scheme is known from the drawings numbered 6 to 10 (a plan, a drawing with a section and a slightly different plan, a transverse section, and a section; figs. 7–10; also see Wilton-Ely, fig. 15). On the plan, the basic elements are only slightly larger than in the first scheme (with a complete ambulatory), but their function is turned upside down. The former presbytery wall is lowered and turned into a semicircular columnar screen of Piranesi's own invention. The previous low external ambulatory wall is raised to

Tavola Ottava

Sezione ortografica di fianco della Tribuna, del Presbiterio
e dell'Esedra della Basilica Lateranense
immaginati con architettura corrispondente a quella della gran Nave.

8. TRANSVERSE SECTION
OF THE SANCTUARY, VIEWED
FROM THE TRANSEPT, AND
GROUND PLAN (TAVOLA 7)
Pen and gray and brown ink
on off-white laid paper

9. LONGITUDINAL SECTION
SHOWING SOUTH WALL
OF SANCTUARY WITH TRANSEPT
AND BEGINNING OF NAVE
(TAVOLA 8)
Pen and gray and brown ink
on off-white laid paper

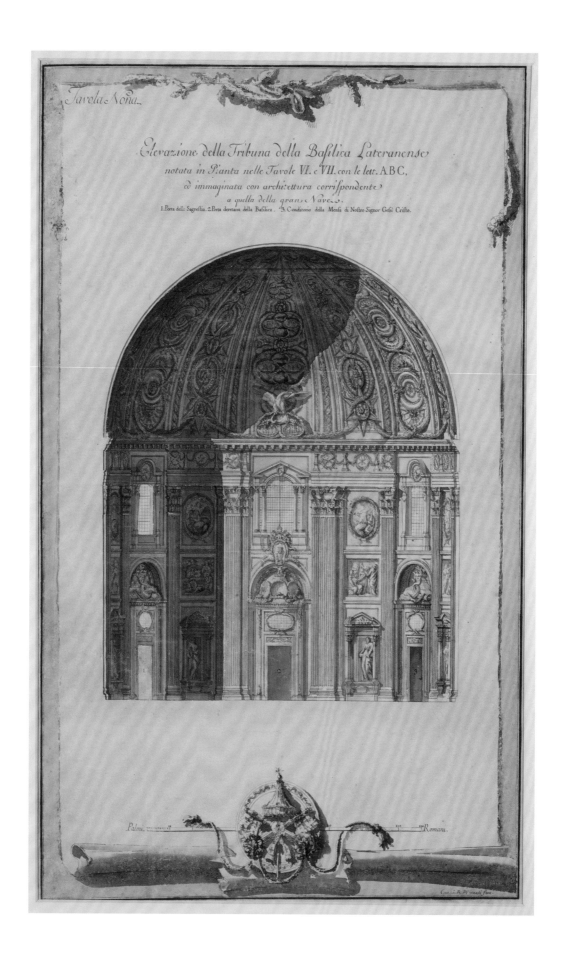

THE PROJECTS FOR THE RECONSTRUCTION OF THE LATERAN BASILICA IN ROME

the height of the ceiling of the nave. This colossal arrangement of space also involved raising the ceiling of the sanctuary in two stages: the barrel vault of the forechoir is raised considerably above the height of the ceiling of the nave and transept, and the half-dome of the presbytery and ambulatory higher still, supported by an arch with three clerestory windows, allowing the presbytery area to be lit by windows not visible from the crossing. The weight of his half-dome on the supporting structure would have been considerable; nonetheless, nothing is changed in the plan, which has the same hollowed out piers as in the previous schemes.

The fifth scheme is known from the drawings numbered 11 to 13 (figs. 11, 12) and the one unfinished drawing (a plan, a section, and an unfinished section; but there are no transverse sections). This scheme repeats the main articulation, as seen in the preceding plan with its arrangement of space. The most important changes concern the lateral doorways that are aligned with Borromini's large arched openings between the aisles and the transept. To achieve this, Piranesi diminished the thickness of the walls, apparently without taking into consideration that they are utterly inadequate to support the weight of his half-dome. The depth of the forechoir is diminished, such that the semicircular columnar screen can be detached from the forechoir wall and stand independent.

Returning to a consideration of the fourth scheme, the presbytery is again seen through a framing arch with another variant of the papal escutcheon of Clement XIII above, surrounded by garlands and a large banderole. Piranesi's semicircular columnar screen—in which the use of figurative reliefs on the columns below the capitals emphasizes his predilection for extravagant ornamentation—overloads convoluted capitals, and statues of angels placed on a half-wall between the columns are seen in the presbytery. Above the altarpiece, the mosaic head of the Savior is inserted into a decorative frame.

In the wall of the apse, Piranesi reuses many elements from Borromini's nave: a large arched opening at center featuring a window frame with double Corinthian columns above that support the pediment; rectangular stucco reliefs above and still higher oval frames for paintings framed on both sides by the tripartite pillar with a superimposed tabernacle niche for statuary; a large arched opening with a window frame and with terms supporting an arcuated lintel that bends up and around the Pamphili dove; and another tripartite pillar. The use of fluted Corinthian double pilasters accentuates the central axis, whereas the other sections are separated with single pilasters.

The overall effect, however, is diametrically opposed to Borromini's nave, where the arched openings support the dynamic rhythms running through the nave. In Piranesi's design, this blind arcade, copied on an

12. TRANSVERSE SECTION
SHOWING WEST WALL OF
TRANSEPT WITH PAPAL ALTAR
AND BALDACCHINO WITHIN
THE SANCTUARY (TAVOLA 12)
Pen and gray and brown
ink over graphite on off-white
laid paper

11. PLAN OF SANCTUARY WITH
SCREEN OF COLUMNS AND
AMBULATORY (TAVOLA 11)
Pen and gray and brown
ink on off-white laid paper

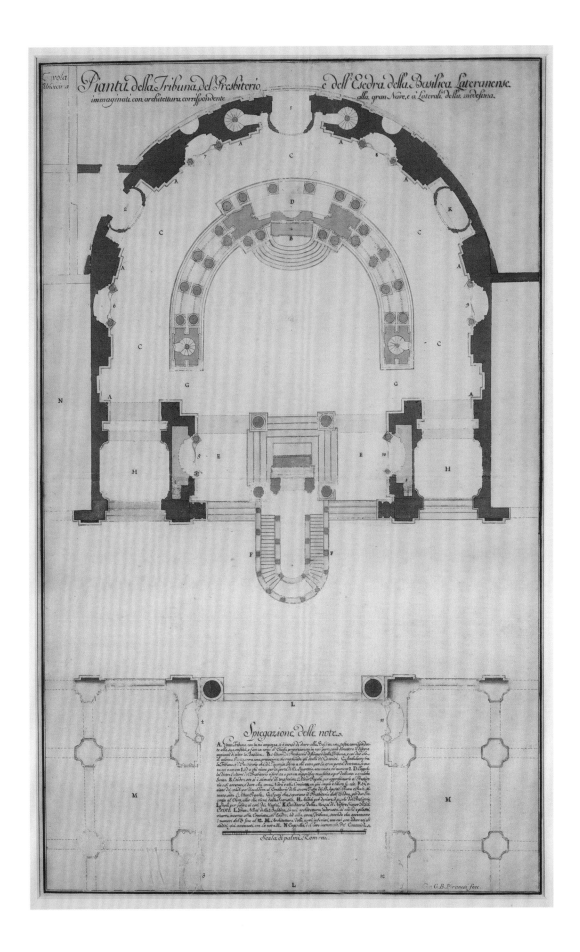

13. PLAN OF SANCTUARY WITH
AMBULATORY (TAVOLA 14)
Pen and gray and brown ink
on off-white laid paper

external wall without openings, loses its raison d'être and becomes purely decorative. Where the large arched openings in Borromini's nave provide circulation and counteract the detailed elements, they are now crammed with details such as a door surrounded by ornamental frames, an oval frame above, three shells, and an eagle with wings outstretched. The apsidal vault, where he gives full rein to his predilection for sumptuous ornamentation, is Piranesi's own design.

In the fifth scheme, Piranesi went even further and, for the first time, proposed a redecoration of the transept's walls, which had been renovated during the pontificate of Clement VIII. Their absence in drawing 12 indicates that he intended to suppress the altar of the Blessed Sacrament on the south wall and the organ on the north wall. Although barely indicated, this scheme furthermore entails the rebuilding of the whole area to the north of the sanctuary. Besides Borromini's nave, the only components of the basilica left untouched are, to the south of the sanctuary, the Colonna family chapel (on the drawings labeled "Capella d'inverno de' Canonici", the winter chapel of the canons), and the sacristy.

The presbytery is again seen through a framing arch with yet another variant of the papal escutcheon of Clement XIII above, surrounded by a large banderole. On both sides are a pair of large arched openings, without the papal escutcheon. A window frame above includes double Corinthian columns supporting the pediment, which are reused from Borromini's nave and separated by single pilasters. The large arched openings on the western wall are changed into rectangular doorways. The arched overdoors are filled with medallion portraits of Pope Clement XIII and medallions of the Holy Ghost, surrounded by a decorative border. The decoration does not fit the available space, however, and Piranesi is left with a small space to the north and a larger space to the south. The reuse of the same four sections of Borromini's nave is, according to the plan, applied to the eastern wall (drawing 11). There are no drawings that show the transept's eastern wall, and the plan does not allow us to determine if the doorways are identical on both sides of the transept. If Piranesi's scheme were identical on both sides, Borromini's large arched openings would have to be deformed into rectangular doorways; if not, the two walls would be very dissimilar. This scheme repeats the main articulation of the half-dome and the apse wall as seen in the preceding scheme. There is only one minor change: in the preceding scheme, only the central axis is accentuated by the use of fluted Corinthian double pilasters. In this plan, the double pilasters are used uniformly around the apse.

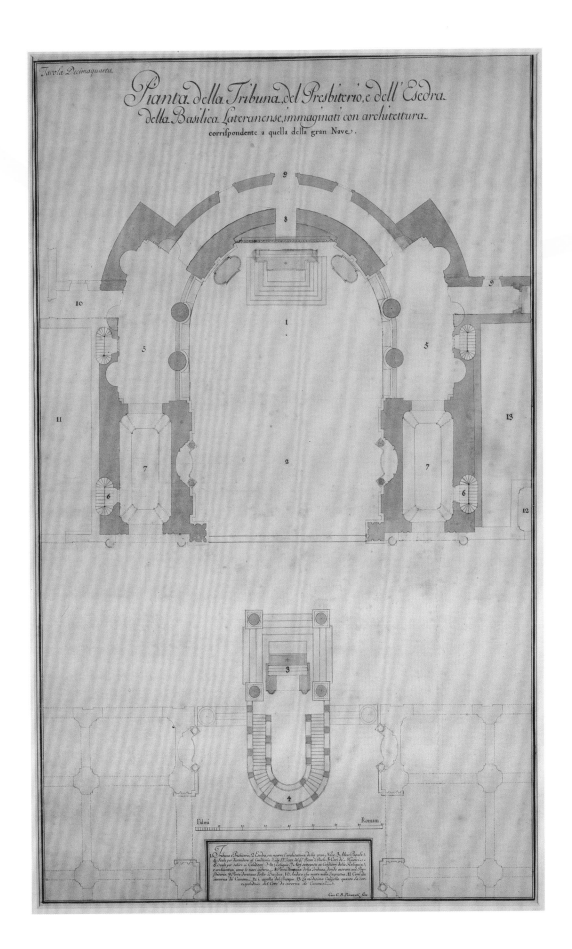

Tavola Decimaquarta.

Pianta della Tribuna, del Presbiterio, e dell'Esedra della Basilica Lateranense, immaginati con architettura corrispondente a quella della gran Nave.

Palmi   Romani

Cav. G. B. Piranesi fec.

The very limited number of changes to the presbytery area compared with the previous scheme is, at first glance, astonishing. In all of the other designs, Piranesi had to relate beyond the separating polychrome transept to Borromini's nave with a continuity of horizontal accents and by recycling some decorative elements from the nave. He now had the unique possibility of creating complete continuity in the basilica, architectural as well as decorative, but he did not pursue this, and it appears that he may not have been interested in doing so. His main preoccupation seems to have been to effect small adjustments to his own architecture, but not the important changes that were necessary to create a unity in the basilica. In connection with the Lateran schemes, Piranesi has sometimes been described as an admiring follower of Borromini, but this design is certainly not evidence for that.

The third group consists of two projects, with two variants. The sixth scheme is poorly represented: the plan numbered 14 (fig. 13) shows two options, the primary solution in which the walls are depicted in black and a secondary solution in which only the outlines are drawn; but the drawings numbered 15 (a section; fig. 14) and 16 (a transverse section; fig. 15) show only the secondary solution. In this scheme, Piranesi returns to the apse and ambulatory concept. If the ambulatory had been completed, this solution would have occupied the same space as the previous plan, but, in order to limit the extension westward, the outermost third of the ambulatory has been cut off. The innermost section is turned into an elevated platform separated from the choir by freestanding columns. The height of the coffered ceiling over the platform is the same as that of the ceiling of the nave. The vault of the presbytery and forechoir is raised a considerable height above. In the forechoir, the tripartite pillars with a superimposed tabernacle niche for statuary are reused, whereas the rectangular stucco relief above is turned into a balcony and oval frames for paintings are placed still higher. This scheme does not assure a convenient circulation. There is no passage to the sacristy, and the only passage to the courtyard and beyond it to the baptistery is through a narrow gap between the altar and the wall, no more than fifty to sixty centimeters wide, quite insufficient for the convenient passage of a well nourished canon of the Chapter of San Giovanni in Laterano. The primary solution, shown only on the plan, has a narrow ambulatory with a passage beyond to the baptistery.

The seventh scheme is also poorly represented. The plan numbered 17 (fig. 16) shows two options, but drawing 18 (a transverse section; fig. 17) shows only the secondary solution. This secondary option is a variant of the preceding scheme, but with an extensive enlargement of the fore-

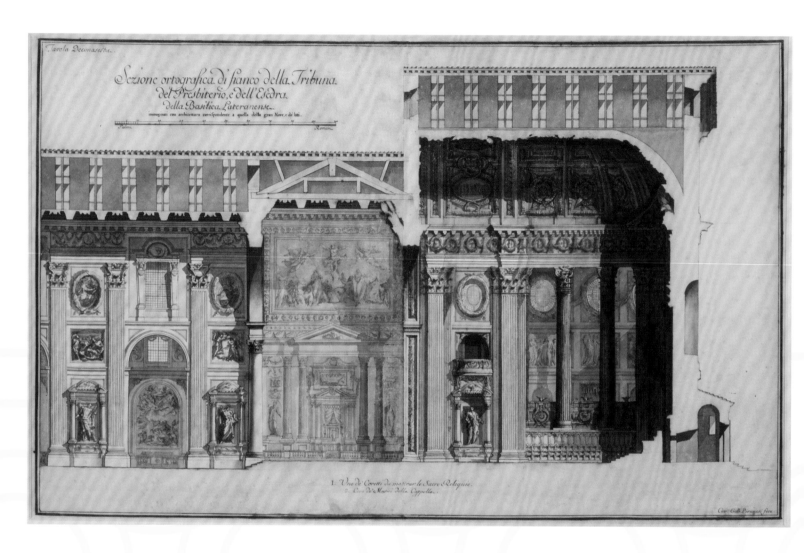

15. LONGITUDINAL SECTION
SHOWING SOUTH WALL OF
SANCTUARY, WITH TRANSEPT
AND BEGINNING OF NAVE
(TAVOLA 16)
Pen and gray and brown ink
on off-white laid paper

16. PLAN OF SANCTUARY
(TAVOLA 17)
Pen and gray and brown ink
on off-white laid paper

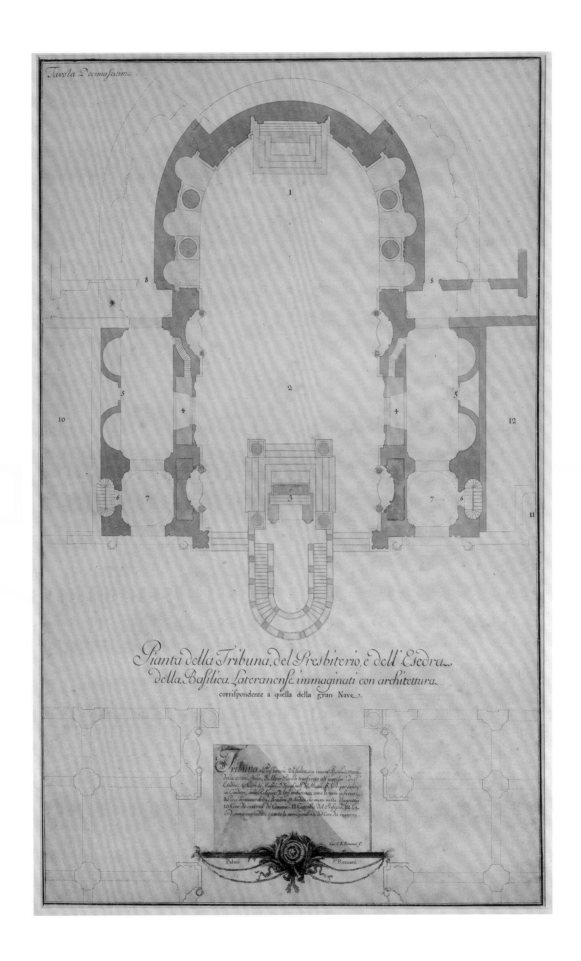

Pianta della Tribuna, del Presbiterio, e dell' Esedra
della Basilica Lateranense immaginati con architettura
corrispondente a quella della gran Nave.

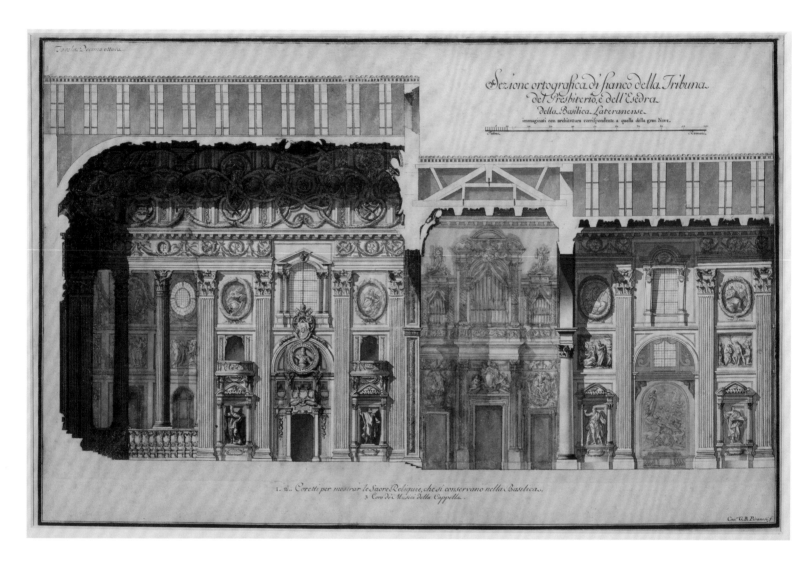

Tavola Decima ottava

Sezione ortografica di fianco della Tribuna del Presbiterio, e dell'Esedra della Basilica Lateranense. immaginati con architettura corrispondente a quella della gran Nave.

1. 2. Coretti per mostrar le Sacre Reliquie, che si conservano nella Basilica. 3 Coro de' Musici della Cappella.

Cav.r G.B. Piranesi f.

17. LONGITUDINAL SECTION
SHOWING NORTH WALL OF
SANCTUARY, WITH TRANSEPT
AND BEGINNING OF NAVE
(TAVOLA 18)
Pen and gray and brown ink
on off-white laid paper

18. ALTERNATIVE DESIGN
FOR PAPAL ALTAR AND
BALDACCHINO (TAVOLA 20)
Pen and brown ink, brush
and brown and gray wash
over graphite on off-white
laid paper

Altro progetto dell'Altar Papale della Basilica Lateranense
veduto dalla parte della gran nave della stessa Basilica
adornato con un'urna da riporvi le Sacre Teste de' Santi Apostoli Pietro e Paolo.

Cav. G.B. Piranesi fece.

choir. In the primary solution, shown only on the plan, the ambulatory arms have been suppressed and the columns are standing against the outer wall. To emphasize his own architecture, Piranesi changes the floor level: He suppresses the steps between the nave and transept, but made four steps between transept and forechoir. The floor in the transept is lowered close to eighty centimeters, which was not without problems of its own, especially for the officiant at the altar of the Blessed Sacrament.

In the sixth scheme, the framing arch is not shown, and the presbytery is seen from within the forechoir area. Set around a huge painted altarpiece, with a distinctive Piranesian frame, an elaborate candelabrum is flanked by double pilasters and columns. The mosaic head of the Savior is again visible above, and even farther above it is the unmistakable vault decoration by Piranesi. In the forechoir and on the external walls, elements from the nave are reused. In the seventh scheme, the presbytery looks very much like the previous design, except for the forechoir, which has now been tripled. In the middle is a large arched opening with a window frame above, and double Corinthian columns support the pediment. Framed on both sides by the tripartite pillar, with a superimposed tabernacle niche for statuary, the rectangular stucco relief above is turned into a balcony, with oval frames for paintings above that. The large arched openings are again changed into rectangular doorways, with arched overdoors filled with a medallion portrait of pope Clement XIII.

The second part of the project concerns the new papal altar and baldacchino, placed in the transitional area between Piranesi's choir and Borromini's nave. Piranesi made no fewer than six different designs that are mainly shown on separate sheets: a preparatory drawing of the lower section of the papal altar and baldacchino mounted as a presentation drawing and numbered 20 (fig. 18), three finished large presentation drawings numbered 21 to 23 (figs. 19–21), and a small preparatory drawing now in the collection of the Morgan Library that shows a design of the ornamental frame containing the two reliquary busts.[11] The essential structure is the same as in the previous drawings: a central oval aperture surrounded by a richly ornamental framework, crowned with the crossed keys of Saint Peter and the papal tiara that Piranesi had used in two of the other project designs (drawings 20 and 22). This variant is not represented in the known presentation drawings, but there is the distinct possibility that it was used in the missing drawing number 24. The last variant is seen integrated into drawing 12.

Piranesi must have known of Borromini's proposals for a new papal altar with its architectonic ciborium. The four projects were engraved in

Uno de progetti dell'Altar Papale, veduto
Dalla parte della mensa, che riguarda. La

Tribuna, ed inventato sul gusto del Boromino,
secondo il quale è stata rinnovata la Basilica.

Cav. C. Batta Piranesi F.

Tavola Vigesimasecunda.

Cav. G. Batta Piranesi fece

one of the best known architectural books of the eighteenth century, Domenico de Rossi's *Studio d'architettura civile sopra gli ornamenti di porte e finestre tratti da alcune fabbriche insigni di Roma*, published in Rome in 1702. There is not, however, the slightest similarity between Borromini's proposals and those of Piranesi. He wrote on two of the drawings that they were *inventato sul gusto del Boromino* and *inventato su lo stile del Boromino*—descriptions that are also appropriate for two other drawings. They look, in fact, more like exaggerated pastiches. It is difficult to imagine any of these pastiches successfully integrated with any schemes for the rebuilding of the basilica. Piranesi may have felt the difficulty himself, as the papal altar is not indicated in the first three schemes. The altar is subsequently shown on the different plans, but only on one section, and it is absent on the drawings numbered 8, 16, and 18.

At first, Piranesi may have been asked to submit proposals for only the new papal altar and baldacchino. This would have given him the chance to assert his inventiveness by making it more Borrominian than Borromini himself. It would also have ensured that those features would be a conspicuous focal point amidst Borromini's nave, the polychrome transept, and the medieval apse with its mosaic. But when he subsequently was asked to submit proposals for the rebuilding—in which he attempted to generate a continuity between the building blocks—any conspicuous focal point would have counteracted the effect he was now seeking. This could explain why they were not integrated into several of the schemes for rebuilding the basilica.

Piranesi's aspirations as an architect have to some extent been blurred by the very drawings by which they are known, thereby contributing to the misunderstanding of his architectural accomplishment. The finished appearance of the presentation drawings, with their multitude of minute details, gives the fallacious impression that the various schemes were worked out in detail, and that these drawings show the final stages of his thinking. In fact, the presence of many errors indicates that they were no more than works in progress. Because a professional architectural draftsman made the very detailed presentation drawings, Piranesi had to decide many nonessential details, without necessarily considering the consequences. It is difficult, as a result, to distinguish between what his main preoccupation was and what was only a fortuitous effect. For instance, the many numbers bearing reference to the detailed legend give the impression that they were solutions to a series of detailed prerequisites, but in some instances, it is unlikely that he set out to solve a specific problem. It appears, rather, that by copying he ended up with spaces for which he then tried to find some use. In the fourth and fifth schemes,

Altro progetto dell'Altar Papale della Basilica Lateranense rappresentato e
veduto dalla parte della mensa, che riguarda la Tribuna, e inventato su lo Stile del Boromino, secondo il quale
è Stata rinnovata la Basilica.

Cav. G. Batta Piranesi Fece.

when he copied Borromini's large arched openings on the external wall, he ended up with three doors; two were used to assure a convenient passage from the church to the sacristy and beyond it to the cloisters, and another passage to the courtyard behind the apse and beyond it to the baptistery, but the third door was of no use. It was then designated the *Conditorio della Mensa di Nostro Signor Gesù Cristo*, a repository for the table thought to have been used by Christ at the Last Supper, one of the most venerable relics in San Giovanni in Laterano. It is hardly believable that it could have been shuffled around merely to fill up an otherwise useless space. It is telling that it was only from the fourth scheme, when the more complicated plan engendered useless spaces, that Piranesi started paying attention to the venerable relics.

There are serious flaws in nearly all the projects, including structural problems, difficulties in assuring a convenient circulation within the basilica and beyond to the baptistery, capricious designations of spaces, and badly adjusted decorations. Nevertheless, Piranesi multiplied the projects, as it was more important to display his inventiveness than to make a single constructable project. In 1763–64, such an expensive rebuilding was probably beyond the reach of the church, already confronted with serious financial problems, but a lack of funds did not hamper "paper" architecture.

If the very detailed and picturesque appearance of these presentation drawings distract from their usefulness as architectural drawings, it adds to their attractiveness as images. Therefore, it is fitting that Giovanni Battista Rezzonico, grand prior of the priory of Rome of the Order of Malta, his patron for the reconstruction of S. Maria del Priorato, chose to hang the drawings for San Giovanni in Laterano—framed in gilded gold frames—on the walls in his apartments.[12]

ALICE JARRARD

PERSPECTIVES ON PIRANESI AND THEATER

PERHAPS NO OTHER ASPECT OF PIRANESI STUDIES IS AS VEXED AS THE RELATIONSHIP BETWEEN HIS PRINTS AND THE THEATER OF HIS TIME. THE PRINTS THEMSELVES, LIKE MANY ARTWORKS OF THE EIGHTEENTH CENTURY, ARE OFTEN DESCRIBED AS "THEATRICAL," "DRAMATIC," EVEN "OPERATIC," most often in general allusion to Piranesi's distinctive deployment of sharply raking perspective, strong contrasts of lighting, and minute human figures cast in gesticulating, rhetorical poses.[1] (fig. 1) Yet beyond evocative adjectives or metaphors, and even more than a shared dependence on techniques of perspective and lighting, Piranesi's work reflects vital debates about the larger role of architecture in contemporary eighteenth-century theater. Like the theater designers of his time, and despite his own interests in construction, Piranesi celebrated architecture as image, designed primarily for visual consumption and effect, in his graphic works.

Toward the end of the eighteenth century, just a few years after Piranesi's death, French architectural critics pronounced theater crucial to modern architecture's inception. They attributed architecture's new ability to inspire profound emotional effects to the onstage experiments of architects earlier in the century.[2] Two of Piranesi's early biographers conveyed something of the prestige accorded to theater design in these later years when, neglecting to mention his actual building experience with his uncle at all, they described only his training with

Gruppo di Scale ornato di magnifica Architettura, le quali stanno disposte in modo che conducano a varj piani, e specialmente ad una Rotonda che serve per rappresentanze teatrali.

1. GRUPPO DI SCALE ORNATO
DI MAGNIFICA ARCHITETTURA
Etching, engraving

painters who were experts in perspective and theater.[3] The reputation of such stage work was still contested during Piranesi's early years, and the celebration of architecture's ideation, rather than its actual practice, remained a running tension in both Piranesi's work and writings. Theatrical design became a lightning rod for debates about professional identity, boundaries, and expertise. No traces survive of Piranesi's personal interest in the stage during this age when theater was the dominant cultural form. No anecdotes describe his attendance at the thriving theaters of the cities where he worked, nor have allusions to dramatic productions been discovered in his work. His compatriot Canaletto was later said to have chosen a different career from his stage-designing father by "excommunicating" theater due to the dubious morality of dramatic texts. There is no such suggestion for why Piranesi never designed for the stage.[4]

Despite this lack of direct participation in theater practice, the evidence of Piranesi's work speaks to a profound and ongoing engagement with theater throughout his life. His etchings engaged critical issues that dominated discussion in the architectural, pictorial, and especially the theatrical circles of his day: the reform of style, the issue of buildability, and the communicative role that architecture might play. While Piranesi's early etchings, notably the *Prima Parte di architettura e prospettive* and the *Carceri*, are now almost universally interpreted in light of their perspectival techniques and typological connections to prints from contemporary theater treatises, the polemical intent of the *Prima Parte* has rarely been explored in relation to the stage.[5] Moreover, the tendency has been to limit the relevance of theater to Piranesi's youth and Venetian connections. Recent research suggests instead that, in the 1760s, when these early prints began to be widely imitated on stages as far afield as Paris, theater again provided the artist with fresh inspiration for a new approach to representing the fragmentary remains of the past.[6] Though the lens of theater provides only one angle on Piranesi's complex oeuvre, a sustained look at two moments of Piranesi's production in the context of theatrical debates shows how, and why, theater is fundamental to understanding his work.

THEATER AND ARCHITECTURAL INVENTION

When Piranesi first picked up his engraving tools, the stage—which had long been a locus for architectural displays—was under fire from new quarters. Alluding to Aristostle's *Poetics*, opera libretti from the previous century had accorded architecture a specific role in the inspiration of feelings of terror and grandeur. Designers had gone far beyond the three basic sets described by the ancient Vitruvius. As a writer explained in 1682, there were sixteen kinds of decoration, but "one might add one hundred decorations of caprice, which can diversify the face of a stage in an infinity of ways."[7] Disconnected from the practicalities of actual construction and submitted to the rather different constraints of the perspective wing stage, architecture became a locus of unbridled invention. A new kind of independent architectural representation arose to celebrate the inventive deployment of buildings in perspective. Now dubbed the "architectural fantasy," but perhaps more properly categorized under its eighteenth-century appellation as a "caprice," Piranesi's early drawings occupied this graphic territory between theater and actual architecture.[8] His first biographer, Legrand, alluded to the theatrical aspect of their creation as well their technical demands when he explained that, by working "in the school" of the theater designers Ferdinando Bibiena and the Valeriani brothers, and by painting in the theaters of Venice and Bologna, Piranesi acquired "that facility in per-

2. Ferdinando Bibiena
L'ARCHITETTURA CIVILE,
PLATE 67
Etching, engraving

spective and that knowledge of lines and theater effects which made the largest and most complex compositions a game for him."[9]

The question of whether stage representations of architecture should be the province of trained architects or simply of painters knowledgeable about perspective was hotly debated during Piranesi's youth. Stage design was an acknowledged route to fame for both architects and painters. From Rome, after conceiving sets and teaching perspective drawing in the French Academy, the architect Filippo Juvarra embarked on a wildly successful career as designer to the duke of Turin and the king of Spain. In Bologna, after training as painters and spending three decades visualizing theaters and scenes for dukes and emperors abroad, Ferdinando Bibiena (who was then practically blind) retired to write and teach at the Accademia Clementina while his equally acclaimed brother Francesco made the city a base for continued Italian operations. In his treatises, Ferdinando celebrated the supremacy of perspective and proclaimed the painter closer to the architect than to the untrained builder because of his mastery of ideation.[10] Bibiena also recognized the inevitable dwindling of the architectural idea as drawing was put into execution onstage. He poignantly acknowledged the conundrum of practice in a way Piranesi would have understood, writing that "sometimes one doesn't recognize it for that idea which one initially formed in the mind's intellect . . . it gradually loses that spirit that was first part of the idea."[11]

Ferdinando Bibiena's *Scena per angolo*, published in 1711 and popularized in a revised octavo edition for students in 1732–33, was first and foremost a mathematical demonstration proving the designer's technical skill, and secondarily a solution to the specific spatial problems of a narrow stage. He himself said nothing of the effect of psychological proximity that modern spectators often describe (fig. 2). The ongoing need for such technical knowledge in theatrical circles was amply attested by Benedetto Marcello, who declared, in his satire of Venetian theater, written around 1721, that "the Engineer, or modern Painter should not know Perspective, Architecture, Drawing, Chiaroscuro, etc., and should make sure that the Architectural Scenes never go towards one, or two Points, but rather that each Wing should have four, or six, situated differently, because the Spectator's eye is better satisfied by this variety."[12] That Piranesi would so rigorously adopt—and manipulate—Bibiena's perspectival formulation throughout his life demonstrates his engagement with the technique. The introduction to his first suite of etchings in 1743 cited Vitruvius on perspective's necessity to the architect, and continued, in Piranesi's own irascible way, "Truthfully I might add that anyone who does not see the use and necessity of perspective in Architecture does not yet know whence she draws her greatest and most enduring (sodo) beauty."[13]

Despite their widespread popularity, the scenes of the Bibiena brothers and their many students were under fire upon architectural grounds during Piranesi's youth. In Paris, a new valuation of "buildable," "enduring," and "virile" stage designs appeared by 1730 in newspaper descriptions of works by Giovanni Nicolo Servandoni, the latest Italian stage designer at the Paris Opera.[14] The trickle-down of such criteria into Italy paralleled a revival of interest in Palladio and Vitruvius there. By 1739, Ferdinando Bibiena's first biographer, for example, found it necessary to defend his ornate architectural style, stating that "true and enduring architecture pleased him, and not little curlicues (cartocci), leaves, and other modern frivolities."[15] In the Veneto, Francesco Bibiena was practically the house scenographer (as well as the architect) of the new Teatro Filarmonico in Verona, the first modern theater built with a temple-like façade, patronized by the enlightened Scipione Maffei. Despite Francesco's prominence, a production of his nephew Giuseppe's *Bajazet* at San Giovanni Crisostomo was received with derision in 1742, while Piranesi was in Rome preparing the *Prima Parte*.[16] "One saw nothing but columns, and even in the middle of the sea there were rocks with columns raised on them, so that commonly one called it the persecution of the columns," wrote Girolamo Zanetti of Giuseppe's production. He went on to note, "There was also a strange agglomeration of Gothic, Greek, and Roman architecture that was a most ugly sight to the eyes of knowledegable viewers."[17]

The first issue of Piranesi's *Prima Parte*, in 1743, in which each plate was carefully signed "Architectus," provided his own answer to the debate regarding the theatrical imagining of architecture. Though often likened to Giuseppe Bibiena's *Architettura e prospettive* of 1740, its contents systematically critiqued the Bibiena style.[cl] A self-promotional work, it was published in Rome—where the Bibiena family's students also dominated stage design—at a moment when the most talented stage painters in Venice (notably the Roman painter Giuseppe Valeriani, with whom Piranesi is said to have worked, and the Modenese painter Antonio Iolli) had just decamped to work at the Russian court and in London, respectively.[18] In its dedication, Piranesi extolled the ideation of architecture, condemned its present practice, and challenged patrons to alter the situation.

Piranesi manipulated perspective creatively in three landscape views of ruins and exploited the techniques of *scena per angolo* in six of the tract's ten architectural plates. He methodically deployed the grand an-

Vestibolo d'antico Tempio, oltre il quale s'entra nella Cella, per cui si gira all'intorno con tre Navate principali. Si scuopre pure in lontano la gran Cappella ove sta situata l'Ara principale pè Sagrifizj.

Gio. Batta Piranesi Archit.º Veneto inv. ed incise in Roma

13.

3. VESTIBULE OF AN ANCIENT
TEMPLE—PRIMA PARTE
Etching, engraving

cient settings for tragedy that are now known primarily from their titles as listed in opera libretti, as few images survive. A separate sheet originally listed the titles of Piranesi's plates in a manner similar to an opera libretto, though at the end of his publication: gallery, prison, sepulcher, ruin, hall, courtyard, temple interior, vestibule, and atrium, for example (fig. 3). (Captions were only added to each plate four years later.) The prevalence of interiors far surpassed the usual number found in contemporary productions, and they emphasized heroic magnificence and, in the case of the prison, terror. By comparison with Ferdinando Bibiena's etchings, or a maquette attributed to the Valeriani brothers, Piranesi's designs represented a clear declaration of independence from the decors dominating Italian stages (fig. 4). In their rejection of the heavy brackets, ornamented column shafts, curving fronds, and impossible vaults rampant on the stages of his day, these settings showed a notable decorative restraint and simplicity reminiscent of Palladio. They served as Piranesi's stylistic manifesto.

THE THEATER OF ARCHAEOLOGY: OBJECTS

In Piranesi's day, due to a longstanding misinterpretation of Vitruvius's writings, the term *scenografia* designated not stage painting, but rather a mode for representing buildings on paper using perspective. Perspective, as a representational means that became popular in the sixteenth century at the same time as the new perspective stage, was long critiqued for its inaccuracies and considered useful only for clients. Only in the late eighteenth century, and apparently first in England, was the term applied to modern—rather than ancient—stage design.[19] When the Latin term began to appear in the inscriptions accompanying Piranesi's plates, first in the *Antichità Romane* and with increasing frequency in the so-called "archaeological" works begun in the 1750s, it signified not a connection to the stage, as one might think, but the use of perspective. It reflected Piranesi's increasing attention to a varied repertoire of architectural representations. Alongside "ichnographic," "hypsographic," and "orthographic" images, "views," "fragments," "remains," and elevations, perspectives like his view of the Campus Martius served to present an imaginary dimension of ancient Rome. Piranesi's contact with the *pensionnaires* of the French Academy in Rome almost certainly inspired this new variety of representation. Although the *Prima Parte*'s perspectives deeply impressed these architectural students, they charged Piranesi "with ignorance of plans," according to the visiting William Chambers, who intimated that Piranesi only "styled himself an architect."[20]

Piranesi's response was to multiply his graphic arsenal, and he immediately conceived a magnificent plan for a college, complete with theater. Ever a voracious consumer of other printmakers' works, Piranesi digested the French architecture students' bible, Charles Perrault's *Vitruvius*, in order to present a new array of visual arguments about the grandeur of ancient Rome.[21] Besides including his own provocative footnotes about antiquity, Perrault's work had already introduced graphic conventions and luscious perspectival engravings to an earlier generation of printmakers in Rome, especially Pietro Santi Bartoli. The latter was an early explorer in the new archaeological genre, whose reconstructions of Roman tombs were republished under papal auspices in

Facciata delli Sepolcri antichi ricoperti di Terra Senz altre ruine, ritrouati nella Villa Corsini, fuori la Porta Aurelia. Sono singolarizati per la conseruatione, che rende più
marauigliosa la loro bellezza in ogni parte, benche alcuni nelle Volte fanno conoscere l'Eda-
cità del Tempo ueggendosi laceri. Si osseruano fatti di mattoncini arotati, bianchi, e rossi
nelle parti esteriori, con Ornamenti, e membri di Architettura sublime laurati con somma
intelligenza, le parti anteriori sono fregiate di Stucchi, Pitture, e Mosaichi bellissimi contra
segno che in quel Secolo le arti erano nel grado maggiore della loro perfettione A.B.C.D.
Ornamenti di Architettura composti di mattoncini intagliati di artificio Eccellente.

5. Pietro Santi Bartoli
FACCIATA DELLI SEPOLCRI...
Etching, engraving

1727. Perhaps even more than the evocative depictions of ruins by contemporary perspectival painters like Panini, with whom Piranesi is often compared, these works tempered Piranesi's new approach to antiquity. Bartoli's perspectives often invoked the aura of ancient theater, as when he filled a tomb-lined stage with a cast of gesturing tragedians, gravediggers, and architectural fragments thrown into dramatic shadow for effect (fig. 5). Like Piranesi, who later sought to preserve Rome's supremacy among ancient cultures, Bartoli deployed perspective toward rhetorical ends, buttressing these images with crisp plans and elevations to "preserve the grandeur of ancient Rome from the ravages of time."[22]

In Rome, where public stages continued to attract foreign visitors and magnificent ephemeral architecture was often staged on the streets, there is no record of Piranesi developing more than an antiquarian's interest in theater.[23] In the *Antichità Romane,* fourteen plates explored the canonical elevation and orders of the famed Theater of Marcellus, but they also imagined its invisible substructures and construction (fig. 6). In the next decade, as Piranesi was occupied with the first actual building projects of his career, he banished the distortions of perspective when presenting his own ornamental designs in clearly legible elevations.

Despite his own lack of interest in producing scenery, Piranesi's early prints soon influenced stage design outside Rome. By 1760, Pierre-Antoine de Machy's prison set at the Paris Opéra, of which no images survive, was pronounced by a reviewer to be "one of the most beautiful examples of perspective that we have seen on the stage . . . taken from the engravings of the celebrated Piranesi."[24] In 1776, an intrepid Bolognese scenographer named Vincenzo Mazzi entitled a suite of his own prints *Capricci di carceri tea[trali]*, linking Piranesi's visions of prisons to the stage by partially including the word "theatrical" in his frontispiece.[25] (fig. 7)

The tremendous public success of Piranesi's early prints meant pressures to invent anew, and may have helped push the artist's theatrical concerns in new directions. Piranesi's long overlooked final compilation of archaeological depictions, *Vasi, candelabri, cippi...* (1778), has long been interpreted in light of contemporary collecting practices. Piranesi's own *museo,* the display room of his shop, was represented with twenty-seven objects; the suite's contents were much like those found in the recently founded Museo Clementino, and "Vases," as Josiah Wedgwood wrote to a friend in 1760, "is the thing."[26] The work's commercial tone was explicit in the dedication of each plate to Piranesi's past or anticipated clients, the availability of many of the objects represented for sale, and their mode of address. More than one third of the etchings submitted these ancient objects to the virtuosic deformations of perspective, frequently

6. VIEW OF THE
FOUNDATION OF THE
THEATER OF MARCELLUS
Etching, engraving

7. Vincenzo Mazzi
CAPRICI DI SCENE...
Etching, engraving

CAPRICI DI SCENE TEA

INVEN; DISSEG:, & INTAGL

DA

VINCENZO MAZZI

BOLOGNESE

1776

215

necessitating the inclusion of a separate, more strictly legible elevation (fig. 8). Andrew Robison's research has cast new light on these prints, demonstrating that Piranesi returned to and reworked the plates of the *Prima parte* several times in the 1770s, and that many of his large architectural sketches after Juvarra's set designs, once thought to be early works, were instead probably sketched in these late years.[27] An early sketch of a vase, posed in similar perspective but designed with more rococo flourishes, confirms that the *Vasi* marked Piranesi's explicit return to an earlier fascination.[28] Despite the spatial isolation of many of these objects, it is perhaps not so farfetched to see in these unusual prints of objects the final manifestation of Piranesi's theatrical concerns.

It has rarely been noted just how radically these perspectives depart from the traditions of archaeology, as well as from the conventions for representing ornamental inventions. Though Piranesi's suite was no doubt inspired by a whole panoply of eighteenth-century prints of vases—from reprints of Bartoli's depictions of ancient Roman urns and Petitot's inventive creations to the recent publication of Hamilton's collection of Greek and Etruscan vases (itself notably indebted to Piranesi's archeological caprices)—he used entirely different means to portray them.[29] The works must be understood instead in the context of perspectival treatises, as authors from the sixteenth-century Serlio to the eighteenth-century Bibiena had done when they celebrated vases as exemplars of "more difficult" and "most irregular" shapes, to be attempted only by "the man of judgment" and "experience."[30] Unlike his predecessors, who relied on strict elevation to present their vessels close up, Piranesi used complex techniques analogous to those found in stage design to transform these objects into monuments worthy of veneration.

Whether showing a simple ancient marble vase raised on a balustrade, an ornate candelabrum, or a humble clay lamp, Piranesi applied the laws of perspective and illumination in the *Vasi* to situate objects in relation to individual viewers. Like prints of a theater stage or views of urban settings, these etchings explicitly appeal to the viewer's location in space. Presented on folio sheets far exceeding the usual size for such prints, the images sometimes reach two full feet in height and practically demand the use of perspective to accommodate the viewer's physical presence. Piranesi raised up marble vases so that we examine them from below; and applied two diverging perspectival points, one above and one below, to situate viewers midpoint to appreciate elongated forms like the Newdigate candelabrum, one of the most remarkable objects in his museo, and turned it in space, like a computer manipulation, to present additional information (see Wilton-Ely, fig. 57).

Vaso antico di marmo di gran mole, che si rende particolare per
l'eleganza de suoi manichi, quali formano tutto il principale ornamento
di esso, e si vede nel cortile del Monistero di S. Cecilia in Trastevere.

Cavalier Piranesi del. e inc.

9. Pietro Santi Bartoli
OIL LAMP IN THE FORM
OF A CROUCHING FIGURE
Etching, engraving

Piranesi's virtuoso staging of objects went beyond the abstracted images of popular compendia of antiquities like Montfaucon's *Antiquité expliquée* (1719–24) to inspire deeper meditation, developing trompe l'oeil effects first introduced by Bartoli in his publication of ancient lamps in order to situate antique remains powerfully in space (figs. 9, 10). Yet Piranesi's settings were deliberately indecipherable. Though ancient lamps were lined up on ledges, their chains suspended from iron nails driven into the wall as if in a catacomb or a grotto, the mural surface itself appears decorated with lush vegetation, perhaps painted like a pastoral or arcadian wall from a Roman villa. In the creation of such enigmatic scenarios at the end of his life, in an inversion of his first prints, Piranesi deployed his capricious invention and perspectival knowledge to create private, intimate dramas.

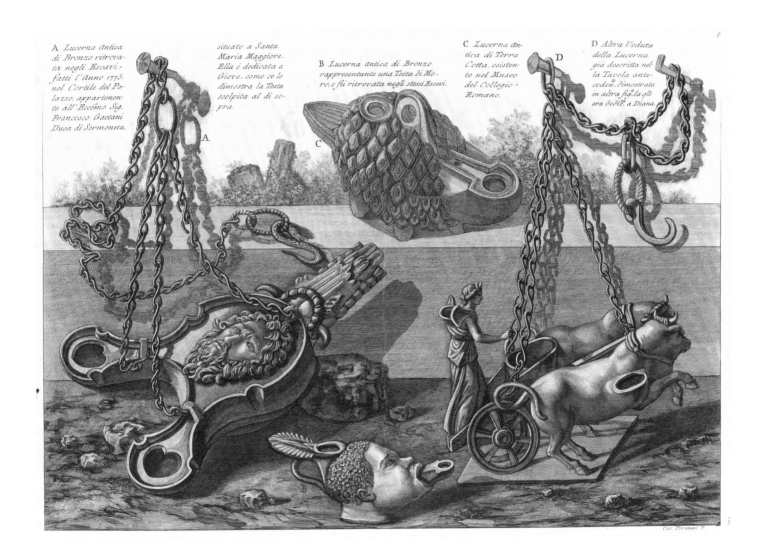

A *Lucerna Antica di Bronzo ritrova-ta negli Escavi-fatti l'Anno 1773. nel Cortile del Pa-lazzo, appartenen-te all'Eccmo Sig. Francesco Gaetani Duca di Sermoneta.*

situato a Santa Maria Maggiore. Ella è dedicata a Giove, come ce lo dimostra la Testa scolpita al di so-pra.

B *Lucerna antica di Bronzo rappresentante una Testa di Mo-ro, e fù ritrovata negli stessi Escavi.*

C *Lucerna an-tica di Terra Cotta. esisten-te nel Museo del Collegio Romano.*

D *Altra l'eduta della Lucerna già descritta nel-la Tavola ante-cedeñ. dimostrata in altra fig. la qle era dedic. a Diana.*

10. VARIOUS LAMPS OF BRONZE
AND TERRA-COTTA
Etching, engraving

In the final analysis, the connections between Piranesi and the the-ater of his age may appear more a matter of technique than of sub-stance. Sets of ancient Rome, prisons, and ruins were popular long before he began making prints. Instead, it was his powerful formulation of traditional subject matter, through the use of perspective and sharp lighting as first popularized on the stage, that allowed him to make even the smallest objects, as one contemporary observed, "grandioso."[31] Walpole's comment that Piranesi "imagined scenes that would startle geometry" beautifully conveys the emotional effects provoked by such mathematical means, in an age when the forces of rationalism were cel-ebrated alongside more mysterious ones.[32]

ALVAR GONZÁLEZ-PALACIOS

PIRANESI AND FURNISHINGS

1. Laurent Pécheux
THE MARCHESA MARGHERITA
GENTILI BOCCAPADULI, 1777
Oil on canvas

WITH THE EXCEPTION OF PIRANESI'S *DIVERSE MANIERE D'ADORNARE I CAMMINI* (1769), ONLY ONE RELIABLE SOURCE MENTIONS, ALBEIT BRIEFLY, THE WORK OF PIRANESI AS A FURNITURE DESIGNER AND DECORATOR: THE *NOTICE HISTORIQUE SUR LA VIE ET LES OUVRAGES DE G. B. PIRANÈSE* (1799), written twenty years after the designer's death by J. G. Legrand, an architect and contemporary of the artist.[1] However, a careful examination of a painting of the period reveals much about Piranesi's interior and design work. *The Marchesa Margherita Gentili Boccapaduli* (fig. 1) by Laurent Pécheux (1729–1821), a French artist who worked in Piranesi's circle, is a portrait of a lady who was a notable personality of the period and whom Piranesi knew well. Executed in oil on panel, signed, and dated in Rome in 1777, the work was included in a list drawn up by the artist of his paintings completed in Rome.[2] The Marchesa Boccapaduli (1735–1820) lived in the family palace in Via in Arcione, near the Quirinal, which contained numerous important artworks, notably *The Sacraments* by Nicolas Poussin. The Marchesa, a cultivated lady with a passion for the sciences, is portrayed in her natural-history cabinet, decorated in a distinctively neoclassical style.

In the painting, one immediately notices the table supported by Egyptian telamons, two of which, in the foreground, are shown frontally while the one in the rear is seen obliquely. These figures, modeled after the famous statues from Tivoli, now at the entrance of the

Museo Pio Clementino,[3] bear a frieze with hieroglyphics surrounding a tabletop inlaid with specimens of colored marble. The Marchesa unveils with her right hand a small framed collection of butterflies, which rests on a stand whose shaft corresponds exactly to the shape of an antique candelabrum formerly in the Gualtieri Collection.[4] Nearby on the floor there appears to be something resembling a stool, which in fact turns out to be a small table, as indicated by the wooden support. (Since small tables like these did not exist in Rome at the time, it must be assumed that it was privately commissioned.) The table rests on monopod griffins that are clearly derived from antique prototypes, possibly from an altar decoration or a *trapezoforo* (marble table). Piranesi used monsters of this kind in the *Diverse maniere* and in his *Vasi e candelabri*.[5] On the right side of the painting, in the background, there is a glimpse of a small, circular piece of furniture with open shelves used to display natural wonders, antique classical vases, and even a stuffed bird. This étagère, painted blue, is supported by a carved gilt tripod composed of goat-like legs with ram's heads linked by a wreath. Such figures, particularly popular with Piranesi, refer to antiquity and were frequently used in Roman furniture in the late eighteenth century. To the left of the Marchesa is a basin containing goldfish, also fashioned after the antique with short, goat-like legs and lion's heads with rings for ease of carrying. (Many containers of this kind, in silver, were used, particularly in England, to chill wine bottles.[6]) The scientific interests of the Marchesa are made evident by the *macchina a disco* (electricity-generating machine) that rests on the small low table, as well as by the pump with a glass bell on the shelf at the rear of the painting.

LEGRAND: THE REZZONICO

At that time, the revival of antiquity was all the rage, and the taste for the so-called "picturesque" resulted in curious productions such as the room with *faux* ruins painted by Clérisseau at the Trinità dei Monti (still in existence),[7] as well as various decorations commissioned by the Ambassador of Malta, the Bali de Breteuil, for his apartments. According to Legrand, the painters Etienne Lavallée-Poussin and Hubert Robert and the architect Giuseppe Barberi—who took advantage of Piranesi's advice in this project—were all involved in the works carried out for Breteuil. Subsequently, Legrand stated, "The Marchesa Boccapaduli followed that example and had her town and country residences similarly decorated in that manner, which mingled attractive objects among those beautiful ones in a severe and virile style which was so plentiful in Rome."

A severe and virile style: one could hardly improve on this description of Piranesi's manner. We are still just only a few years after the *Diverse maniere* was published: Pécheux's painting, again, is from 1777; Piranesi had only one more year to live. Legrand comments on how Piranesi may have intended to engrave "these different decorations," but was held back due to his work on producing the *Vasi e Candelabri*—it was, in fact, left unfinished—and his great work on the Trajan and Antonine columns (1775, 1776).

Besides the portrait of the Marchesa, which may depict, as we have seen, three pieces of furniture designed by Piranesi at the end of his life (though none has so far been identified as such), we only have two other works in wood produced by his genius: the tables now in the Rijksmuseum in Amsterdam and in the Minneapolis Institute of Arts. These well-known masterpieces of European Neoclassicism, distinguished by their quality and provenance, were created for the Quirinal apartment of Giovanni Battista Rezzonico, one of the nephews of the pope, to whom Piranesi dedicated the *Diverse maniere* (and in which this furniture is illustrated). Contrary to what is commonly stated, Rezzonico at the time was still not a cardinal—a title that he only acquired in September 1770 after the death of his uncle, the pontiff.[8] Rezzonico, however, had been grand prior of the Order of Malta since 1761 and maggiordomo to the pope since July 1766; the latter position provided him with the apartment in the Quirinal Palace. Following the death of Clement XIII in 1769, Rezzonico went to live with his brother, the senator of Rome, Don Abbondio Rezzonico, in his sumptuous apartment at the Capitol. According to the posthumous inventory of the Cardinal Rezzonico (who died in July 1783 in the Senatorial Palace), the "two tables of seven by three and a half, carved with tops veneered in Montauto alabaster with gilt metal frames, with claw feet all carved with festoons and other gilt ornaments" designed by Piranesi were in his room.[9]

Legrand asserted that Piranesi, at the beginning of his career, still in in Venice before 1740, was involved in the decoration of palace interiors for various senators and Venetian nobility, but "l'ennui le gagnait" ("boredom got the upper hand")—he could not think of anything but Rome. Legrand continued: "Through the Pope's favor he was commissioned to decorate various magnificent apartments in the pontifical palaces, both in the city and the country, and was encouraged to live as a member of the Rezzonico household," presumably after the election of Clemente XIII in 1758. Between 1764 and 1766, Piranesi, at the request of Monsignor Giovanni Battista, completed his only architectural work, the piazza and embellishment of Santa Maria del Priorato. The captions that accompany the plates in the *Diverse maniere* show that some particularly fanciful decorative objects were created for the senator of Rome. They were possibly in the apartment of Don Abbondio, but, when the senator's position came to an abrupt end at the arrival of the French in 1798, everything was dispersed and transferred to various locations.[10]

PALAZZO SENATORIO

Some documents discovered by the late Bruno Contardi throw fresh light on Piranesi's work during the redecoration of the apartment on the Capitol for Senator Rezzonico.[11] These documents, which date back to 1769, just after the marriage of Don Abbondio and Ippolita Boncompagni Ludovisi, who lived at the Palazzo Senatorio, refer to the Piombino, or Boncompagni Ludovisi, coat of arms, coupled with that of the Rezzonico, on the apartment ceiling.[12] The documents in question, from April 15 and July 5, are accounts of "works done by the painter Rocco Feltrini" for the enlargement of the Senatorial Palace toward the Campo Vaccino. They refer to decorative paintings for ceilings, friezes, and skirting boards in several rooms, which presumably were not among the most important in the apartment. (Other works were carried out in 1767, but the relevant evidence has not yet been found.) What is particularly interesting here is the fact that the accounts of Feltrini record that he had been "in the house of Signor Piranesi" for the purpose of creating the designs for decorations subsequently transferred to canvas stretched over the ceiling. The document refers to the "third large room that follows where the fireplace is." The same occurs in the fifth room, where Feltrini prepared the design for the ceiling according to the drawing "provided by Piranesi." The painter, at least according to these documents, was not apparently responsible for the walls of these rooms. We are not able to say, therefore, if the delicate decorations that we see on the background of some engravings in the *Diverse maniere* were meant to be painted on walls, as was apparently done in the famous Caffè degli Inglesi.

In another document published by Contardi, from November 28, 1767, payment was made for a "chimneypiece in the French style in *bigio antico* marble," executed by two well-known master stonecutters (*scalpellini*), the brothers Filippo and Nicola Cartoni, and installed in a room of the Senatorial apartment. It appears, however, that this does not refer to the mantelpiece designed by Piranesi, since the name of the artist is missing. The only name mentioned is that of the architect responsible for the work at the Campidoglio, Carlo Puri de Marchis. Nonetheless, it is reasonable to infer that the chimneypiece illustrated in the *Diverse maniere* would have been produced around that time.[13] It is almost cer-

2. Francesco Giardoni
BRONZE SIDE-TABLE WITH
AN ANCIENT MOSAIC TOP, 1742

tain that Piranesi's chimneypieces were created in his studio under his direct supervision, as suggested indirectly by Legrand. In fact, the biographer recounted how the artist had acquired a considerable number of fragments from Villa Adriana, which he had restored and partly completed by skillful craftsmen to whom he gave designs of what he wanted done. These were, according to Legrand, "Cardelli, Pronzoni, and Jacquietti": the first was likely Lorenzo Cardelli, to whom we will turn shortly; the second is Francesco Antonio Franzoni; and the third is, perhaps, Antonio Guglielmo Grandjacquet.[14]

As some of Piranesi's chimneypieces have been identified, either through contemporary documents and invoices or a simple comparison with the engravings in the *Diverse maniere*, their influence throughout Europe has become undeniable. Among the first to be influenced by Piranesi's designs and ideas was, as has often been pointed out, Robert Adam. During the 1780s, Antonio Asprucci also followed in the footsteps of Piranesi, both in the palace as well as the villa of Prince Borghese, as happened with other architects in several Roman residences, such as the Palazzo Caetani. Some of the craftsmen employed by Piranesi continued the work on their own, including Lorenzo Cardelli, who also served under the Borghese and other foreign nobles.[15]

TRANSCRIPTIONS, COPIES, SUGGESTIONS

Piranesi's obsession with archaeology had its origins in Roman scholarship and academic studies, and he could count on a vast iconographic repertoire. Topographers, numismatists, artists, and craftsmen of every kind had contributed, in various degrees and ways, in conveying the magnificence of Rome. For instance, Francesco Giardoni executed two bronze tables in 1742, when Piranesi had just arrived in Rome. Benedict XIV had them made as supports for two fragments of floor mosaics from the Villa Adriana discovered by Cardinal Furietti (fig. 2). We do not know the name of the designer of these tables, which include both archaeological elements, such as the winged monopod lions inspired by antique Roman *trapezofori*, and baroque ones such as female masks and garlands. Nothing made at that time was closer to Piranesi's taste for the monumental. As the pope donated these solemn objects to the Capitoline Museum in the same year, Piranesi would undeniably have seen them.[16]

Perhaps the first "Piranesian" was his friend and colleague Robert Adam. While scholars continue to debate the degree of reciprocal influence between the two, they cannot fail to recognize that the genius of Piranesi always triumphed in the end. Adam possessed a delicate touch and unmistakable style, more logical and distinctly less grandiose than his friend's. As he himself wrote to his brother James in 1755, Adam, despite the admiration that he felt for his friend, found the company of Piranesi extremely disturbing and his manner of expression "furious and fantastick."[17] We could not express it better ourselves and, if we look at Adam's interiors of Osterley Park, to give but one example, it is evident that his highly refined, carefully measured, perfectly symmetrical world had very little to do with the "furious" or the "fantastic" as happened with every stroke of the Venetian's pen.

If Adam guessed, or even understood, the nature of Piranesi's ideas, he transformed rather than translated his inventions. There was, however, a considerable amount of work brought to completion in Central Europe that cannot be considered anything else but repetitions, reductions, or transcriptions of the violent forms in Piranesi's inventions and his ideas on decorative design. Two marble candelabra (now in Oxford), sold by Piranesi from his *museo*—which is what he called his studio—to Sir Roger Newdigate, were reproduced on a small scale in metal and marble by the Roman bronzesmith Giuseppe Boschi. The Newdigate candelabra, illustrated by Piranesi himself in *Vasi e Candelabri*, were widely acclaimed.[18] One of them was depicted in Jacques-Louis David's 1783 painting *The Sorrow of Andromache*, and directly copied in an 1816 drawing by Jean-Auguste-Dominique Ingres for the tomb of Lady Jane Montague.[19] (figs. 3, 4)

Piranesi's *Vasi e candelabri* was an authoritative and useful source of designs for English silversmiths. Paul Storr, Rebecca Emes, Edward Barnard, and Benjamin Smith, to name but a few, meticulously copied, with little adaptation, the engravings from these famous volumes.[20] The finest pieces in silver of this type are to be found in the English Royal Collection, which includes an outstanding reduction done by Storr of the famous Warwick Vase (which also originated from the *Museo Piranesi*). The original marble fragments of this celebrated vase were found in the Pantanello area of the Villa Adriana in 1770 and "restored," as only he knew how, by Piranesi and his assistants. It was copied countless times, in varying quality and in many different materials, even by the elusive B. Boschetti, in *rosso antico* marble, dating from the papacy of Pope Pius IX (now at the Toledo Museum in Ohio).[21]

Designs from the *Vasi e candelabri* were also translated into porcelain. One of the most spectacular engravings in this work, a monument in the form of a curious rhyton, or drinking cup, with a boar's head, an object that belonged to Piranesi himself, was subsequently sold to Gustav III of Sweden, and is now in the Stockholm Royal Palace.[22] An 1805 watercolor by Théodore Brongniart derived from this engraving, with the addition of a floral wreath which functions as a support for the object, was rendered in porcelain at Sèvres and was part of the Service Olympique given to Czar Alexander I in 1807, and now displayed in Moscow.[23] Two other engravings were inspired by another marble from Piranesi's *museo*. It represents an ancient ship with three banks of oars, now at Brocklesby Park, Lincolnshire. Likely dating back to the Restoration period, this truly bizarre object was copied precisely in porcelain in Paris, bearing no marks and painted in brilliant colors.[24] (fig. 5)

ELLE ETOIT DE CE MONDE OU LES PLUS BELLES CHOSES
ONT LE PIRE DESTIN,
ET ROSE ELLE A VÉCU CE QUE VIVENT LES ROSES
L'ESPACE D'UN MATIN.

3. Jacques-Louis David
LA DOULEUR
D'ANDROMAQUE, 1783
Oil on canvas

4. Jean-Auguste-Dominique
Ingres
DESIGN FOR THE TOMB OF
LADY JANE MONTAGUE, 1816
Sepia and ochre

Charles Heathcote Tatham, an architect and connoisseur who acted as an agent in Rome for Henry Holland, architect of the Prince of Wales, was another enthusiast of Piranesi's work, but viewed his achievements from the standpoint of a less original designer. In his *Etchings*, produced in Rome between 1794 and 1796, Tatham wrote of Piranesi, "Fired with a genius which had defiance to control, and rejected with disdain the restraint of minute observation, he has sometimes sacrificed accuracy to what he conceived the richer productions of a more fertile and exuberant mind." Tatham's admiration probably inspired him to copy, more or less mechanically and in outline, one of the marble Barberini candelabra, now at the Vatican and previously engraved by Piranesi. He also had his own engraving rendered in mahogany, with results that recall the décor of English clubs in their slavish accuracy.[25]

To Regency connoisseur Thomas Hope, who did not mention Piranesi in the introduction to his book on decoration in 1807, every ornament had a tinge of the pedantic, more an architectural study than a work of art. The distance that separated Piranesi from interior designers of that time and beyond is the same distance from Italian sculptor Antonio

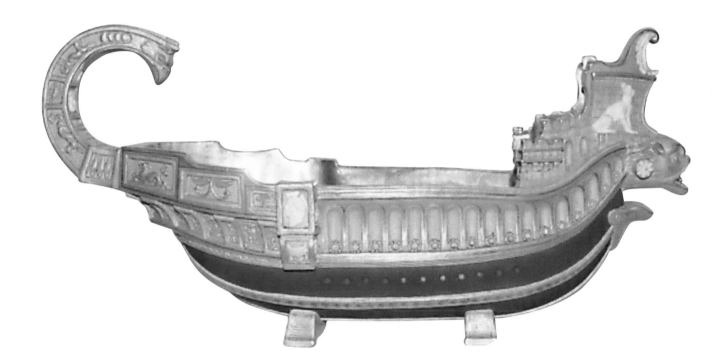

Canova to Charles Percier and Fontaine: the soul is lacking; instead, the soul is so dressed up with abstract concepts that it becomes a philosophical arabesque. For example, a design by Percier, who lived and worked in Rome between 1786 and 1791, shows a picturesque garden, with cypresses and umbrella pines in a shady wood, strewn with various remains of antiquity. In the foreground is a *tazza baccellata*, richly carved with figures, which is a direct quotation from the *Vasi e candelabri*; in fact, it is a conflation of two tripods that belonged to Cardinal Albani, both depicted in the same plate by Piranesi.[26] (fig. 6) The difference between Piranesi's engraving and the design by Percier resides in the solemn portrayal of an ancient marble as opposed to the elegance of a garden ornament.

Piranesi's influence on other artists of his time was less immediate. Ennemond-Alexandre Petitot, a Frenchman who knew Piranesi well during his long stay in Rome before serving under the Duke of Parma, kept him in mind in the geometric fabrications of his *Mascarade à la Grècque* or in his *Suite des Vases* (Parma, 1764). They corresponded though to his own invention, often excessively ornate, with a touch of self-consciousness that fails to match the inexhaustible virility of the master but are always charming in their boundless imagination. One of the first images by Petitot, an amphora with long handles that extend to the base, recalls in a more domestic key the dramatic image of the *cantharos*, or two-handled vase, in the courtyard of Santa Cecilia in Trastevere, illustrated in the *Vasi e candelabri*.[27] The architect François-Joseph Bélanger, who never met Piranesi, nonetheless echoed his taste, but he did so in the manner of Robert Adam, with a levity that was fundamen-

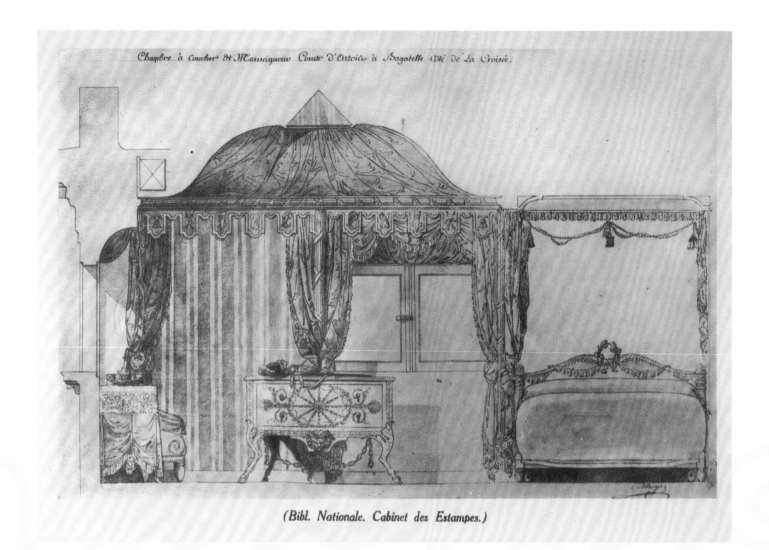

Chambre à coucher de Monseigneur Conte d'Artois à Bagatelle Cité de la Croisée.

(Bibl. Nationale. Cabinet des Estampes.)

7. François-Joseph Belanger
PROJECT FOR THE COMTE
D'ARTOIS'S BEDROOM AT THE
BAGATELLE, 1777

tally antithetical to the character of ancient Rome. In Bélanger's spare designs for the bedroom of the Count d'Artois (the future Charles X) at Bagatelle, there is a hint of Piranesi in the chest of drawers resting on tall animal legs (fig. 7). It has been suggested that one can also see here the hand of another famous designer of the time, Bélanger's brother-in-law, Jean-Démosthène Dugourc. It is possible, but were one to go down this path, one could become trapped in the gilded web at the close of the ancien régime.[28]

ROME

After the publication of the *Diverse maniere*, Piranesi's influence tended to be confused with that of many ornamental expressions of Neoclassicism already in place throughout Europe at the time. It is not always easy to isolate his own specific language from those of his apprentices and disciples. One artist as famous as Piranesi in Rome, the painter Pompeo Batoni, included in certain portraits from the end of his career some bizarre furnishings in an antiquarian style for which he had previously shown little interest. For instance, in his 1772 portrait of Thomas Escourt, the gentleman leans on a piece of furniture, halfway between a fireplace and a writing desk; in his 1775 portrait of the Elector Karl Theodore, one sees a table supported by harpies. Neither piece of furniture—if they can be called that—is taken from Piranesi's ideas or from antiquity.[29]

Even if Batoni reflected, in his own way, the atmosphere created by Piranesi, Italian, and particularly Roman decorative arts depended directly on Piranesi's imagination. Not every detail of every ornament can be attributed to his productions, but it is always possible to say whether a work dates from before or after his inventions. Piranesi was fully associated with the rebirth of the ancient world, but his unique type of Neoclassicism was deeply personal, at once enamored yet freely interpretative of antiquity. This is what is meant by the phrase coined by Henri Focillon—the "Piranesi Style."

Luigi Valadier, without question the best Roman goldsmith of the eighteenth century, created works after his own designs. Conditioned by the French Rococo (he perfected his craft in Paris), Valadier adapted himself to the peculiar style of Piranesian classicism and, in fact, found his own formula in the symbiotic relation between typical eighteenth-century forms and other examples taken from the archaeological repertoire. Some of his *surtouts de table* (table centerpieces) could be defined as Piranesian, even though there were no specific models to follow. However, one should bear in mind the recently identified minature bath that formed part of the Braschi *surtout*, completed in 1783 for the Duke of Braschi, nephew of Pius VI. This object in gilt bronze and white marble adorned with heads of crouching bulls derives from designs in the *Vasi e candelabra*.[30] (fig. 8)

The bull is hardly rare in the ornamental vocabulary of antiquity. During the late eighteenth century, a bull was the heraldic animal of the King of Poland, Stanislas Augustus Poniatowski. Two Roman tables, with mosaic tops donated by the papal nuncio, were sent to Warsaw; while a third one, circular in shape and topped with a mosaic of a bull, was ordered by the king through his agent in Rome.[31] I have known for many years a magnificent Roman chest of drawers of considerable size, beautifully inlaid with rare woods, topped with a slab of *verde antico* marble, and with gilt bronze mounts in the form of bull's heads (fig. 9). Upon identifying this piece of furniture, I suggested that it could, in some way, be linked to Giovanni Battista Piranesi and the king that ruled Poland from 1764 to 1795.[32] I have not seen that important piece again recently, but, in examining the photographs once more, it came to mind that these bronzes could have been executed by Luigi Valadier. On the

other hand, Valadier prepared some metal ornaments during the 1780s for furniture pieces destined for Prince Borghese.[33]

I am unsure to whom should be attributed a support that I saw a few years ago on the market (fig. 10). This unusual work was obviously intended for a sacred context, indicated by the symbols of the Four Evangelists and the Sacred Tablets shown at the center. The decoration is unquestionably Piranesian, and the most likely date would be the last quarter of the eighteenth century in Rome.

Three important pieces of furniture conceived under the aegis of Piranesi were executed in Rome around this time. The first one was a papal commission, a pedestal (from a group of six) intended to support a vase of Oriental porcelain (fig. 11). It bears the coat of arms of Clement XIV and was made for the pontiff's residence in the Quirinal. It is the work of Giovanni Grespi, a wood carver who had a workshop in the Piazza di Spagna; the surviving artisan's accounts mention it in the entry for May 8, 1774. Grespi had made a wax model for his work, following the instructions of the papal architects Giovanni Stern and Pietro Camporese. The pedestal is supported by three birds: the original account specified that they were to be crows, "an allusion to peace," a curious idea that does not correspond to the *Iconologia* of Cesare Ripa, in

which crows were associated only with vengeance and hesitation, being more commonly known as the bearers of misfortune.[34]

The second piece of furniture was a side table (fig. 12), one of a pair, carried out by a wood carver, Antonio Landucci, whose work is gradually being rediscovered. He died in Rome in 1783. The tables, documented on May 17, 1773, were intended for the Palazzo Borghese, where they remained until the dispersal of the collection in 1892. Their design, obviously derived from the *Diverse maniere*, was produced by the architect Antonio Asprucci, in the service of Prince Marcantonio Borghese, the principal patron at the time responsible for one of the most beautiful interiors in Europe, the Villa Borghese.

Finally, the third piece of furniture, documented just slightly later, was a table (fig. 13) by a wood carver practically forgotten today, Nicola Freddi, who had a workshop at San Romualdo in Rome. Freddi sent a bill for the table to the Duke of Caserta, the head of the Caetani family, on March 26, 1776.[35] This table can now be found at the Palazzo Caetani, and may be considered a simplified version of a masterpiece (still anonymous) in the Palazzo Senatorio.

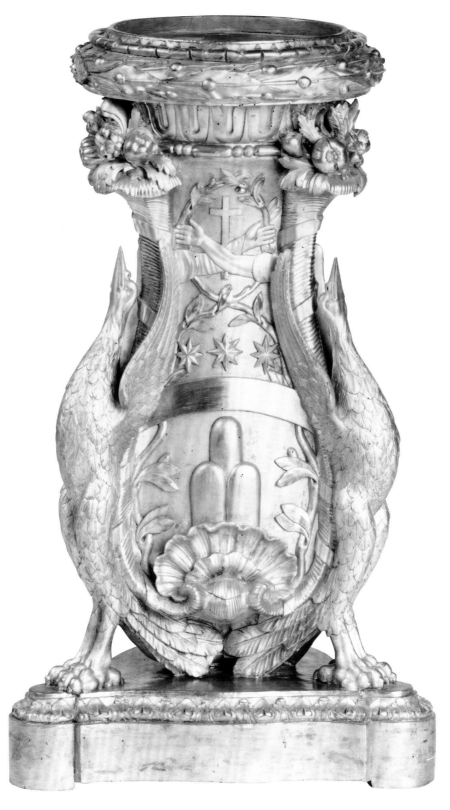

10. PEDESTAL WITH SYMBOLS
OF THE EVANGELISTS, 1770–85
Silver, gilt-bronze, brass

11. Giovanni Grespi
PEDESTAL WITH THE COAT OF
ARMS OF CLEMENT XIV, 1774
Gilt wood

12. Antonio Landucci
SIDE TABLE FROM THE
PALAZZO BORGHESE, 1773
Gilt wood

13. Nicola Freddi
SIDE TABLE, 1776
Gilt wood
Palazzo Caetani

RONALD DE LEEUW

DEALER AND CICERONE
PIRANESI AND THE GRAND TOUR

**TRAVELERS TO ROME IN THE SECOND HALF OF THE EIGH-
TEENTH CENTURY COULD NOT AVOID ENCOUNTERING THE
FIGURE OF PIRANESI. EVEN BEFORE THEY STEPPED INTO
THEIR CARRIAGES TO EMBARK ON THE LONG AND OFTEN
HAZARDOUS JOURNEY ACROSS THE ALPS, MOST OF THEM**
studied Piranesi's famous *Vedute* to prepare themselves for the city's
architecture—to many, the apotheosis of their "Grand Tour." The Grand
Tourist, a young man of good family, usually undertook this educa-
tional trip, which would last anywhere from nine months to two years,
after completing his university studies and before getting married.
Amidst this flood of English *milordi* and German *kavaliere* were also
Dutch travelers, members of the highest ranks of the then Republic of
the Seven United Provinces.

Of his second trip to Italy in 1792, the Dutch collector Johan
Meerman (1753–1815) wrote: "The manner of the Knight Piranesi, of
recording for posterity with robust strokes and uncommon power the
magnificent memorials of Rome or the neighbouring places, albeit
sometimes embellished a little, is known throughout all Europe from
the numerous Volumes in which his plates have been collected. His
heirs continue somewhat in the same way to swell this multitude; and
one can come by his works, either all together or each one of them separately, for a reasonable price."[1] (fig. 1)

Piranesi's first set of Roman views were published in 1748. More than a quarter century later, in 1776, the Dutch traveler Gerrit Johannes, Baron de Hochepied, reported that the series had grown to an impressive total of 123 prints. No tourist left Rome without having spent the last few days of his stay there choosing prints in Piranesi's print shop on Strada Felice. The most exalted visitors were sometimes presented with Piranesi prints by the pope as a goodwill gift. Some, like the Dutch magistrate Hendrik Fagel the Elder, found that the prints themselves were enough, and enjoyed the splendor of Rome at home, as armchair travelers. When anyone made the journey to Italy, friends or acquaintances often asked them to bring back the latest Piranesi prints.

It comes as no surprise that the artist dubbed "the Rembrandt of the ruins" by architect Carlo Bianconi (1732–1802) appealed so strongly to the Dutch. The prints were often sold separately as soon as they were made; later, they were officially collected and published in book form. Some travelers pasted them into their travel journals; others drew copies of them. Most people would have known from the signature he appended to many of his books, "Piranesi the Elder. Famous architect and engraver of the excellent works *Vedute di Roma* (views of Rome)," that Piranesi was also an architect. But few were prepared for the astonishingly singular character of Piranesi's own architectural feat—the Church of the Order of Malta on the Aventine Hill, which he restored between 1764 and 1767. The extraordinary architectural fantasy style known as *capriccio* evoked admiration among his patrons, among them Pope Clement XIII Rezzonico and his nephews, but it also met with considerable disapprobation. Not everyone was able to appreciate Piranesi's quest for an individual, eclectic style. In 1787, the Dutch traveler Adriaan Gillis Camper (1759–1820) judged one of Piranesi's creations as being "in execrable taste."

Many travelers took advantage of their stay in Italy to acquire objects to adorn their townhouses or country mansions. As a rule, people bought things that were easily portable, such as antique or pseudo-antique cameos, coins, and medals. Miniature mosaics, most often used on *tabatières* (snuffboxes), were also very popular. But visitors also stocked up on heavier items, such as tabletops featuring sophisticated compositions of mosaics or marble inlays. As early as the seventeenth century, the Dutch traveler Coenraad Ruysch bought tops inlaid with "artificial marble" in Italy, and had them shipped home.[2]

The majority of the items purchased came into the category of decorative sculpture. The marble chimneypieces, columns, vases, and tables were usually made up of antique fragments, or what passed for them. Mantelpieces were particularly in vogue. In the eighteenth century they

2. Narcisse Garnier
PORTRAIT OF JOHAN FREDERIK
WILLEM, BARON VAN SPAEN
Oil on canvas

were the *pièces de résistance* in the formal rooms of many country mansions and townhouses. The lavishly carved mantelpieces found in virtually every sculptor's workshop were especially popular, even if not everything was precisely to the taste of the Northern Europeans. Hendrik Fagel the Younger, who explored Rome in 1786–87 with, like Goethe, Johann Friedrich von Reiffenstein as his *cicerone* (guide), condemned numerous fireplaces as "in bad taste." His Uncle Boreel, in contrast, was very much taken with everything he was offered in Rome. He could imagine his house, Elswout, furnished from top to bottom, although the high prices did give him pause. He wrote to his brother, "You cannot imagine how richly ornamented and in what quantities chimneypieces may be obtained here, but then one is talking about 20 or 30 *zecchini*, for one can get nothing decent for less." At the urging of his wife, who was traveling with him, he bought two marble tables to replace two older mahogany ones, lamenting he had "actually made more purchases that I had intended, since I wanted to furnish a room in Elswout with marble vases and other small ornaments like drawings, prints, etc."[3]

In Biljoen Castle, the country estate of Johan Frederik Willem, Baron van Spaen (1746–1827) (fig. 2) in the eastern Netherlands, one could likewise find among the loot from his 1769 tour to Italy "tables of lava, various types of fine foreign marble, and rare mosaics." More curious, and possibly unique, is the way the baron used his prints of buildings of Ancient Rome as the inspiration for the decoration of his house.[4] Van Spaen conducted his tour of Italy in the company of his friend Derk de Leeuw, calling at the very best addresses. He met with Cardinal Albani and spent time in Rome in the company of Baron de Breteuil, Cardinal de Bernis, and the Marchioness Bocapaduli, all celebrities on the Grand Tour circuit of the day. His principal cicerone was the well-known antiquarian Orazio Orlandi. Before leaving for Naples, where he called on Sir William Hamilton, he went to Piranesi's print shop to select and buy engravings, and had his servant at Biljoen send him a list of all the topographical prints he already owned so as to avoid duplication.

The impact of the *Vedute* was later reflected in the decorations of the Great Hall at Biljoen Castle, decorated in 1781–82, in which the most striking feature was the abundant decorative plasterwork done by Herman Bader, who copied eight Piranesi prints in stucco. Piranesi's famous prints of the Pantheon (fig. 3), the tomb of Caecilia Metella, the Temple of the Sybil in Tivoli, and the Pyramid of Gaius Cestius functioned as *supraportes* (panels above the doors), while a view of the Ponte Molle crowned two monumental semi-circular niches (figs. 4, 5). The photographs (fig. 6) show vases in these niches, but in van Spaen's time they probably held a bust of Julia (fig. 7) and a replica of the renowned Aphrodite Anadyomene. (The two classical sculptures, restored in the eighteenth century, are now in the National Museum of Antiquities in Leiden, the Netherlands.) Piranesi's prints of triumphal arches and obelisks were also used between the pilasters and the niches. The scenes were originally white against a green background, but the room has since been whitewashed. In Blickling Hall, in Norfolk, England, Caroline Connolly, Duchess of Buckingham, had Piranesi *vedute* pasted on the walls of her print room, but, to the best of my knowledge, Biljoen Castle's stucco *vedute* were unique.

Veduta del Ponte Molle sul Tevere due miglia lontan da Roma
A Ristauri del Pontefice Niccolo V. B Rovine del Ponte supplite con
due ponti levatoj C.Torre fabbricata ne'tempi bassi per custodia del Ponte

Si vendono posti due a motte appo l'Autore nel palazzo del Sig.r Co.Tomati a Strada Felice   Piranesi F.

5. VIEW OF THE
PONTE MOLLE, ROME
Etching

3. GREAT HALL OF
BILJOEN CASTLE, VELP,
THE NETHERLANDS,
PLASTERWORK DECORATION
OF THE PANTHEON,
ROME (AFTER PIRANESI)

4. GREAT HALL OF BILJOEN
CASTLE, PLASTERWORK
DECORATION OF THE PONTE
MOLLE, ROME

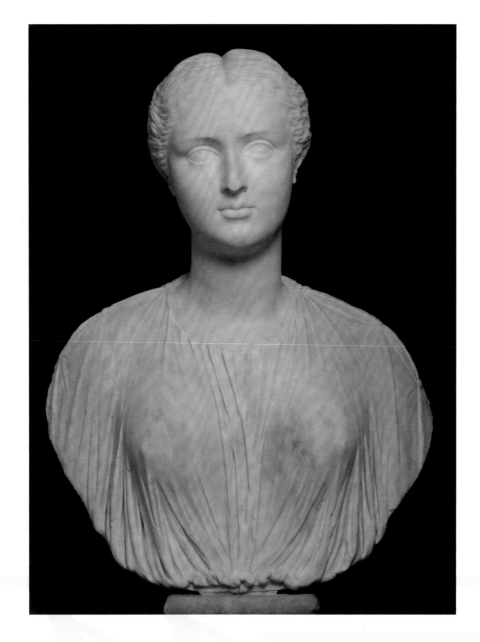

Countless travel journals testify to the fact that Piranesi was also known to the tourists as a dealer and restorer of antiques. While he was selecting his prints, van Spaen took the opportunity to investigate "Monsieur Piranesi's cabinet," but he considered the prices of the antiquities exorbitant. Johan Meerman, when he dropped by Piranesi's to pick up his catalogue of prints, saw "in his garden a very large antique vase, fine, heavily restored, which an Englishman has bought." While these gentlemen contented themselves with just looking, one of Piranesi's most important Dutch clients was John Hope (1737–1784), the father of Thomas Hope, and the last wholly Dutch forefather of the later entirely anglicized Hope family of bankers (fig. 8). Hope was a *grand seigneur* who owned a considerable collection of paintings, including masterpieces by Rembrandt van Rijn, Jan Vermeer, and Gabriel Metsu.[5]

9. After Giovanni
Battista Piranesi
CHIMNEYPIECE MADE FOR
JOHN HOPE, CA. 1769
White marble

In 1761, on his grand tour, he did a great deal of shopping—certainly the Pichlers and Sirletti supplied him with cameos in that year.

We know from Hope's inventory that he later owned no fewer than nine inlaid tabletops, including one of "antique green Egyptian marble, known to the Italians by the name of *verde antico*." Two of them were "excavated in my presence from beneath the ruins of the Villa Hadriani in Tivoli in the year 1761 & with purchase, excavation, making up into Tables & suchlike, cost me about f 500."[6] He was Piranesi's client for his famous chimneypiece, to which Piranesi devoted a magnificent print, but we do not know whether he also went to Piranesi for these two tables, or led the excavations himself. Piranesi may well have had a hand in refurbishing the tables. Among Hope's most remarkable acquisitions of 1761 were two large basins in Carrara marble intended for the gardens of Groenendaal, his country estate. His son, the brilliant designer Thomas Hope, later owned a large candelabrum by Piranesi (now at Lady

10. DESIGN FOR
A CHIMNEYPIECE
Engraving

Lever Gallery, Port Sunlight). Many years after his grand tour, John Hope was still making purchases in Italy on a grand scale. In 1778, for instance, the Scottish sculptor Colin Morison, who worked in Rome, made a monumental Venus Pudica for him. Morison moved in the same circles as Winckelmann, Mengs, and Piranesi, and may well have been the link between Hope and Piranesi.

Hope bought from Piranesi an "uncommonly fine antique mantelpiece of white Paros marble" for the sum of f. 400, including expenses. In 1769, with the publication of his *Diverse maniere d'adornare i Cammini*, Piranesi firmly established his supremacy as the virtuoso of the chimneypiece (figs. 9, 10). Although Piranesi optimistically noted under the print that his masterpiece could be seen in the cabinet of "Cavaliere Giovanni Hope" in Amsterdam, the mantelpiece was not there for long. For years it was left packed in crates at Groenendaal along with countless other treasures Hope had acquired on his Italian travels. It was not until after

11. Cornelis Ploos van Amstel
PORTRAIT OF
ARNOUT VOSMAER, 1792
Watercolor in a decorative
etched border

12. AERNOUT VOSMAER'S
VISITING CARDS, BOUGHT
FROM GIUSEPPE DELLA SANTA
DURING HIS TRIP IN 1776

his death in 1784 that the mantelpiece was installed in the house known as Welgelegen, near Haarlem. Welgelegen belonged to Henry Hope (1735–1811), John Hope's cousin, also a considerable collector, who had ordered a group of lead garden statues after famous classical sculptures from Francesco Righetti in Rome.

In 1776, Johan Meerman reported that the antiquities he had seen at Piranesi's that year had "mostly been found in the Villa Hadriani and all for sale." In 1771, James Grinston wrote about Piranesi, "This Man is exceedingly clever as an Antiquarian…; it is immense the sum of money he has got by the Statue, Vases, Tripodes &c that he has found by searching among the Ruins of the Villa Adriana."[7] At around the same time, Aernout Vosmaer (figs. 11, 12), Keeper of the Cabinet to Prince William V of Orange, was also in Italy. His diary tells us that, on January 15, 1776, he bought "a fine antique bas relief from Piranesy" depicting Perseus and Andromeda. This, too, as Vosmaer tells us, was found at the Villa Hadriana while he was staying in Rome, and subsequently sold to him by Piranesi.[8]

These were clearly enterprising times, and Piranesi was not the only one to emerge as a cultural entrepreneur. Numerous artists and cognoscenti were referred to in the literature of the day as Piranesi's partners. Englishmen Thomas Jenkins and James Byres were important agents who brought in customers, and many others earned a pretty penny as go-betweens between tourists and suppliers of antiquities, genuine or alleged. Jenkins himself also dealt in cameos, running his own little factory in a corner of the Colosseum, where "he sold 'em as fast as they made 'em."[9] It was Byres who sold the famous Portland Vase to Sir William Hamilton in 1783 (now at the British Museum). As a young man, English sculptor Joseph Nollekens, to whom we owe a magnificent bust of Piranesi (in the Gallery of the Accademia di San Luca in Rome), kept the wolf from the door by dealing in antiquities: "[Gavin] Hamilton, and I, and Jenkins, generally used to go shares in what we bought; and as I had to match the pieces as well as I could, and clean 'em, I had the best part of the profits."[10] This may well have been Piranesi's motive for taking on the work on the sculptures himself.

Among the restorers with whom Piranesi collaborated were the brilliant sculptor and restorer Bartolomeo Cavaceppi (fig. 13) and his pupil Carlo Albacini (1735–1813). The German Baron de Krudemer had particular praise for Albacini's "skill at adding to the antique statues, and at whose premises we found a quantity of (marble) chimneypieces, bas reliefs, small reproductions, etc., ready for sale."[11]

Although Vosmaer bought a sculpture from Piranesi, there is no doubt that this was not the artist's specialty. Strict papal export laws meant that important sculptures were essentially unobtainable. From Gavin Hamilton's *Account of Ancient Marbles found…*, it is clear that Piranesi was able to get his hands on very few important pieces of classical statuary ("A great number of Fragments of Vases, Animals of different sorts, and some elegant ornaments and one Colossal head"). He concentrated primarily on the sale—and manufacture—of decorative items; in the process, classical fragments were made important in the hands of his assistants.[12] On closer examination, the candelabra sold to Sir Roger Newdigate in 1775 (now in the Ashmolean Museum in Oxford), proved to be ingenious pastiches, cheerfully quoting elements from Piranesi's own *Diverse maniere*. Thanks to the outstanding quality produced by his sculptors Francesco Antonio Franzoni and Lorenzo Cardelli, Piranesi had no trouble keeping his contemporaries happy. They were highly skilled in patinating the new marble to hide the fact that it was not antique material. Piranesi's masterpiece in this regard was the Warwick Vase, found in Pantanello in 1770, which was restored and filled in by his partner in crime, the sculptor Grandjacquet, and lavishly praised by Piranesi himself in his prints (fig. 14). The vase is utterly convincing as a composition in one piece, but numerous elements actually sprung entirely from Piranesi's fertile imagination. John Wilton-Ely described these objects constructed of antique fragments as "elaborate fabrications," but Piranesi's detractors less kindly called them "*pasticcios*."[13] The painter James Barry (1741–1806) strongly disapproved of the restoration practices of the day. He saw capitals carved "in so fantastic a manner,

with so little of the true forms remaining, that they serve indifferently for all kinds of things, and are with ease converted into candelabra, chimney pieces, and what not. Examples of this kind of trash may be seen in abundance in the collections of Piranesi."[14]

Not only Piranesi's "classical" decorative objects were viewed with distaste by some people. Piranesi was also known as a tough negotiator. In 1780, Frenchman Roland de la Platière complained about Piranesi's aggressive sales tactics, claiming that "with him it's a continual marketplace where one is embarrassed to see his talent constantly being doubly debased by a greed which is both grasping and mean."[15] From a modern perspective, Piranesi's dealings can be described as unscrupulous, and he was remarkably sophisticated in the way he gave his creations authority and credibility by including them in his publications, such as *Vasi, candelabri, cippi*. It meant that his own creations were effectively vouched for by similar pieces that really were entirely original. This is why Jonathan Scott called *Vasi, candelabri, cippi*. "a sales catalogue." In the captions to the prints, Piranesi took great pains to come across as seriously as possible. The nature of the restorations was described at length, as was the spot where the objects had been discovered and the collections, public or private, which held them.

In the second volume of *Vasi, candelabri, cippi*, Piranesi illustrated one of two marble altars. Their original elements dated from around AD 140–60, but Piranesi's workshop was let loose on them. At the time of Piranesi's death in 1778, they were still in his estate, possibly because he had set the price too high. In 1782, they found their way to the Museo Pio Clementino (figs. 15, 16). As well as vases, Piranesi also published designs for commodes, console tables, mirrors, sconces, clocks, and sedan chairs. Lord Carlisle even went to Piranesi in June 1768 for a design for a coach with antique ornaments.[16]

As we have seen, Piranesi was not without competitors. Inventive in everything he did, he employed his marketing skills on several different fronts. Piranesi's manifold activities—printmaker and publisher, architect, designer of decorative arts, and dealer—and his catering to rich foreigners on the Grand Tour made it almost inevitable that he would also regularly act as a cicerone for the travelling milordi. Piranesi's biographer, J.-G. Legrand, wrote that "his flights of imagination made him a very entertaining companion." He was by nature an irrepressible talker, bubbling over with information and speculative theories, and he was often viewed as tiresome, volatile, and disorganized in the Roman academic circles. The architect Luigi Vanvitelli called him "*Perfettissimo matto in tutto*"—the most perfect madman in everything—and he drove

15. TRIPOD, CA. AD 140–60
Marble

16. ONE OF TWO
IDENTICAL ALTARS
Engraving

Si rappresenta in questa Tavola una delle due grandiose Are del tutto simili in
ogni lor parte, ed anche uguali nella
lor grandezza. Esse furono ritrova-
te in Albano nella Villa di Pompeo Ma-
gno. Queste sono dedicate ad Apollo,
tanto più per vedersi in esse scolpita la
Lira, sopra la quale appoggia con la
zampa un Ipogrifo nel luogo indicato
dalla Let.ª A. Le Baccanti B indicano,
come se fossero intorno all'Ara di
questa Divinità danzando.

Sono architettato queste due Are con par-
ticolar gusto. Frà le principali Colonne
si veggono altre disposte in simetria,
l'una d'Ordine Jonico, e l'altra ep-
posta d'Ordine Dorico. Ogni lavoro
è diligentem. scolpito, nè v'è cosa alcuna trascurata. La parte superiore
C è incavata, per ricevere il Focolare
di Bronzo, che si metteva per li Sagri-
ficii. Queste Are si vedevano una volta in Albano; al presente sono nel Museo dell'Autore.

Cav. Piranesi F.

Al Nobile Uomo il Sig. Giambattista Collicola Montioni Foriere Maggiore
Dei Sagri Palazzi Apostolici amatore delle belle Arti
In atto d'Ossequio il Cav. Gio. Batta Piranesi D.D.D.

his colleague Robert Adam crazy if he spent too much time in his company.[17] However, these same qualities may have endeared him to the foreigners for whom he acted as cicerone. Aernout Vosmaer thoroughly enjoyed the artist's services when he was in Rome and Pompeii. They had known each other since September 1775, when Vosmaer visited Piranesi's *museo* in Palazzo Tomati, near the famous Spanish Steps. We know about their contact thanks to the diary of Vosmaer's travelling companion D. J. de Hochepied and the superb *Album Amicorum*, which contains three pasted-in drawings, one of Pompeii by Piranesi (fig. 17) and two by Piranesi's sons Francesco and Angelo. Francesco made a vivid wash drawing of the Campo Vaccino, with the three monumental columns of the Temple of Jupiter Stator that dominate most depictions of the Roman Forum (fig. 18). Angelo, proudly specifying his tender age of twelve in the drawing's dedication, chose as his subject a relief with two griffins from the Villa Albani (fig. 19). Both drawings were inscribed by Vosmaer with the date January 10, 1776. The same date figures on the drawing by the elder Piranesi himself, another testimony of the friendship between the Dutchman and the Italian. From de Hochepied's journal, we know that Vosmaer and Piranesi bumped into each other again during an excursion to Pompeii, and that the two men dined with him and viewed the antiquities there under his expert guidance. In general, guides rapidly earned the trust of the visitors they showed around and, as the logical next step, became their advisers when it came to buying antique souvenirs. Inevitably, visitors would be taken to the emporia where the guides had commercial dealings. Thus many a young nobleman on an instructive tour not only acquired enlightening information about classical antiquity, but was also given a "unique opportunity" to take a piece of that antiquity home with him. Or, as someone once wrote to the painter George Romney, "Virtue however is to be purchased, like other superfluities, and in the end their *cicerone* lays them in for a bargain, perhaps a patchwork head or Trajan set upon a modern pair of shoulders, and made up with Caracalla's nose and Nero's ears."[18]

Taken together, the travel journals of eighteenth-century Dutch travelers and the sometimes tangible evidence of their shopping give us a good idea of Piranesi's activities, but it was of course first and foremost the British *milordi* who made up the greater part of his clientele. Of the clients Piranesi mentioned by name in his *Vasi…*, for instance, more than fifty were British. However, Frenchmen, Russians, Swedes, Germans, and the occasional Dutchman were also featured. Piranesi and his Roman colleagues had a sophisticated and effective international network and, once someone was a client, Piranesi saw to it that he was

Vedeta del Tempio d'Iside a Pompei
Il Cavalier Piranesi dà in atto
d'amicizia al Sr. Vosmaer

Rome 10 Jan. 1776.

Piranesi. de Vader.
Beroemd Architekt en graveur
van de excellente werken Veduta
de Roma &c. 06.17.

263

Francesco Piranesi 1776

Veduta del Tempio di Giove Statore in Campo Vaccino
Dedicato al Sig.ᵉ Vosmaer
In Atto d'ossequio da Francesco Piranesi

Rome 10. Jan. 1776.

Zoon van voorgaande
Piranesi.

18. Francesco Piranesi
**VIEW OF THE
FORUM IN ROME**, 1771
Pen and brush in grey
over a sketch in pencil

19. Angelo Domenico Piranesi
**DRAWING OF A MARBLE
RELIEF OF GRIFFONS FROM
THE VILLA ALBANI**, 1776
Pencil

*Fregio Antico di Marmo, che si vede nella Villa Albani
Dedicato al Sig.e Vosmaer
In atto d'ossequio da Angelo Piranesi*

Roma 10 Jan. 1776.

*Zoon van gem. Piranesi
12 Jaar oud.*

kept informed by way of his sales catalogues and multilingual publications. His best customer was Edward Walter of Bury Hall, whose name appears seven times in the plates in the *Vasi*.

Piranesi died quite suddenly in 1778, leaving a large stock. The inventory of his museo, drawn up after his death, listed more than one hundred items, and there were at least as many more stored in a warehouse on the Campo Vaccino. The collection ended up, virtually as a job lot, in Stockholm when, in 1783, King Gustav III of Sweden took over the whole of the estate from Piranesi's heir Francesco in return for an annuity of 630 zecchini. Piranesi's artistic legacy, however, was to have a long afterlife. The book of illustrations of Paestum, on which the artist had been working until shortly before his death, was published posthumously by his heirs (fig. 20). The impact of his oeuvre, not least in the field of the decorative arts, was to make itself felt for centuries, and the products of his rich invention, so despised by some, inspired designers for many generations.

MICHAEL GRAVES

DRAWING FROM PIRANESI

AS AN ARCHITECT WHO VALUES DRAWING AS A FUNDAMEN-TAL PART OF THE CREATIVE PROCESS, I AM FASCINATED BY THE DRAWINGS OF OTHER ARCHITECTS. DRAWING IS BOTH A MNEMONIC AND A REPRESENTATIONAL ACT, INTERNALLY SOLIDIFYING OUR VISUAL IMPRESSIONS WHILE SIMULTANEOUSLY revealing to others our point of view and influences. As artifacts, draw-ings thus convey more than simply information; they convey traces of the speculative inquiry that leads to the very conception of architec-ture. At various levels of specificity, they might reveal the *parti*, the con-ceptual organization of a composition, or simply a characteristic detail. Considering the connection between mind and act that occurs in the process of drawing, what architects choose *not* to draw is just as impor-tant as what they choose to draw.

I have also been a longtime student of Rome, starting in the 1960s, when I spent two years at the American Academy.[1] Like many archi-tects on their personal "Grand Tours," I have made drawings of build-ings that I thought held important lessons. No matter what the subject or the medium, my drawings have always been analytical, and in-tended to reveal characteristics that I wanted to recollect. During my Rome fellowship, I was not specifically conscious of the ways in which other architects and artists had rendered those key monuments. However, I have since enjoyed analyzing the varied depictions of the same architectural topics by architects as divergent as Piranesi and Le

Corbusier, as well as by artists such as Jean-Baptiste-Camille Corot and Jean-Auguste-Dominique Ingres.

Le Corbusier, like many practicing architects, drew to remember, to capture a discovery or an idea, or to conceive and develop an architectural scheme and communicate it to others. In contrast, the painters often placed the monuments in the context of the landscape or the city, focusing on the effects of their formal compositions, coloration, and surface lighting. Piranesi, of course, is best known as an architect who produced a prodigious number of etchings depicting various architectural subjects, which were destined to be sold throughout the world. Whatever the commercial purpose of the drawings, they were fundamentally the product of an inquisitive and engaging architectural mind interested in how buildings are constructed, their contextual existence, and, in the case of ruins, the grand vision produced in their sublime state. Piranesi's virtuosic drawing style and the breadth of his subject matter in pictorial series such as the *Vedute* have had an enduring influence on admirers of architecture and, in particular, on admirers of the architecture of Rome.

In researching Piranesi's work for this essay, I have appreciated the opportunity to reacquaint myself with his views. I was struck by his depictions of various buildings I know well compared with others' interpretations of them. Therefore, I have constructed my contribution to this volume on Piranesi as a series of comparisons. Through this method, I have made a number of gratifying discoveries about Piranesi's point of view and his interests. Although I cannot say that his drawings had any direct effect on the specific examples chosen for the comparisons, I have identified several common themes in order to highlight the similarities and differences.

WHAT TO DRAW OR NOT TO DRAW

While one experiences the architectural monuments of Rome in the contextual fabric of the city, architects may either choose to document a building in isolation in order to understand its formal characteristics; or instead include the surroundings to explain contextual influences, which in turn may emphasize an aspect of the primary subject through the composition. An example of the latter, Piranesi's drawing of the Church of Santa Maria in Aracoeli contrasts dramatically with my own quick sketches and with Ingres's more painterly view. What we each chose to draw, or not to draw, reveals our perception of the building and its attributes.

When approaching the stairway leading to the Aracoeli church, one is startled by the extraordinary number of steps and of their steepness.

Veduta del Romano Campidoglio con Scalinata che va alla Chiesa d'Araceli
Architettura di Michelangelo Bonaroti

1. THE CAPITOLINE HILL
WITH STEPS TO S. MARIA
ARACOELI, ca. 1751
Etching on white laid paper

The viewer immediately wonders about the history and present use of this tour de force, specifically, what degree of ascent a human body can tolerate. According to tradition, nuns of a certain sect climb the stair on their knees once a year as penance. Piranesi's composition creates juxtapositions that amplify the great sweep of the Aracoeli stair through its adjacency to the gently stepped ramp leading to the Campidoglio and the gradually sloping road that carriages take up to the square (fig. 1). It is as if Piranesi were building the composition upward from right to left, pivoting about the open space in front of the Aracoeli stair. Clearly, Piranesi was intrigued by both the steepness of the stair and the curious façade of the church, which together create an unexpected, arresting ensemble in the context of the city. Their juxtaposition with the comparatively ordered group of buildings of the Campidoglio poses a comment about the immediate urban condition.

2. Michael Graves
SANTA MARIA IN ARACOELI,
NO. 2, 1960
Pen and brown
ink on white paper

When I visited the Aracoeli, I tried several ways of depicting the afore-mentioned condition, but eventually felt satisfied by more painterly, quick sketches of the stair itself (fig. 2). Even more than in my versions, the viewpoint from which Ingres drew the stair almost obliterates one's sense of the surroundings. As one looks toward the Campidoglio, the wall that bounds the stair blocks the view. Looking at this drawing makes me speculate how Ingres painted this image, specifically, how he rendered the stair given his typical meticulous attention to detail. The drawing offers a small hint of his painterly vision through the silhouette of a nun approaching the church, mid-flight on the stair.

What to draw or not to draw in a building's interior similarly illustrates an architect's point of view. While in Rome in the early 1960s, I was eager to see for myself the interiors of the church of Santa Maria in Cosmedin, purported to be Le Corbusier's favorite interior in Rome. When I was there, I thought I understood what interested him: for example, the way that the row of columns separating the nave from the aisle supports a massive second floor. Even though the surface is made only of stucco over rubble, its visual weight is astonishing, made more so by the juxtaposition of columns to broad surface.

In comparing my sketch of Cosmedin (fig. 3) with Piranesi's drawing of the interior of the church of San Paulo fuori le Muri (fig. 4) or his other drawings of church interiors with the same viewpoint, I see an obvious compositional similarity in the way the columns support the second story and separate the nave from the aisle. However, in contrast to what I chose not to draw, Piranesi created, by what he chose to draw, a similar effect, albeit grander than the Cosmedin example. I thought I was dematerializing the wall by depicting its surface as an abstract, and therefore seemingly weightless, plane. Piranesi dematerialized the apparent weight of the wall through his elaborate treatment of its elevation. The gridded, decorative surface, punctured by arched openings, diverts attention from the mass of the wall supported by the columns. While the geometries and typology of Piranesi's wall are similar to mine at Cosmedin, the effect for me is dramatically different because of the way the wall is drawn.

PROPORTION AND CONTEXT: THE VIEWPOINT REVEALS THE POINT OF VIEW

In most of Piranesi's *Vedute*, the buildings or objects are shown in perspective. The diagonal inflection of those views creates a pictorial quality that allows Piranesi to render the buildings or objects in their urban context. It also allows us as observers to locate ourselves within the urban spaces, the piazzas or squares, which share a reciprocal relation-

S. Maria in Cosmedin, Rome
10.61 Michael Graves

Veduta interna della Basilica di
S. Maria Maggiore
Cavall Piranesi inc.

3. Michael Graves
SANTA MARIA
IN ARACOELI, 1960
Pen and brown
ink on white paper

4. INTERIOR VIEW OF
THE BASILICA OF S. MARIA
MAGGIORE, ca. 1751
Etching on white laid paper

5. VIEW OF THE FAÇADE
OF SAN GIOVANNI
IN LATERANO, Ca. 1751
Etching on white laid paper

ship with the architecture. Piranesi's view of San Giovanni in Laterano, for example, juxtaposes the imposing building with the vast open space in front and to its side (fig. 5).

An opposite technique of rendering the buildings frontally permits us to understand the proportions of the composition. My own drawing of the same church (fig. 6) depicts the façade frontally. I thought that was the most appropriate view, not only because I was studying the proportions and play of the rich Roman sunlight on the articulated façade, but also because the building terminates a long urban axis and is often seen in that manner. The same analysis applies to Piranesi's and my approach to other subjects, such as the fountain known as the Acqua Paola.

6. Michael Graves
SAN GIOVANNI
IN LATERANO, 1960
Pen and brown
ink on white paper

In other instances, when Piranesi and I drew the same subject, for example, the Palazzo Senatorio on the Campidoglio (figs. 7, 8), we assumed a similar viewpoint. The ascending staircase is so prominent in this building that it almost compels a three-quarter view. The angle allows us to comprehend how the paired stairs move above the central Neptune Fountain to the front door at the *piano nobile*. In addition, the chiaroscuro effect produced by the diagonal glancing light reveals the richness of the façade's surface. Piranesi's version, however, goes beyond mine to address the building's urban condition. By drawing the shadow of the adjacent museum in the foreground and up onto the palazzo's façade, he subliminally acknowledged the museum's twin structure on the opposite side of the piazza, and captured the urban space between, putting the three buildings in the context of their shared piazza.

FRAMING: AT THE THRESHOLD

Framing is a device many architects use as a way of forming a threshold to a space, creating tension between inside and outside. The frame's symmetrical disposition identifies our own bodily position. In drawings, the viewpoint an architect chooses and the location of the

Veduta della Piazza del Campidoglio
1. Abitazione di Sua Ecc.ª il Sig.ʳ Senatore di Roma . 2. Museo Capitolino . 3. Chiesa e Convento d'Aracoli . 4. Statua Equestre di
Marco Aurelio . 5. Trofeo d'Ottaviano Augusto

Cavalier Piranesi F.

**7. VIEW OF THE PIAZZA
DEL CAMPIDOGLIO, ca. 1751**
Etching on white laid paper

8. Michael Graves
PALAZZO SENATORIO, 1960
Pen and ink on white paper

picture plane create a frame that poises the viewer between the inside and the outside of the composition.

In looking at the collected *Vedute*, it appears that the time Piranesi spent in Paestum yielded more studies than almost any other subject. Most of these are viewed from a three-quarter perspective, looking from one temple to another, which is typically how one experiences the place in person. For example, in one view, we see the Temple of Juno in the foreground and the Temple of Neptune beyond (fig. 9). Today, without the temple interiors in place, the columns and the relationships among them create the interest, and thus one sees their juxtaposition as a kind of hypostyle condition, in which the roof rests on the columns.

I too did many drawings while in Paestum in 1961, but, unlike Piranesi, I was motivated to see the flank of the Temple of Juno in

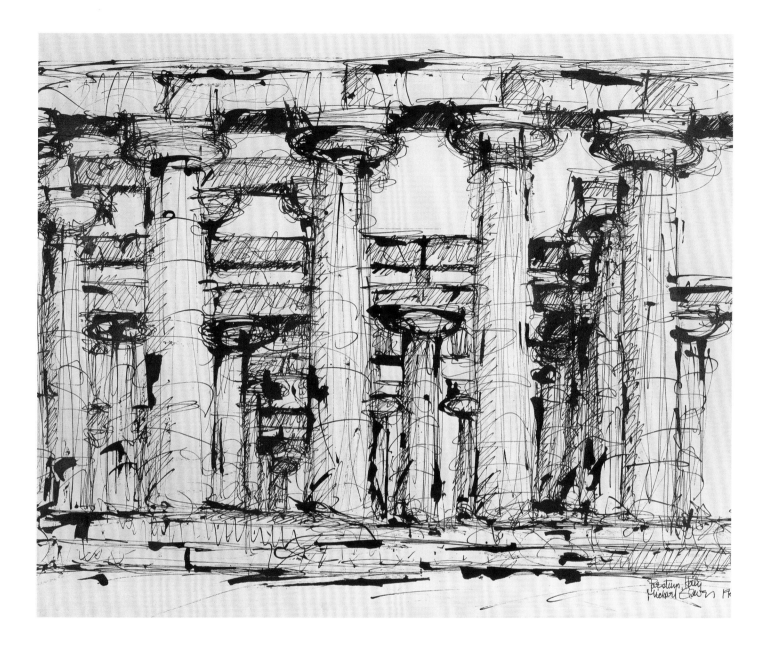

10. Michael Graves
PAESTUM, ITALY, 1960
Pen and ink on white paper

elevation (fig. 10) for two reasons: to understand the proportions of the columns and the spaces between them; and to see the columns as a framing device through which I could see past the first temple to the others on the site. I was, and remain, interested in the true proportion of architectural elements, and when that is my primary goal, I draw the building in elevation. Piranesi, on the other hand, created less analytical, more picturesque compositions by drawing the temples in three-quarter view. He was also interested in framing views through and beyond the columns. However, rather than the clear framing a frontal view allows, his renderings of the temples at Paestum remind us of his training in contemporary scenography, with its characteristic diagonally oriented perspectives, such as those seen in his etching series known as the *Carceri*.

The device of framing also produces a kind of symbolic occupation of the spaces beyond, as we can imagine ourselves crossing the threshold visually, if not physically. In Piranesi's wonderful view of the interior of the Pantheon (fig. 11), the paired columns in the foreground frame the threshold to the grand rotunda. Because of the columns, we can imagine ourselves poised at that threshold, just outside the room. In addition, due to the axial relationship of those columns to their counterparts at the other side of the rotunda, we can also imagine occupying the space itself.

I attempted a similar strategy, using two of the columns of the arcade that surrounds the piazza in front of St. Peter's to frame an axial view toward one of the fountains in the center (fig. 12). In this case, we identify ourselves with the fountain that occupies the center. Any pair of columns in this colonnade, which acts as a collection device surrounding the piazza, could be used to frame the fountain's axial position. I had to set up my view to miss the other fountain and the obelisk in the center of St. Peter's Piazza, and also to capture the building behind in order to close the composition and focus on the fountain.

12. Michael Graves
SAN PIETRO, ROME, 1960
Pen and ink on white paper

BLOCK BY BLOCK: A FASCINATION WITH CONSTRUCTION

Piranesi's interest in construction is striking throughout his etchings, particularly in the *Vedute*, but also in the more archaeological series documenting Roman antiquities in plan, section, elevation, and detail. The surfaces of antique buildings and ruins typically reveal, for example, the corbelling of an arch or vault or the coursing of brick that would have been the under-layer for the application of stone veneer.

Piranesi's view of the Remains of the Temple of Minerva Medica (fig. 13), for example, reveals his interest in archaeology, particularly in Roman (as opposed to Greek) architecture. Piranesi elected to depict the object quality of the temple, presumably to show us the interior with light streaming in and resting on the void of the window. As in Giovanni Paolo Panini's great painting of the interior of the Pantheon, the lighting is a way of seeing the drama and depth of the cylindrical form. In his painting of a similar view, Corot also communicated the liveliness of the interior through the animated shadows resting on the interior face. It is somewhat rare to find artists like Corot painting a single object like this, rather than seeing it as one of several objects in the open landscape, and therefore one assumes the light falling on the curving interior surfaces captivated him.

In my own small ink sketch of Minerva Medica dating from 1977, I depicted the building from the closed side, emphasizing the opacity of the object-like figure rather than the void. The power of the temple's cylindrical form is best conveyed in this view. My drawing also speaks of the progression from the outside through the pronounced doorway and into the vestibule, which reveals the interior beyond. I was also interested in seeing the back-up masonry and the brick in relationship to the stone surface revealed in the entrance façade. In another of his views of the temple, Piranesi painstakingly revealed the coursing of the brick and the corbelling of the roof, again demonstrating his interest in architectural construction and archaeological authenticity.

In Piranesi's view of the Pantheon, the brick construction of the outer wall of the great rotunda occupies fully half of the composition and shows the construction of the courses and arches that make up the wall.[2] (fig. 14) In my drawing of the Pantheon, I too was interested in showing the juxtaposition of porch and rotunda, but also wanted to depict the building's urban relationships (fig. 15). Seeing the side street along the flank of the rotunda as a pedestrian has always interested me, as I can, from a very close vantage point, look at the construction techniques used in the rotunda's outer wall, much as Piranesi did.

Veduta del Tempio ottangolare di Minerva Medica

A Egli era interiormente ornato di marmi, B e di musaici bianchi, ed esteriormente coperto d'stucco. C Rovine d'altre edifizio congiunte posteriormente col Tempio.

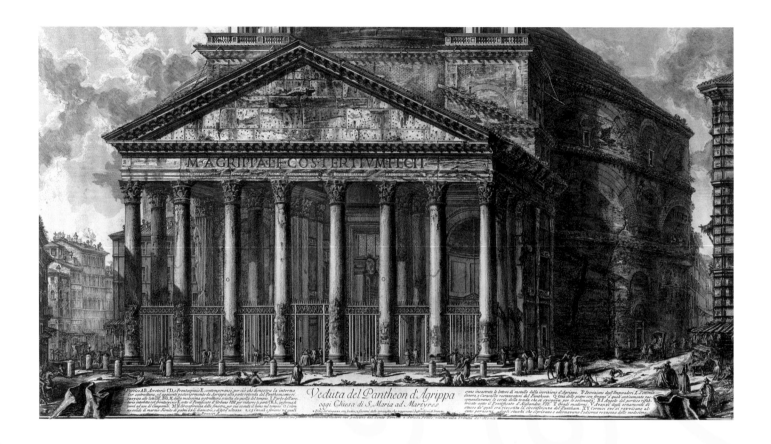

Veduta del Pantheon d'Agrippa
oggi Chiesa di S. Maria ad Martyres

14. THE PANTHEON
(LE ANTICHITÀ ROMANE), 1756
Etching on white laid paper

15. Michael Graves
THE PANTHEON, 1960
Pen and ink on white paper

FIGURE AND GROUND: FRAGMENTS IN CONTEXT

Another theme that occurs throughout Piranesi's etchings, as well as in anyone's comprehension of Rome, is the idea of the fragment as it alludes to the whole. Certainly, the romantic ideas associated with ruins are derived in part from their fragmentary nature, which encourages the imagination to complete the composition. The result is an engagement between the architectural fragment and the landscape or urban space. The two develop a reciprocal relationship that is sometimes real and sometimes speculative.

The three remaining arches of the Basilica of Maxentius (which is known by many names) were frequently documented by artists and architects of Piranesi's time and thereafter. He himself made several drawings of this magnificent fragment (fig. 16). Architects are captivated by the basilica because so much of the articulation of the undersides of the arches remains. Realizing that this is only one side aisle of a much larger building, one is awestruck by the grand scale. It is no wonder that Piranesi emphasized the enormity of the building through his vantage point and his dramatic etching technique. My version from 1960 expresses the grandeur in much the same way Piranesi did (fig. 17).

16. THE BASILICA OF
MAXENTIUS (CALLED VIEW
OF THE BATHS OF DIOCLETIAN),
ca. 1751
Etching on white laid paper

17. Michael Graves
THE BASILICA OF
MAXENTIUS, 1960
Pen and ink on white paper

18. Jean-Baptiste-Camille Corot
THE COLISEUM (SEEN THROUGH
THE BATHS OF MAXENTIUS)
Oil on canvas

It was one of the first drawings that allowed me to describe chiaroscuro, which was only an abstract concept to me before I went to Rome. The painter Corot selected a very different vantage point in the Basilica of Maxentius (fig. 18). He used the small arched wall at the end of the building to frame the view of the Colosseum. Because of the framing, Corot saw, as a painter would, not only the context of the two buildings, but also their picturesque value.

The Colosseum was a favorite subject of Corot's. In another version, he used a rather muted palette and made the Colosseum seem aqueduct-like.[3] Corot did not try to take advantage of the cylindrical form of the Colosseum; rather, he saw the curving walls of the inner and outer rings as two flat planes. Only our memory of the form allows us to read the shadows as an indication of curvature. Piranesi's drawing of the Colosseum similarly causes it to be seen as a "ground" against which the Arch of Constantine is read as a figural object (fig. 19). This juxtaposition reminds us that these and many other structures are seen in context, and the vantage point he chose for his drawing shows that Piranesi did

not want us to forget that contextual relationship. Furthermore, in drawing the building itself, he revealed the structural and spatial relationship of the outer and inner shell with a glimpse of the glorious intermediary vomitory, the entrance piercing the seats.

In my own view of the Colosseum, I elected, after another painting of Corot's, to see into the void from the two ruined corners of the outer shell (fig. 20). The inner building, which defines the edge of the vomitory, has always intrigued me as a picturesque condition of the ruin. As in Piranesi's version, this vantage point gave me the chance to draw the Arch of Constantine in the foreground, which again allows both the Colosseum and the arch to be understood formally in their contextual stance.

Fragments of buildings, because of their inherent incompleteness, create an engagement with the immediately adjacent open space. In some cases, such as the long wall in the remains of the Praetorium Camp at Hadrian's Villa, drawn by both Piranesi and Le Corbusier, the plane of the wall acts as a reference against which the open space is read (figs. 21, 22). This condition continued to interest Le Corbusier, and he incorpo-

20. Michael Graves
THE COLISEUM, 1960
Pen and ink on white paper

21. HADRIAN'S VILLA, ca. 1751
Etching on white laid paper

22. Le Corbusier
(Charles-Edouard Jeanneret)
HADRIAN'S VILLA
Black chalk on paper

293

23. VIEW OF THE REMAINS
OF THE SECOND FLOOR OF
THE BATHS OF TITUS, ca. 1751
Etching on white laid paper

24. Michael Graves
SANT'ANASTASIA AND DOMUS
AUGUSTANA, 1960
Pen and ink on white paper

rated it both in his architectural work and in the way he represented his buildings in drawings.

Fragments of buildings can also create a reciprocal relationship between the building and an opposing solid. As with Le Corbusier's interest in juxtaposing the barrier of the long wall with adjacent open space, the concave surface also became a compositional device in his buildings. There are numerous examples among Piranesi's *Vedute* of partially ruined buildings where a curving surface, covered by an overhanging roof, starts to engage the adjacent space. His view of the remains of the second floor of the Baths of Titus is one of several such examples (fig. 23). While the wall that I drew at Sant'Anastasia and the Domus Augustana is actually flat with a curved profile, I used it here to illustrate the effect of perceived concavity on the adjacent space (fig. 24). One of the most interesting examples of this effect is Ingres's small painting of the so-called House of Raphael, where the overhang of the roof highlights the concave wall surface below. The circular shape of the painting further reinforces the reading of the curving façade. This compositional interest occurs within Le Corbusier's work, particularly in one of the façades at the Chapel at Ronchamp.

MAN AND LANDSCAPE: REAL AND METAPHORIC

I have thought of traditional or figurative architecture as having roots in both man and the landscape. Certainly, the symmetry of our own bodily stance influences how we approach and read a façade and how we orient ourselves in a space. The relationship is thus both literal and metaphoric. The same holds true for the landscape, where, for example, a pyramidal form can be interpreted as a metaphorical mountain.

In my several versions of the façade and stairs of Santa Maria Maggiore, I tried to demonstrate that the stairs assume a landscape presence: they appear to be a great hill or mound on which the church stands (fig. 25). Approaching the great curving staircase, one cannot help but think for a moment that the entire façade is sitting within the open landscape, and that the stairs create a separation between the city and that landscape. In both of my renditions, one senses the metaphor of the landscape through the active manner in which I drew the stairs. The vantage point from which Piranesi described the rear façade of Santa Maria Maggiore allows one to think of the great mound of stairs as simply a way to enter the aisle doors (fig. 26). However, to achieve this view, he would have had to be high in the air; therefore, it is possible that he constructed, rather than observed, his vantage point.

There are also instances where buildings are seen as objects within

25. Michael Graves
SANTA MARIA MAGGIORE,
APSE, 1960
Pen and ink on white paper

the *campagna*, the landscape itself. Examples include the aqueducts seen throughout Rome and the region and the Ponte Nomentano, which are documented by Piranesi and by painters such as Corot and Ingres in highly different ways. In the compositions of the aqueducts by Corot and Ingres (and in my drawing after Corot), we see the painter or architect viewing the scene as a dramatic contrast between linear, man-made architecture and the natural landscape (figs. 27, 28). As in many other versions of this scene, one starts with the horizontality of the landscape, the sky, and the aqueduct. Yet when the aqueducts are seen from a closer vantage point, one understands not only their horizontality, but also their almost columnar verticality. In contrast, it is the construction of these landscape walls that interested Piranesi (fig. 29). Piranesi drew with great precision the coursing and corbelling and the structure of the arches in a way that would rarely interest the painter. He showed himself not only as an architect but also as an archaeologist. The objects in the foreground are part of his archaeology, and Piranesi lends them an importance metaphorically by allowing them to project

past the picture plane and even throw a shadow on the text, as if to say that the object supersedes the narrative.

Throughout his etchings in the *Vedute* series, Piranesi frequently populated the foreground of his views of buildings with people engaged in a variety of activities. Contemporary architects such as Leon Krier often include such fictional people in their drawings as an indication of the character of a place. Le Corbusier, in his drawing of the *Ville Contemporaine*, used a convivial setting of tables and chairs as a foreground from which to view his vision of the modern city with its residential towers in the landscape beyond. In Piranesi's case, some of his figures, intentionally dwarfed by the grand scale of the architecture, exhibit the same curiosity about the ruins as Piranesi does, with their ladders, ropes, and measuring devices. Others are romantic, almost mythical figures strolling about in pastoral scenery, and yet others are everyday people engaged in everyday activities, reminding us that the great monuments are part of the normal surroundings of Rome. The people thus impart an immediacy to the architectural scenes, bridging the glorious past with Piranesi's view of the present, as well as his hope for a future that would affirm the values of the ancient Romans.

Veterum [Aquae] Marciae ductuum, muris Urbis ab Aureliano constructis inter se...ruinae, a Porta Majori ad Portam S. Laurentii; prout habetur in Tom. I. Antiqu. Rom. num. 119, 120, 121 Indic. gener. vestig. Romae veteris.

27. Jean-Baptiste-Camille Corot
THE ROMAN COMPAGNA WITH
THE CLAUDIAN AQUEDUCT
Oil on canvas

28. Michael Graves
AQUEDUCT, 1960
Pen and ink on white paper

29. ANCIENT AQUEDUCT
OF THE ACQUA MARCIA
AT THE CITY WALLS ERECTED
BY AURELIAN..., page CXCIX,
Vignette, DELLA MAGNIFIC-
ENZA ED ARCHITETTURA
DE'ROMANI, 1761
Etching on white laid paper

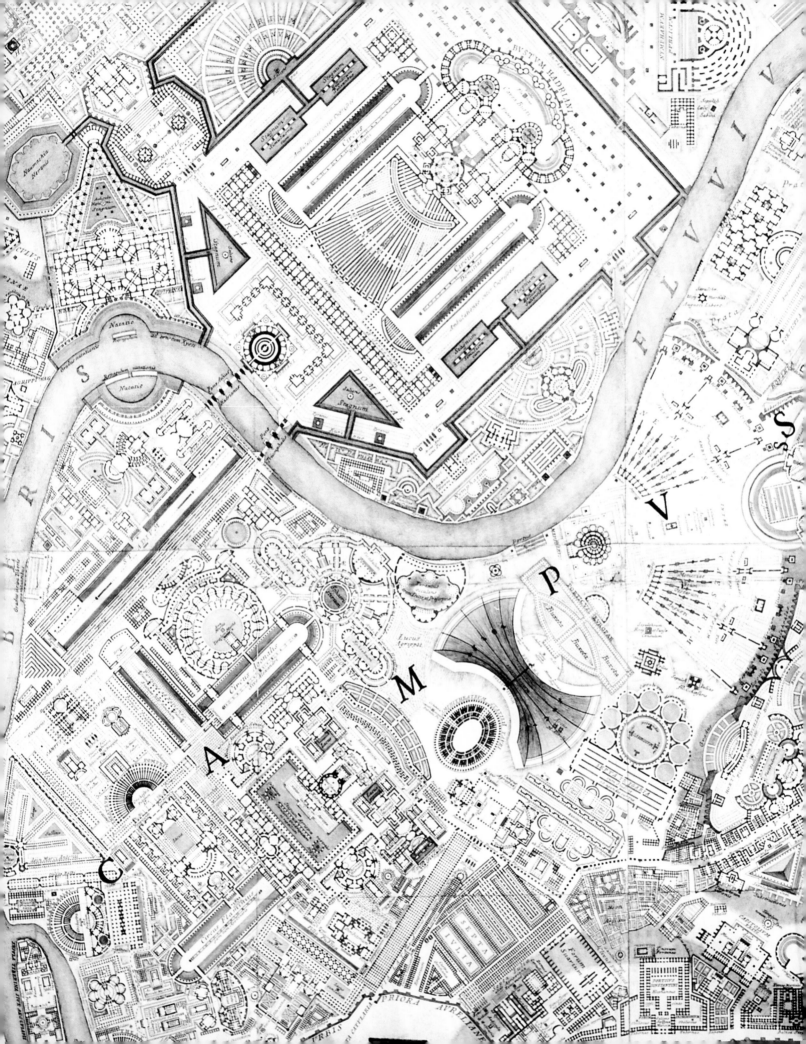

PETER EISENMAN

PIRANESI AND THE CITY

IF THERE ARE TWO ICONS THAT REPRESENT THE PERIOD FROM 1980 TO 2000 NOW KNOWN AS POSTMODERNISM, ONE IS GIAMBATTISTA NOLLI'S MAP OF ROME (FIG. 2) AS THE ICON OF REACTION; THE OTHER IS PIRANESI'S 1762 MAP OF THE *CAMPO MARZIO* (FIG. 1), THE ICON OF TRANSGRESSION.

The Nolli map also figured in one of two important exhibitions, mounted at nearly the same time in Italy, which became the touchstones of postmodernism. The first, in Rome in 1978, called *Roma Interrotta* (*Rome Interrupted*), took the Nolli map as its starting point; while the other, *Strada Novissima* (*The Latest Path*), at the second international Venice architectural *Biennale* in 1980, concentrated mainly on iconic façades. These two exhibitions remain a faint memory today, yet several of its artifacts, including Colin Rowe and Fred Koetter's *Collage City* and Leon Krier's and others' New Urbanist schemes, continue to attract interest. However, Piranesi's map of the Campo Marzio, especially in its relation to Nolli's map of Rome, was seen to have proposed, in its questioning of the sedimented conventions of viewing the city, a critical moment for architecture. The Campo Marzio asked in the eighteenth century, Is the city the sum of its parts? on entirely different terms than those in effect at the time, and which today are becoming increasingly relevant.

The Nolli map, produced in 1748, was also radical for its time. One only has to compare it to other maps of the period, in particular to Buffalino's sixteenth-century map of Rome, to understand the powerful political and social critique the Nolli map contained in its unique rendering of the city. The Nolli map showed the context of Rome as it was in the eighteenth century, but delineated it in a new way by representing the interiors of public buildings with the same coloration—that is, the paper color—as the streets. Since the buildings were drawn in densely hatched black lines, this map became the first figure/ground drawing, as well as the first articulation of the figure and ground concept in a map. More important was the differentiation between public and private space. The hatched black of the buildings represented private space and white was public space; black was figure and white was ground. These two conditions became the dominant mode of representation in what became postmodernism's return to the question of figure versus ground, and the dialectical relationship of solid and void, poché and space, and its implication for presence and absence.

Piranesi's map of the Campo Marzio was a direct response to Nolli's map of Rome, on which Piranesi had also worked as a delineator, transposing his drawing to the copperplate for engraving. Piranesi's strategy not only put into question the idea of figure/ground, but also, more significant, questioned the idea of a map as a single moment in space and time. There are two important issues in considering Piranesi's Campo Marzio. The first is the critique of baroque town planning and the idea of the mass subject, as opposed to the individual subject, which became fully articulated during the French Revolution. The second issue, a new idea in terms of the persistencies of architecture, is the question of time. Time becomes differentiated from the time that it takes to walk through a building, a time known as the apperception of a subject. Traditionally, when a subject walks into a (usually symmetrical) building, walks through a central space, enters a central door, sees a colonnade on the right, turns around at the back of the building, comes back and sees a colonnade again on his or her right, and returns to the front, the subject realizes through apperception that he or she is walking in a symmetrical space. Thus the time of understanding this symmetry and the time of experience are considered one and the same thing. This persistency existed from the sixteenth through the eighteenth centuries, when the question of time and the fragmentation of the relationship of time to a particular moment became problematized.

The Campo Marzio is important in this context. Piranesi's drawing of the Campo Marzio was made in 1762, almost twenty years after Nolli's map. Piranesi's drawing anticipated an entirely different idea of the urban. It did so with a dense layering of different times, places, and scales so that it was impossible to say which was the base or original condition. The Campo Marzio map was etched on what Piranesi represented as stone tablets, held together with a series of stone clips. The map therefore was made of parts as well as fragments; his purpose was to show this as a fragment of a larger entity he had reassembled. Certain landmarks remained: the Tiber River, the Piazza Navona, and a Colosseum-like structure, which was in the wrong location and, in a sense, at the wrong scale. Certain structures from imperial Rome, as well as elements that still existed in the 1760s, could be recognized. Other buildings resembled giant baths, *agora* (marketplaces), or *fora* (forums) that might have existed in imperial times or were just creations of Piranesi's imagination. The map also included some buildings from imperial Rome still standing in 1762, but not in their actual locations. Finally, it included buildings drawn at different scales so that an existing building was rendered significantly larger than its actual size. In a single map, Piranesi suggested that there was no one scale, no one time, no one location, and no one reality to his project—a clear transgression of the conventions of mapmaking.

The buildings populating the Campo Marzio are joined in multiple symmetrical compositions, joined in a cascading set of axes. A symmetrical composition linked to the flank of another building includes two giant raceways, picked up by a pair of paired rectangles, which lead to a secondary pair of symmetrical compositions. This produces a condition in which no axis clearly dominates and organizes the city into a coherent, visible whole. Instead, each axis leads to another set of axes in a constant system of destabilization. The interconnection of buildings through such shifting axes produces in the residual spaces a set of interstitial figures to which smaller structures are appended. Such interstitial figures occupy the space that would have been the ground on the Nolli map; in Piranesi's map, there is no ground and no street, only figures. Analyses of the buildings and how they relate to the next scales and their connections to other axes reveal that the figures in Piranesi's map, while they look like buildings, in fact do not function as buildings. In Piranesi's Campo Marzio, there is an equal play between the hard material of architecture—stone—and its more fluid elements, such as the numerous waterworks that create a network across Rome.

To study the Campo Marzio is to understand that there are whole figures which come partly from actual Roman figures and partly from invention, which then relate to other whole figures, and together they constitute a figural fabric. This fabric includes the figures of buildings, the interstitial traces of vanished streets, and even partial figures, which attach one figure, linking a secondary axis in the first figure to a primary axis in the second, thereby attaching the largest scale to an ever-decreasing chain of scale. There are whole figures that fill in between the larger scale figures and diminish in scale to become what could be called interstitial figures or poché. Previously, poché was thought to be a

NEXT SPREAD
Giambattista Nolli
LA NUOVA TOPOGRAFIA
DI ROMA, 1748

ALLA SANTITA'
DI NOSTRO SIGNORE
PAPA
BENEDETTO XIV
LA NUOVA TOPOGRAFIA
DI ROMA

ROME 1748   BEING A ONE-HALF SCALE REDUCTION OF
GIAMBATTISTA NOLLI'S *PIANTA GRANDE DI ROMA*

figure/ground exercise, similar to Nolli's articulating the difference between buildings and open space in black and white in his map of Rome. But here Piranesi suggested that there is no "black," that everything is both figure and ground at the same time—in other words, it is a figured ground. This was a radical vision for an urban fabric that saw the city as a series of figures, as opposed to a series of figures on a ground.

Piranesi's map presented the idea of a figure/figure urbanism. His Campo Marzio is a critique of baroque Rome, and the idea of what would become baroque Rome in relationship to medieval Rome. The latter was captured in the plan of Sixtus V, who cut diagonal streets through the medieval fabric, placing a series of piazzas with obelisks to mark significant places in Rome, usually related to the major churches or the routes to the major churches. Rome became a context that could be understood visually by a Christian pilgrim. Piranesi's map envisioned Rome instead as another kind of invention, a terrain for questioning the persistencies of architecture.

That is, is the city the sum of its parts? Does Leon Battista Alberti's idea of the Renaissance City as a large house and a house a small city still have meaning? It could be argued that modern architecture accepted this idea of a relationship of parts to the whole. Later generations of architects, including Mathias Ungers and Rem Koolhaas, have begun, however, to question whether the parts need to relate to the whole. New ideas coming forward today question the validity of the part-to-whole relationship. This is one of the lessons of Piranesi.

One of the projects that remain unanswered for today's generation of architects and those to come is, What is a model for the contemporary city? The Nolli and Piranesi maps are relevant to this question in that they stand as icons of the two ways of looking at the relationship of architecture to the city during the eighteenth century, when the question of an urban model had to encompass enormous political change and social revolution. The Nolli plan represented a different ideology than Piranesi's plan. All architecture has within it persistencies, some of which may no longer be operative—the detritus of former points of view. It is not possible merely to reinfuse a point of view into an old work and make it come alive. What is necessary today is to look at the past to see if there is anything from that past that can help us understand how to manifest a point of view today. Persistencies—such as those between subject and object, organism and disassociation, transgression and acceptance of norms—fluctuate over time, yet these same fluctuations may reoccur today. The problem of the relationship between the past and the present, between differing scales, the meaning of buildings, the relationships of buildings—all of these issues remain active in the contemporary city.

The following works are featured in Cooper-Hewitt, National Design Museum's *Piranesi as Designer* exhibition, but are not illustrated in the essays. For a complete list of works included in Cooper-Hewitt's exhibition as well as that of the Teylers Museum, Haarlem, the Netherlands, please see the List of Illustrations on p. 331.

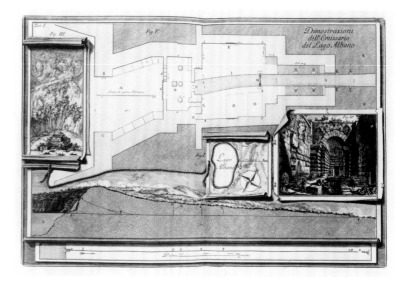

DIMOSTRAZIONE
DELL'EMISSARIO DEL LAGO
ALBANO, 1762
Etching on off-white laid paper

PIANTA DEL SEPOLCRO DI
ALESSANDRO SEVERO, SITUATO
FUORI DI PORTA S. GIOVANNI,
plate XXXI from LE ANTICHITÀ
ROMANE, vol. 2, 1756
Etching on off-white laid paper

OPPOSITE

ARCHITECTURAL FANTASY
WITH MONUMENTAL PORTICO
BEFORE A PALACE, ca. 1763
Pen and brown ink,
brown wash over red chalk
on off-white laid paper

Joseph Michael Gandy
VIEW OF CONSULS
TRANSFER OFFICE FOR THE
BANK OF ENGLAND, n.d.
Pen and watercolor

Robert Adam and
Charles-Louis Clérisseau
IMAGINARY INTERIOR BASED
ON ROMAN BATHS, 1755–1756
Pen and ink with wash

VEDUTA INTERNA DELLA
BASILICA DI S. GIOVANNI
LATERANO, from the series
VEDUTE DI ROMA, 1768
Etching on white laid paper

Jean-Charles Delafosse
TEMPLE OF JUSTICE, ca. 1765
Pen and black ink,
brush and pink, blue,
and gray wash on paper

CENTRAL VIEW OF A
CHURCH INTERIOR WITH
TOMBS AND URNS ALONG
EITHER WALL AND A
FREESTANDING MONUMENT
IN THE CENTER, n.d.
Pen and brown ink with gray
and brown wash over black
chalk, with red chalk additions

STUDY OF AN ORNAMENTAL
SWORD FOR THE DECORATIVE
PILASTERS ON THE FAÇADE
OF S. MARIA DEL PRIORATO,
mid-18th century
Pen and ink on off-white
laid paper

SHEET OF VARIOUS
SKETCHES FOR CHIMNEYPIECES
AND CANDELABRA WITH
COMPUTATIONS AND NOTES
ON MATERIALS / THEMES, n.d.
Pen and brown ink with
written annotations
on off-white laid paper

Robert Adam
TWO SKETCH DESIGNS FOR
PORTIONS OF CHIMNEYPIECES
DERIVED FROM THOSE IN
"DIVERSE MANIERE," ca. 1777
Pencil and ink on paper

PREPARATORY DESIGN
FOR CHIMNEYPIECE WITH
MONOPODS, n.d.
Red and black chalk with
additions in pen and brown
ink on two sheets of off-white
laid paper, joined

WORKING STUDY FOR A
CHIMNEYPIECE WITH CENTRAL
TABLET LINKED BY FESTOONS
TO WREATHS, WITH COMPUTA-
TION AND SIDE ELEVATION
OF STILE, n.d.
Black chalk on off-white
laid paper

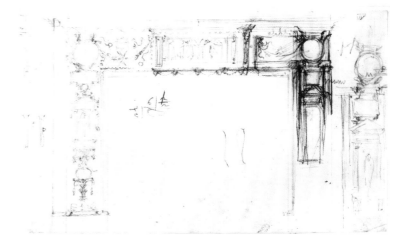

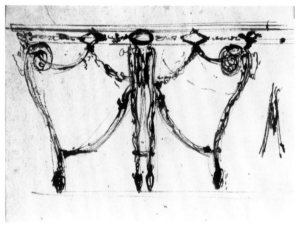

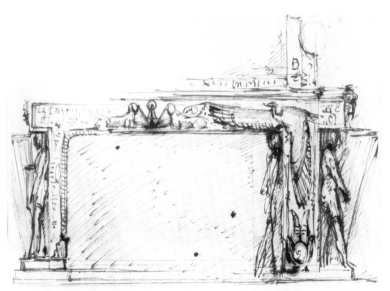

DESIGN FOR A CHIMNEYPIECE
AND CHAIR, n.d.
Pen and brown ink over black
chalk on off-white laid paper

DESIGN FOR A SIDE TABLE
Pen and brown ink on
off-white laid paper

SKETCH DESIGN FOR
CHIMNEYPIECE IN THE EGYPTIAN
TASTE WITH STANDING
FIGURES AND BIRD, n.d.
Pen and brown ink on
off-white laid paper (irregular)

Carlo Marchionni
DESIGN FOR A DOORWAY
TO THE GRAND GALLERY
OF THE VILLA ALBANI, 1755–56
Pen and brown ink, brush
and brown and gray wash,
graphite on cream laid paper

Robert Adam
A DESIGN OF A CHAIR
FOR THE ETRUSCAN DRESSING
ROOM AT OSTERLEY, 1776
Pen and ink with watercolor

Robert Adam
DESIGN FOR A CONFIDANTE,
AN ETRUSCAN ARM CHAIR,
AND A SILVER CUP, 1777
Black chalk, brush and
white gouache on oatmeal-
colored laid paper

CHIMNEYPIECE IN THE
EGYPTIAN STYLE: SEATED
FIGURES IN PROFILE ON
EITHER SIDE, FROM THE
DIVERSE MANIERE..., 1769
Etching on off-white laid paper

CHIMNEYPIECE IN THE
EGYPTIAN STYLE: GIANT
FIGURES SUPPORTING
THE LINTEL FLANKED BY
CHAIRS, FROM THE DIVERSE
MANIERE..., 1769
Etching on off-white laid paper

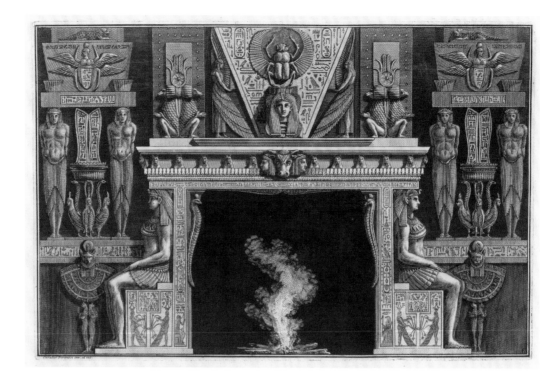

Louis-Jean Desprez
**SEPULCHER WITH DEATH
SEATED AND CROWNED,
IMAGINARY TOMB DESIGN
IN THE EGYPTIAN STYLE,**
ca. 1779–84
Pen and black ink, brush
and brown, gray, blue-gray
wash, traces of graphite
on off-white paper

Filippo Marchionni
**SANTA MARIA DEL PRIORATO,
ROME, ALTERNATIVE DESIGN
FOR THE HIGH ALTAR,** 1724–30
Pen and black ink, gray wash,
black chalk on white laid paper

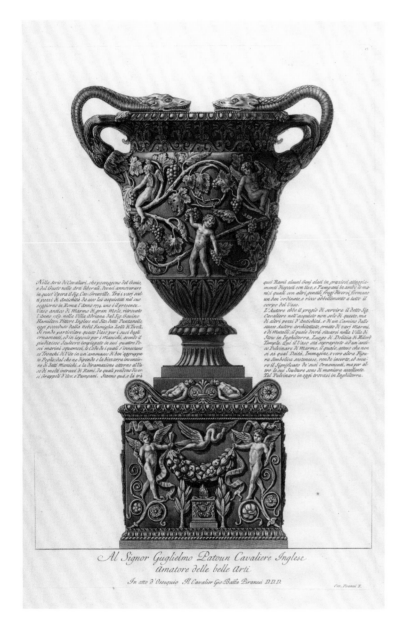

Al Signor Guglielmo Patoun Cavaliere Inglese
Amatore delle belle Arti

In atto d'Ossequio Il Cavalier Gio Batta Piranesi D.D.D.

Alla Sig. Marchesa Margarita Sparapani Gentili Boccapaduli Amatrice delle belle Arti.

In atto di Ossequio il Cavalier Gio. Batta Piranesi. D. D. D.

BUCKINGHAM VASE,
"THE DONCASTER CUP,"
from VASI, CANDELABRA,
CIPPI, SARCOPHAGI..., 1778
Etching on off-white laid paper

PERSPECTIVE VIEW OF AN
ANTIQUE MONUMENT FOUND
IN A TOMB ON THE VIA APPIA,
late 18th century
Etching on off-white laid paper

OPPOSITE

DESIGN FOR A MIRROR
FRAME, n.d.
Pen and brown ink, brush
and gray wash over graphite
on off-white laid paper
(squared for transfer)

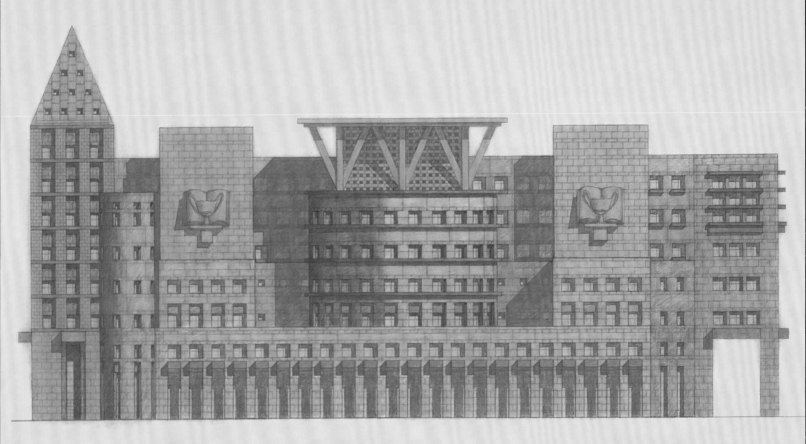

Denver Central Library
Thirteenth Avenue

Graves

Michael Graves
DENVER CENTRAL LIBRARY,
SOUTH ELEVATION, 1991
Graphite and colored pencil
on yellow tracing paper

One of the characteristics of Piranesi's compositions is his depiction of architecture as a collection of pieces rather than as singular objects. The individual parts often add up to a complex whole, particularly in his views of ruins in their sublime, fragmentary state. We adopted a similar approach in our design for the Denver Central Library. In the early 1990s, we won a design competition to expand the existing library, a two-story, 1950s-era modern building on Civic Center Park, to nearly triple its size. We composed the massing and façades— including the bold, new south-facing elevation—as a collection of functional and symbolic parts. This strategy maintained the proportions of the original building and allowed it to be read as one of the fragments that make up the whole composition.

Another major theme in Piranesi's compositions is his interest in revealing the construction techniques used in the buildings he drew. In my own work, I have often tried to incorporate what Piranesi has taught us: using traditional construction materials such as stone not only creates wonderful surfaces articulated by chiaroscuro, but also imparts a sense of scale. For example, the size of a cut stone might suggest that one or two masons could lift it into place within a wall, and thus the architecture is made by man and not by a machine. Even when a building is made of pre-cast concrete, due to budgetary concerns, we try to use coursing, as we did in the south elevation of the library, to mediate between the large scale of the building and the smaller, human scale of those who use it.

ROBERT VENTURI AND DENISE SCOTT BROWN

Venturi, Scott Brown and Associates

Venturi, Scott Brown
and Associates
EPISCOPAL ACADEMY CHAPEL,
2006
Plotted inkjet on wove paper

Viva Piranesi! for his Romantic-
dramatic-historical spaces,
forms, and light.

Love him and employ him
in natural and urban contexts—
but only where appropriate.

Viva, too, electronic iconography
for an architecture of the
Information Age!

Piranesian Episcopal Chapel:
Light reveals a soaring structure.

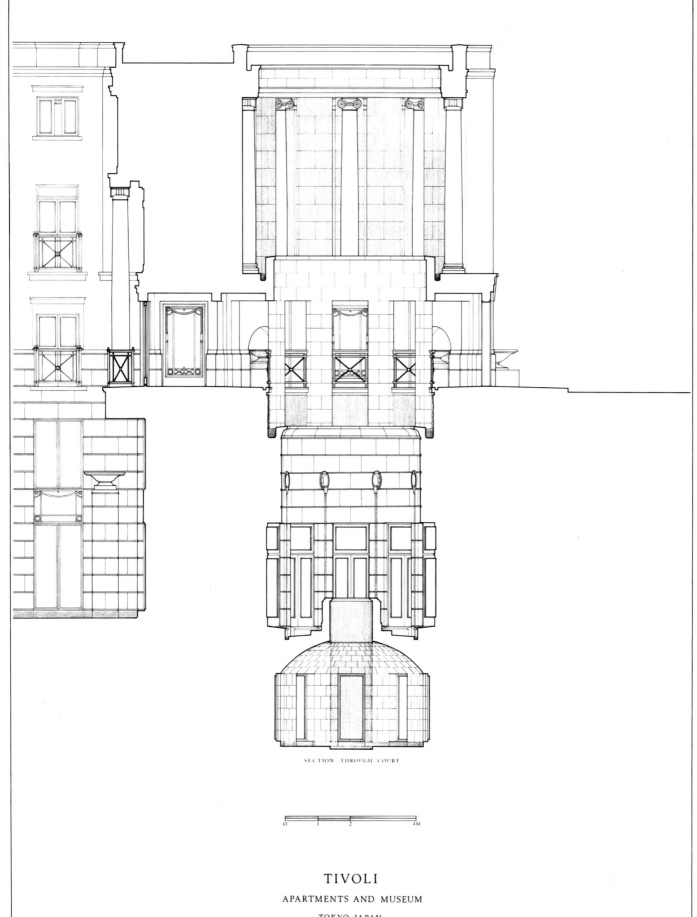

SECTION THROUGH COURT

O   1   2   4M

TIVOLI
APARTMENTS AND MUSEUM
TOKYO, JAPAN

ROBERT A. M. STERN

Robert A. M. Stern Architects

Robert A. M. Stern
PLAN DESIGN FOR THE
TOKYO TIVOLI APARTMENTS
Ink on Mylar

Piranesi's idiosyncratic sceno-graphic illustrations have influenced figures in architecture as diverse as the Adam brothers; Sir John Soane and his enigmatic delineator Joseph Gandy; and, in America a century and a half later, Louis Kahn and Philip Johnson. Piranesi's vision was founded on his rediscovery of the architectural forms and details of ancient Rome. My partners and I may not often look directly to him for inspiration, but, in our approach to history, we carry forward his outlook: our office's work is predicated on the study and interpretation of precedent, and our oeuvre owes much to those whom he directly influenced.

Perhaps the most Piranesian of our designs is a 1991 project for a three-story luxury apartment building located in Harajuku, in the heart of Tokyo, Japan, which accommodated apartments, a rooftop garden, a dining terrace above grade, office space, a small private museum, and a restaurant below grade.

The need for the vertical compression of these spaces led us to a solution not dissimilar to some of Piranesi's drawings: A water garden on the south side of the building brings light and views to the building's various public spaces. A sequence of water spills from a fountain surrounded by smooth stone columns down over terraces to a serene reflection pool. In an adjacent "temple grotto," a circle of water cascades from an upper pool to a lower pool, offering a dramatic view from the entry court. Our ink-on-Mylar illustrations are likewise Piranesian in their choice of viewpoints, which exaggerate the verticality of the parti and emphasize the penetration of light and water through the mass of the building.

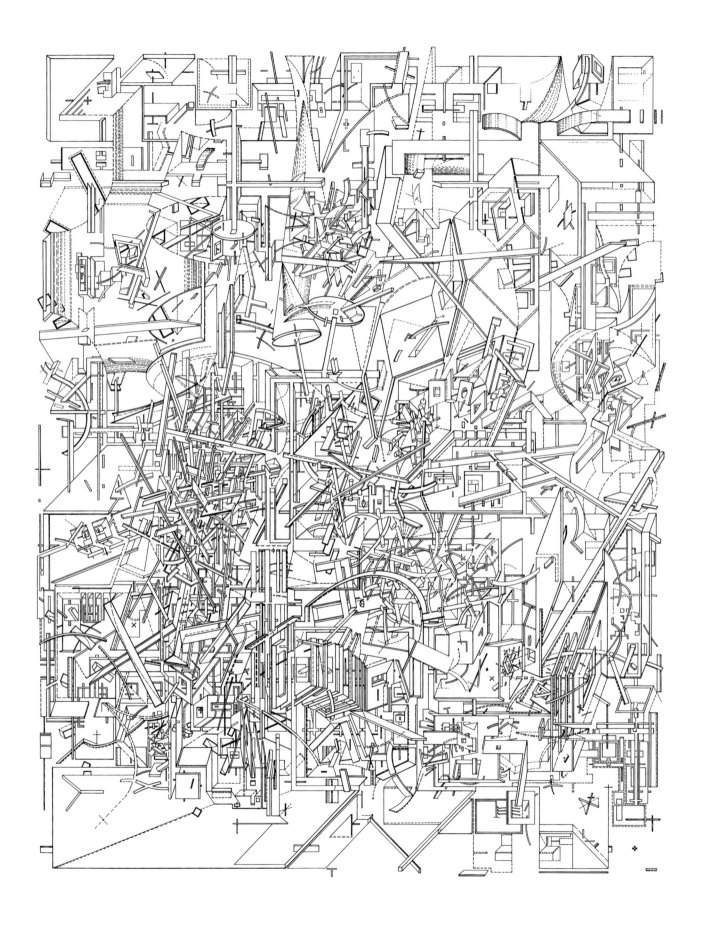

DANIEL LIBESKIND
Studio Daniel Libeskind

Daniel Libeskind
MALDOROR'S EQUATION,
from the series MICROMEGA,
21st century
Silkscreen

Piranesi and My Work*

What links Piranesi's work to my own efforts is the fact that he did not view architecture as a means in the service of external ends. For him, it was possessed by its own truth, as his engraver's stroke bore the whole burden of its construction. The revelatory essence of Piranesi's truth is that architecture is far more akin to the "voice of spirit" than a means of pleasure and utility. It is analogous to philosophy, literature, poetry, and political meditation far more than to mechanics, materials, or physics.

In its raw and latent state, architecture is a source of meaning more potent and enduring than its "ideal," and that is why Piranesi's drawings never cease to amaze us. The symbols they provide can be developed only indeterminately and undeterminably because they refer to the topology of a dwelling, and not only to topography.

Finally, the interest I have in Piranesi's work stems from the realization that it addresses the present in a profound and mysterious manner, that it is both message and demand. This architecture withdraws itself from every definition, conception, fixation. It becomes accessible only in the decision to grant its claim by accepting and preserving in faith a new experience of the world: a new being of architecture, which is revealed as historical.

* *Excerpted from* Piranesi und Architecturphantasien in der Gegenwart, *an exhibition at the Kunstverein, Hanover, Germany (1982)*

PETER EISENMAN
Eisenman Architects

Peter Eisenman
DESIGN FOR THE
CARDINALS' STADIUM,
GLENDALE, ARIZONA, 2006
Digital rendition print

Piranesi's drawings of prisons, called the *Carceri*, produce a different idea of thinking about perspectival space and the relationship of a viewer subject to an object. In these drawings, space impedes the viewer from understanding the picture plane or the perspectival whole. Space that was once architecturally legible becomes fragmented, undecided, and, in some sense, transgressive. There is the breakdown of the picture plane, of monocular perspective, and of scale. The *Carceri*'s tangle of bridges, balconies, stairways, and ruins seems to dispense with the picture frame; rather, it subsumes the viewer. Subject and object occupy the same space within a picture plane.

It has always been my desire to find a way to produce in my work such Piranesi-like space, a fragmented conception where people are moving in different kinds of vectorial space. This was the generative idea for the interstitial spaces at the Arizona stadium—the spaces between the exterior skin and the concourses, the places of vertical movement, and spaces where one can look down and up on people on different levels. Like the *Carceri* drawings, these spaces are not seen from a single view, but present a series of fractured views which give an idea, an affect, not a literal rendition of something, but something that in fact approximates an imagined series of spaces of movement and interchange.

1709 Ruins of the ancient city of Herculaneum are discovered. Excavations progress intermittently until 1738, when Charles III orders full-scale operations to commence under Roque Joaquín de Alcubierre.

1709–10 Venetian Cardinal Pietro Ottoboni (1667–1740), an active patron of the arts, commissions Filippo Juvarra (1678–1736) to construct a theater in the Cancelleria. Juvarra's lavish set designs for productions there will inspire Piranesi's drawn and engraved fantasies.

1711 Ferdinando Galli Bibiena (1657–1743) publishes *L'architettura civile*, one of several works on stage design which profoundly influence Piranesi.

1720 Giovanni Battista Piranesi is born on October 4 at Mojano di Mestre, near Venice, to Laura Lucchesi and Angelo Piranesi, a prosperous stone mason and master builder. Baptized on November 8 in the church of San Moisé, Venice.

1721 Johann Bernhard Fischer von Erlach (1656–1723), publishes *Entwurf einer historischen Architektur*, an important influence on Piranesi's imaginative reconstructions of antiquity.

Charles-Louis de Secondat, Baron de Montesquieu (1689–1755) anonymously publishes *Lettres persanes*—one of the first major works of the Enlightenment.

1724 A series of systematic excavations at Hadrian's Villa begins under Giuseppe Fede, Liborio Michilli, and Francesco Antonio Lolli, and continues until 1742.

1726 Completion of the Spanish Steps, a complex system of stairs and terraces in Rome designed by Francesco de' Sanctis (d. 1731), which connects Piazza di Spagna to S. Trinità dei Monti.

Members of the Accademia dell'Arcadia (to which Piranesi will be elected in the mid-1740s) hold their first meeting in the Bosco Parrasio on the Janiculum, designed by Antonio Canevari.

François Boucher arrives in Rome, where he will study at the Académie de France until 1731.

1730 Marco Ricci (1676–1730) publishes *Varia Marci Ricci pictoris prestantissimi experimenta*, which will inspire Piranesi's development of the architectural fantasy.

1732 Italian architect Nicola Salvi (1697–1751) begins work on his Fontana di Trevi in Rome. The fountain is later continued by Giuseppe Pannini and inaugurated in 1762.

1734 The Museo Capitolino is founded by Pope Clement XII, under the direction of Alessandro Gregorio Capponi.

1735 Piranesi is apprenticed to his maternal uncle, Matteo Lucchesi, an architect and hydraulics engineer in the Magistrato delle Acque, and studies perspective under Carlo Zucchi. After disagreements with Lucchesi, Piranesi is transferred to the studio of the neo-Palladian architect Giovanni Antonio Scalfurotto (ca. 1700–1764), where he may have been involved in the final stages of the church of SS. Simeone e Guida (built 1718–38), Venice.

Work begins on Alessandro Galilei's façade of S. Giovanni in Laterano and Ferdinando Fuga's Palazzo della Consulta.

Antonio Viscentini publishes *Prospectus Magni Canalis…*, containing engravings of the Grand Canal based on paintings by Canaletto.

William Hogarth (1697–1764) produces *A Rake's Progress*, an episodic series of paintings illustrating the decline of a corrupt young man from riches to death in a madhouse. This work is eventually incorporated by the Regency architect Sir John Soane into the Piranesian interior of his London house (now Sir John Soane's Museum).

1740 Piranesi moves to Rome as a draftsman in the retinue of the Venetian ambassador, Marco Foscarini (1696–1763). He is befriended by Monsignor Giovanni Bottari, librarian to the Corsini, and uses the library of the Venetian builder Niccola Giobbe. He studies stage design under the Valeriani brothers and learns graphic techniques, particularly etching, in the studio of Giuseppe Vasi (1710-1782), the leading purveyor of engraved views of Rome.

Prospero Lambertini (1675–1758) is elected Pope Benedict XIV, a great patron of the arts. He will found new schools, establish chairs for the study of science, mathematics, and medicine, and expand the Vatican Library and archives. Giuseppe Galli Bibiena publishes *Architetture e Prospettive*, a work of considerable influence on Piranesi's architectural fantasies.

1741 Piranesi begins collaboration with young French artists studying at the Académie de France in Rome on a series of plates for guidebooks to the city, which had become a focal point of the Grand Tour.

Work begins on Fuga's façade of S. Maria Maggiore.

Canaletto publishes imaginary views of Venice in *Vedute altre prese dai luoghi, altre ideate*.

1743 Piranesi publishes the *Prima parte di architetture e prospettive*, a book of imaginary buildings of monumental scale and originality. This first independent production is dedicated to Niccola Giobbe.

1743–44 Piranesi returns several times to Venice, where he encounters, and possibly studies, under Giambattista Tiepolo (1695–1770), who issues his engraved *Capricci*.

1744 Piranesi travels to Naples and visits the excavations at Herculaneum. He returns to Venice, where he produces interior designs for certain palaces.

1747 After a substantial stay in Venice, Piranesi finally returns to Rome as an agent for the print dealer Joseph Wagner (1706–1780) and opens his establishment in the Via del Corso, opposite the Académie de France. He produces the four plates of the *Grotteschi*.

Giuseppe Vasi issues the first volume of his *Delle magnificenze di Roma antica e moderna*, a ten-volume work completed in 1761.

Cardinal Alessandro Albani begins construction of his celebrated villa on the Via Salaria (to the designs of Carlo Marchionni), which is completed in 1767. A print of the exterior will be included by Piranesi among his *Vedute di Roma* in 1769.

1748 Piranesi publishes his first independent set of *vedute*, entitled *Antichità Romane de' tempi della Repubblica e de' primi Imperatori* (later reissued in the early 1760s as *Alcune Vedute di Archi Trionfali…*), dedicated to Giovanni Bottari. He moves from more modest plate size to the larger format as he initiates his major series, the *Vedute di Roma*, in separate plates and in batches throughout the remainder of his career.

Italian cartographer and architect Giovanni Battista Nolli (1701–1756) publishes his definitive map of Rome, providing the most accurate survey of Roman monuments, ancient and contemporary, to date. Piranesi provdes vignettes for a reduced version of the map.

Excavations begin at Pompeii under Alcubierre.

1750 Piranesi issues the first edition of *Invenzioni capric di Carceri...Opere Varie...* (the latter being a reprinting of *Prima parte di Architettura* with additional fantasies). The latter influences a new generation of students at the Académie de France, including Charles de Wailly (1730–1798) and Marie-Joseph Peyre (1730-1785).

He issues the folio *Camere sepolcrali degli antichi Romani le quali esistono dentro e di fuori di Roma*.

The Scottish architect William Chambers (1723–1796) arrives in Rome, where he meets Piranesi and remains until 1755. The English painter Joshua Reynolds (1723–1792) arrives in Rome, staying until 1752.

1751 The first volume is published of the *Encyclopédie, ou Dictionnaire raisonné des sciences, des arts et des métiers...* The French philosopher Denis Diderot (1713–1784) assumes the role of general editor by 1747, and more than one hundred leading intellectual figures of the day contribute by the time it is completed in 1780.

1752 Piranesi marries Angelica Pasquini, daughter of the gardener to Prince Corsini.

1753 Piranesi publishes *Trofei de Ottaviano Augusto* to provide outstanding examples of Roman architectural decoration as "useful to painters, sculptors and architects."

The initial phase of the Graeco-Roman controversy opens when the *Essai sur l'architecture* is published by French Jesuit Marc-Antoine Laugier (1713–1769). In this work, he asserts that the first fundamental dwelling, the rustic hut, was developed by Ancient Greece and that the pure ideals of the Greeks displayed were corrupted and debased by the Romans.

1754 The view painter Gian Paolo Pannini becomes Principe of the Accademia di San Luca.

The French painter Hubert Robert (1733–1803) arrrives in Rome, where he will stay until 1765.

The French architect Julien-David Le Roy (1724–1803) visits Greece.

1755 Birth of Piranesi's daughter, Laura, who later works in the family print business and subsequently publishes reduced versions of her father's *vedute*. The Scottish architect Robert Adam (1728–1792) arrives in Rome with the French architect Charles-Louis Clérisseau (1721–1820), whom he had met in Florence. The latter introduces him to Piranesi, who will critically influence the development of Adam's career and subsequent works in Britain. The Scottish architect Robert Mylne (1733–1811), together with his brother William, arrives in Rome and stays until 1759. The impact of Piranesi's archaeological ideas contributes to his winning design for Blackfriars Bridge, London, in 1760 (etched under construction by Piranesi in 1764 from the working drawings).

Johann Joachim Winckelmann (1717–1768), the greatest advocate for the Hellenists' claims, publishes *Gedanken über die Nachahmung der Griechischen Werke in der Malerei und Bildhauerkunst* (*On the Imitation of the Painting and Sculpture of the Greeks*), shortly before arriving in Rome to be librarian to Cardinal Alessandro Albani.

The French painter Jean-Honoré Fragonard (1732–1806) arrives in Rome, where he will remain until 1761.

1756 After intensive archaeological studies, Piranesi publishes the four-volume *Le Antichità romane* with more than 250 plates as a comprehensive survey of ancient Roman architecture. In it, he criticizes contemporary architects for failing to use the remains of antiquity as inspiration.

1757 Piranesi is made an honorary member of the Society of Antiquaries of London. He issues his first polemical work, *Lettere di giustificazione...a Milord Charlemont*, a pamphlet addressed to the Irishman Lord Charlemont, the promised patron of *Le Antichità romane*, who failed to provide financial support. Piranesi circulates this to colleagues and influential patrons.

Adam and Clérisseau make detailed studies of the ruins of the Emperor Diocletian's Palace at Spalato (now Split) before the former returns to London.

A folio on this subject is published in 1764, dedicated to George III.

Edmund Burke (1729–1797) publishes *A Philosophical enquiry into the origin of our ideas of the Sublime and Beautiful*.

1758 Birth of Piranesi's first son, Francesco, who later trains to be an engraver and collaborates with his father in his later works. George Dance the Younger (1741–1825) arrives in Rome, where he will remain until 1764. Piranesi has a profound effect on the former's highly original design of Newgate Prison, London (1770–80).

Julien-David Le Roy publishes *Les ruines des plus beaux monuments de la Grèce*, the first published evidence, based on the Athenian monuments, in support of claims to the Greeks' architectural superiority.

The Venetian Carlo della Torre Rezzonico (1693–1769) is elected Pope Clement XIII. The Pope and his family will become Piranesi's key patrons.

1759 Charles III of Naples initiates the publication of *Le Antichità di Ercolano esposte* in eight volumes (1757–92).

1761 Piranesi formally enters the Graeco-Roman debate with the publication of *Della magnificenza ed architettura de'Romani*, which defends the cultural origins of Rome. The work is dedicated to Clement XIII. This work is followed by the publication of his study of the ancient Roman aqueduct system in *Le Rovine del Castello dell'Acqua Giulia*.

Piranesi establishes his own printmaking business and showrooms in Palazzo Tomati, on Via Sistina, as the leading topographical engraver in Rome. He is elected to the Accademia di San Luca, the leading artistic institution in Rome, an event commemorated in the Accademia by a portrait bust produced by the British sculptor Joseph Nollekens.

Piranesi reissues the heavily reworked *Invenzioni capric di carceri*, with two additional plates, now titled *Carceri d'invenzione*.

Anton Raphael Mengs completes his ceiling fresco *Parnassus* in the Villa Albani as a major statement of the new classicism in contemporary painting.

1762 Piranesi publishes further archaeological folios with a polemical edge: *Lapides Capitolini*, featuring a vast inscription from the Forum Romanum; *Descrizione e disegno dell'emissario del lago Albano*, featuring the design and construction of the drainage outlet to Lake Albano (with the appendix *Di due spelonche ornate dagli antichi alla riva del lago Albano*); and *Il Campo Marzio dell' Antica Roma*, dedicated to Robert Adam, which celebrates the Romans' originality in urban design.

The Trevi Fountain is completed.

1763 Pope Clement XIII commissions designs for a new pontifical altar and tribune for S. Giovanni in Laterano from Piranesi, who draws up several schemes.

Winckelmann is made Prefect of Roman Antiquities.

The Treaty of Paris ends the Seven Years' War with the victory of England and Prussia.

1764 Piranesi is commissioned by Cardinal Giambattista Rezzonico (Grand Prior of the Order since 1761) to renovate and embellish the Church of the Knights of Malta, S. Maria del Priorato. The only architectural work that Piranesi will execute, the project is completed in 1766.

Piranesi publishes the folios *Antichità di Albano e di Castelgandolfo* and *Antichità di Cora*, as well as *Raccolta di alcuni disegni del...Guercino*.

Pierre-Jean Mariette publishes a critical letter in the *Gazette littéraire de l'Europe* attacking Piranesi's arguments in *Della magnificenza*.

Winckelmann publishes *Geschichte der Kunst des Altertums* (*The History of the Art of Antiquity*), the first survey of ancient art.

1765 Piranesi responds to the criticisms of *Della magnificenza* in a three-part apologia: *Osservazioni sopra la letter de M. Mariette*, outlining his artistic beliefs; *Parere su l'architettura* (*Opinions on Architecture*), a dialogue between two rival architects in which he puts the case for a new and eclectic system of design; and *Della Introduzione e del progresso delle belle arti in Europa nei tempi antichi*, which includes a discussion on Etruscan art.

MID-1760S Piranesi designs a painted decorative scheme for the Caffè degli Inglesi in Piazza di Spagna, the first complete Egyptian Revival interior. During this decade, he designs interiors for Pope Clement XIII at Castelgandolfo, in Palazzo Quirinale for Cardinal Giambattista Rezzonico, and in Palazzo Senatorio on the Capitoline Hill for Senator Abbondio Rezzonico (none of these schemes survive).

1766 Piranesi is invested as a knight of the Sperone d'Oro when Pope Clement XIII visits the completed Priory Church in October 1766.

1768 The Royal Academy of Arts is founded in London, with the painter Joshua Reynolds (1723–1792) as its president. Its mission is to raise the status of the artistic profession through academic training, free exhibition of works, and the promotion of a national school of art.

1769 Piranesi's *Diverse maniere d' adornare I cammini ed ogni altra parte degli edifizi desunte dall' architettura Egiza, Etrusca e Greca* (*Diverse ways of ornamenting chimneys and all other parts of houses taken from Egyptian, Tuscan and Grecian architecture*) is published and dedicated to Cardinal Giambattista Rezzonico. It will be Piranesi's final polemical and theoretical work, as well as his principal publication concerning design.

Pope Clement XIII dies and is succeeded by Giovan Vincenzo Antonio Ganganelli, Clement XIV. As the Rezzonicos' patronage decreases, Piranesi develops his printmaking business to attract foreign customers, especially British collectors on the Grand Tour. For the same market, he continues the production of chimneypieces, involving classical fragments, and the imaginative restoration of decorative antiquities such as vases and candelabra, displayed in his "museo," or showrooms. Much of his material comes from excavations at Hadrian's Villa undertaken with the artist and dealer Gavin Hamilton.

1770 Piranesi makes a series of expeditions to record the excavations at Pompeii.

The Museo Clementino opens to check the quantity of ancient art exported from Rome, initiating a major restructuring of the Vatican collection of antiquities.

1771 Original fragments of the monumental Warwick Vase (now in the Burell Collection, Glasgow) are excavated by painter Gavin Hamilton (1723–1798) in the Pantanello area of Hadrian's Villa, and restored to Piranesi's design before its sale to the connoisseur Sir William Hamilton.

1774 While on his Grand Tour, George Grenville, nephew and heir to Lord Temple, commissions a chimneypiece from Piranesi for his country house at Stowe, Buckinghamshire (later transferred to the Banco de Santander, Spain). He also acquires a restored antiquity from the artist, the Buckingham Vase (now in Los Angeles). In the same year, the connoisseur Patrick Home acquires from Piranesi's showrooms in Rome a marble chimneypiece, which is incorporated by Robert Adam into his interior design for Wedderburn Castle, Scotland.

1774–79 With considerable studio help, Piranesi issues the composite publication *Trofeo o sia magnifica colonna coclide…*, which meticulously records three monumental relief columns in Rome: of Trajan, Marcus Aurelius (the Antonine Column), and Antoninus and Faustina.

1775 Sir Roger Newdigate acquires from Piranesi two highly ornamental candelabra, originally found in fragments at Hadrian's Villa, and presents them to the University of Oxford (now in the Ashmolean Museum).

Pope Clement XIV dies and is succeeded by Giovan Angelo Braschi as Pius VI.

1776 Piranesi's four etched plates of interiors at Syon House (dated 1761), the Duke of Northumberland's country seat outside London, which was remodeled by Robert Adam in the 1760s, first appear in an installment to volume two of *The Works in Architecture of Robert and James Adam* (republished in 1779).

Edward Gibbon publishes the first volume of *The Decline and Fall of the Roman Empire*.

Work is begun on the Teatro alla Scala, Milan, designed by Guiseppe Piermarini (1734–1808).

Major architectural projects are initiated at the Vatican by Pope Pius VI, including the New Sacristy of St Peter's by Carlo Marchionni and two branches of the Museo Pio-Clementino by Michelangelo Simonetti.

1777 Piranesi visits and sketches the Greek temples at Paestum, accompanied by his son Franceso, assistant Benedetto Mori, and the architect Augusto Rosa.

1778 Piranesi's recreation of decorative antiquities, recorded in individual prints over the decade, are issued in two volumes as the *Vasi, candelabri, cippi, sarcofagi, tripodi, lucerne, ed ornamenti antichi*. Returning from Paestum to Rome (where he meets the young English architect John Soane), he begins etching the plates of *Différentes vues de quelques restes de trois grands édifices qui subsistent encore dans l'ancenne ville de Pesto*. This is completed and published posthumously by Francesco.

Piranesi dies on November 9 in Rome, and is initially buried in S. Andrea delle Fratte. At the orders of Cardinal Rezzonico, he is finally laid to rest in his only executed work of architecture, the priory church of the Knights of Malta on the Aventine. His intended funerary monument, a large marble candelabrum (now in the Louvre), is placed nearby, but is replaced sometime after 1786 by Giovanni Angelini's full-length statue of the artist.

1781 Francesco Piranesi issues his father's plan of Hadrian's Villa, *Pianta delle fabriche esistenti nella Villa Adriana*, based on surveys made by his father throughout his career, particularly between 1765 and 1774. This is dedicated to Stanislaus Augustus, King of Poland.

1791 Francesco publishes his father's *Dimostrazione dell'Emissario del Lago Fucino*. The large double-plate, showing the drainage tunnel dug by the Emperor Claudius (AD 41–54), is dedicated to Ferdinand IV and Maria Carolina of Naples.

1804–07 Francesco etches and publishes his father's views of the excavations of Pompeii, made in 1770, in *Les antiquités de la Grande Grèce*.

LIST OF ILLUSTRATIONS

Full information on the images in this publication are provided below. CH denotes objects featured in the *Piranesi as Designer* exhibition at Cooper-Hewitt, National Design Museum; T denotes objects featured in the exhibition at the Teylers Museum, Haarlem, the Netherlands.

Unless otherwise stated, all works are by Giovanni Battista Piranesi (Italian, 1720–1778).

COVER

CH|T

PIER TABLE, ca. 1768
Oak, lime wood, marble, gilt
90.2 x 149.9 x 74.3 cm
(35 1/2 x 59 x 29 1/4 in.)
Lent by the Rijksmuseum,
Amsterdam, the Netherlands

HALF-TITLE
AND FOREWORD

CH|T

Carlo Labruzzi
(Italian, 1748–1817)
PORTRAIT OF GIOVANNI
BATTISTA PIRANESI, 1779
Oil on canvas
710 x 580 mm
(27 15/16 x 22 13/16 in.)
Lent by the Museo di Roma,
Palazzo Braschi

DESIGN THROUGH FANTASY:
PIRANESI AS DESIGNER

Frontispiece.
DESIGN FOR A CHIMNEYPIECE
AND CHAIR, n.d.
Pen and brown ink over black
chalk on off-white
laid paper
18.9 x 35.6 cm (7 7/16 x 14 in.)
Lent by The Pierpont Morgan Library.
Bequest of Junius S. Morgan
and gift of Henry S. Morgan.
Acc. no. 1966.11:86

CH|T

1. Francesco (Felice) Polanzani
(Italian, 1700–after 1783)
PORTRAIT OF GIOVANNI BATTISTA
PIRANESI AS AN ANTIQUE BUST, 1750
Etching and engraving
on off-white laid paper
610 x 460 mm (24 x 18 1/8 in.)
Lent by John Wilton-Ely

CH|T

2. THE IMPERIAL MAUSOLEUM
(MAUSOLEO ANTICO), plate III from
PRIMA PARTE DI ARCHITETTURE

E PROSPETTIVE, 1743
Etching on off-white laid paper
350 x 250 mm
(13 13/16 x 9 7/8 in.)
Lent by Smithsonian Institution
Libraries, Cooper-Hewitt,
National Design Museum

CH|T

3. DESIGN FOR A "BISSONA,"
OR FESTIVAL GONDOLA, n.d.
Pen and brown ink, over black chalk,
on paper; (verso) graphite
297 x 683 mm (11 11/16 x 26 7/8 in.)
Lent by The Pierpont Morgan Library.
Bequest of Junius S. Morgan and gift
of Henry S. Morgan. Acc. No.
1966.11:10

CH|T

4. TOMB OF NERO, from the series
GROTTESCHI, 1750
Etching on off-white laid paper
395 x 520 mm (15 1/2 x 20 1/2 in.)
Lent by Smithsonian Institution
Libraries, Cooper-Hewitt,
National Design Museum

5. HALL IN THE CORINTHIAN ORDER...
(SALA ALL'USO DEGLI ANTICHI
ROMANI CON COLONNE...), plate VI
from PRIMA PARTE DI ARCHITETTURE
E PROSPETTIVE, 1743
Etching on off-white laid paper
245 x 365 mm (9 5/8 x 14 3/8 in.)
Lent by Smithsonian Institution
Libraries, Cooper-Hewitt,
National Design Museum

CH|T

6. ARCHITECTURAL FANTASY
WITH COLOSSAL ARCADED FAÇADE
OVERLOOKING A PIAZZA WITH
MONUMENTS, n.d.
Pen and brown ink, with brown
wash, over graphite, perspective lines
and details in red chalk, on paper;
irregularly trimmed along lower edge
270 x 428 mm (10 9/16 x 16 7/8 in.)

Lent by The Pierpont Morgan Library,
Purchased as the gift of Miss Alice
Tully. Acc. No. 71.4

7. ORNEMENTI DI STUCCO, ESISTENTI
NELLA VOLTA DELLS STANZE
SEPOLCRALE DI L. ARRUNZIO
(STUCCO DECORATIONS ON THE
VAULT OF THE TOMB CHAMBER
OF L. ARRUNTIUS), plate XII, vol. 2,
LE ANTICHITÀ ROMANE, 1756–57
Etching on off-white laid paper
390 x 595 mm (15 3/8 x 23 7/16 in.)
Lent by Smithsonian Institution
Libraries, Dibner Library

CH|T

8. William Chambers
(Scottish, 1723–1796)
SECTIONAL PERSPECTIVE OF
PROJECTED MAUSOLEUM FOR
FREDERICK, PRINCE OF WALES,
February 1752
Pen and ink, brush and watercolor
on off-white laid paper executed
by John Yenn
324 x 483 mm (12 3/4 x 19 in.)
Lent by The British Architectural
Library, Drawings and Archives
Division, Victoria and Albert Museum

CH|T

9. ROMAN IONIC CAPITALS COMPARED
WITH GREEK EXAMPLES BY LE ROY,
plate 20 from DELLA MAGNIFICENZE
ED ARCHITETTURA DE' ROMANI, 1761
Etching on off-white laid paper
390 x 590 mm (15 3/8 x 23 1/4 in.)
Lent by Smithsonian Institution
Libraries, Cooper-Hewitt, National
Design Museum

CH|T

10. FRONTISPIECE WITH DEDICATION
TO ROBERT ADAM, from IL CAMPO
MARZIO DELL'ANTICA ROMA,
published in Rome, 1762
445 x 235 mm (17 1/2 x 9 1/4 in.)
Lent by Smithsonian Institution
Libraries, Cooper-Hewitt,
National Design Museum

T

11. "ICHNOGRAPHIA," OR PLAN
OF THE CAMPUS MARTIUS OF THE
ANCIENT CITY, plate V–X from
IL CAMPO MARZIO DELL'ANTICA

ROMA, published in Rome, 1762
1350 x 1170 mm (53 x 46 in.)
Cooper-Hewitt, National Design
Museum, Smithsonian Institution

CH|T

12. PREPARATORY DRAWING
FOR PLATE IV OF THE SERIES
"CARCERI D'INVENZIONE," ca. 1749
Pen and light brown ink, brush
and brown wash over black chalk
on off-white laid paper
218 x 252 mm (8 1/2 x 10 in.)
Lent by The National Gallery
of Scotland

CH|T

13. THE DRAWBRIDGE, plate VII
for the series CARCERI D'INVEN-
ZIONE (early state), ca. 1749
Etching on off-white laid paper
550 x 410 mm (21 11/16 x 16 1/8 in.)
Lent by the Arthur Ross Foundation

CH|T

14. THE DRAWBRIDGE, plate VII
for the series CARCERI D'INVEN-
ZIONE (late state), ca. 1760s
Etching on off-white laid paper
550 x 410 mm (21 11/16 x 16 1/8 in.)
Lent by the Arthur Ross Foundation

CH

15. ELEVATION LOOKING EAST SHOWING
THE COLONNADE SEPARATING THE
AMBULATORY FROM THE PRESBYTERY
(TAVOLA 10)
Pen and brown ink, brush
and brown wash over graphite
on off-white laid paper
876 x 564 mm (34 1/2 x 22 3/16 in.)
Lent by the Avery Architectural and
Fine Arts Library, Columbia University

CH|T

16. ARCHITECTURAL FANTASY WITH
MONUMENTAL PORTICO BEFORE
A PALACE, ca. 1763
Pen and brown ink and wash
over red chalk
500 x 360 mm (19 11/16 x 14 3/16 in.)
Lent by Biblioteca Comunale
dell'Archiginnasio, Bologna

CH|T

17. DESIGN FOR THE RELIQUARY
IN THE BALDACCHINO

Pen and brown ink, with grey
and brown wash over black chalk
on off-white laid paper
337 x 184 mm (13 1/4 x 7 1/4 in.)
Lent by The Pierpont Morgan Library.
Bequest of Junius S. Morgan
and gift of Henry S. Morgan.
Acc. no. 1966.11:110

CH

18. PIAZZALE DE'CAVALIERI
DI MALTA looking southwest
(modern photograph)
Lent by John Wilton-Ely

19. PRELIMINARY DESIGN FOR
ENTRANCE SCREEN TO S. MARIA DEL
PRIORATO, ROME (DETAIL), 1764
Pen and brown ink on off-white
laid paper
506 x 741 mm (19 15/16 x 29 3/16 in.)
Lent by Kunstbibliothek, Berlin,
Hdz 6303

CH|T

20. DESIGN FOR DECORATIVE RELIEF
PANEL BELOW CENTRAL STELA
OF SOUTH WALL, PIAZZALE DE'
CAVALIERI DI MALTA, ROME, 1765-66
Pen and brown ink over black chalk,
additional work in black chalk
on off-white laid paper
216 x 379 mm (8 1/2 x 14 5/16 in.)
Lent by The Pierpont Morgan Library.
Bequest of Junius S. Morgan
and gift of Henry S. Morgan.
Acc. No.1966.11:54

CH|T

21. DESIGN FOR A VERTICAL WALL
PANEL WITH MALTESE CROSS
AND INSIGNIA OF THE REZZONICO
FAMILY FOR S. MARIA DEL PRIORATO,
ROME, 1765-66
black chalk, pen and brown ink
on off-white laid paper
297 x 683 mm (11 11/16 x 26 7/8 in.)
Lent by The Pierpont Morgan Library.
Bequest of Junius S. Morgan and gift
of Henry S. Morgan. Acc. No.1966.11:53

CH

22. DETAIL OF FAÇADE, S. MARIA DEL
PRIORATO (modern photograph)
Lent by John Wilton-Ely

23. DETAIL OF SPHINX CAPITAL, plate XIII
from DELLA MAGNIFICENZA ED
ARCHITETTURA DE'ROMANI, 1761
Etching on off-white laid paper
395 x 255 mm (15 9/16 x 10 1/16 in.)
Smithsonian Institution
Libraries, Cooper-Hewitt,
National Design Museum

CH

24. INTERIOR OF THE NAVE, S. MARIA
DEL PRIORATO (modern photograph)
Lent by John Wilton-Ely

CH|T

25. PREPARATORY DRAWING FOR
THE HIGH ALTAR OF S. MARIA
DEL PRIORATO, ROME, FLANKED
BY CANDLESTICKS, 1764-65
Pen and brown ink on off-white
laid paper
118 x 117 mm (4 5/8 x 4 9/16 in.)
Lent by The Pierpont Morgan Library.
Bequest of Junius S. Morgan and gift
of Henry S. Morgan. Acc. No.1952.26

CH|T

26. PRELIMINARY DESIGN FOR
HIGH ALTAR, S. MARIA DEL
PRIORATO, ROME, 1764
Black chalk with traces of pen
and ink on off-white laid paper
304 x 186 mm (11 15/16 x 7 5/16 in.)
Lent by The Kunstbibliothek, Berlin

CH|T

27. DESIGN FOR THE HIGH ALTAR,
S. MARIA DEL PRIORATO, ROME,
1765-66
Pen and brown ink, brush with
gray and brown wash, over black
chalk on off-white laid paper
472 x 365 mm (18 1/2 x 14 3/8 in.)
Lent by The Pierpont Morgan Library.
Bequest of Junius S. Morgan and gift
of Henry S. Morgan. Acc. No.1966.11:51

CH|T

28. DESIGN FOR THE CENTRAL RELIEF
PANEL OF THE VAULT, S. MARIA
DEL PRIORATO, ROME, 1765-66
Pen and brown ink, with gray
wash over black chalk on off-white
laid paper, framing line in pen
and brown ink
534 x 318 mm (21 1/16 x 12 1/2 in.)
Lent by The Pierpont Morgan Library.
Bequest of Junius S. Morgan and
gift of Henry S. Morgan. Acc.
No.1966.11:50

CH|T

29. DETAIL OF THE TOMB OF ADMIRAL
FRÀ SERIPANDO SHOWING
PIRANESI'S ORNAMENTAL RELIEF
INVOLVING NAVAL SYMBOLS
(modern photograph)
Lent by John Wilton-Ely

30. CHIMNEYPIECE DESIGNED
FOR LORD EXETER, from DIVERSE
MANIERE D'ADORNARE...,
published in Rome, 1769
Etching on off-white laid paper

340 x 240 mm (13 3/8 x 9 7/16 in.)
Smithsonian Institution
Libraries, Cooper-Hewitt,
National Design Museum

CH|T

31. CHIMNEYPIECE DESIGNED
FOR JOHN HOPE, from DIVERSE
MANIERE D'ADORNARE...,
published in Rome, 1769
Etching on off-white laid paper
383 x 245 mm (15 1/16 x 9 5/8 in.)
Lent by Smithsonian Institution
Libraries, Cooper-Hewitt,
National Design Museum

CH|T

32. Charles Percier (French, 1764–1838)
and Pierre-François-Léonard Fontaine
(French, 1762–1853)
DESIGN FOR A TABLE WITH
MONOPODS, from RECUEIL
DES DÉCORATIONS INTÉRIEURES,
published in Paris, 1812
Etching on white laid paper
Cooper-Hewitt, National Design
Museum, Smithsonian Institution
Purchased for the Museum by the
Advisory Council, 1921-6-377-39

CH|T

33. Jean-Démosthène Dugourc
(French, 1749–1825) after François-
Joseph Bélanger (French, 1744–1818)
DESIGN FOR TWO ANDIRONS AND
A SCONCE OF GILT BRONZE FOR THE
PAVILLON DE BAGATELLE, PARIS, 1777
Pen and ink, brush and yellow, green,
blue, and brown watercolor on white
laid paper, lined and mounted
205 x 293 mm (8 1/16 x 11 9/16 in.)
Cooper-Hewitt, National Design
Museum, Smithsonian Institution
Purchased for the Museum by
the Advisory Council, 1921-6-61

CH|T

34. SKETCH DESIGN FOR CHIMNEYPIECE
WITH CONFRONTED ELEPHANT
HEADS, before 1769
Pen and brown ink over black chalk
on off-white laid paper
213 x322 mm (8 1/2 x 12 1/2 in.)
Lent by The Pierpont Morgan Library.
Bequest of Junius S. Morgan and
gift of Henry S. Morgan. 1966.11:61

CH|T

35. SKETCH DESIGN FOR PART OF
AN INTERIOR SCHEME WITH
CHIMNEYPIECE, n.d.
Pen and brown ink with inscriptions
710 x 532 mm (27 15/16 x 20 15/16 in.)
Lent by The Kunstbibliothek, Berlin

36. Robert Adam
(Scottish, 1728–1792)
ETRUSCAN DRESSING ROOM,
OSTERLEY PARK, MIDDLESEX,
ENGLAND, ca. 1775
The National Trust for Places of
Historic Interest or Natural Beauty

CH|T

37. Louis-Jean Desprez
(French, 1743–1804; active in Sweden)
SEPULCHER IN EGYPTIAN STYLE WITH
CARYATIDS AND A LION, ca. 1779–84
Pen and black ink; brush and brown,
gray, blue-gray wash; traces of
graphite on off-white laid paper
145 x 289 mm (5 11/16 x 11 3/8 in.)
Cooper-Hewitt, National Design
Museum, Smithsonian Institution
Museum purchase through gift
of various donors and from Eleanor
G. Hewitt Fund, 1938-88-3950

38. EGYPTIAN DECORATION OF THE
CAFFÈ DEGLI INGLESI: ADDORSED
SPHINXES AT THE CENTER OF THE
CORNICE, from DIVERSE MANIERE
D'ADORNARE I CAMMINI..., 1769
Etching on off-white laid paper
210 x 270 mm (8 1/4 x 10 5/8 in.)
Smithsonian Institution
Libraries, Cooper-Hewitt,
National Design Museum

39. EGYPTIAN DECORATION OF THE CAFFÈ
DEGLI INGLESI: ANIMALS ON THE
CORNICE, INCLUDING A BULL AT
THE CENTER, from DIVERSE MANIERE
D'ADORNARE I CAMMINI..., 1769
Etching on off-white laid paper
210 x 320 mm (8 1/4 x 12 5/8 in.)
Smithsonian Institution
Libraries, Cooper-Hewitt,
National Design Museum

CH|T

40. Thomas Hope (Scottish, 1769–1831)
EGYPTIAN OR BLACK ROOM,
DUCHESS STREET, from HOUSEHOLD
FURNITURE AND INTERIOR DECORA-
TION, published in London, 1807
305 x 483 x 584 mm (12 x 19 x 23 in.)
Lent by Smithsonian Institution
Libraries, Cooper-Hewitt,
National Design Museum

CH|T

41. Thomas Hope (Scottish, 1769–1831)
SETTEE IN THE EGYPTIAN TASTE
FROM THE EGYPTIAN ROOM,
DUCHESS STREET, LONDON, 1800–04
Mahogany, painted black
and gold with bronze mounts
76.2 x 172.7 x 71 cm (30 x 68 x 28 in.)
Lent by The Powerhouse Museum.

Purchased with the assistance of the patrons of the Powerhouse Fund, 1987. Bronze lions reproduced courtesy of Lord Faringdon, Buscot Park, England. The assistance of George Levy, H. Blairman & Sons, London, is gratefully acknowledged.

CH|T

42. DESIGN FOR SCONCES, n.d.
Red chalk over black chalk on off-white laid paper
234 x 132 mm (9 1/4 x 5 1/4 in.)
Lent by The Pierpont Morgan Library. Bequest of Junius S. Morgan and gift of Henry S. Morgan. Acc. No. 1966.11:106

CH|T

43. DESIGN FOR A WALL PANEL IN THE FORM OF A ROCOCO SHIELD WITH SCONCES, n.d.
Pen and brown ink, brush and brown wash, over black chalk on off-white laid paper
293 x 237 mm (11 9/16 x 9 5/16 in.)
Lent by The Pierpont Morgan Library. Bequest of Junius S. Morgan and gift of Henry S. Morgan. Acc. No. 1966.11:11

CH|T

44 PIER TABLE, ca. 1768
Oak, lime wood, marble, gilt
90.2 x 149.9 x 74.3 cm
(35 1/2 x 59 x 29 1/4 in.)
Lent by the Rijksmuseum, Amsterdam, the Netherlands

CH|T

45. SKETCH DESIGNS FOR PART OF A TABLE, n.d.
Pen and brown ink over red chalk on off-white laid paper
20 x 146 mm (7 7/8 x 5 3/4 in.)
Lent by The Victoria and Albert Museum

CH|T

46. FURNITURE INCLUDING A SIDE TABLE DESIGNED FOR MONSIGNOR REZZONICO, from DIVERSE MANIERE..., published in Rome, 1769
Etching on cream laid paper
19.1 x 83.8 x 58.4 cm (7 1/2 x 33 x 23 in.)
Lent by Smithsonian Institution Libraries, Cooper-Hewitt, National Design Museum

CH|T

47. DESIGN FOR A CLOCK IN THE FORM OF A PINEAPPLE, n.d.
Red and black chalk on off-white laid paper
115 x 620 mm (4 1/2 x 24 7/16 in.)

The Pierpont Morgan Library. Bequest of Junius S. Morgan and gift of Henry S. Morgan. Acc. No. 1966.11:103

CH|T

48. SKETCH DESIGNS FOR TWO COMMODES, n.d.
Pen and brown ink on off-white laid paper
240 x 186 mm (9 7/16 x 7 5/16 in.)
Lent by the Gahlin Collection

CH|T

49. SKETCH DESIGN FOR A COMMODE, n.d.
Pen and brown ink on off-white laid paper
122 x 154 mm (4 13/16 x 6 1/16 in.)
Lent by the Gahlin Collection

CH|T

50. SHEET OF SKETCH DESIGNS FOR BODYWORK OF COACHES, n.d.
Pen and brown ink with traces of graphite on off-white laid paper
231 x 345 mm (9 1/8 x 13 9/16 in.)
The Pierpont Morgan Library. Bequest of Junius S. Morgan and gift of Henry S. Morgan. Acc. No. 1966.11:100

CH|T

51. Thomas Hope (Scottish, 1769–1831)
CLOCK IN THE EGYPTIAN STYLE, n.d.
Bronze, ormolu, and rosso antico marble
50.2 x 29.5 x 19.7 cm
(19 3/4 x 11 5/8 x 7 3/4 in.)
Lent by The Royal Pavilion, Library & Museum, Brighton & Hove

CH|T

52. PERSPECTIVE VIEW OF THE WARWICK VASE, FOUND AT THE PANTANELLO, HADRIAN'S VILLA, TIVOLI, IN 1771, from VASI, CANDELABRI, CIPPI, SARCOFAGI..., 1778
Etching on off-white laid paper
720 x 475 mm (28 3/8 x 18 11/16 in.)
Lent by Smithsonian Institution Libraries, Cooper-Hewitt, National Design Museum

CH|T

53. AUTOGRAPH LETTER FROM GIOVANNI BATTISTA PIRANESI TO CHARLES TOWNLEY, WITH DRAWING OF THE WARWICK VASE ACCOMPANIED BY DIMENSIONS, 3 August 1772
Pen and ink on off-white laid paper
The Pierpont Morgan Library, Purchase; Mr. John P. Morgan II, Miss Julia P. Wightman, and Mrs. Charles Wrightsman, in memory of Mrs. J. P. Morgan, 1985. Acc. No. MA 4220

54. Unknown Roman, restored by Giovanni Battista Piranesi
SERPENT-HANDLED VASE WITH EROTES AMONG GRAPEVINES
Hadrianic period, AD 117–38
Marble
116.84 x 99.06 x 73.66 cm
(46 x 39 x 29 in.)
William Randolph Hearst Collection, Los Angles County Museum of Art

CH|T

55. Rebecca Emes and Edward Barnard (English, active 1804–ca. 1829)
THE DONCASTER RACE CUP OF 1828
Silver gilt
H: 39.25 cm (15 1/2 in.)
Lent by The Leeds Art Galleries, Lotherton Hall

CH|T

56. Joseph Barnard, Edward Barnard & Sons (English, est. ca. 1680) after Giovanni Battista Piranesi
WINE COOLER, 1828
Silver gilt
36.2 x 30.5 x 22.2 cm
(14 1/4 x 12 x 8 3/4 in.)
Lent by the Minneapolis Institute of Arts, Gift of Ruth and John Huss

CH|T

57. PERSPECTIVE OF NEWDIGATE CANDELABRUM WITH CRANES, from VASI, CANDELABRI. CIPPI, SARCOFAGI..., 1778
Etching on off-white laid paper
665 x 415 mm (26 3/16 x 16 1/4 in.)
Lent by Smithsonian Institution Libraries, Cooper-Hewitt, National Design Museum

CH|T

58. ELEVATION OF PIRANESI'S OWN FUNERARY CANDELABRUM WITH PUTTI, from VASI, CANDELABRI. CIPPI, SARCOFAGI..., 1778
Etching on off-white laid paper
655 x 415 mm (25 13/16 x 16 3/8 in.)
Lent by Smithsonian Institution Libraries, Cooper-Hewitt, National Design Museum

CH|T

59. DESIGN FOR AN OVERDOOR DECORATION WITH TROPHIES IN THE LUNETTE AND WINGED SERPENTS AND DOLPHINS IN SPANDRELS FOR MAIN SALON OF VILLA ALBANI, ROME, n.d.
Red and black chalk on off-white laid paper
266 x 560 mm (10 1/2 x 22 1/16 in.)
Lent by The Pierpont Morgan Library. Bequest of Junius S. Morgan and

gift of Henry S. Morgan. Acc. no. 1966.11:35

CH|T

60. FOUNTAIN WITH UPPER BASIN TOPED BY A PINE CONE SUPPORTED BY WINGED HARPYIES, DOLPHIN SPOUTS EMPTYING INTO LOWER BASIN, n.d.
Black chalk on paper; (verso) red chalk
248 x 136 mm (9 3/4 x 5 5/16 in.)
Lent by The Pierpont Morgan Library. Bequest of Junius S. Morgan and gift of Henry S. Morgan. Acc. No. 1966.11:112

CH|T

61. Robert Adam (Scottish, 1728–1792)
CANDLE STAND FROM THE EATING ROOM, 20 ST. JAMES'S SQUARE, n.d.
Pine and mahogany with carved decoration applied
122 x 57.2 cm (48 1/16 x 22 1/2 in.)
Lent by The Victoria and Albert Museum

CH

62. Claude-Nicolas Ledoux (French, 1736–1806)
FRAGMENTS DES PROPYLÉES, plate 29 from ARCHITECTURE DE C.-N. LEDOUX, VOL.1 [BEING LEDOUX'S L'ARCHITECTURE CONSIDERÉE SOUS LE RAPPORT DES MOEURS ET DE LA LÉGISLATION, 1804], published in Paris, 1847
Lent by Avery Architectural and Fine Arts Library, Columbia University

CH|T

63. Etienne-Louis Boullée (French, 1728–1799)
PROJECT FOR A METROPOLE, 1782
Pen and gray wash
330 x 630 mm (13 x 24 13/16 in.)
Lent by RIBA Library Drawings and Archives Collections

CH|T

64. Sir John Soane (English, 1753–1837)
BANK OF ENGLAND. PERSPECTIVE OF THE 3% CONSOLS OFFICE, 1799 and September 1800
Pen and ink, brush and watercolor on off-white laid paper
455 x 605 mm (18 x 23 3/4 in.)
Lent by The British Architectural Library, Drawings and Archives Division, Victoria and Albert Museum

PIRANESI AND HIS AESTHETIC OF ECLECTICISM

Frontispiece.
ANTIQUUS BIVII VIARUM
ET ARDEATINAE PROSPECTUS
AD IL LAPIDEM EXTRA PORTAM
CAPENAM (detail), frontispiece from
LE ANTICHITÀ ROMANE, vol. 2, 1765
Etching on off-white laid paper
Smithsonian Institution Libraries,
Cooper-Hewitt, National Design
Museum

1. ANTIQUUS BIVII VIARUM ET
   ARDEATINAE PROSPECTUS AD IL
   LAPIDEM EXTRA PORTAM CAPENAM,
   frontispiece from LE ANTICHITÀ
   ROMANE, vol. 2, 1765
   Etching on off-white laid paper
   Smithsonian Institution Libraries,
   Cooper-Hewitt, National Design
   Museum

   CH|T

2. SHEET OF SKETCHES WITH TEMPLES,
   TOMBS, SARCOPHAGI, VASES, ETC.,
   AFTER FISCHER VON ERLACH'S
   "ENTWURFF EINER HISTORISCHEN
   ARCHITEKTUR," 1721
   Pen and brown ink on off-white
   laid paper
   418 x 283 mm (16 ⅜ x 11 ⅛ in.)
   Lent by The Pierpont Morgan Library.
   Bequest of Junius S. Morgan
   and gift of Henry S. Morgan. Acc.
   No. 1966.11:17

3. ANCIENT SCHOOL BUILT IN THE
   EGYPTIAN AND GREEK MANNER,
   from OPERE VARIE D'ARCHITETTURE,
   PROSPETTIVE, GROTTESCHI,
   ANTICHITÀ, 1761
   Etching on off-white laid paper
   Smithsonian Institution Libraries,
   Cooper-Hewitt, National Design
   Museum

4. ARCHITECTURAL ELEMENTS
   OF ANCIENT BATHS THAT LEAD
   TO THE GYMNASIUM AND THEATRE,
   from OPERE VARIE D'ARCHITETTURE,
   PROSPETTIVE, GROTTESCHI,
   ANTICHITÀ, 1761
   Etching on off-white laid paper
   Smithsonian Institution Libraries,
   Cooper-Hewitt, National Design
   Museum

5. CHAPTER OPENING from PARERE
   SU L'ARCHITETTURA, 1765
   Etching on off-white laid paper
   Smithsonian Institution
   Libraries, Cooper-Hewitt,
   National Design Museum

6. VIGNETTE from PARERE
   SU L'ARCHITETTURA, 1765
   Etching on off-white laid paper
   Smithsonian Institution
   Libraries, Cooper-Hewitt,
   National Design Museum

7. Plate IV from PARERE
   SU L'ARCHITETTURA, 1765
   Etching on off-white laid paper
   Smithsonian Institution
   Libraries, Cooper-Hewitt,
   National Design Museum

8. Plate V from PARERE
   SU L'ARCHITETTURA, 1765
   Etching on off-white laid paper
   Smithsonian Institution
   Libraries, Cooper-Hewitt,
   National Design Museum

9. Plate VII from PARERE
   SU L'ARCHITETTURA, 1765
   Etching on off-white laid paper
   Smithsonian Institution
   Libraries, Cooper-Hewitt,
   National Design Museum

10. Plate VIII from PARERE
    DU L'ARCHITETTURA, 1765
    Smithsonian Institution
    Libraries, Cooper-Hewitt,
    National Design Museum

11. Plate IX from PARERE
    SU L'ARCHITETTURA, 1765
    Etching on off-white laid paper
    Smithsonian Institution
    Libraries, Cooper-Hewitt,
    National Design Museum

12. FRONTISPIECE from DIVERSE
    MANIERE D'ADORNARE…,
    published in Rome, 1769
    Etching on off-white laid paper
    Smithsonian Institution
    Libraries, Cooper-Hewitt,
    National Design Museum

13. COMPARATIVE DIAGRAM OF
    ETRUSCAN VASES AND SHELL
    FORMS, Table 2, page 21, from
    DIVERSE MANIERE D'ADORNARE…,
    published in Rome, 1769
    Etching on off-white laid paper
    Smithsonian Institution
    Libraries, Cooper-Hewitt,
    National Design Museum

14. MANTELPIECE IN THE EGYPTIAN
    STYLE, from DIVERSE MANIERE
    D'ADORNARE…, published
    in Rome, 1769
    Etching on off-white laid paper
    Smithsonian Institution

Libraries, Cooper-Hewitt,
National Design Museum

15. MANTELPIECE IN THE EGYPTIAN
    STYLE, from DIVERSE MANIERE
    D'ADORNARE…, published
    in Rome, 1769
    Etching on off-white laid paper
    Smithsonian Institution
    Libraries, Cooper-Hewitt,
    National Design Museum

PIRANESI AND THE ANTIQUARIAN IMAGINATION

1. Jean-Baptiste-Siméon Chardin
   (French, 1699–1779)
   THE ANTIQUARIAN MONKEY
   (LE SINGE ANTIQUAIRE), 1743
   Oil on canvas
   285 x 235 mm (11¼ x 9¼ in.)
   Musée des Beaux-Arts,
   Chartres, France

2. VEDUTA DELL'ANTICA VIA
   APPIA (VIEW OF THE VIA APPIA),
   figure VII, vol. 2, LE ANTICHITÀ
   ROMANE, 1756–57
   Etching on off-white laid paper
   315 x 232 mm (12 ⁷⁄₁₆ x 9 ⅛ in.)
   Smithsonian Institution Libraries,
   Dibner Library

3. SPACCATO DEL SEPOLCRO DI
   ALESSANDRO SEVERO (SECTION OF
   THE TOMB OF ALEXANDER SEVERUS),
   figure XXXII, vol. 1, LE ANTICHITÀ
   ROMANE, 1756–57
   345 x 460 mm (13 ⁹⁄₁₆ x 18 ⅛ in.)
   Etching on off-white laid paper
   Smithsonian Institution Libraries,
   Dibner Library

4. MODO, QUALE FURONO ALZZATI
   I GROSSI TRAVERTINI… (MEANS
   BY WHICH THE LARGE BLOCKS
   OF TRAVERTINE AND MARBLE…),
   figure LIII, vol. 2, LE ANTICHITÀ
   ROMANE, 1756–57
   Etching on off-white laid paper
   350 x 520 mm (13 ¹³⁄₁₆ x 20 ½ in.)
   Smithsonian Institution Libraries,
   Dibner Library

5. DOPO DI AVER'ESPOSTO NELLA TAV.
   PASSATA IL MODO… (AFTER HAVING
   SHOWN IN THE PREVIOUS PLATE
   THE MEANS…), figure LIV, vol. 2,
   LE ANTICHITÀ ROMANE, 1756–57
   Etching on off-white laid paper
   335 x 590 mm (13 ³⁄₁₆ x 23 ¼ in.)
   Smithsonian Institution Libraries,
   Dibner Library

6. CONCERNING THE FOUNTAINHEAD
   OF THE ACQUA GIULIA (LONGITUDI-

NAL SECTION; PLAN AND DETAILS
OF PLUMBING) fig. 15, LE ROVINE DEL
CASTELLO DELL'ACQUA GIULIA, 1761
Etching on off-white laid paper
385 x 210 mm (15 ³⁄₁₆ x 8 ¼ in.)
Mark J. Millard Architectural
Collection, National Gallery of Art,
Washington, D.C.

7. CONCERNING THE FOUNTAINHEAD
   OF THE ACQUA GIULIA (DETAILS OF
   THE SLUICES), fig. 14, LE ROVINE DEL
   CASTELLO DELL'ACQUA GIULIA, 1761
   Etching on off-white laid paper
   385 x 212 mm (15 ³⁄₁₆ x 8 ⅜ in.)
   Mark J. Millard Architectural
   Collection, National Gallery of Art,
   Washington, D.C.

COL SPORCAR SI TROVA: PIRANESI DRAWS

CH|T
Frontispiece.
TOMB OF NERO (detail),
from the series GROTTESCHI, 1750
Etching on off-white laid paper
680 x 930 mm (26 ¾ x 36 ⅝ in.)
Lent by John Wilton-Ely

1. DIAGONAL VIEW OF TWO
   COLONNADED COURTYARDS, n.d.
   Pen and brown ink and gray wash
   over ruled black chalk sketch
   on off-white laid paper
   141 x 210 mm (5 ⁹⁄₁₆ x 8 ¼ in.)
   The British Museum, London

2. TOMB OF THEODORIC
   AT RAVENNA, n.d.
   Pen and brown ink on off-white
   laid paper
   110 x 167 mm (4¼ x 6½ in.)
   Courtauld Institute of Art Gallery,
   London

3. ARCHITECTURAL SKETCHES, n.d.
   Pen and deep brown ink
   on off-white laid paper
   141 x 210 mm (5 ⁹⁄₁₆ x 8 ¼ in.)
   British Museum, London

4. PRIMA PARTE:
   TITLE PAGE–STATE I, 1743
   Etching, engaving, drypoint,
   and scratching
   362 x 257 mm (14¼ x 10 in.)
   Smithsonian Institution
   Libraries, Cooper-Hewitt,
   National Design Museum

   CH|T

5. DESIGN FOR A WALL PANEL
   WITH ROCOCO SHIELD, SMALLER
   FLANKING SHIELDS, AND WINGED
   FEMALE FIGURE AT LEFT

Pen and brown ink with gray-brown wash over black chalk on off-white laid paper
293 x 237 mm (11 9/16 x 9 5/16 in.)
Lent by The Pierpont Morgan Library. Bequest of Junius S. Morgan and gift of Henry S. Morgan. Acc. no. 1966.11:11

6. DECORATIVE SHELL, n.d.
Pen and brown ink and wash over black chalk on off-white laid paper
246 x 184 mm (9 11/16 x 7 1/4 in.)
The Pierpont Morgan Library

CH

7. DESIGN FOR A FESTIVAL GONDOLA, n.d.
Pen and brown ink and wash over black chalk on off-white laid paper
297 x 683 mm (11 11/16 x 26 7/8 in.)
The Pierpont Morgan Library

8. DECORATIVE DESIGN, n.d.
Pen and brown ink and wash on off-white laid paper
305 x 229 mm (12 x 9 in.)
CCA

9. DECORATIVE DESIGNS AND RECLINING FIGURE, n.d.
Pen and brown ink and wash on off-white laid paper
305 x 229 mm (12 x 9 in.)
CCA

10. Giovanni Battista Tiepolo
(Italian, 1692–1770)
SCHERZI DI FANTASIA: FIGURES REGARDING AN EFFIGY ….
Etching on off-white laid paper
232 x 183 mm (9 1/4 x 7 1/4 in.)
Cooper-Hewitt, National Design Museum, Smithsonian Institution

11. Giovanni Battista Tiepolo
(Italian, 1692–1770)
SCHERZI DI FANTASIA: TITLE PAGE, UNLETTERED
Etching on off-white laid paper
National Gallery of Art, Washington, D.C.

CH|T

12. DESIGN FOR A FRONTISPIECE WITH SCROLL, CROWN, AND SARCOPHAGUS
Pen, brown ink and wash over black chalk
395 x 519 mm (15 9/16 x 20 7/16 in.)
Lent by The Pierpont Morgan Library. Bequest of Junius S. Morgan and gift of Henry S. Morgan. Acc. no. 1966.11:7

13. DESIGN FOR A TITLE PAGE WITH SCROLL, CHAIN OF MEDALLIONS, AND PULPIT
Pen and brown ink with brown wash and pink water color over

black chalk on off-white laid paper
508 x 749 mm (20 x 29 1/2 in.)
The Pierpont Morgan Library

14. THE MONUMENTAL TABLET–STATE I from the series GROTTESCHI, 1750
Etching, engraving, drypoint, and scratching on off-white laid paper
396 x 547 mm (15 1/2 x 21 1/2 in.)
National Gallery of Art, Washington, D.C.

15. ARA ANTICA: PRIMA PARTE –plate 7 of first edition
Etching on off-white laid paper
247 x 353 mm (9 3/4 x 14 in.)
Smithsonian Institution Libraries, Cooper-Hewitt, National Design Museum

CH

16. TOMB OF NERO, from the series GROTTESCHI, 1750
Etching on off-white laid paper
680 x 930 mm (26 3/4 x 36 5/8 in.)
Lent by John Wilton-Ely

17. CARCERI: TITLE PAGE, FIRST EDITION
Etching and engraving on off-white laid paper
553 x 419 mm (21 3/4 x 16 1/2 in.)
National Gallery of Art, Washington, D.C.

18. INTERIOR OF A PRISON, n.d.
Pen and brown ink and wash over black chalk sketch on off-white laid paper
256 x 189 mm (10 1/16 x 7 7/16 in.)
Bildarchiv Preussischer Kulturbesitz/Art Resource, NY /Kunsthalle, Hamburg

19. CARCERI: TITLE PLATE, STATE III, SECOND EDITION
Etching and engraving on off-white laid paper
553 x 419 mm (21 3/4 x 16 1/2 in.)
National Gallery of Art, Washington, D.C.

20. RACCOLTA DI ALCUNI DISEGNI DEL BARBERI DA CENTO DITTO IL GUERCINO: FRONTISPIECE
Etching and engraving on off-white laid paper
480 x 354 mm (19 x 14 in.)
Avery Architectural and Fine Arts Library, Columbia University

21. TWO FIGURES, n.d.
Black and red chalk on off-white laid paper
216 x 210 mm (8 1/2 x 8 1/4 in.)
Louvre, Paris

22. TWO MEN
(DRAWN OVER FOOT), n.d.
Pen and brown ink; foot in red chalk on off-white laid paper
195 x 271 mm (7 5/8 x 10 5/8 in.)
Ashmolean Museum, Oxford

CH

23. SKETCH DESIGN FOR A MONUMENTAL CANDELABRUM, n.d.
Pen and brown ink on off-white laid paper
248 x 890 mm (9 3/4 x 35 1/16 in.)
British Museum, London

THE PROJECTS FOR THE RECONSTRUCTION OF THE LATERAN BASILICA IN ROME

CH

Frontispiece.
DETAILED DESIGN FOR PANEL OF VAULTING COFFERS IN APSE, CORRESPONDING TO NUMBER 9 (TAVOLA 19)
Pen and brown ink over pencil, with brown washes
862 x 537 mm (33 15/16 x 21 1/8 in.)
Lent by Avery Architectural and Fine Arts Library, Columbia University

1. LONGITUDINAL SECTION BEGINNING AT TRANSEPT OF THE PROPOSED TRIBUNE OF S. GIOVANNI IN LATERANO
Pen and brown ink, brush and brown wash with traces of graphite on off-white laid paper
(12 9/16 x 21 1/8 in.)
The Pierpont Morgan Library

2. TITLE PAGE OF PRESENTATION DRAWINGS EMBODYING PROPOSALS FOR A NEW SANCTUARY (TAVOLA 1)
Pen and gray and brown ink on off-white laid paper
889 x 561 mm (35 x 22 1/8 in.)
Avery Architectural and Fine Arts Library, Columbia University

3. CROSS SECTION SHOWING WEST WALL OF TRANSEPT AND VIEW INTO SANCTUARY (TAVOLA 2)
Pen and gray and brown ink on off-white laid paper
553 x 855 mm (21 3/4 x 33 5/8 in.)
Avery Architectural and Fine Arts Library, Columbia University

4. LONGITUDINAL SECTION SHOWING SOUTH WALL OF SANCTUARY, WITH TRANSEPT AND BEGINNING OF NAVE (TAVOLA 3)
Pen and gray and brown ink on off-white laid paper
557 x 902 mm (21 15/16 x 35 1/2 in.)
Avery Architectural and Fine Arts Library, Columbia University

5. PLAN AND VIEW OF SANCTUARY FROM THE TRANSEPT (TAVOLA 4)
Pen and gray and brown ink on off-white laid paper
887 x 560 mm (34 15/16 x 22 1/16 in.)
Avery Architectural and Fine Arts Library, Columbia University

6. LONGITUDINAL SECTION SHOWING SOUTH WALL OF SANCTUARY, WITH TRANSEPT AND BEGINNING OF NAVE (TAVOLA 5)
Pen and gray and brown ink on off-white laid paper
553 x 865 mm (21 3/4 x 34 1/16 in.)
Lent by Avery Architectural and Fine Arts Library, Columbia University

7. PLAN OF SANCTUARY WITH SCREEN OF COLUMNS AND AMBULATORY (TAVOLA 6)
Pen and gray and brown ink on off-white laid paper
896 x 562 mm (35 5/16 x 22 1/8 in.)
Avery Architectural and Fine Arts Library, Columbia University

CH

8. TRANSVERSE SECTION OF THE SANCTUARY, VIEWED FROM THE TRANSEPT, AND GROUND PLAN (TAVOLA 7)
Pen and gray and brown ink on off-white laid paper
887 x 566 mm (34 7/8 x 22 5/16 in.)
Lent by Avery Architectural and Fine Arts Library, Columbia University

9. LONGITUDINAL SECTION SHOWING SOUTH WALL OF SANCTUARY WITH TRANSEPT AND BEGINNING OF NAVE (TAVOLA 8)
Pen and gray and brown ink on off-white laid paper
587 x 898 mm (23 1/8 x 35 5/16 in.)
Avery Architectural and Fine Arts Library, Columbia University

CH

10. TRANSVERSE SECTION OF THE SANCTUARY SHOWING REAR VIEW OF APSE FACING WEST (TAVOLA 9)
Pen and gray and brown ink on off-white laid paper
881 x 562 mm (34 11/16 x 22 1/16 in.)
Lent by Avery Architectural and Fine Arts Library, Columbia University

11. PLAN OF SANCTUARY WITH SCREEN OF COLUMNS AND AMBULATORY (TAVOLA 11)
Pen and gray and brown ink on off-white laid paper
890 x 562 mm (35 1/16 x 22 1/8 in.)
Avery Architectural and Fine Arts Library, Columbia University

CH

12. TRANSVERSE SECTION SHOWING
WEST WALL OF TRANSEPT WITH
PAPAL ALTAR AND BALDACCHINO
WITHIN THE SANCTUARY (TAVOLA 12)
Pen and gray and brown ink over
graphite on off-white laid paper
567 x 885 mm (22 ⅜ x 34 ⅞ in.)
Lent by Avery Architectural and
Fine Arts Library, Columbia University

13. PLAN OF SANCTUARY WITH
AMBULATORY (TAVOLA 14)
Pen and gray and brown ink
on off-white laid paper
882 x 563 mm (34 ¹¹/₁₆ x 22 ³/₁₆ in.)
Avery Architectural and Fine Arts
Library, Columbia University

14. CROSS SECTION THROUGH
THE CHOIR, CORRESPONDING
TO NUMBER 14 (TAVOLA 15)
Pen and gray and brown ink
on off-white laid paper
897 x 572 mm (35 ⁵/₁₆ x 22 ½ in.)
Avery Architectural and Fine Arts
Library, Columbia University

15. LONGITUDINAL SECTION SHOWING
SOUTH WALL OF SANCTUARY,
WITH TRANSEPT AND BEGINNING
OF NAVE (TAVOLA 16)
Pen and gray and brown ink
on off-white laid paper
556 x 893 mm (21 ⅞ x 35 ⅛ in.)
Avery Architectural and Fine Arts
Library, Columbia University

16. PLAN OF SANCTUARY (TAVOLA 17)
Pen and gray and brown ink
on off-white laid paper
891 x 565 mm (35 ¹/₁₆ x 22 ¼ in.)
Avery Architectural and Fine Arts
Library, Columbia University

17. LONGITUDINAL SECTION SHOWING
NORTH WALL OF SANCTUARY,
WITH TRANSEPT AND BEGINNING
OF NAVE (TAVOLA 18)
Pen and gray and brown ink
on off-white laid paper
582 x 906 mm (22 ⅞ x 35 ¹¹/₁₆ in.)
Avery Architectural and Fine Arts
Library, Columbia University

CH

18. ALTERNATIVE DESIGN FOR
PAPAL ALTAR AND BALDACCHINO
(TAVOLA 20)
Pen and brown ink, brush and
brown and gray wash over graphite
on off-white laid paper
741 x 474 mm (29 ³/₁₆ x 18 ¹¹/₁₆ in.)
Avery Architectural and Fine Arts
Library, Columbia University

19. PLAN AND ELEVATION OF
PAPAL ALTAR AND BALDACCHINO
(TAVOLA 21)
Pen and gray and brown ink
on off-white laid paper
895 x 597 mm (35 ¼ x 23 ½ in.)
Avery Architectural and Fine Arts
Library, Columbia University

CH

20. PAPAL ALTAR AND BALDACCHINO,
FLANKED BY ELABORATE
CANDELABRA (TAVOLA 22)
Pen and gray and brown ink
on off-white laid paper
900 x 597 mm (35 ⁵/₁₆ x 23 ½ in.)
Lent by Avery Architectural and
Fine Arts Library, Columbia University

21. PAPAL ALTAR AND BALDACCHINO,
FLANKED BY ELABORATE
CANDELABRA (TAVOLA 23)
Pen and gray and brown ink
on off-white laid paper
906 x 594 mm (35 ¹¹/₁₆ x 23 ⅜ in.)
Avery Architectural and Fine Arts
Library, Columbia University

PERSPECTIVES ON PIRANESI AND THEATER

Frontispiece.
GRUPPO DI SCALE ORNATO DI
MAGNIFICA ARCHITETTURA (detail)
Etching, engraving
250 x 374 mm (9 ¾ x 14 ¾ in.)
Smithsonian Institution
Libraries, Cooper-Hewitt,
National Design Museum

1. GRUPPO DI SCALE ORNATO
DI MAGNIFICA ARCHITETTURA
Etching, engraving
250 x 374 mm (9 ¾ x 14 ¾ in.)
Smithsonian Institution
Libraries, Cooper-Hewitt,
National Design Museum

2. Ferdinando Bibiena
(Italian, 1657–1743)
L'ARCHITETTURA CIVILE, plate 67
Etching, engraving
340 x 255 mm (13 ½ x 10 in.)
National Gallery of Art,
Washington, D.C.

3. VESTIBULE OF AN ANCIENT
TEMPLE—PRIMA PARTE
Etching, engraving
240 x 355 mm (9 ½ x 14 in.)
Smithsonian Institution
Libraries, Cooper-Hewitt,
National Design Museum

4. Giuseppe Valeriani
(Italian, 1720–1761)

SET OF DESIGNS FOR
A STAGE SET, MODEL
Pen and brown ink,
watercolor, gold leaf on paper
Courtauld Institute of Art
Gallery–Willt Collection

5. Pietro Santi Bartoli
(Italian, 1635–1700)
FACCIATA DELLI SEPOLCRI...
Etching, engraving
Arc. 1070.202*F, Department of
Printing and Graphic Arts, Houghton
Library, Harvard College Library

6. VIEW OF THE FOUNDATION
OF THE THEATER OF MARCELLUS
Etching, engraving
590 x 395 mm (23 ¼ x 15 ½ in.)
Smithsonian Institution Libraries,
Dibner Library

7. Vincenzo Mazzi
CAPRICI DI SCENE...
Etching, engraving
Typ 725.76.563.F, Department of
Printing and Graphic Arts, Houghton
Library, Harvard College Library

8. VASO ANTICO DI MARMO
Etching, engraving
530 x 385 mm (20 ¾ x 15 ¼ in.)
Smithsonian Institution
Libraries, Cooper-Hewitt,
National Design Museum

9. Pietro Santi Bartoli
(Italian, 1635–1700)
OIL LAMP IN THE FORM
OF A CROUCHING FIGURE
Etching, engraving
344 x 235 mm (13 ½ x 9 ¼ in.)
FIC6 B2857 691 aca, Department of
Printing and Graphic Arts, Houghton
Library, Harvard College Library

10. VARIOUS LAMPS OF BRONZE AND
TERRA-COTTA
Etching, engraving
387 x 535 mm (15 ¼ x 21 in.)
Smithsonian Institution
Libraries, Cooper-Hewitt,
National Design Museum

PIRANESI AND FURNISHINGS

1. Laurent Pécheux
(French, 1729–1821)
THE MARCHESA MARGHERITA
GENTILI BOCCAPADULI, 1777
Oil on canvas
Private collection, Turin

2. Francesco Giardoni
(Italian, 1692–1757)
BRONZE SIDE-TABLE WITH AN
ANCIENT MOSAIC TOP, 1742
Museo Capitolini, Rome

3. Jacques-Louis David
(French, 1748–1825)
LA DOULEUR D'ANDROMAQUE, 1783
Oil on canvas
275 x 203 mm (10 ¾ x 8 in.)
Musée du Louvre, Paris, 1969-1

4. Jean-Auguste-Dominique Ingres
(French, 1780–1867)
DESIGN FOR THE TOMB OF LADY
JANE MONTAGUE, 1816
Sepia and ochre
410 x 560 mm (16 ¼ x 22 in.)
National Gallery of Victoria,
Melbourne, Australia. Acc.no. 1066-3

5. PORCELAIN (PORCELAINE DE PARIS)
BOAT AFTER A ROMAN TRIREME,
1815–20
Painted and gilt porcelain
Private collection

6. MAHOGANY PEDESTAL AFTER A
ROMAN MARBLE CANDELABRUM
London, Kenwood House

7. François-Joseph Bélanger (1744–1818)
PROJECT FOR THE COMTE D'ARTOIS'S
BEDROOM AT THE BAGATELLE, 1777
Pen, ink, and brush and wash on paper
Bibliothèque Nationale de France,
Cabinet des Estampes

8. Luigi Valadier (Italian, 1726–1785)
VASE FROM THE BRASCHI SURTOUT-
DE-TABLE, 1783
Marble and gilt bronze
Private collection

9. COMMODE INLAID IN VARIOUS
WOODS WITH GILT BRONZE
MOUNTS AND A VERDE ANTICO
TOP, ROME, ca. 1785
Present whereabouts unknown

10. PEDESTAL WITH SYMBOLS
OF THE EVANGELISTS, 1770–85
Silver, gilt-bronze, and brass
Present whereabouts unknown

11. Giovanni Grespi (Italian,
active Rome, late 18th century)
PEDESTAL WITH THE COAT OF ARMS
OF CLEMENT XIV, 1774
Gilt wood
Palazzo del Quirinale

12. Antonio Landucci (Italian,
active Rome, late 18th century)
SIDE TABLE FROM THE PALAZZO
BORGHESE, 1773
Gilt wood
Palazzo del Quirinale

13. Nicola Freddi (Italian,
active Rome, late 18th century)

SIDE TABLE, 1776
Gilt wood
Palazzo Caetani

PIRANESI AS DESIGNER

1. CATALOGUE OF WORKS
   PUBLISHED TO DATE BY
   GIO. BATTISTA PIRANESI, ca. 1671
   Engraving
   396 x 294 mm (15¹/₂ x 11¹/₂ in.)
   Roma, Istituto Nazionale per
   la Grafica per gentile concessione
   del Ministero per i Beni e le Attività
   Culturali

2. Narcisse Garnier
   PORTRAIT OF JOHAN FREDERIK
   WILLEM, BARON VAN SPAEN
   (1746–1827)
   Oil on canvas
   790 x 640 mm (31 x 25¹/₄ in.)
   Dutch private collection

3. GREAT HALL OF BILJOEN CASTLE,
   VELP, THE NETHERLANDS, PLASTER-
   WORK DECORATION OF THE PAN-
   THEON, ROME (AFTER PIRANESI)
   Dutch private collection

4. GREAT HALL OF BILJOEN CASTLE,
   PLASTERWORK DECORATION
   OF THE PONTE MOLLE, ROME
   Dutch private collection

5. VIEW OF THE PONTE MOLLE, ROME
   Etching
   440 x 673 mm (17¹/₄ x 26¹/₂ in.)
   Teylers Museum, Haarlem, Collection
   Teding van Berkhout

6. GREAT HALL OF BILJOEN CASTLE
   Dutch private collection

7. BUST OF JULIA
   White marble with some blue veining
   Height 70 cm (27¹/₂ in.)
   Leiden, Rijksmuseum van Oudheden

8. Jacques Henri Sablet
   (French, 1749–1803)
   THOMAS HOPE OF AMSTERDAM, 1792
   Oil on canvas
   622 x 501 mm (24¹/₂ x 19¹/₄ in.)
   London, Marylebone Cricket Club

9. After Giovanni Battista Piranesi
   CHIMNEYPIECE MADE
   FOR JOHN HOPE, ca. 1769
   White marble
   Height 133 cm (52¹/₄ in.)
   Amsterdam, Rijksmuseum, BK-15449

10. DESIGN FOR A CHIMNEYPIECE
    Etching
    270 x 270 mm (10¹/₂ x 10¹/₂ in.)
    Roma, Istituto Nazionale per
    la Grafica per gentile concessione
    del Ministero per i Beni e le Attività
    Culturali

11. Cornelis Ploos van Amstel
    (Dutch, 1726–1798)
    PORTRAIT OF ARNOUT VOSMAER
    (1720–1799), 1792
    Watercolor in a decorative
    etched border
    207 x 266 mm (8¹/₄ x 10¹/₂ in.)
    Vosmaer heirs

12. AERNOUT VOSMAER'S VISITING
    CARDS, BOUGHT FROM GIUSEPPE
    DELLA SANTA DURING HIS TRIP
    IN 1776
    Vosmaer heirs

13. Bartolomeo Cavaceppi
    (Italian, 1716–1799)
    VIEW OF THE INTERIOR
    OF THE WORKSHOP, from
    RACCOLTA, vol. 1, 1769
    Etching
    215 x 164 mm (8¹/₂ x 6¹/₂ in.)

14. WARWICK VASE DRAWING (copy
    of a print), from VOYAGIE DE LA
    ITALYE PAR LA FRANCE, SUISSE,
    L'ITALIE, TIJROL, ET L'ALLEMAGNE,
    EN HOLLANDE. L'ANNÉE 1775–1776
    by J. A. de Hochepied
    210 x 275 mm (8¹/₄ x 10³/₄ in.)
    Leiden, University Library, ms. BLP
    2058, drawing between ff. 127-128

15. TRIPOD, ca. AD 140–60
    Marble
    Height 131 cm (51¹/₂ in.), diameter
    48 cm (19 in.), base 58 cm (22³/₄ in.)
    Vatican Museums, inv.nr. 2323

16. ONE OF TWO IDENTICAL ALTARS
    Etching
    670 x 420 mm (26¹/₄ x 16¹/₂ in.)
    Roma, Istituto Nazionale per
    la Grafica per gentile concessione
    del Ministero per i Beni e le
    Attività Culturali

17. THE TEMPLE OF ISIS IN POMPEII,
    1776, from Aernout Vosmaer's ALBUM
    AMICORUM II, 1781, page 197
    80 x 132 mm (3¹/₄ x 5¹/₄ in.)
    Vosmaer heirs

18. Francesco Piranesi (ca. 1758/9–1810)
    VIEW OF THE FORUM IN ROME,
    1776, from Aernout Vosmaer's ALBUM
    AMICORUM II, page 199

Pen and brush in grey over a sketch
in pencil
104 x 145 mm (4 x 5³/₄ in.)
Vosmaer heirs

19. Angelo Domenico Piranesi (1763–?)
    DRAWING OF A MARBLE RELIEF OF
    GRIFFONS FROM THE VILLA ALBANI,
    1776, from Aernout Vosmaer's ALBUM
    AMICORUM II, 1781, page 201
    Pencil
    65 x 160 mm (2¹/₂ x 6¹/₄ in.)
    Rijksmuseum, Amsterdam,
    on loan from Vosmaer heirs

20. THE TEMPLE OF JUNO
    AT PAESTUM, 1776–78
    Pen, brush, and Indian ink over
    a sketch in black and red chalk
    465 x 675 mm (18¹/₄ x 26¹/₂ in.)
    Amsterdam, Rijkmuseum,
    RP-T-1960-205

DRAWING FROM PIRANESI

Frontispiece.
PAESTUM, ITALY (PLATE XVII–
DIFFERENT VIEWS OF PESTO
AT PAESTUM) (detail), 1778
Etching on white laid paper
RIBA Library Drawings
and Archives Collections

1. THE CAPITOLINE HILL WITH STEPS
   TO S. MARIA ARACOELI, ca. 1751
   Etching on white laid paper
   RIBA Library Drawings
   and Archives Collections

2. Michael Graves (American, b. 1934)
   SANTA MARIA IN ARACOELI, NO.2
   Pen and brown ink on white paper
   Courtesy of Michael Graves

3. Michael Graves (American, b. 1934)
   SANTA MARIA IN ARACOELI, 1960
   Pen and brown ink on white paper
   Courtesy of Michael Graves

4. INTERIOR VIEW OF THE BASILICA
   OF S. MARIA MAGGIORE, ca. 1751
   Etching on white laid paper
   RIBA Library Drawings
   and Archives Collections

5. VIEW OF THE FAÇADE OF SAN GIO-
   VANNI IN LATERANO, ca. 1751
   Etching on white laid paper
   RIBA Library Drawings
   and Archives Collections

6. Michael Graves (American, b. 1934)
   SAN GIOVANNI IN LATERANO, 1960
   Pen and brown ink on white paper
   Courtesy of Michael Graves

7. VIEW OF THE PIAZZA
   DEL CAMPIDOGLIO, ca. 1751
   Etching on white laid paper
   RIBA Library Drawings
   and Archives Collections

8. Michael Graves (American, b. 1934)
   PALAZZO SENATORIO, 1960
   Pen and ink on white paper
   Courtesy of Michael Graves

9. PAESTUM, ITALY (PLATE XVII–
   DIFFERENT VIEWS OF PESTO
   AT PAESTUM), 1778
   Etching on white laid paper
   RIBA Library Drawings
   and Archives Collections

10. Michael Graves (American, b. 1934)
    PAESTUM, ITALY, 1960
    Pen and ink on white paper
    Courtesy of Michael Graves

11. INTERIOR VIEW OF THE
    PANTHEON, XV. FIGURE II
    (LE ANTICHITÀ ROMANE, VOL. 1)
    Etching on white laid paper
    RIBA Library Drawings
    and Archives Collections

12. Michael Graves (American, b. 1934)
    SAN PIETRO, ROME, 1960
    Pen and ink on white paper
    Courtesy of Michael Graves

13. TEMPLE OF MINERVA MEDICA,
    ROME, ca. 1751
    Etching on white laid paper
    RIBA Library Drawings
    and Archives Collections

14. THE PANTHEON
    (LE ANTICHITÀ ROMANE), 1756
    Etching on white laid paper
    RIBA Library Drawings
    and Archives Collections

15. Michael Graves (American, b. 1934)
    THE PANTHEON, 1960
    Pen and ink on white paper
    Courtesy of Michael Graves

16. THE BASILICA OF MAXENTIUS
    (CALLED VIEW OF THE BATHS
    OF DIOCLETIAN), ca. 1751
    Etching on white laid paper
    RIBA Library Drawings
    and Archives Collections

17. Michael Graves (American, b. 1934)
    THE BASILICA OF MAXENTIUS, 1960
    Pen and ink on white paper
    Courtesy of Michael Graves

18. Jean-Baptiste-Camille Corot
(French, 1796–1875)
THE COLISEUM (SEEN THROUGH
THE BATHS OF MAXENTIUS)
Oil on canvas
Louvre, Paris

19. COLISEUM AND ARCH
OF CONSTANTINE, ca. 1751
Etching on white laid paper
RIBA Library Drawings
and Archives Collections

20. Michael Graves (American, b. 1934)
THE COLISEUM, 1960
Pen and ink on white paper
Courtesy of Michael Graves

21. HADRIAN'S VILLA, ca. 1751
Etching on white laid paper
RIBA Library Drawings and
Archives Collections, JWE 227

22. Le Corbusier (Charles-Edouard
Jeanneret) (French, 1887–1965)
VILLA ADRIANA, from CARNET DU
VOYAGE D'ORIENT, NO 5, p.34, 1911
Black chalk on paper
Courtesy of La Fondation
Le Corbusier/ARS

23. VIEW OF THE REMAINS OF
THE SECOND FLOOR OF THE BATHS
OF TITUS, ca. 1751
Etching on white laid paper
RIBA Library Drawings and Archives
Collections

24. Michael Graves (American, b. 1934)
SANT'ANASTASIA AND
DOMUS AUGUSTANA, 1960
Pen and ink on white paper
Courtesy of Michael Graves

25. Michael Graves (American, b. 1934)
SANTA MARIA MAGGIORE,
APSE, 1960
Pen and ink on white paper
Courtesy of Michael Graves

26. VIEW OF THE REAR ENTRANCE
OF THE BASILICA OF S. MARIA
MAGGIORE, ca. 1751
Etching on white laid paper
RIBA Library Drawings and Archives
Collections

27. Jean-Baptiste-Camille Corot
(French, 1796-1875)
THE ROMAN CAMPAGNA WITH
THE CLAUDIAN AQUEDUCT, 1826
Oil on canvas
National Gallery, London, NG3285

28. Michael Graves (American, b. 1934)
AQUEDUCT, 1960
Pen and ink on white paper
Courtesy of Michael Graves

29. ANCIENT AQUEDUCT OF THE
ACQUA MARCIA AT THE CITY WALLS
ERECTED BY AURELIAN... Page CXCIX,
Vignette, DELLA MAGNIFICENZA
ED ARCHITETTURA DE'ROMANI, 1761
Etching on white laid paper
RIBA Library Drawings and Archives
Collections

PIRANESI AND THE CITY

1. "ICHNOGRAPHIA," OR PLAN OF THE
CAMPUS MARTIUS OF THE ANCIENT
CITY (detail), plate V–X from
IL CAMPO MARZIO DELL'ANTICA
ROMA, published in Rome, 1762
Cooper-Hewitt, National Design
Museum, Smithsonian Institution
Purchased in memory of Eleanor
and Sarah Hewitt, 1956-15-1

2. Giovanni Battista Nolli
(Italian, 1701–1756)
LA NUOVA TOPOGRAFIA DI ROMA,
1736–48
12 cooperplate engravings
1780 x 2080 mm (70 x 82 in.)
Courtesy of J.H. Aronson

SELECTED
EXHIBITION OBJECTS

CH|T
DIMOSTRAZIONE DELL'EMISSARIO
DEL LAGO ALBANO, 1762
Etching on off-white laid paper
405 x 505 mm (15 15/16 x 19 7/8 in.)
Lent by the Robison Collection

CH|T
PIANTA DEL SEPOLCRO
DI ALESSANDRO SEVERO, SITUATO
FUORI DI PORTA S. GIOVANNI,
plate XXXI from LE ANTICHITÀ
ROMANE, vol. 2, 1756
Etching on off-white laid paper
360 x 350 mm (14 3/16 x 13 3/4 in.)
Lent by the Robison Collection

CH|T
ARCHITECTURAL FANTASY
WITH MONUMENTAL PORTICO
BEFORE A PALACE, ca. 1763
Pen and brown ink, brown wash over
red chalk on off-white laid paper
500 x 360 mm (19 11/16 x 14 3/16 in.)
Lent by the Biblioteca Comunale
dell'Archiginnasio, Bologna

CH|T
Joseph Michael Gandy
(English, 1771–1843)

VIEW OF CONSULS TRANSFER OFFICE
FOR THE BANK OF ENGLAND, n.d.
Pen and watercolor
719 x 1018 mm (28 5/16 x 40 1/16 in.)
Lent by The Trustees of Sir John
Soane's Museum, London

CH|T
Robert Adam (Scottish, 1728–1792)
and Charles-Louis Clérisseau
(French, 1721–1820)
IMAGINARY INTERIOR BASED
ON ROMAN BATHS, 1755–56
Pen and ink wash
279 x 399 mm (11 x 15 11/16 in.)
The Trustees of Sir John Soane's
Museum, London

CH|T
VEDUTA INTERNA DELLA BASILICA
DI S. GIOVANNI LATERANO, from
the series VEDUTE DI ROMA, 1768
Etching on white laid paper
433 x 680 mm (17 1/16 x 26 3/4 in.)
Lent by the Arthur Ross Foundation

CH|T
Jean-Charles Delafosse
(French, 1734–1791)
TEMPLE OF JUSTICE, ca. 1765
Pen and black ink, brush and pink,
blue, and gray wash on paper
153 x 238 mm (6 x 9 3/8 in.)
Cooper-Hewitt, National Design
Museum, Smithsonian Institution
Purchased for the Museum by
the Advisory Council, 1911-28-64

CH|T
CENTRAL VIEW OF A CHURCH
INTERIOR WITH TOMBS AND
URNS ALONG EITHER WALL AND
A FREESTANDING MONUMENT
IN THE CENTER, n.d.
Pen and brown ink with gray
and brown wash over black chalk,
with red chalk additions
187 x 247 mm (7 3/8 x 9 3/4 in.)
Lent by The Pierpont Morgan Library.
Purchased as the gift of the Fellows.
Acc. no. 1959.14

CH|T
STUDY OF AN ORNAMENTAL SWORD
FOR THE DECORATIVE PILASTERS
ON THE FAÇADE OF S. MARIA
DEL PRIORATO, mid-18th century
Pen and ink on off-white laid paper
147 x 55 mm (5 13/16 x 2 3/16 in.)
Lent by The British Museum
[1908-6-16-34]

CH|T
SHEET OF VARIOUS SKETCHES FOR
CHIMNEYPIECES AND CANDELABRA

WITH COMPUTATIONS AND NOTES
ON MATERIALS/THEMES, n.d.
Pen and brown ink with written
annotations on off-white laid paper
439 x 640 mm (17 5/16 x 25 3/16 in.)
Lent by The Pierpont Morgan Library.
Bequest of Junius S. Morgan and gift
of Henry S. Morgan. ACC. No. 1966.11:92

CH|T
Robert Adam (Scottish, 1728–1792)
TWO SKETCH DESIGNS FOR
PORTIONS OF CHIMNEY-PIECES
DERIVED FROM THOSE IN
"DIVERSE MANIERE," ca. 1777
Pencil and ink on paper
122 x 196 mm (4 13/16 x 7 11/16 in.)
Lent by The Trustees of Sir John
Soane's Museum, London

CH|T
PREPARATORY DESIGN
FOR CHIMNEYPIECE
WITH MONOPODS, n.d.
Red and black chalk with additions
in pen and brown ink on two sheets
of off-white laid paper, joined
232 x 364 mm (9 1/8 x 14 5/16 in.)
Lent by The Pierpont Morgan Library.
Bequest of Junius S. Morgan
and gift of Henry S. Morgan.
Acc. no. 1966.11:63

CH|T
WORKING STUDY FOR
A CHIMNEYPIECE WITH CENTRAL
TABLET LINKED BY FESTOONS
TO WREATHS, WITH COMPUTATION
AND SIDE ELEVATION OF STILE, n.d.
Black chalk on off-white laid paper
238 x 415 mm (9 3/8 x 16 5/16 in.)
Lent by The Pierpont Morgan Library.
Bequest of Junius S. Morgan
and gift of Henry S. Morgan.
Acc. no. 1966.11:77

CH|T
DESIGN FOR A CHIMNEYPIECE
AND CHAIR, n.d.
Pen and brown ink over black chalk
on off-white laid paper
189 x 356 mm (7 7/16 x 14 in.)
Lent by The Pierpont Morgan Library.
Bequest of Junius S. Morgan
and gift of Henry S. Morgan.
Acc. no. 1966.11:86

CH|T
DESIGN FOR A SIDE TABLE
Pen and brown ink on off-white
laid paper
125 x 165 mm (4 15/16 x 6 1/2 in.)
Lent by Sven Gahlin, London

CH|T

SKETCH DESIGN FOR CHIMNEYPIECE IN THE EGYPTIAN TASTE WITH STANDING FIGURES AND BIRD, n.d.
Pen and brown ink on off-white laid paper (irregular)
218 x 310 mm (8 9/16 x 12 3/16 in.)
Lent by The Pierpont Morgan Library. Bequest of Junius S. Morgan and gift of Henry S. Morgan. Acc. no. 1966.11:68

CH|T

Carlo Marchionni
(Italian, 1702–1786)
DESIGN FOR A DOORWAY TO THE GRAND GALLERY OF THE VILLA ALBANI, 1755–56
Pen and brown ink, brush and brown and gray wash, graphite on cream laid paper
405 x 193 mm (15 15/16 x 7 5/8 in.)
Cooper-Hewitt, National Design Museum, Smithsonian Institution Museum purchase through gift of various donors and from Eleanor G. Hewitt Fund, 1938-88-486

CH|T

Robert Adam (Scottish, 1728–1792)
A DESIGN OF A CHAIR FOR THE ETRUSCAN DRESSING ROOM AT OSTERLEY, 1776
Pen and ink with watercolor
500 x 355 mm (19 11/16 x 14 in.)
Lent by The Trustees of Sir John Soane's Museum, London

CH|T

Robert Adam (Scottish, 1728–1792)
DESIGN FOR A CONFIDANTE, AN ETRUSCAN ARM CHAIR, AND A SILVER CUP, 1777
Black chalk, brush and white gouache on oatmeal-colored laid paper
231 x 269 mm (9 1/8 x 10 9/16 in.)
Cooper-Hewitt, National Design Museum, Smithsonian Institution Museum purchase through gift of Jacques Seligmann, 1946-14-1

CH|T

CHIMNEYPIECE IN THE EGYPTIAN STYLE: SEATED FIGURES IN PROFILE ON EITHER SIDE, from the DIVERSE MANIERE..., 1769
Etching on off-white laid paper
240 x 380 mm (9 7/16 x 14 15/16 in.)
Lent by the Robison Collection

CH|T

CHIMNEYPIECE IN THE EGYPTIAN STYLE: GIANT FIGURES SUPPORTING THE LINTEL FLANKED BY CHAIRS, from the DIVERSE MANIERE..., 1769
Etching on off-white laid paper

245 x 380 mm (9 5/16 x 14 15/16 in.)
Lent by the Robison Collection

CH|T

Louis-Jean Desprez
(French, 1743–1804)
SEPULCHER WITH DEATH SEATED AND CROWNED, IMAGINARY TOMB DESIGN IN THE EGYPTIAN STYLE, ca. 1779–84
Pen and black ink, brush and brown, gray, blue-gray wash, traces of graphite on off-white paper
180 x 287 mm (7 1/16 x 11 5/16 in.)
Cooper-Hewitt, National Design Museum, Smithsonian Institution Museum purchase through gift of various donors and from Eleanor G. Hewitt Fund, 1938-88-3951

CH|T

Filippo Marchionni
(Italian, 1732–1805)
SANTA MARIA DEL PRIORATO, ROME, ALTERNATIVE DESIGN FOR THE HIGH ALTAR, 1724–30
Pen and black ink, gray wash, black chalk on white laid paper
671 x 459 mm (26 7/16 x 18 1/16 in.)
Cooper-Hewitt, National Design Museum, Smithsonian Institution Friends of the Museum Fund, 1938-88-3497

CH|T

BUCKINGHAM VASE, "THE DONCAST-ER CUP," from VASI, CANDELABRA, CIPPI, SARCOPHAGI..., 1778
Etching on off-white laid paper
959 x 756 mm (37 3/4 x 29 3/4 in.)
Lent by Smithsonian Institution Libraries, Cooper-Hewitt, National Design Museum

CH|T

PERSPECTIVE VIEW OF AN ANTIQUE MONUMENT FOUND IN A TOMB ON THE VIA APPIA, late 18th century
Etching on off-white laid paper
680 x 420 mm (26 3/4 x 16 9/16 in.)
Lent by Smithsonian Institution Libraries, Cooper-Hewitt, National Design Museum

CH|T

DESIGN FOR A MIRROR FRAME, n.d.
Pen and brown ink, brush and gray wash over graphite on off-white laid paper (squared for transfer)
501 x 386 mm (19 3/4 x 15 3/16 in.)
Lent by The Pierpont Morgan Library. Bequest of Junius S. Morgan and gift of Henry S. Morgan. Acc. no. 1966.11:109

ARCHITECTS' STATEMENTS

CH|T

Michael Graves (American, b. 1934)
DENVER CENTRAL LIBRARY, SOUTH ELEVATION, 1991
Graphite and colored pencil on yellow tracing paper
635 x 864 mm (25 x 34 in.)
Courtesy of Michael Graves

CH|T

Venturi, Scott Brown and Associates
EPISCOPAL ACADEMY CHAPEL, 2006
Plotted inkjet on wove paper
610 x 610 mm (24 x 24 in.)
Courtesy of Venturi, Scott Brown and Associates, Inc.

CH|T

Robert A. M. Stern (American, b. 1939)
PLAN DESIGN FOR THE TOKYO TIVOLI APARTMENTS, n.d.
Ink on Mylar
914 x 610 mm (36 x 24 in.)
Courtesy of Robert A. M. Stern Architects, LLP

CH|T

Daniel Libeskind (American, born in Poland, b. 1946)
MALDOROR'S EQUATION, from the series MICROMEGA, 21st century
Silkscreen
910 x 540 mm (35 13/16 x 21 1/4 in.)
Courtesy of Daniel Libeskind

CH|T

Peter Eisenman (American, b. 1932)
DESIGN FOR THE CARDINALS' STADIUM, GLENDALE, ARIZONA, 2006
Digital rendition print
Courtesy of Eisenman Architects

NOTES

DESIGN THROUGH FANTASY:
PIRANESI AS DESIGNER

1. For the Venetian architectural world of Piranesi's early years, see E. Bassi, *Architettura del sei e settecento a Venezia* (Naples, 1962); and R. Wittkower, *Art and Architecture in Italy, 1600–1750* (Harmondsworth and Baltimore, 1973), 386ff. See also Lionello Puppi, "Appunti sulla educazione veneziana di Giambattista Piranesi," in Alessandro Bettagno, ed., *Piranesi tra Venezia e l'Europa* (Florence, 1983): 217–64.

2. The Magistrato delle Acque was the state organization responsible for the sea defenses and harbor works of the Venetian Republic.

3. The polemical atmosphere of the Lucchesi circle and, in particular, the dominant influence of the radical theorist and priest Carl Lodoli are examined in Joseph Rykwert, *The First Moderns. The Architects of the Eighteenth Century* (Cambridge, MA, 1983): 288–90; also see Emil Kaufmann, "Piranesi, Algarotti and Lodoli. A Controversy in 18th-century Venice," in *Gazette des Beaux-Arts*, XLVI (1955): 21–28. See also Francis Haskell, *Patrons and Painters. A Study in the Relations between Italian Art and Society in the Age of the Baroque* (New Haven and London, 1980), passim; and Ennio Concina, "Storia, archaeologia, achitettura dal Maffei a M. Lucchesi," in Bettagno (1983): 361–76.

4. After his first arrival in Rome in 1740, Piranesi would also have derived inspiration from the set designs by Juvarra for Cardinal Ottoboni's private theater at the Cancelleria. At least two of Piranesi's early pen studies (now in the British Museum) are freely based on engravings of Juvarra's set in the published libretto of Filippo Amadei's 1711 opera *Teodosio il Giovane*. See Hylton Thomas, *The Drawings of Piranesi* (London, 1954), p. 43, no. 54; and the exhibition catalogue *Giovanni Battista Piranesi, His Predecessors and His Heritage*, edited by Edward Croft Murray (London: British Museum, 1968), nos. 26–27.

5. For Marco Foscarini as patron and collector, see Haskell, 258–60.

6. For the cultural and artistic world of eighteenth-century Rome, see the following exhibition catalogues: Edgar Peters Bowron and Joseph J. Rishel, eds., *Art in Rome in the Eighteenth Century* (Philadelphia Museum of Art, 2000); and Andrew Wilton and Illaria Bignamini, eds., *Grand Tour. The Lure of Italy in the Eighteenth Century* (London: Tate Gallery, 1996).

7. Elisabeth Kieven, "Roman Architecture in the Time of Piranesi, 1740–1776," in the exhibition catalogue *Exploring Rome: Piranesi and His Contemporaries*, edited by Cara D. Denison, Myra Nan Rosenfeld, and Stephanie Wiles (New York and Montréal: Pierpont Morgan Library and the Centre Canadien d'Architecture, 1993), XV–XXIV. See also John Pinto, "Architecture and Urbanism," in Bowron and Joseph 2000.

8. Giuseppe Vasi's achievements as a leading *vedutista* are discussed in Paolo Coen, *Le Magnificenze di Roma nelle incisioni di Giuseppe Vasi* (Rome, 1996).

9. For the early etched *vedute*, including those produced with the French *pensionnaires* of the French Academy, see John Wilton-Ely, *Piranesi. The Complete Etchings*, 2 vols. (San Franciso, 1994), vol. 1.

10. For Piranesi's predecessors in imaginative and fanciful reconstructions of antiquity, see John Wilton-Ely, *Piranesi* (exhibition catalogue), Arts Council of Great Britain, Hayward Gallery (London, 1978), 15, 45–46.

11. For the *Prima Parte* and its sources of inspiration, see Andrew Robison, *Piranesi. Early Architectural Fantasies. A Catalogue Raisonné of the Etchings* (Chicago, 1986), 12–24, 65–112.

12. The influence of earlier graphic artists on Piranesi is discussed extensively in Robison 1986.

13. Piranesi's critical impact on the *pensionnaires* of the French Academy in Rome is examined in John Harris, "Le Geay, Piranesi and International Neo-classicism in Rome, 1740–50," in *Essays in the History of Architecture Presented to Rudolf Wittkower*, edited by Douglas Fraser, Howard Hibberd, and Milton J. Lewine (London, 1967): 189–96. See also Richard Wunder, "Charles M.-A. Challe. A Study of his Life and Work," in *Apollo* LXXXV (January 1968): 22ff.

14. For Paderni and the Herculaneum museum at Portici, see Wolfgang Leppmann, *Winckelmann* (New York, 1970): 169; and Jonathan Scott, *Piranesi* (London, 1975): 14.

15. Alessandro Bettagno, "*Incontro veneziano*: Piranesi and Tiepolo," in Bettagno 1983, 397–400.

16. Thomas 1954, 17. Both Tiepolo and Francesco Guardi also drew *bissone*—the large ornamental gondolas used in Venetian water festivals.

17. A discussion of the various interpretations of the four plates of the *Grotteschi* are provided in Robison 1986, 25–32.

18. In the fourth state of the *Prima Parte* title plate, the full reference to Piranesi's association with this literary society of the Arcadians, which met in the Bosco Parrhasio on the Janiculum, is "*fra gli Arcadi/ Salcindio Tiseio*" (the last two words are Piranesi's name as an Arcadian). See Robison 1986, 68, which dates the fourth state of the title plate to 1748–49. For a discussion of the nature and extensive influence of the Accademia dell'Arcadia, see Liliana Barroero and Stefano Susinno, "Arcadian Rome, Universal Capital of the Arts," in Bowron and Rishel 2000, 47–75.

19. Piranesi's use of the architectural fantasy as medium for personal experiment is examined in John Wilton-Ely 1978, 24–26; Wilton-Ely, "El diseño a traves de la fantasia: los dibujos 'capricci' de Piranesi," in *Arquitecturas Dibujadas. I jornadas internacionales sobre el estudio y conservacion de las fuentes de arquitectura*, edited by M.-J. Ruiz de Ael (Vitoria-Gasteiz, 1994): 81–92; and Wilton-Ely, "Design through Fantasy: Piranesi as Architect," in *Giovanni Battista Piranesi. Die Wahrnehmung von Raum und Zeit*, edited by Corinna Höper, Jeannette Stoschek, and Elisabeth Kieven (Marburg, 2002): 65–88.

20. Robison 1986, 126–31.

21. For Piranesi's development of the *veduta* from the small plates of the 1740s onward, see Wilton-Ely 1978, 25–44.

22. Piranesi's remarkable survey and plan of the Villa Adriana site is discussed in William L. Macdonald and John Pinto, *Hadrian's Villa and Its Legacy* (New Haven, 1995), 246–65. Fig. 318 reproduces his signature of 1741 on the vault of the cryptoportico of the Peristyle Pool Building, and another has been found for 1763.

23. Piranesi's early volume on the tomb of the household of Augustus, *Camere sepolcrali*, is considered in Wilton-Ely 1978, 46–47; and Robison 1986, 46.

24. Piranesi's revolutionary use of images in communicating the past in *Le Antichità Romane* is considered in John Wilton-Ely, "Piranesi and the Role of Archaeological Illustration," in *Piranesi e la Cultura Antiquaria : gli Antecedenti e il Contesto : Atti del Convegno*, Assessorato alla Cultura, Comune di Roma; Istituto Storia dell'Arte, Università degli Studi di Roma (Rome, 1983): 317–38.

25. Chambers's relationship and debts to Piranesi in the 1750s are discussed in John Harris, *Sir William Chambers* (London, 1970); John Harris and Michael Snodin, eds., *William Chambers. Architect to George III* (London, 1996); and in John Wilton-Ely, *Piranesi as Architect and Designer* (New Haven, 1993): 18–22. However, later in his career, Chambers criticized Piranesi's *Collegio Magnifico* fantasy plan: "A celebrated Italian architect whose taste and luxuriance of fancy were unusually great, and the effect of whose compositions on paper has seldom been equalled, knew little of construction or calculation, yet less of the contrivance of habitable structures, or the modes of carrying real works into execution, though styling himself an architect. And when some pensioners of the French Academy at Rome, in the Author's hearing, charged him with ignorance of plans, he composed a very complicated one, since published in his work ; which sufficiently proves, that the charge was not altogether ground-

less." From *Treatise on the Decorative Part of Civil Architecture* (London, 1791), introduction, 10. However, Chambers had been far more favorable to Piranesi in 1774, when he advised his pupil Edward Stevens to see the Venetian when in Rome since "he is full of matter, extravagant 'tis true, often absurd, but from his overflowings you may gather much information." See Harris 1972, 22.

26. For Piranesi's well-documented relationship with Robert Adam, see John Fleming, *Robert Adam and His Circle in Edinburgh and Rome* (London, 1962), passim. See also Damie Stillman, "Robert Adam and Piranesi," in Fraser, Hibberd, and Lewine 1967, 197–206; A.A. Tait, *Robert Adam: Drawings and the Imagination* (Cambridge, 1993), passim; John Wilton-Ely, "Antiquity Applied: Piranesi, Clérisseau and the Adam Brothers," in *Bulletin de l'Association des Historiens de l'Art Italien* (Paris, 1995–96), no. 2, 15–24; John Wilton-Ely, "Amazing and Ingenious Fancies: Piranesi and the Adam Brothers," in Fabio Barry, Mario Bevilacqua, and Heather Hyde Minor, eds., *The Serpent and the Stylus: Image and Idea in the Art of Piranesi* (Ann Arbor: University of Michigan Press, forthcoming). The significant role of Adam's French colleague Clérisseau in this relationship is extensively discussed in Thomas J. McCormick, *Charles-Louis Clérisseau and the Genesis of Neo-Classicism* (Cambridge, MA, 1990).

27. For Piranesi's vendetta against Charlemont, see Scott 1975, 108–16.

28. For the theoretical background to the Greek Revival and Graeco-Roman debate, see D. Wiebenson, *Sources of Greek Revival Architecture* (London, 1968), 47–61; J. M. Crook, *The Greek Revival. Neo-Classical Attitudes in British Architecture: 1760-1870* (London, 1972); H. Honour, *Neo-Classicism* (Harmondsworth, 1977); and Robin Middleton and David Watkin, *Neo-classical and Nineteenth-century Achitecture* (New York, 1980).

29. Wolfgang Herrmann, *Laugier and Eighteenth-century French Theory* (London, 1962); and Joseph Rykwert, *On Adam's House in Paradise. The Idea of the Primitive Hut in Architectural History* (Cambridge, MA, 1981).

30. Alex Potts, *Flesh and the Ideal. Winckelmann and the Origins of Art History* (New Haven, 1994). For a selection of Winckelmann's writings, see *Winckelmann. Writings on* Art, selected and edited by David Irwin (London, 1972); and Johann Joachim Winckelmann, *History of the Art of Antiquity*, introduction by Alex Potts, translated by Harry Francis Mallgrave (Los Angeles, 2005).

31. Julien-David Le Roy, *The Ruins of the Most Beautiful Monuments of Greece*, introduction by Robin Middleton, translation by David Britt (Los Angeles, 2004).

32. The plates and full Italian text of *Della Magnificenza de' Romani* are reprinted in *Piranesi. The Polemical Works*, edited and introduced by John Wilton-Ely (Farnborough, 1972). For a discussion of the literary sources of Piranesi's folio and its philosophical significance, see Sarah F. Maclaren, *La Magnificenza e il suo Doppio. Il Pensiero Estetico di Giovanni Battista Piranesi* (Milan, 2005).

33. For Piranesi's involvement in the Graeco-Roman debate and his use of literary sources, see Wilton-Ely, "Vision and Design: Piranesi's 'fantasia' and the Graeco-Roman controversy," in Georges Brunel, ed., *Piranèse et les Français: Actes du Colloque tenu à la Villa Médicis* (Rome: Académie de France à Rome, 1978): 529–52. For a challenging reappraisal of Piranesi's involvement in the debate, see Lola Kantor-Kazovsky, *Piranesi as Interpreter of Roman Architecture and the Origins of his Intellectual World* (Città di Castello, 2005).

34. For a discussion of Piranesi's polemical-archaeological folios of the 1760s, see Wilton-Ely 1978, 65–80.

35. The origins and character of the folio *Il Campo Marzio dell'Antica Roma* is examined in John Wilton-Ely, "Utopia or Megalopolis? The 'Ichnographia' of Piranesi's Campus Martius reconsidered," in Bettagno 1983, 293–304.

36. Giovanni Battista Piranesi, *Observations on the Letter of Monsieur Mariette with Opinions on Architecture, and a Preface to a New Treatise on the Introduction and Progress of the Fine Arts in Europe in Ancient Times*, introduction by John Wilton-Ely, translated by Caroline Beamish and David Britt (Los Angeles, 2002). The significance of the *Parere su l'Architettura* was first explored in Rudolf Wittkower, "Piranesi's 'Parere su l'Architettura,' " in *Journal of the Warburg Institute* II (1938–39): 147–58, republished as "Piranesi's Architectural Creed," in Wittkower, *Studies in the Italian Baroque*, 235–46.

37. The surviving drawings for the additional *Parere* plates, together with those recently discovered (now in the collection of the National Gallery of Art,

Washington, D.C.) are discussed in John Wilton-Ely, "The Art of Polemic: Piranesi and the Graeco-Roman Controversy," in Philippe Boutry et al., eds., *La Grecia Antica : Mito e Simbolo per l'Eta della Grande Rivolution* (Milan, 1991): 121–30. The two signed drawings in Washington are full-scale studies in pen, ink, and wash with chalk for the fourth and fifth additional plates to the *Parere*.

38. The plates and texts of the introductory essay in Italian, French, and English of the *Diverse Maniere* are reprinted in Wilton-Ely 1972.

39. For a bibliography of publications on the *Carceri* up to 1994, see Wilton-Ely 1994, vol. 1, 1209–18; and for a discussion of their genesis and impact, see Wilton-Ely 1978, 81–91, 126. Among the most challenging of recent interpretations is Manfredo Tafuri," 'The Wicked Architect': G. B. Piranesi, Heterotopia, and the Voyage," in *The Sphere and the Labyrinth. Avant-Gardes and Architecture from Piranesi to the 1970s* (Cambridge, MA, 1987): 25–40. A detailed analysis of the etchings, their sources, and various states is provided in Robison 1986, 37–53, 139–210.

40. The formal and perpectival complexity of the *Carceri* is examined in Ulya Vogt-Göknil, *Giovanni Battista Piranesi: Carceri* (Zurich, 1958).

41. The Roman symbolism and inscriptions, especially of the later state of the *Carceri*, are examined in Silvia Gavuzzo-Stewart, *Nelle Carceri di G.B. Piranesi* (Leeds, 1999).

42. Renato Barilli, "Piranesi and Burke," in Bettagno 1983, 325–38.

43. For Simone Quaglio's *Fidelio* set design (Theatre Museum, Munich), see Wilton-Ely 1978, 124, fig. 235.

44. Piranesi's biographer J.-G. Legrand commented on the artist's friendly relationship with Clement XIII and members of the Rezzonico family. Among other things, Legrand mentioned that Piranesi had taught the Pope's nephews to draw, but did not specify which of the four were involved. See *Notice historique sur la vie et les ouvrages de J.B. Piranesi . . . Redigée sur les notes et les pièces communiqueés par ses fils* (1799), transcribed in G. Erouart and M. Mosser, "A propos de la 'Notice historique sur la vie et les ouvrages de J.-B. Piranesi': origine et fortune d'une biographie," in Brunel 1978: 227.

45. Borromini's modernization of the Lateran and the surviving drawings for this in the Biblioteca Apostolica Vaticana are discussed and illustrated by Joseph Connors in Joseph Connors and John Wilton-Ely, *Piranesi Architetto* (exhibition catalogue), American Academy in Rome, 1992, 97–105. See also Rudolf Wittkower 1973, 212–13.

46. Manfred F. Fischer, "Die Umbauplane des G.B. Piranesi fur Chor von S. Giovanni in Laterano, Rom," in *Munchne Jahrbuch der Bildenden Kunst XVIII* (1968): 207–26.

47. The twenty-three presentation drawings are discussed in detail and fully reproduced in Dorothea Nyberg and Herbert Mitchell, eds., *Piranesi. Drawings and Etchings at the Avery Architectural Library* (exhibition catalogue). They are also discussed and fully reproduced in Connors and Wilton-Ely 1992. Another presentation drawing from the set, *Tavola Decimterza*, which shows a version with modifications of the transverse sectional view of the sanctuary looking west in *Tavola Nona*, has been discovered recently in the Hermitage Museum, St. Petersburg. See Bent Sørensen, "Two Overlooked Drawings by Piranesi for S. Giovanni in Laterano in Rome," in *Burlington Magazine* CXLIII, no.1180 (2001): 430–33. The same article discusses a hitherto unidentified study by Piranesi in the Morgan Library & Museum for the reliquary containing the heads of Saints Peter and Paul in the papal altar at the Lateran.

48. For this aspect of Venetian design, see Rudolf Wittkower, "S.Maria della Salute: Scenographic Architecture and the Venetian Baroque," in *Journal of the Society of Architectural Historians* 16 (1975): 3ff, reprinted in *Studies in the Italian Baroque* (London, 1975): 126ff.

49. For Cardinal Giambattista Rezzonico's tomb and Hewetson's career, see Terence Hodgkinson, "Christopher Hewetson, An Irish Sculptor in Rome," in *Walpole Society XXXIV* (1952–54): 42–54.

50. Canova's tomb for Clement XIII is discussed and reproduced in Hugh Honour, "Canova e i suoi incisori," in Sergej Andrisov, Mario Guderzo, and Giuseppe Pavanello, eds., *Canova* (exhibition catalogue), Milano, 2003: 415–16, 429.

51. A detailed discussion of the design and execution of Piranesi's complex of buildings for S. Maria del Priorato can be found in *Piranesi e l'Aventino* (exhibi-

tion catalogue), edited by Barnara Jatta (jointly arranged by the Biblioteca Apostolica Vaticana and Sovrano Militare Ordine di Malta in the Priory; Milan, 1998), which includes the essays by John Wilton-Ely, "Piranesi Architetto," 63–78; "Piranesi: designer e antiquario," 95–104; with related catalogue entries in "L'intervento di Piranesi per il Priorato," 172–89. See also Connors and Wilton-Ely 1992. The majority of the surviving drawings, which were shown in both Rome exhibitions, are discussed in Felice Stampfle, *Giovanni Battista Piranesi: Drawings in the Pierpont Morgan Library* (exhibition catalogue; New York, 1978).

52. Attention was first directed to the significance of the Pelosini account book in Rudof Wittkower, "Piranesi as Architect," in the exhibition catalogue *Piranesi*, edited by O. Parks (Northampton, MA, Smith College, 1961): 99–109, reprinted in Wittkower, *Studies in the Italian Baroque* (London, 1975): 247–58.

53. For a detailed discussion of Piranesi's iconographic program and its sources, see John Wilton-Ely, "Piranesi's Symbolic Images on the Aventine: The Piazza and Priory Church of the Knights of Malta, Rome," in *Apollo* CIII (March 1976): 214–27.

54. The appearance of the original façade is recorded in an elevational drawing of S. Maria del Priorato, now in Sir John Soane's Museum, London. It appears to have been acquired from the office of Robert Adam, who finally left Rome in 1757. No documentary evidence has yet been found to establish when and by whom the drawing was made, but it may have been acquired by his brother James during his visit to Rome in 1761–63. This is reproduced in Jata 1998, 71.

55. For the researches and excavations of Etruscan tombs at Tarquinia and other sites by James Byers and Thomas Jenkins, in which Piranesi was also partly involved, see Mauro Cristofani, *La Scoperta degli etruschi, archeologia e antiquaria nel '700* (Rome, 1983). See also Mauro Cristofani, "Le opere teoriche di G.B. Piranesi e l'etruscheria," in Lo Bianco 1983: 211–20; Rykwert 1980: 409–10, n. 170; and the respective entries for Byers and Jenkins in *Encyclopedia of the History of Classical Archaeology*, edited by Nancy T. de Grummond (Westport, CT, 1996).

56. The design by Marchionni for the Aventine altar, now in Cooper-Hewitt, National Design Museum (1938-88-4193), is reproduced in Jatta 1998, 73. Bent Sørensen, in discussing a recently identified presentation drawing by Piranesi in the Hermitage Museum, for a projected allegorical figure to be placed on the pedestal which originally supported the column of Antoninus Pius, has thrown considerable light on the genesis of the Apotheosis group on Piranesi's Aventine altar. See Sørensen, "An Unpublished Project by Piranesi for Clement XIII," in *Burlington Magazine* CXLII , no. 1169 (2001): 497–501.

57. All three versions of Piranesi's *Apologetical Essay* of the *Diverse Maniere* in Italian, French, and English are reprinted in Wilton-Ely 1972, together with the etched plates.

58. Susan Dixon, "Giovanni Battista Piranesi's *Diverse maniere d'adornare i cammini* and Chimneypiece Design as a Vehicle for Polemic," in *Studies in the Decorative Arts*, Bard Graduate Center for Studies in the Decorative Arts I (Fall 1993): 76–98.

59. For the Burghley House chimneypiece, see Wilton-Ely 1993, 129, plate 7. See also Scott in Bettagno 1983, 55–56. No documentation has so far come to light about this commission, but the ninth Earl of Exeter made an important second visit to Rome in March 1769, where he acquired some sculpture and a marble tabletop from Piranesi. (Information kindly provided by Charles Pugh.) It has been suggested that Robert Adam was involved in this transaction; see Alison Kelley, *The Book of English Fireplaces* (1968), fig. 80.

60. John Hope, for whom Piranesi produced the chimneypiece sometime before 1769, entered the family banking business in Amsterdam in 1762 and, two years later, married the daughter of the Burgomaster of Rotterdam, Philippina van der Hoeven. Their eldest son, Thomas, the famous Regency collector and designer, was born in 1769. The Hopes were outstanding patrons and collectors. Sir Joshua Reynolds praised "Mr. Hope's Cabinet, not only because it is acknowledged to be the first in Amsterdam, but because [he] had an opportunity (by the particular attention and civility of its possessors) of seeing it oftener, and considering it more my leisure, than any other collection." (Reynolds, *The Literary Works* II (1835), 207–80.) This cabinet is possibly the one to which Piranesi referred in giving the location of the chimney

piece in his etching. See David Watkin, *Thomas Hope and the Neo-Classical Idea* (London, 1968), 208, 292.

61. William Rieder, "Piranesi at Gorhambury," in *Burlington Magazine* 117 (September 1975): 582–91; and Alastair Rowan, "Wedderburn Castle, Berwickshire," in *Country Life* 156 (Aug. 8, 1974): 356. The chimneypiece, formerly at Stowe House, Buckinghamshire, was produced by Piranesi for George Grenville, later the first Marquess of Buckingham. The latter acquired the restored marble Buckingham Vase from the artist in 1774, and the caption in the etched plate of the object in *Vasi, Candelabri, Cippi, Sarcofagi...* refers to the chimneypiece, reproduced in Wilton-Ely 1994, 978, no. 901). See Jonathan Scott, "Another Chimneypiece by Piranesi," in Bettagno 1983, 51–57, in which the author traced the work to the boardroom of the Banco de Santander in Spain.

62. Stillman 1967.

63. While Bélanger's design is currently attributed to his commission for the Comte d'Artois at the Pavilion of Bagatelle, near Paris, Dr. Alain Gruber, in a communication to the author, considers that the initials "M.A." on the andirons connect it to a residence of Queen Marie Antoinette.

64. Bruno Contardi, "Piranesi in Campidoglio," in *'700 Disegnatore: incisioni, progetti, caricature,' Studi sul Settecento Romano* 12, edited by Elisa Debenedetti (Rome, 1997): 161–78.

65. For the Etruscan Rooms of Adam, see Stillman 1967, 197–206; John Wilton-Ely, "Pompeian and Etruscan Tastes in the Neo-Classical Country House Interior," in G. Jackson-Stops et al., eds., *The Fashioning and Functioning of the British Country House* (Washington, D.C., 1989), 61–64; Eileen Harris, *The Genius of Robert Adam. His Interiors* (New Haven, 2001); John Wilton-Ely, "Le 'Stanze Etrusche' di Robert Adam: una rivoluzione stilistica," in *Atti dell'Accademia dei Lincei* (Rome, forthcoming).

66. Piranesi's plates for Egyptian chimneypieces and for the walls of the Caffè degli Inglesi, Rome, are reproduced in Wilton-Ely 1994, vol. 2, 936–38, nos. 863–75.

67. For Piranesi's significance in the Egyptian Revival, see Nikolaus Pevsner and Susan Lang, "The Egyptian Revival," in Nikolaus Pevsner, *Studies in Art, Architecture and Design* I (London, 1968): 215–16; James Stevens Curl, *The Egyptian Revival* (London, 1982), 79–81.

68. Piranesi's source material for his Egyptian designs, chimneypieces, and interiors, are discussed in Wittkower, "Piranesi e il gusto egiziano," in *Sensibilità e razionalità nel Settecento*, edited by Vittore Branca (Florence, 1967): 659–74; republished as "Piranesi and Eighteenth-century Egyptomania," in Wittkower, *Studies in the Italian Baroque* (London, 1975): 260–73.

69. Pevsner 1968, 231.

70. Pevsner 1968, 216. "*Vederete in quest'Opera usato ciò che peranche in questo genere non era conosciuto. L'Architettura Egiziana, per la prima volta apparisce; la prima volta, dico, perchè in ora il mondo ha sempre creduto non esservi altro che piramidi, guglie, e giganti, escludendo non esservi parti sufficienti per adornare e sostenere questo sistema d'architettura.*"

71. See *Piranèse et les Français: 1740-1790* (exhibition catalogue), edited by Georges Brunel et al. (Rome: Académie de France à Rome, 1976), 49–50, fig. 9.

72. In December 1776, the Welsh painter Thomas Jones (1742–1803) criticized the Caffè degli Inglesi as "a filthy vaulted room the walls of which were painted with sphinxes, obelisks and pyramids from capricious designs of Piranesi, and fitter to adorn the inside of an Egyptian sepulchre, than a room of social conversation." B. Ford, ed., "The Memoirs of Thomas Jones," in *Walpole Society* XXXII (1946–48): 54.

73. James Barry to Edmund Burke, April 8, 1769; quoted in James Barry, *The Works of James Barry, Esq., Historical Painter...Containing His Correspondence from France and Italy with Mr. Burke...To Which is Prefixed Some Account of the Life and Writings of the Author* (London: 1809), 160–61.

74. Watkin 1968, 114–18.

75. For Hope's surviving Egyptian furniture, see *Treasure Houses of Britain* (exhibition catalogue), edited by G. Jackson-Stops (Washington, D.C.: National Gallery of Art, 1985), 590, no. 525.

76. A major and far-reaching assessment of Piranesi as a designer of furniture and the decorative arts is provided in Alvar González-Palacios, *Il Tempio del*

Gusto: Roma e il Regno delle Due Sicilie: Le Arti Decorative in Italia fra Classicismi e Barocco, 2 vols. (Milan, 1984), Vol. 1, 115–48.

77. Francis J. Watson, "A Side Table by Piranesi: A Masterpiece of Neo-classic Furniture," in *Minneapolis Institute of Arts Bulletin* 54 (1965): 19–29; expanded in Watson, "A Masterpiece of Neo-classic Furniture: A Side-Table designed by Piranesi," in *Burlington Magazine* CVIII (1965): 102; and Hugh Honour, *Cabinet Makers and Furniture Designers* (London, 1969), 146–47.

78. See Watson 1965; *Age of Neo-Classicism* (exhibition catalogue; London: Arts Council of Great Britain, 1972), no. 1576, 733.

79. "Nature and Antiquity: Reflections on Piranesi as a Furniture Designer," in *Furniture History* XXVI (1990; festschrift issue for Geoffrey Beard): 191–97.

80. William Rieder, Piranesi's "Diverse Maniere," in *Burlington Magazine* CXV (May 1973): 309–17. See also the same author's contribution to *Age of Neo-Classicism*, nos. 1577 and 1578, 733–34.

81. Scott 1975, 226, 315. The Earl of Carlisle's letter of January 1768 is quoted in John Heneage Jesse, *George Selwyn and His Contemporaries* (London, 1882).

82. Watkin 1968, 112, 256; *Age of Neo-Classicism*, 777 (no. 651); Wilton-Ely 1978 (catalogue), 111 (no. 282a).

83. For the context of Hope's clock in the Flaxman Room at his house in Duchess Street, London, see Watkin 1968, 112–14.

84. For the antiquarian market of eighteenth-century Rome as a context to Piranesi's creation of chimneypieces and his activities as a restorer, see "An Antiquarian Handlist and the Beginnings of the Pio Clementino," in Seymour Howard, *Antiquity Restored: Essays on the Afterlife of the Antique* (Vienna, 1998): 142–53; Damie Stillman, "Chimneypieces for the English Market: a Thriving Business in Late Eigheenth-Century Rome," in *Art Bulletin* 59 (March 1977): 85–94. See also Wilton and Bignamini 1997, passim.

85. John Wilton-Ely, "Antiquity for the Designer: Piranesi as a Restorer of Classical Antiquities" (paper in the symposium *Roma, Piranesi e l'Effetto Piranesi*, Istituto Svedese di Studi Classici a Roma, in collaboration with the Swedish Academy and National Museum, Stockholm, 2001, forthcoming). See also Jonathan Scott, *The Pleasures of Antiquity: British Collectors of Greece and Rome* (New Haven, 2003): 104–09.

86. For Charles Townley as a collector, see Scott 2003, 193–208; B. F. Cook, *The Townley Marbles* (London: British Museum, 1985). For Thomas Hope as a collector, see Scott 2003, 237–45; and for Thomas Hope's marble candelabrum by Piranesi, see Watkin 1968, 208, fig. 7 and plate 65.

87. Richard Marks and Brian L. Blench, *The Warwick Vase* (The Burrell Collection, Glasgow Museums and Art Galleries, 1979); Scott in Anna Lo Bianco 1983, 339–47. For Piranesi and the eighteenth-century excavations at Hadrian's Villa, Tivoli, see also MacDonald and Pinto 1995, 294–97.

88. Denison, Rosenfeld, and Wiles 1993, 119–20 (no. 65).

89. David Udy, "Piranesi's *Vasi*, the English Silversmith and His Patrons," in *Burlington Magazine* CXX (December 1978): 820–37.

90. Scott in Bettagno 1983, 55.

91. *Leeds Art Calendar*, no. 59 (1966), 2; Scott in Bettagno 1983, 53–54; Wilton-Ely 1972 (catalogue), 119–20 (no. 316). Another pair of silver gilt wine coolers by Barnard to the same design, in the British Museum, bear the coat of arms of the Beaumont family from Whitley in Yorkshire.

92. Michael McCarthy, "Piranesi and Sir Roger Newdigate," in *Burlington Magazine* CXIV (July 1972): 466–72. Wilton-Ely 1978 (catalogue), 117, (nos. 306–07); Macdonald and Pinto 1995, 296. See also Alvar González-Palacios, "Sir Roger Newdigate and Piranesi" (correspondence), in *Burlington Magazine* CXIV (1972): 716–19.

93. The function of Piranesi's funerary candelabrum is discussed in John Wilton-Ely, "A Bust of Piranesi by Nollekens," in *Burlington Magazine* CVIII (August 1976): 593–95. The candelabrum's journey from its original setting in S. Maria del Priorato to its current location in the Louvre is traced in Carlo Gasparri, "La Galleria Piranesi da Giovanni Battista a Francesco," in *Xenia* 3 (1982): 91–107. See also Wilton-Ely in Jatta 1998, 188–89. The three erotes shown at the base of the candelabrum in the etched plates in the *Vasi, candelabri, cippi, sarcofagi…* were acquired by Gustav III from Francesco Piranesi and are now in the Royal Palace, Stockholm. See Anne-Marie

94. For the ornamental lunette in the Galleria del Parnaso in Villa Albani, Denison, Rosenfeld, and Wiles 1993, 46–47 (no. 28); Wilton-Ely 1993, 140–43; Carlo Gaspari, "Piranesi a Villa Albani," in *Artisti e Mecenati: dipinti, disegni, sculture e carteggi nella Roma curiale: Studi sul Settecento Romano 12*. The fountain at Villa Albani was identified and discussed in Paolo Gasparri, "Una fontana ritrovata. Ancora su Piranesi a Villa Albani," in *Studi sul Settecento Romano 12 (Artisti e Mecenati. Dipinti, disegni sculture e carteggi nella Roma curiale)* 1996, 193–206.

95. Eileen Harris, *The Furniture of Robert Adam* (London, 1963), 102 (no. 139); Wilton-Ely 1978 (catalogue), 106 (no. 272); and Harris 2001, 268–69.

96. For the circumstances which led to the works remaining in Piranesi's "museo" in Rome being acquired by Gustav III from Franceso Piranesi, see Touati 1998, vol. I, 51–59; vol. II, *The Piranesi Collection*, is in preparation.

97. James Lomax, "Piranesi, Mr. Messenger and the Duke of Newcastle: Supereminent art applied to industry," in *Leeds Art Calendar* 98 (1986): 26–32.

98. John Wilton-Ely, "Ledoux et Piranèse: Speculation et Communication," in *Claude Nicolas Ledoux et le Livre d'Architecture en Français. Etienne Louis Boulée: L'Utopie et la Poésie de l'Art* (Paris: Centre des Monuments Nationaux, 2006): 110–19.

99. Francesco Milizia, *Roma, delle belle arti del disegno: Parte prima: Dell'architettura civile* (Bassano, 1787), 197. Giovani Lodovico Bianconi, *Opere*, vol.2, *Lettere al marchese Filippo Hercolani* (Milan, 1802), 275: "Oh, quanto è diverso Il disegnar dall'eseguir le imprese ! L'opera riuscì troppo carica d'ornamenti, e questi pure, benchè presi dall'antico, non sono tutti d'accordo fra di loro. La Chiesa del Priorato piacerà certo a molti, come piaceva sommamente al Piranesi, che la riguardò mai sempre per un capo d'opera, ma non piacerebbe nè a Vitruvio, nè al Palladio, se tornassero in Roma."

100. Sylvia Lavin, *Quatremère de Quincy and the Invention of a Modern Language of Architecture* (Cambridge, MA, 1992), 133.

101. John Wilton-Ely, "Soane and Piranesi," in *Late Georgian Classicism: Papers Given at the Georgian Group Symposium, 1987*, Roger White and Caroline Lightburn, eds. (London: The Georgian Group, 1987), 45–57; John Wilton-Ely, *Piranesi, Paestum and Soane* (London: Sir John Soane's Museum, 2002).

102. David Watkin, *Sir John Soane and Enlightenment Thought and the Royal Academy Lectures* (Cambridge, 1996), 605.

103. For a range of writers influenced by Piranesi's *Carcere*, see Wilton-Ely 1978 (book), 126. Also see in particular J. Andersen, "Giant Dreams: Piranesi's Influence in England," in *English Miscellany*, vol. 3 (1952): 49–60; Luzius Keller, *Piranèse et les Romantiques Français. Le mythe des escaliers en spirale* (Paris, 1966); Marguerite Yourcenar, "The Dark Brain of Piranesi," in Yourcenar, *The Dark Brain of Piranesi and Other Essays* (Henley-on-Thames, 1985): 88–128.

104. Maurizio Calvesi, "Saggio introduttivo," in Henri Focillon, *Giovanni Battista Piranesi*, edited by Maurizio Calvesi and Augusta Monferini (Bologna, 1967): iii–xlii; Tafuri 1987; Rykwert 1980.

105. Robert Venturi, *Complexity and Contradiction in Architecture* (New York, 1966).

PIRANESI AND HIS AESTHETIC OF ECLECTICISM

1. I am extremely grateful for the support of the Peter Krueger Foundation in the research and writing of this essay. This generous grant is but one of the many ways in which the Krueger family has shown support for my work on Piranesi, and I remain deeply indebted to them for their enthusiasm for and encouragement of scholarship in the decorative arts.

2. The most significant early study of Piranesi's writings is Rudolf Wittkower, "Piranesi's *Parere su l'architettura*," in *Journal of the Warburg and Courtauld Institutes* 2: 147–58. An excellent critique of Wittkower's characterization of Piranesi's *volte-face* is given by Aline Payne, "Rudolf Wittkower and Architectural Principles in the Age of Modernism," in *Journal of the Society of Architectural Historians*, 53 (1994): 322–42. The suggestion that Piranesi relied heavily on a ghostwriter was malevolently given by Giovanni Lodovico Bianconi in his obituary of Piranesi; see G. L. Bianconi, "Elogio storico del cavaliere Giambatista Piranesi," in *Antologia romana*, no. 34 (1779): 274. The suggestion has been given some credence by current scholars, as cautiously

noted by Andrew Robison, 1986, 57, note 80, and more recently in Mario Bevilaqua, Heather Hyde Minor, and Fabio Barry, eds., *The Serpent and the Stylus: Essays on G. B. Piranesi* (Ann Arbor: University of Michigan Press, 2006): 7.

3. Two valuable essays on Piranesi's writings are John Wilton-Ely, "Introduction," in *Giovanni Battista Piranesi, Observations on the Letter of Monsieur Mariette, with Opinions on Architecture, and a Preface to a New Treatise on the Introduction and Progress of the Fine Arts in Europe in Ancient Times* (Los Angeles: Getty Publications, 2002): 1–83; and an important new study of the intellectual context of Piranesi's writings by Lola Kantor-Kazovsky, *Piranesi as Interpreter of Roman Architecture and the Origins of his Intellectual World* (Florence: Leo S. Olschki, 2006). See also Didier Laroque, *Le discours de Piranèse: l'ornement sublime et le suspens de l'architecture, suivi d'un tableau de l'oeuvre écrit de Piranèse et d'une nouvelle traduction de 'Ragionamento apologetico in difesa dell' architettura Egizia e Toscana'* (Paris, 1999).

4. An interesting discussion on the relation of text to image in Piranesi's work is given in Corinna Hoper, "Die 'Legende zum Bild'—Uber das Verhaltnis von Schrift und Darstellung in der Radierungen Piranesis," in C. Hoper et al., eds., *Giovanni Battista Piranesi: Die Wahrnehmung von Raum und Zeit* (Marburg, 2002): 9–20. Another study of Piranesi's interaction of words and images is given in Heather Hyde Minor, "Engraved in Porphyry, Printed on Paper: Piranesi and Lord Charlemont," in Bevilaqua, Minor, Barry, eds., *The Serpent and the Stylus* (2006): 123–47.

5. On the *Prima parte*, see Andrew Robison, *Piranesi, Early Architectural Fantasies: A Catalogue Raisonné of the Etchings* (Chicago and London: University of Chicago Press, 1986), 12–24, 65–112.

ii. On Nicola Giobbe and his relation to the *Prima parte*, see Jorg Garms, "Considérations sur la prima parte," in Georges Brunel, ed., *Piranèse et les Français* (1976): 265–80.

iii. "La doviziosa, e scelta raccolta, che Voi avete di Pitture, di disegni, di Libri, e di Carte intagliate, di cui non v' e forse in queste dominante la piu copiosa, o unita almeno con piu squisito gusto." *Prima parte* (1743), dedication page, verso. An interesting discussion of the contents of Giobbe's library can be found in Kantor-Kazovsky 2006, 19.

6. "Io vi diro solamente, che di tali immagini mi hanno riempiuto lo spirito questi parlanti ruine, che di simili non arrivai a potermene mai formare sopra I disegni, benche accuratissimi, che di queste stesse ha fatto l'immortale Palladio, e che io pur sempre mi teneva innanzi agli occhi. Quindi e ch'essendomi venuto in pensiero do farne palesi al Mondo alcune di queste: ned essendo sperabile a un Architetto do questi tempo , di poterne effettivamente eseguire alcuna: … ned apparendo ne' principi, o ne' private disposizione a farneli vedere; altro partito non veggo restare a me, e a qualisivoglia altro Architetto moderno, che spiegare con disegni le proprie idée." *Prima parte* (1743), dedication page, recto. Translation from "Original Text of *Prima parte* and English Translation," in Dorothea Nyberg, ed., *Giovanni Battista Piranesi: Drawings and Etchings at Columbia University* (exhibition catalogue; New York: Columbia University, 1972): 117.

7. "Piu di tutto pero io conosco di dovere a gl' insegnamenti vostri, avendomi Voi non solo d' ogni rarita di questo genere antica, o moderna, che si trova in Roma, fatto osservare le piu singolari belleze a parte a parte: ma con gli esempi de' vostri eccelenti disegni ancora dimostrato, come si possa in nuove forme fare un lodevole uso de' ritrovati de' nostril maggiori." *Prima parte* (1743), dedication page, verso. Translation in "Original Text of *Prima parte* and English Translation," in Nyberg 1972: 118.

8. The significance of the dedicatory letter has been addressed previously in John Wilton-Ely, "Vision and Design: Piranesi's 'Fantasia' and the Graeco-Roman controversy," in Brunel 1976: 530; and Robison 1986: 12.

9. Marc-Antoine Laugier, *An Essay on Architecture*, W. and A. Hermann, trans. (Los Angeles: Hennesy & Ingalls, 1977), 8.

10. Julien-David Le Roy, *The Ruins of the Most Beautiful Monuments of Greece* (Getty Trust Publications, 2004), with an important introduction by Robin Middleton; and Alastair Smart, *Allan Ramsey: Painter, Essayist, and Man of the Enlightenment* (New Haven: Yale University Press, 1992): 115–48. See also Middleton's thorough and insightful study of these early writings on Greek architecture, "The Abbé de Cordemoy and the Graeco-Gothic Ideal: A Prelude to Romantic Classicism," in *Journal of the Warburg and Courtauld Institutes* 25 (1962): 278–320; 26 (1963): 90–123.

11. On Winkelmann's place within this debate, see Lola Kantor-Kazovsky, "Pierre Jean Mariette ad Piranesi," in Bevilaqua Barry 2006: 150–51. She correctly emphasizes the preeminence of Mariette among the Philhellenics and the particular significance of his *Traité des pierres gravées* (Paris, 1750) in this context. See also Ralph Stern, "Winkelmann, Piranesi, and the Graeco-Roman Controversies: A Late Exchange in the *Querelle des anciens et des modernes*," in *Architectura* 33, no. 1 (2003): 62–94; Krzysztof Pomian, "Mariette et Winckelmann," in *Révue Germanique Internationale* 13 (2000): 24–37; Norbert Miller, "Winkelmann und der Griechenstreit. Uberlegungen zur Historisierung der Antiken–Anschauung im 18. Jahrhundert," in Thomas Gaehtgens, ed., *Johann Joachim Winkelmann, 1717–1768* (Hamburg, 1986): 239–64; and Lionello Sozzi, "La polemique anti–Italienne en France au XVIème siècle," in *Atti dell' Accademia delle scienze di torino. Clase di scienze morali, storiche e filologiche* 106, no. 1 (1972): 99–190.

12. On eighteenth-century Etruscan studies in Italy, see Mauro Cristofano, *La scoperta degli etuschi: Archeologia e antiquarian nel '700* (Rome: Consiglio Nazionale delle Ricerche, 1983); and Nancy Thomson de Grummond, "Rediscovery," in Larissa Bonfante, ed., *Etruscan Life and Afterlife: A Handbook of Etruscan Studies* (Detroit: Wayne University Press, 1986): 37–40. On Piranesi's particular interest, see Mauro Cristofano, "Le opere teoreticche di G. B. Piranesi e l'etrusceria," in Anna Lo Bianco, ed., *Piranesi e la cultura antiquarian, gli antecedenti e il contesto* (Rome: Multigrafica, 1983).

13. "Perciò non sempre si dee stare alle regole di Vitruvio, qual legge inalterabile; Poichè se si farà osservazione sopra I monumenti antichi, si troverà una gran varietà di proporzioni, le quail, parlando de' monumenti piu insigni in architettura, so conoscono dirette sempre dale circostanze del sito, e delle stesse fabbriche, come spiegherò nell' opera mia architettura," *Le Antichità Romane*, II, plate 5; Kantor-Kazovsky 2006, 114.

14. Kantor-Kazovsky discusses the specific importance of these works for an understanding of Piranesi's writings, and notes that books by both authors were in the library of Nicola Giobbe. See Kantor-Kazovsky 2006, 114ff. On the subject of creative license in Renaissance architectural theory, see Alina Payne, *The Architectural Treatise in the Italian Renaissance: Architectural Invention, Ornament and Literary Culture* (Cambridge and New York: Cambridge University Press, 1999), especially chapter one, "License and Archaeology," 15–33; and with particular reference to Piranesi, Terry Kirk, "Piranesi's Poetic License: His Influence on Modern Italian Architecture," in Bevilacqua, Minor, Barry, eds., *The Serpent and the Stylus* (2006): esp. 239–40 and note 4.

15. For a range of views on the *Campo marzio dell' Antica Roma*, see John Wilton-Ely, "Utopia or Megapolis? The 'Ichnographia' of Piranesi's 'Campus Martius' Reconsidered," in Allesandro Bettagno, ed., *Piranesi tra Venezia e l'Europa: Civita Veneziana Saggi* (Florence, 1983): 293–304; Norbert Miller, "Verteidigung des Erhabenen. Der Griechen–Streit," in *Archaologie des Traumes: Versuch uber Giovanni Battista Piranesi* (Munich, 1978): 221–90; and Manfredi Tafuri, *The Sphere and the Labyrinth*, trans. P. d'Acierno and R. Connolly (Cambridge, MA, 1987; first Italian edition, 1980), 33–35; Marcel Baumgarten, "Topografie als Medium der Erinnerung in Piranesis 'Campo Marzio dell' Antica Roma,' " in Wolfram Martini, ed., *Architektur und Erinnerung* (Gottingen, 2000): 71–102; and, most recently, Susan M. Dixon, "Illustrating Ancient Rome, or the *Ichnographia* as Uchronia and Other Time Warps in Piranesi's *Il Camp Marzio*," in Sam Smiler and Stephanie Moser, eds., *In Envisioning the past: Archaeology and the Image* (London: Blackwell, 2005): 115–32.

16. "Sebbenecio do che io piuttosto temer debbio, si e, che non sembrino inventate a capriccio, piu che prese dal vero, alcune cose di questa delineazione del Campo; le quail de taluno contronta coll' antica maniera di architettare, compredera, che molto da essa di discostano, e s'avvicinano all'usanza de' nostril tempi. Ma chiumnque egli sia, prima dui condonnare alcuno d'impostura, osservi di grazia l'antica piñata di Roma…osservi le antiche ville del Lazio, quella d'Adriano in Tivoli, le terme, i sepolcri, e gli altri edifizi di Roma, che rimangono, in ispezie poi fuori di Porta Capena: non ritrova

inventate piu cose dai moderni, che dagli antichi contra le piu rigide leggi dell'architettura. O derive pertanto dalla natura e condizione delle arti, che cuando sono giunte al sommo, vanno a poco a poco in decadenza e in rovina, o cosi porti l'indole degli uomini, che nelle professioni ancora reputansi lecita qualsisia cosa, che nelle fabricche nostrale talvolta biasimiamo." *Il Campo Marzio dell'Antica Roma*, 1762, dedicatory letter, xi.

17. *Trofei di Ottaviano Augusto* (1753), pl. iii; Kantor-Kazovsky 2006, 91.

18. *Antiquus Bivii Viarum Appiae et Ardeatinae ad il Lapidem Extra Portam Capenam* (1756).

19. "La seconda Tavola posta alla testa del secondo Volume, che tratta de' Sepolcri antichi, rappresenta la Via Appia presso Roma nel Bivio, che dava principio all' Ardeatina. Cicerone ci narra, che quivi la magnificenza e'l desiderio de' Romani di far passare il nome loro alla posterita, avevano eretti quegl' immensi Sepolcri, alcuni de' quali rassomigliavano piuttosto a de' templi, o a de' palazzi, che a de' luoghi consecrati alla morte. L'autore ha cercato di dare un' idea della confusione, che Cicero dice essere stata da per tutto." *Lettere de Giustificazione scritte a Milord Charlemont* (1756), ii, note 3.

20. Kantor-Kazovsky similarly underscores the significance of this note. I elaborate here on her articulation of the notion of Piranesi's aesthetic of confusion; Kantor-Kazovsky 2006, 90.

21. "Cosi in fatto fecero i Romani, che dopo avere usata per piu secoli l'estrusca architettura, adottarono poi anche la greca, e l'una a l'altra unirono insieme," *Diverse Maniere d'adornare i cammini* (1769), dedication.

22. "Quella pazza liberta di lavorare a capriccio," Piranesi, *Parere su l'architettura* (1765), 10.

23. Charles de Secondat, baron de Montesquieu, "Un batiment d'ordre gothique dans les choses est une espèce d'énigme pour l'oeil qui le voit, et l'âme est embarrassée, comme quand on lui présente un poème obscure." From *Essai sur le goût dans les choses de la nature et de l'art.*

24. Translation from Piranesi, *Observations* (2002), 104.

25. "Mostratemi de' disegni fatti da qualsivoglia rigorista, da chiunque si crede d'aver coneputo un progetto de' piu maravigliosi per far un'opera; e se non sara piu sciocco costui di chi opera da libero, mio danno: piu sciocco si; imperciocche potra idearsi un edifizio senza irregolatira, quando Quattro pali ritti con un coperto soprappostovi, che sono tutto il prototipo dell' Architettura, potan sussistere interi ed uniti nell' atto medesimo che saran dimezzati, distracti, e disposti per mille versi; in soma, quando il semplice sara un composto, e l'uno sra quella moltitudine che si vuole." Piranesi, *Parere su l'architettura*, 11; translation from Piranesi, *Observations* (2002), 106.

26. Translation from Piranesi, *Observations* (2002), 107.

27. Translation from Piranesi, *Observations* (2002), 108.

28. "Ma ammettiano l'impossibile; supponghiamo, che il Mondo, sebben e ristucco, di tutto quell che non varia di giorno a giorno, facesse alla vostra monotonia la grazia di sosserirla, l'Architettura a che sarebb'ella ridotta? *A un vil métier ou l'on ne feroit que copier*, a detto un certo Signore: talche voi altri non solamente sareste Architetti ordinari ordinarissimi, com' io v' ho detto poc' anzi, ma da meno de' muratori. Imperocche questi dal porre in opera sempre una cosa, oltre che, la imparerebbono a mente, avrebbono di piu di voi altri il vantaggio del meccanismo: anzi finireste affato di essere Architetti: imperocche i padroni, qualora volessero fabbricare, sarebbero sciocchi a chieder anche dall' Archtetto quel che non tanto meno spesa potrebbono avere dal muratore." Piranesi, *Parere su l'Architettura*, 14. Translation from Piranesi, *Observations* (2002), 110–11.

29. Translation from Piranesi, *Observations* (2002), 111.

30. Piranesi indicates that the Roman capital in the vignette at the start of the *Osservazioni* was found in the courtyard of the Palazzo Gabrielli; and the Etruscan antefix at the *Introduzione* belongs to the artist Matthew Nultry.

31. See Peter Murray, *Piranesi and the Grandeur of Ancient Rome* (London: Thames and Hudson, 1971), 46.

32. Because three of these plates are signed "Cavaliere," they must postdate the conference on Piranesi by Clement XIII of the order of the golden spur, which occurred in 1767. Robison gives the dates of 1769, *Woodner Collection* (2006), no. 84. Rykwert, *First Moderns*, 279–82, suggests that the plates convey a theoretical progression. See John Wilton-Ely, "Introduction," in Piranesi,

Observations (2002), 45–51.

33. An iconographic reading of Piranesi's dense imagery is attempted by Matteo Calvesi, "Introduzione," in Henri Focillon, *Giovanni Battista Piranesi, 1720–1778* (Bologna: Alfa, 1967): xxiv–xxvii.

34. "AEQUUM EST VAS COGNOSCERE ATQUE IGNOSCERE QUAE VETERES FACTITARUNT SI FACIUNT NOVI," Terrence, *Eunuchus*, prologue, 41–43.

35. "Rerumque novatrix ed aliis alias reddit natura figures." Ovid, *Metamorphoses*, 15.252–253.

36. Julien-David Le Roy, "Pour ne pas faire de cet art sublime un vil métier ou l'on ne ferait que copier sans choix," in *Les Ruines des Plus Beaux Monuments de la Grèce* (1758). This same quotation is also included in the text of the *Parere*.

37. "NOVITATEM MEAM CONTEMNUNT, EGO ILLORUM IGNAVIAM." *Bellum Igurthinum*, 85.14.

38. Translation from Piranesi, *Observations* (2002), 112–13.

39. The most important discussion of the *Diverse maniere* remains William Rieder, "Piranesi's *Diverse maniere*," in *Burlington Magazine*, vol. 115 (May 1973): 309–17, which situates both the essay, the etchings, and the related drawings within the context of Piranesi's prior work. See also Susan M. Dixon, "Giovanni's Battista Piranesi's *Diverse maniere d'adornare i cammini* and the Chimneypiece Design as a Vehicle for Polemic," in *Studies in the Decorative Arts I/1* (Fall 1993); and Roberta Battaglia, "Le 'Diverse maniere d'adornare i cammini...' di Giovanni Battista Piranesi: Gusto e Cultura Antiquaria," in *Saggi e Memorie di storia dell' arte*, vol. 19 (1994): 193–273.

40. "Ho ravvisato in essa, O Signore, che poco contento delle moderne maniere di abbellire le opera archittoniche avreste anzi voluto, che i nostril Architetti nelle loro opere non le greche maniere usassero soltanto, ma le Egizie altresi, e l'Etrusche, e con saggio, e avveduto temperamento, prendessero da costoro monumenti, quanto essi ci presentano di vago, e di bello... Cosi in fatti fecero I Romani, che dopo avere usata per piu secoli l'estrusca architettura, adottarono poi anche la greca: e l'una, a l'altra unirono insieme." *Diverse Maniere d'adornare i cammini*, 1769, dedication. On Piranesi and his relation to the Rezzonico, see Susanna Pasquali, "Piranesi Architect, Courtier, and Antiquarian: The Late Rezzonico Years (1762–1768)," in Bevilacqua, Minor, Barry 2006: 171–194.

41. *Diverse Maniere d'adornare i cammini* (1769), p. 2.

42. Ibid.

43. Ibid.

44. Ibid.

45. Ibid. Piranesi was certainly aware of the consideration given to character by Sebastiano Serlio in his sixteenth-century treatise on domestic architecture (written, it should be noted, for his French patrons), as well as the currency of the issue in French writings on domestic interiors. On Serlio's treatise, see Myra Rosenfield, *Sebastiano Serlio: On Domestic Architecture* (Cambridge, 1978). On the subject of character and its prominence in eighteenth-century architectural theory, see Werner Szambien, *Symétrie, goût, caractère : théorie et terminologie de l'architecture à l'âge classique, 1550–1800* (Paris: Picard, 1986).

46. *Diverse Maniere d'adornare i cammini* (1769), p. 4.

47. Ibid., p. 6.

48. Ibid., p. 8.

49. On this discovery, see Wolfgang Liebenwein, "Der Porticus Clemens XI und sein Statuenschmuck. Anitkenrezeption und Kapitolsidee im fruhen 18. Jahrhundert," in Beck et al., eds., *Forschungen zur Villa Albani. Antike Kunst und die Epoche der Aufklarung* (Berlin, 1982): 73–105. On the eighteenth-century Egyptian revival, see Jurgis Baltrusaitis, *La Quete d'Isis: Essai sur la légende d'un mythe. Introduction à l'egyptomanie* (Paris, 1967); and Nikolaus Pevsner and Susanne Lang, "The Egyptian Revival," in Pevsner, *Studies in Art, Architecture, and Design*, vol. 1: *From Mannerism to Romanticism* (London and New York, 1968): 213–35; Michael Pantazzi, "Le voyage d'Italie," in *Egyptomania: L'Egypte dans l'art occidental, 1730–1930* (exhibition catalogue; Paris, 1994): 38–45.

50. "Vederete in quest' Opera usato cio che peranche in questo genere non era conosciuto. L'Architettura Egiziana, per la prima volta apparisce; la prima volta, dico, perche in ora il mondo ha sempre creduto non esservi altro che piramidi, guglie, e giganti, escludendo non esservi parti sufficienti per

adornare e sostenere questo sistema d'architettura." As quoted in Nikolaus Pavsner and Susanne Lang, "The Egyptian Revival," in Pevsner 1968: 216; *Egyptomania: L'Egypte dans l'art occidental, 1730–1930* (exhibition catalogue; Paris, 1994). See also Wilton-Ely 2002, p. 54.

51. *Diverse Maniere d'adornare i cammini* (1769), p. 9.

52. Ibid., p. 10. The question of whether Piranesi created his own hieroglyphic vocabulary, most notably in the *Parere*, is addressed by Maurizio Calvesi, *Giovanni Battista e Francesco Piranesi* (exhibition catalogue; Rome: Calcografia Nazionale, 1967), 22; and later by Rykwert, *The First Moderns*, p. 380.

53. *Diverse Maniere d'adornare i cammini* (1769), p. 14.

54. The significance given by Piranesi to the formative influence of the shell in Etruscan design is undoubtedly in response to Vitruvius identifying the same source for Greek architectural ornament. See Vitruvius, *The Ten Books on Architecture* (New York, 1960), book 4, chapter 2, 107. Rykwert suggests that Piranesi is the first decorative artist to provide a repertoire of shell forms for ornamental use in *The First Moderns*, 413, note 203.

55. Rykwert, *The First Moderns*, 389.

56. *Diverse Maniere d'adornare i cammini* (1769), p. 22.

57. Ibid., p. 23.

58. Susan M. Dixon, "Giovanni's Battista Piranesi's *Diverse maniere d'adornare i cammini* and the Chimneypiece Design as a Vehicle for Polemic," in *Studies in the Decorative Arts* I/1 (Fall 1993): 76–98.

59. *Diverse Maniere d'adornare i cammini* (1769), p. 15.

60. This mantle is given particular attention as well by Susan M. Dixon, "Giovanni's Battista Piranesi's *Diverse maniere d'adornare i cammini* and the Chimneypiece Design as a Vehicle for Polemic," in *Studies in the Decorative Arts* I/1 (Fall 1993), fig. 7.

61. *Diverse Maniere d'adornare i cammini* (1769), pp. 34–35.

PIRANESI AND THE ANTIQUARIAN IMAGINATION

1. Jean Seznec, *Essais sur Diderot et l'Antiquité* (Oxford: Clarendon Press, 1957).

2. The classic text is Arnaldo Momigliano, "Ancient History and the Antiquarian," in *Contributo alla storia degli studi classici* (Rome: Edizioni di Storia e letteratura, 1955). See *Momigliano and Antiquarianism: Foundations of the Modern Cultural Sciences*, ed. Peter N. Miller (Toronto: University of Toronto Press, 2007).

3. Pierre Gassendi, *The Mirrour of True Nobility and Gentility* (London, 1657), year 1600, p. 30. Robert Burton poked fun at just this sort of learned fantasy: "Your supercilious criticks, grammatical triflers, notemakers, curious antiquaries, find out all the ruines of wit, *ineptiarum delicias*, amongst the rubbish of old writers; and what they take they spoil, all fools with them that cannot find fault; they correct others, & are hot in a cold cause, puzzle themselves to find out how many streets in Rome, houses, gates, towers...what clothes the Senator did wear in Rome, what shoes, how they sat, where they went to the close stool." *The Anatomy of Melancholy* (New York: George H. Doran, 1927): 95–96.

4. For Cyriac, see *Ciriaco d'Ancona e la cultura antiquaria dell'Umanesimo*, ed. Gianfranco Paci and Sergio Sconocchia (Reggio Emilia: Edizioni Diabasis, 1998); Francesco Scalamonti, *Vita Viri Clarissimi et Famosissimi Kyriaci Anconitani*, ed. and trans. Charles Mitchell and Edward W. Bodnar, S. J. (Philadelphia: American Philosophical Society, 1996); Karl August Neuhausen, "Die vergessene 'göttliche Kunst der Totenerweckung', Cyriacus von Ancona als Begründer der Erforschung der Antike in der Frührenaissance," in *Antiquarische Gelehrsamkeit und Bildende Kunst. Die Gegenwart der Antike in der Renaissance* (Köln: Buchhandlung Walther König, 1996): 51–68; Cyriac of Ancona, *Later Travels*, ed. and trans. Edward W. Bodnar (Cambridge, MA, and London: Harvard University Press, 2003).

5. Sigmund Freud, *Civilization and Its Discontents* (London: Hogarth Press, 1930).

6. Anthony Grafton, "The Bright Book of Strife," in *The New Republic* (May 22, 2000).

7. See Charles Mitchell, "Archaeology and Romance in Renaissance Italy," in *Italian Renaissance Studies*, ed. E. F. Jacob (London: Faber & Faber, 1960): 455–83.

8. The most important recent work on Ligorio is Anna Schreurs' monumental, *Antikenbild und Kunstanschauungen des Pirro Ligorio (1513–1583)* (Köln: Walther König, 2000). See also David R. Coffin, *Pirro Ligorio: The Renaissance Artist, Architect, and Antiquarian* (University Park: The Pennsylvania State University

Press, 2003), and the essays collected in *Pirro Ligorio: Artist and Antiquarian*, ed. Robert W. Gaston (Florence: Silvana Editoriale, 1988). For an assessment of his place in the Roman antiquarian tradition, see Ingo Herklotz, *Cassiano dal Pozzo und die Archäologie des 17. Jahrhundert* (Munich: Hirner, 1999), chaps. 10–11.

9. Howard Burns, "Pirro Ligorio's Reconstruction of Ancient Rome: The *Antiquae Uribs Imago* of 1561," in Gaston, *Pirro Ligorio*, p. 37. Even Burns does not, however, go the further step of examining the interaction of imagination and erudition that actually makes "restoration" possible.

10. The first of these questions is asked and answered by Gaston in his introduction to *Pirro Ligorio*, p. 14. The second is asked but not answered (p. 15), and the third is not asked at all.

11. Henri Focillon, *Giovanni Battista Piranesi, 1720–1778* (Paris: H. Laurens, 1918).

12. John Wilton-Ely, *The Mind and Art of Piranesi* (London: Thames and Hudson, 1978).

13. *Piranesi e la cultura antiquaria: gli antecedenti e il contesto*, ed. Anna Lo Bianco (Rome: Multigrafica, 1985); Norbert Wolf, *Giovanni Battista Piranesi Der Römische Circus. Die Arena als Weltsymbol* (Frankfurt: Fischer Verlag, 1977); Lola Kantor-Kazovsky, *Piranesi as Interpreter*.

14. Augusta Monferini, "Le 'Antichità Romane,' fulcro della visione archeologica del Piranesi," in *Piranesi. Antichità Romane. Vedute di Roma*, ed. Raffaella Resch (Milano: Edizioni Gabriele Mazzotta, 2000): 19–20.

15. Susan M. Dixon, "The Image and Historical Knowledge in Mid-Eighteenth-Century Italy: A Cultural Context for Piranesi's Archaeological Publications" (Ph.D. diss., Cornell University, 1991).

16. Quoted in Pablo Schneider, "Il Campo Marzio dell'Antica Roma und seine Antikenrekonstruktion," in *Giovanni Battista Piranesi: Bilder von Orten und Räumen*, ed. Annelie Lütgens (Hamburg: Hamburger Kunsthalle, 1994): 30–31.

17. Piranesi, *Le Antichità Romane* (Rome, 1756), I.

18. William Wordsworth, *Lines Composed a Few Miles Above Tintern Abbey*, line 49.

19. For too long Piranesi's images obscured his words, but even now that his words are considered relevant, the captions remain dismissed or ignored.

20. I am grateful to Louise Rice for beautifying my translation.

21. Kantor-Kazovsky, *Piranesi as Interpreter*, pp. 85–87, 99.

22. See Irène Aghion, "Collecting Antiquities in Eighteenth-Century France. Louis XV and Jean-Jacques Barthélémy," in *Journal of the History of Collections* 14 (2002): 196.

23. Mark Phillips, *Society and Sentiment: Genres of Historical Writing in Britain, 1740–1820* (Princeton: Princeton University Press, 2000).

COL SPORCAR SI TROVA: PIRANESI DRAWS

1. The literature on Piranesi's drawings, the study of which has lagged behind the scholarship on his prints, begins effectively with Felice Stampfle's publications of the drawings in the Pierpont Morgan Library: "An Unknown Group of Drawings by Giovanni Battista Piranesi," in *Art Bulletin* 30 (1978): 122–41, reprinted as an exhibition catalogue the following year and reissued as *Drawings by Giovanni Battista Piranesi: Drawings in the Pierpont Morgan Library* (New York: Dover Publications, 1978). It was followed by Hylton Thomas, *The Drawings of Giovanni Battista Piranesi* (New York: Beechhurst Press, 1954), based on his Harvard dissertation of 1949 and still a fundamental survey. Naturally, connoisseurship of the drawings is closely tied to scholarship on Piranesi's prints, and here the most important work is that of Andrew Robison, who is preparing the catalogue raisonné of the drawings: see especially *Piranesi*, and, most recently, "Piranesi's Later Drawings of Architectural Fantasies," in *Giovanni Battista Piranesi: Die Wahrnehmung von Raum und Zeit* (Marburg: Jonas Verlag, 2002): 49–64.

2. For further discussion and references, see Alice Jarrard's essay in this volume, "Perspectives on Piranesi and Theater." A general introduction to Piranesi's early education can be found in John Wilton-Ely, "Apprenticeship: Venice and Rome, 1720–1750," in *Mind and Art of Piranesi*. See also Lionello Puppi, "Appunti sulla educazione veneziana di Giambattista Piranesi," in Bettagno, *Piranesi tra Venezia e l'Europa*, pp. 217–64.

3. For a richly illustrated survey of this visual culture, see the informative exhibition catalogue *The Glory of Venice: Art in the Eighteenth Century*, ed. Jane Martineau and Andrew Robison (New Haven and London: Yale University Press, 1994).

4. See David Rosand, *"Disegni a stampa: The Printed Line," in Drawing Acts: Studies in Graphic Expression and Representation* (Cambridge and New York: Cambridge University Press, 2002).

5. From the dedication to the *Prima Parte di Architetture e Prospettive* (1743), quoted in Robison, *Piranesi*, pp. 96–97. A translation is available in Nyberg, *Giovanni Battista Piranesi*, pp. 117–18.

6. "Per questo fine io ho proccurato nel mio soggiorno in questa gran Metropoli d'accoppiare alle cognizioni, che qualunqu'elle sieno ho acquistate d'Architettura l'arte di disegnare non solo le mie invenzioni, ma d'intagliarle ancora nel rame."

7. For the clarification of this chronology, see Lino Moretti, "Nuovi document piranesiani," in Bettagno, *Piranesi tra Venezia e l'Europa*: 127–53, and Robison, *Piranesi*: 9–10.

8. Adriano Cavicchi and Silla Zamboni, "Due 'taccuini' inediti di Piranesi," in Bettagno, *Piranesi tra Venezia e l'Europa*: 177–216.

9. The group includes drawings in the collections of the Ashmolean Museum, Oxford (inv. 1038), the Kunsthalle, Hamburg (1915/638), the Pierpont Morgan Library, New York (1968.13), and the Ratjen Foundation, Vaduz (R 814, R 910). For further discussion of the dismembered sketchbook, see David Lachenmann, *Italian Drawings from the Ratjen Foundation, Vaduz* (Bern: Benteli Publishers, 1996), cat. nos. 45, 46 (the latter a copy by Piranesi of Titian's ceiling painting *Cain Slaying Abel*, in Santa Maria della Salute). Felice Stampfle and Cara D. Denison, *Drawings from the Collection of Mr. & Mrs. Eugene V. Thaw* (New York: The Pierpont Morgan Library, 1975), cat. no. 54, notes that the signature on the Morgan Library drawing flows from drawing to mount, suggesting that the artist himself or one of his sons mounted it. The drawing in Hamburg is rather different in subject; it depicts masked figures at a Punch and Judy show, and yet the spread of wash across the sky adds a particularly ominous mood to this carnival scene. A good color illustration is available in Martineau and Robison, *Glory of Venice*, p. 376.

10. J.-G. Legrand, "Notice historique sur la vie et les ouvrages de J. B. Piranesi architecte, peintre et graveur né à Venise en 1720 mort à Rome en 1778," reprinted as an appendix to Gilbert Erouart and Monique Mosser, "A propos de la 'Notice historique sur la vie et les ouvrages de J.-B. Piranesi': Origine et fortune d'une biographie," in Brunel, *Piranèse et les français*: 221–52. See the Vasi quotation on page 223: "A la patience prèsque Vasi ne pouvait obtenir de sa fougue, aussi disait-il toujours: *Vous êtes trop peintre, mon ami, pour être jamais graveur*."

11. The reclining figure in figure 12 seems clearly inspired by Tiepolo. See also the seated soldier in one of the capricci (H. Diane Russell, *Rare Etchings by Giovanni Battista Piranesi and Giovanni Domenico Tiepolo* [Washington, D.C.: National Gallery of Art, 1972], p. 42).

12. For further discussion of Tiepolo's capricious graphic style and inventive iconographic transformations, see Rosand, *Drawing Acts*, pp. 302–27, with previous bibiliography, and for a good introduction to the series, see *Giambattista Tiepolo 1696–1770*, ed. Keith Christiansen (New York: Metropolitan Museum of Art, 1996), pp. 348–69.

13. Tiepolo's own title page remained without text; only after his death did his son add the title *Scherzi di Fantasia*.

14. Robison, *Piranesi*, cat. nos. 21–24.

15. Ibid., cat. no. 18.

16. Two sheets of sketches recording Piranesi's study of Fischer von Erlach's publication are in the Morgan Library: Stampfle, *Giovanni Battista Piranesi*, nos. 17 and 18.

17. *Diverse maniere d'adornare i cammini ed ogni altra parte degli edfizj…*(Rome, 1769), p. 18; two engraved plates illustrate a variety of shells and their relationship to the forms of vases (pp. 21 and 22). The volume was published with both English and French translations.

18. On the *Grotteschi* in relation to Piranesi's imaginative practice, see Rosand, *Drawing Acts*, pp. 278–84, with further references, and, for the relevance to Piranesi's spiral of Hogarth's serpentine, see pp. 265–78.

19. G. L. Bianconi, "Elogio storico del Cavalier Giambattista Piranesi, celebre antiquario ed incisore di Roma," in *Antologia romana* 34–36 (February–March 1779): 265–84, especially p. 273; reprinted in *Grafica* 2 (1976): 127–35.

20. For the history of the editions and states, see Robison, *Piranesi*, pp. 37–53, 130–210, nos. 29–44. The following remarks draw upon my discussion in Rosand, *Drawing Acts*, pp. 284–98.

21. See "Disegno: The Invention of an Art," in Rosand, *Drawing Acts*.

22. For the related drawings see Patricia May Sekler, "Giovanni Battista Piranesi's *Carceri* Etchings and Related Drawings," in *Art Quarterly* 25 (1962): 330–63, and Robison, *Piranesi*, pp. 37–44.

23. The problems of perspective and architectural construction in the *Carceri* have been graphically analyzed in Ulya Vogt-Göknil, *Giovanni Battista Piranesi: "Carceri"* (Zurich: Origo Verlag, 1958).

24. Legrand, "Notice historique," in Brunel, *Piranèse et les français*: 246–47.

25. ". . . et si on lui demandait pourquoi il ne faisait pas de dessins plus terminés, et où toutes les ombres fussent exprimées? *J'en serais bien fâché*, répondit-il, *ne voyez-vous pas que si mon dessin était fini ma planche ne deviendrait plus qu'une copie; lorsqu'au contraire je crée l'effet sur le cuivre, j'en fait un original.*" Ibid., p. 246.

26. On the generic status of the *Carceri*, see Werner Busch, "Piranesis 'Carceri' und der Capriccio-Begriff im 18. Jahrhundert," in *Wallraf-Richartz-Jahrbuch* 39 (1977): 210–24, and Norbert Miller, "Giovanni Battista Piranesis Entdeckung der Imagination: Das Capriccio in den Zeichnungen und Radierungen seines Frühwrks," in *Das Capriccio als Kunstprinzip: Zur Vorgeschichte der Moderne von Arcimbolo und Callot bis Tiepolo und Goya*, ed. Joachim Rees (Milan: Skira, 1966): 141–55.

27. "Piranesi ne faisait point de dessins finis, un gros trait à la sanguine, sur lequel il revenait ensuite avec la plume ou le pinceau et par parties seulement lui suffisait pour arrêter ses idées, mais il est presque impossible de distinguer ce qu'il croyait fixer sur le papier, ce n'est qu'un chaos dont il démêlait seul les elements sur le cuivre avec un art admirable.
   "Le peintre Robert avec lequel il dessinait quelques fois aussi d'après nature, et qui était si bien en état d'apprécier son talents, ne concevait pas ce qu'on pouvait fare de croquis aussi peu arrêtés; Piranesi, voyant son étonnement, lui disait: *le dessin n'est pas sur mon papier, j'en conviens, mais il est tout entire dans ma tête, et vous le verrez par la planche*, elle était fidèle, en effet, et rien n'y était omis."

28. John Wilton-Ely, *Piranesi* (London: Arts Council of Great Britain, 1978), no. 291; Robison, "Piranesi's Later Drawings of Architectural Fantasies," pp. 50–51.

29. Giorgio Vasari, *Le vite de' più eccellenti pittori, scultori ed architettori* (1550, 2nd ed. 1568), ed. Gaetano Milanesi (Florence, 1878–85), 1:174.

30. For the *Raccolta di alcuni disegni*, not often discussed in the Piranesi literature, see Alessandro Bettagno, *Piranesi: Incisioni-rami-legature-architetture* (Vicenza: Neri Pozza Editore, 1978), pp. 53–55, nos. 306–09. The significance of the motto was suggestively explored by Michelangelo Muraro, "Giambattista Piranesi o dell'espressione," in Bettagno, *Piranesi tra Venezia e l'Europa*: 75–87.

31. For more information on Leonardo's discovery, see Rosand, *Drawing Acts*, pp. 50–54.

32. Such figures among antique ruins make their appearance in an early, Tiepolesque drawing in Hamburg (Kunsthalle, inv. 1915/653), dated to the mid-1740s by Thomas, *Drawings*, no. 10.

33. This drawing in the Louvre, like many of Piranesi's drawings, is executed on the back of a fragment of a proof or discarded impression of a print: here one by Giovanni Ottaviano after a drawing by Guercino, part of the *Raccolta di alcuni disegni…*, published in 1754. See Roseline Bacou, "À propos des dessins de figures de Piranèse," in Brunel, *Piranèse et les français*: 33–34; see also Alessandro Bettagno, *Disegni di Giambattista Piranesi* (Vicenza: Neri Pozza Editore, 1978), no. 60.

34. For further discussion of Piranesi's figure drawings, see Thomas, *Drawings*, pp. 25–27, and Bacou, "À propos des dessins de figures," pp. 33–41.

THE PROJECTS FOR THE RECONSTRUCTION OF THE LATERAN BASILICA IN ROME

1. For Piranesi's activities as an architect, see M. F. Fischer, "Die Umbaupläne des Giovanni Battista Piranesi für den Chor von S. Giovanni in Laterano," in *Münchner Jahrbuch der Bildenden Kunst* 19 (1968): 207–28; Nyberg, *Giovanni Battista Piranesi*; John Wilton-Ely and J. Connors, *Piranesi Architetto: Disegni 1764–67* (Rome: Edizioni dell'Elefante, 1992); John Wilton-Ely, *Piranesi as Architect and Designer* (New York: Pierpont Morgan Library; New Haven: Yale University Press, 1993); Elisabeth Kieven, *Von Bernini bis Piranesi. Römische Architekturzeichnungenn des Barock* (Stuttgart: Hatje, 1993); Pierluigi Panza, *Piranesi architetto* (Milano: Guerni Studio, 1998); John Wilton-Ely, "Piranesi architetto," in *Piranesi e l'Aventino*, ed. Barbara Jatta (Milan: Electa, 1998), pp. 63–78; F. Barry, "San Giovanni che non c'è': La strategia Piranesiana per il coro di San Giovanni in Laterano," in *Francesco Borromini: Atti del convegno internazionale Roma 13–15 gennaio 2000*, ed. Christoph L. Frommel and Elisabeth Sladek (Milan: Electa, 2000): 458–63; L. Finocchi Ghersi, "Piranesi architetto: La formazione veneziana e i progetti romani," in *Antonio Canova e il suo ambiente artistico a Venezia, Roma e Parigi*, ed. Giuseppe Pavanello (Venice: Istituto veneto di scienze lettere ed arti, 2000): 193–217; Bent Sørensen, "An unpublished project by Piranesi for Clement XIII," in *The Burlington Magazine* 142, no. 1169 (August 2000): 497–501; Bent Sørensen, "Two Overlooked Drawings by Piranesi for S. Giovanni in Laterano in Rome," in *The Burlington Magazine* 143, no. 1180 (July 2001): 430–33; R. Middleton, "The Case of the Missing Baptistery—Piranesi's S. Giovanni in Laterano," in *Architektur weiterdenken: Werner Oechslin zum 60. Geburtstag*, ed. Sylvia Claus et al. (Zürich: gta, 2004): 182–200.

2. According to unspecified documents, Carl Justi, in his *Winckelmann und seine Zeitgenossen* (Leipzig, 1866; reprint, 1898), 2:329, states that Carlo Marchionni in 1763 was invited to submit projects for the new choir in the Lateran basilica.

3. "Sa Sainteté, voulant orner la basilique de Saint-Jean-de-Lateran d'un maître-autel qui réponde à la magnificence de cette église, elle a ordonné sieur Piranesi, célèbre architecte-sculpteur, de composer un dessein propre à l'exécution de ce projet." *Correspondance des Directeurs de l'Académie de France à Rome avec les Surintendants des Bâtiments*, ed. Anatole Montaiglon and Jules Guiffrey (Paris: Charavay Freres, 1901), 11:489.

4. "In vero, se faranno fare qualche fabrica al Piranesi, si vedrà cosa puol produrre la testa di un matto, che non à verun fondamento. Né ci vuole un pazzo per terminare la tribuna di San Giovanni in Laterano, abenché il Boromino, che ristaurò la chiesa, non fosse uomo molto savio e se sarà il Pannini la cosa serà un quid simile del Piranesi."

5. Stampfle, "An Unknown Group of Drawings," pp. 122–41; Stampfle, *Giovanni Battista Piranesi*.

6. For the twenty-seventh drawing, unrelated to the Lateran projects and for the provenance of the presentation drawings, see Sorensen, "Unpublished Project by Piranesi." For the twenty-three drawings in the Avery, see Nyberg, *Giovanni Battista Piranesi*.

7. The State Hermitage Museum, St. Petersburg, Inv. 18875. See Sørensen, "Two Overlooked Drawings."

8. Ibid.

9. A. Foscari, "Disegni inediti dell'archivio Rezzonico," *Palatino* 12, no. 2, (1968): fig. 10.

10. See J. Connors and A. Roca de Amicis, "A New Plan by Borromini for the Lateran Basilica, Rome," in *The Burlington Magazine* Volume 146, no. 1217 (August 2004): 526–33.

11. It has been suggested by Barry, "San Giovanni che no c'è," and Middleton, "Case of the Missino Baptistery," that one of the determining factors in the planning was an obligation to ensure a passage for a processional route to the baptistery; to my knowledge such a route is not mentioned in any eighteenth-century source.

12. The drawing (Pierpont Morgan Library, 1966.11:110) is illustrated in Stampfle, "An Unknown Group of Drawings," p. 139; Stampfle, *Giovanni Battista Piranesi*, no. 110; See also Sørensen, "Two Overlooked Drawings."

13. B. Contardi, "Piranesi in Campidoglio," in *Studi sul Settecento Romano* 13 (1997): 166, notes 36 and 37.

PERSPECTIVES ON PIRANESI AND THEATER

1. For a lucid critique of the problem in relation to painting, see Keith Christiansen, "Tiepolo, Theater, and the Notion of Theatricality," in *Art Bulletin* 81/4 (1999): 665–89.

2. Nicolas Le Camus de Mézières, *The Genius of Architecture, or, The Analogy of That Art with Our Sensations*, 1782, trans. David Britt (Santa Monica: Getty Center for the History of Art and the Humanities, 1992), p. 71.

3. J.-G. Legrand, transcribed in Brunel, *Piranèse et les Français*, pp. 223–24, and Bianconi, in 1779, as reprinted in *Grafica grafica* (Rome: Edizione dell'Elefante, 1976), 2:127. Piranesi's compatriot Tomaso Temanza says he learned the "principi di disegno" from his engineer uncle, and perfected his drawing skills in Rome. *Zibaldon*, ed. N. Ivanoff (Firenze: Istituto per la Collaborazione Culturale, 1981), p. 51. Focillon, *Giovanni Battista Piranesi*, p. 58, relegates analysis of Piranesi's theatrical training to a long footnote, instead emphasizing Roman perspective painters like Panini, pp. 171–80.

4. See Antonio Maria Zanetti, *Della pittura veneziana* (Venezia: Giambattista Abrizzi, 1771), p. 463. Piranesi's drawing for an ephemeral production, the Chinea of 1746, seems never intended for production.

5. See Jorg Garms, "Considérations sur la Prima Parte," pp. 265–80, and "Piranesi e la scenografia," in *La scenografia barocca* (Bologna: CLUEB, 1982). For analysis of the *Carceri* in this light, see Sekler, "Piranesi's *Carceri*," in Vogt-Göknil, *Giovanni Battista Piranesi*, and especially Joseph R. Roach, "From Baroque to Romantic: Piranesi's Contribution to Stage Design," in *Theater Survey* 19, no. 2 (1978): 91–118.

6. Robison, "Piranesi's Later Drawings," 2002, p. 61.

7. Claude-François Menestrier, *Des représentations en musique anciennes et modernes* (1682; Genève: Minkoff Reprint, 1972), p. 174.

8. See Bettagno, *Piranèse et les Français*; Garms, "Considérations sur la Prima Parte"; Robison, *Piranesi*, and Robison, "Piranesi's Later Drawings of Architectural Fantasies."

9. See note 2 above.

10. Since it was a "simple matter to learn the practical mechanics of materials," in *Risposta al capitolo quarto*, 1721, p. 5, as cited in *I Bibiena: una famiglia europea*, ed. Deanna Lenzi and Jadranka Bentini (Venezia: Marsilio, 2000), p. 180. *L'architettura civile, preparata su la geometria, e ridotta alle prospettive* (Parma: Paolo Monti, 1711).

11. *Direzione della prospettiva prattica e teorica…* (Bologna: Lelio dalla Volpe, 1732), p. 115.

12. Benedetto Marcello, *Teatro alla Moda* (Borghi di Belincania, all'insegna dell'Orso in Penta, n.d.), p. 50.

13. First issue texts are reprinted in Nyberg, *Giovanni Battista Piranesi*, pp. 115–17.

14. For excerpts describing the reception of Servandoni's sets from 1730 to 1741, see Christel Heybrock, *Jean Nicolas Servandoni (1695–1766); eine Untersuchung seiner Pariser Bühnenwerke* (N.p., 1970).

15. A. Zanotti, *Storia della Accademia Clementina* (Bologna, 1739), 2:212.

16. For the dominance of Venetian scenography by designers between 1730 and 1742, see *I teatri del Veneto*, ed. Franco Mancini, Maria Teresa Muraro, and Elena Povoledo (Venice: Giunta, 1985–90), specifically, for the Valeriani brothers and Antonio Iolli, vol. 1, tomo II, pp. 16–25, 88–92, 123, 395–98; for the Bibiena in Verona, vol. 2, pp. 77–81. For Francesco's documented scenes in Bologna in 1727, 1730, and 1731, see Corrado Ricci, *Teatri di Bologna nei secoli xvii e xviii* (Bologna: Successori Monti, 1888), pp. 430–35.

17. Girolamo Zanetti, "Memorie per servire all'istoria dell'inclita citta di Venezia," in *Archivio veneto* (1885): 104. Zanetti spoofs the familiar image of Christ's flagellation at the columns.

18. For publication details, see Robison, *Piranesi*, pp. 12–21. Peter Murray, *Piranesi and the Grandeur of Ancient Rome* (London: Thames and Hudson, 1971), p. 20, suggests the work was promotional; Garms, "Considérations sur la Prima Parte," p. 273, disagrees.

19. See note 2. For the Bolognese presence in Rome, see *Il teatro a Roma nel Settecento*, 2 vols. (Rome: Istituto dell'Encyclopedia Italiana, 1989).

20. The term used by Vitruvius, though applied to ancient stage scenery by E. Dante in 1586, was only applied consistently to modern stage design some three centuries later. For other related issues, see W. Oechslin, "Zwischen Malerei und Architektur. Künstlichkeit und Eigenständigkeit der

Bühnenbildkunst," in *Daidalos* 14 (1984): 21–35.

21. Chambers, as excerpted in Robison, *Piranesi*, p. 56, n. 52.

22. The influence of Perrault's text upon printmakers, with its synthesis of ideas drawn from scientific circles, demands further exploration. For Perrault, see Antoine Picon, *Claude Perrault, 1613–1688, ou, La curiosité d'un classique* (Paris: Picard Éditeur, 1988).

23. Pietro Santi Bartoli, *Gli antichi sepolcri ovvero mausolei romani ed etruschi* (1697; Rome: De' Rossi, 1727), p. iii. By contrast, with earlier archaeological reconstructions with figures by Duperac, Ligorio, and Lauro, Bartoli's convey the layering of time with anatomical precision, in keeping with doctor Perrault's example.

24. During Piranesi's years in Rome, seven public and three college theaters were operational; lyric stages were dominated by the works of Metastasio (until the late arrival of opera buffa); and prose stages saw the late introduction of Goldoni's works in 1753. Goldoni was named a member of the Accademia degli Arcadii in 1742 (like Piranesi), and, like Piranesi, profited from the Rezzonico papacy by taking up residence in the city. For a chronicle without mention of scenography, see Filippo Clementi, *Il carnevale romano nelle cronache contemporanee* (Citta di Castello: Unione Art Grafica, 1938), 2:68–196. For street events, see *Le feste a Roma: Il Settecento*, ed. Marcello Fagiolo (Roma: De Luca, 1997).

25. For *Dardanus*, by this student of Servandoni, see *L'Avant-Coureur*, April 21, 1760, cited in A. M. Nagler, *A Source Book in Theatrical History* (New York: Dover Publications, 1952), pp. 319–20.

26. For Mazzi, a little-known student of Bibiena, and for the influence of the *Carceri* on stage design in England, see Roach, "From Baroque to Romantic," p. 104.

27. Rykwert, *First Moderns*, p. 370, first analyzed the *Vasi* in the context of line drawings.

28. For his redating of images first attributed by Croft Murray to early in Piranesi's career, based on analysis of scale copying of large drawings after Juvarra's prints of *Teodosio il Giovane*, see Robison, "Piranesi's Later Drawings," p. 61.

29. Reproduced in Andrew Robison, *The Poetry of Light: Venetian Drawings from the National Gallery of Art* (Washington, D.C.: National Gallery of Art, 2006), p. 19. Thanks to Sarah Lawrence for calling this to my attention.

30. See Oechslin's discussion of vases, "Le groupe des 'Piránésiens' français (1740–50): Un renouveau dans la culture romaine," in Brunel, *Piranèse et les français*, esp. pp. 379–95, noting their importance in views by Fischer van Erlach. Also *Vasemania: Neoclassical Form and Ornament in Europe*, ed. Stephanie Walker (New Haven: Yale University Press, 2004). In Montfaucon's compendium of 1726, only two vases appear in perspective, one seen from above.

31. *Sebastiano Serlio on architecture*, trans. Vaughan Hart and Peter Hicks (1544; New Haven: Yale University Press, 1996), 1:23–25; Bibiena, *Direzione*, 1732, Operazione 112, tav. 6, and p. 40.

32. Legrand, "Notice historique sur la vie," pp. 239–40.

33. Walpole, in *Works of Horatio Walpole, Earl of Oxford*, with an introduction by P. Sabor (1798; reprint, London: Pickering & Chatto, 1999), 3:399; alluding to their magnificence, Walpole continued, they would "exhaust the Indies to realize."

PIRANESI AND FURNISHINGS

1. This essay was translated from the Italian by John Wilton-Ely.

2. G. Morazzoni, *G.B. Piranesi. Notizie biographiche* (Milan, 1921), pp. 47ff. This manuscript, now held by the Bibliothèque Nationale, Paris (Nouv.Acq. Franc., 5968), was previously noted by Focillon, but has not always been given due consideration. The most recent and precise transcription is provided by Gilbert Erouart and Monique Mosser in *Piranèse et les Français* (Rome: Accademia di Francia, 1978), pp. 213–52.

3. Pécheux wrote, "Le portrait de M.me la Marquise Gentili Boccapaduli, peint sur bois, d'environs 4 palmes et demi, où elle est représentée dans son cabinet d'histoire naturelle, levant un voile de dessus un tableau, où sont recueillis les plus beaux papillons." See L. C. Bollea, *Lorenzo Pécheux* (Turin, 1942), p. 398.

4. There exist several derivatives of this piece of furniture that would have been designed after Piranesi around 1775, including a chimneypiece and sev-

eral Tuscan tables in the Pitti Palace; see Alvar González-Palacios, *Il Tempio del Gusto* (Milan, 1984), figs. 242 and 243. E. Colle, in *Il mobile neoclassico in Italia* (Milan, 2005, pp. 134–35), and others associate the portrait of the Marchesa with a large table supported by Egyptian telamons from the Fondazione Magnani Rocca. In my opinion, the table is of a later date and of different dimensions to the one seen in this painting.

5. Recorded in a engraving by Lorenzo Roccheggiani around 1800 and reproduced in González-Palacios, *Il Tempio del Gusto*, fig. 241.

6. John Wilton-Ely, *Giovanni Battista Piranesi: The Complete Etchings* (San Francisco: Alan Wofsy Fine Arts, 1994, 2 vols.), vol. II, nos. 843, 910. In this room we also find two famous statues: a hairy Silenus, now in the Berlin Museum; and a nude boxer, in the niche on the right, first catalogued in the *Musée de Sculpture* by Clarac in 1839 when it was still in the Palazzo Gentili (now there is no trace of it).

7. About Clérisseau, see T. J. McCormick and J. Fleming, "A Ruin Room," in *The Connoisseur* CXLIX (April, 1962): 239–43; and McCormick, "Piranesi and Clérisseau," in *Piranèse et les Français* (Rome, 1978): 303–14.

8. G. Moroni, *Dizionario di erudizione storico-ecclesiastica…*, vol. LVII (Venice, 1852), pp. 166–67; see also A. M. Clark, "Brief Biography of Cardinal Giovanni Battista Rezzonico," in *The Minneapolis Institute of Arts Bulletin* LIV (1965), pp. 30–31.

9. "Due tavolini di sette, e tre e mezzo centinati impelicciati d'alabastro di Montautto con bastoncino di metallo dorato con piedi a zampa tutti intagliati con festoni, ed altri ornamenti dorati." See B. Contardi, "Piranesi in Campidoglio," in *Studi sul Settecento romano* XIII (1997): 167. It should be pointed out that, in 1783, the tables still had a layer of alabaster veneer, with a gilt bronze border and festoons that joined the legs; see *Il Tempio del Gusto*, p. 118. Around 1978, under the aegis of the Minneapolis Institute of Arts, I undertook the task of having a tabletop made in Rome in green Egyptian granite with a gilt bronze edge to replace the modest nineteenth-century slab of marble from a modern quarry (the 1782 inventory was not yet known) similar to the one on the table in Amsterdam. For the Minneapolis table, see F. J. B. Watson, "A Side Table by Piranesi," in *The Minneapolis Institute of Arts Bulletin* LIV (1965): 19–29.

10. Alvar González-Palacios, *Arredi e ornamenti alla corte di Roma* (Milan, 2004), pp. 332–37, especially p. 336.

11. Bruno Contardi, "Piranesi in Campidoglio," in *Studi sul Settecento romano* XIII (1997).

12. C. Pietrangeli, "La Sala Nuova di Don Abbondio Rezzonico," in *Capitolium* XXXVIII (1963): 244–46.

13. Wilton-Ely, *The Complete Etchings*, vol. II, no. 831.

14. See Erouart and Mosser, p. 41. They identify these craftsmen with Pietro Cardelli (of whom little is known in relation to Piranesi), with Franzoni (here we are in agreement), and with Francesco Righetti (who was, however, a bronzesmith and not a sculptor). About Grandjacquet and his role as a restorer for Piranesi, see P. Arizzoli Clémentel, "Charles Percier et la Salle Egyptienne de la Villa Borghese," in *Piranèse et les Français*, p. 10, n. 45, and *passim*. About Franzoni, see Gonzáles-Palacios, *Arredi e ornamenti…*, pp. 243–59.

15. For Lorenzo Cardelli, see Alvar González-Palacios, *Il gusto dei Principi* (Milan, 1993), *passim*; González-Palacios, *Arredi e ornamenti…*, *passim*; for Palazzo Caetani, see "Arredi e ornamenti a Palazzo Caetani," in *Proporzioni* V (2004): 184–228 (the chimneypiece by Antonio Vinelli and Antonio de Rossi is figure 174). For the chimneypieces of Piranesi, see William Rieder, "Piranesi at Gorhambury," in *Burlington Magazine* CXVII (September 1975): 582–91; and John Wilton-Ely, *Piranesi as Architect and Designer* (New Haven: Yale University Press, 1993), with additional information and photographs.

16. See González-Palacios in *Arredi e ornamenti…*, p. 181. The two bronze tables were loosely copied by an anonymous Roman carver in a series of pieces of furniture in the Quirinal, dating to ca. 1825. See Alvar Gonzáles-Palacios, with the collaboration of R. Valeriani, *Il patrimonio artistico del Quirinal. I mobili Italiani* (Milan, 1997), pp. 170–71.

17. See D. Stillman, "Robert Adam and Piranesi," in *Essays in the History of Architecture Presented to Rudolf Wittkower* (London, 1967): 197–206; D. Stillman, *The Decorative Work of Robert Adam* (London, 1966); E. Harris, *The Genius of Robert Adam: His Interiors* (New Haven: Yale University Press, 2001), pp. 222–60, with

a rich bibliography that includes J. Fleming, *Robert Adam and His Circle in Edinburgh and Rome* (London, 1962).

18. Wilton-Ely, *The Complete Etchings*, vol. II, nos. 910, 911, 991, 992.

19. González-Palacios, *Il Tempio del Gusto…*, figs. 281–83, illustrate the reductions by Boschi; figs. 218–19, David and Ingres. For other examples of candlesticks in *rosso antico* marble and gilt bronze by Giuseppe Boschi, similar to those in the Palazzo Pitti, have been published, with an erroneous attribution to Pietro Mertz (*Civiltà dell'Ottocento a Napoli*, Naples, 1997, p. 209). For other reductions of the same model by Boschi and for the wooden pedestal that can be traced back to the same idea, in English collections, see D. Udy, "Le fonti classiche del mobile neoclassico inglese," in *Arte Illustrata* VI (1973), n. 52, p. 29.

20. D. Udy, "Piranesi's *Vasi*, the English Silversmiths, and His Patrons," in *The Burlington Magazine* CXX (December 1978): 820–37.

21. See Wilton-Ely, *The Complete Etchings*, vol. II, nos. 889–91; and R. Marks and B. J. Blench, *The Warwick Vase* (Glasgow, 1979). For Boschetti's vase, see González-Palacios, *Il Tempio del Gusto…*. fig. 287.

22. Wilton-Ely, *The Complete Etchings*, vol. II, no. 993; figure 994 is another image of the same monument dedicated to the Marchesa Boccapaduli.

23. P. Arizzoli-Clémentel, "Les surtouts impériaux en porcelaine de Sèvres," in *Keramik-Freunde der Schweiz* 88 (May 1976): figs. 11–12.

24. Wilton-Ely, *The Complete Etchings*, vol. II, nos. 1000, 1001; the porcelain (15.3 cm x 31 cm x 10.5 cm), painted and gilded, was in the collection of the Dr. Roberto Illuminati.

25. C. H. Tatham, *Etchings Representing the Best Examples of Ancient Ornamental Architecture…in Rome* (London, 1799); in the 1820 edition, figs. 86–88; see also Wilton-Ely, *The Complete Etchings*, vol. II, nos. 935–36; and D. Udy, "Le fonti classche del mobile neoclassico inglese," in *Arte Illustrata* VI (1973), no. 52: fig. 16.

26. See Wilton-Ely, *The Complete Etchings*, vol. II, no. 918. Percier's drawing appeared at a Sotheby's sale in Monaco, June 17, 1988, lot 452. The relationship between the famous cardinal and our artist is somewhat mysterious. Piranesi certainly worked at least in the central room of Villa Albani; see C. Gasparri, "Piranesi a Villa Albani," in *Studi sul Settecento romano*, vols. 1-2, 1985, pp. 211–19; and Wilton-Ely, *Piranesi as Architect and Designer*, pp. 142–43.

27. Wilton-Ely, *The Complete Etchings*, vol. II, no. 922.

28. See J. Stern, *F. J. Bélanger* (Paris, 1930), which includes a study of Bélanger's *Livres des cheminées*, now in the Bibliothèque Nationale; see also J.-L. Gaillemin, ed., *La Folie d'Artois à Bagatelle* (Paris, 1988).

29. A. M. Clark (E. P. Bowron, ed.), *Pompeo Batoni* (Oxford: Oxford University Press, 1985), figs. 317, 343. On the furniture depicted in the portraits by Batoni, see also the work of Francesco Antonio Franzoni; and González-Palacios, *Arredi e ornamenti…*, pp. 242–59.

30. Wilton-Ely, *The Complete Echings*, vol. II, nos. 912, 942, 953; on Valadier, see González-Palacios, *Arredi e ornamenti…*, pp. 313 and 426.

31. L. Ferrara, "Pompeo Salvini, Venceslao Peter e il mobile neoclassico romano," in *Palatino* (July–September 1968): 256–62; see also González-Palacios, *Arredi e ornamenti…*, pp. 218–19. These three objects are now kept in the Royal Castle, Warsaw.

32. A. González-Palacios, "Il mobile di corte italiano," part 4, in *Antiquariato* (January 1986), no. 67, pp. 43 and 50. The chest, measuring 95 cm x 184 cm x 67 cm, was subsequently sold at auction at Semenzato, Venice, July 11, 1987. My ideas were echoed in the auction catalogue; however, it attributed the design of the commode to Piranesi, contrary to what I had written.

33. González-Palacios, *Il Gusto dei Principi*, figs. 451–54. Valadier did have colleagues of equal competence as bronzesmiths and gilders, such as Antonio de Rossi, who worked at the Villa Borghese (and in other places like the Palazzo Caetani) with excellent results (fig. 449).

34. González-Palacios, *Il patrimonio artistico del Quirinale…*; for Grespi pedestals, see pp. 245–46; for Landucci's tables, see pp. 184–85. For Landucci, see also Gonzáles-Palacios, *Il Gusto dei Principi*, passim, and Gonzáles-Palacios, "Lucia Landucci intagliatora e i suoi mariti," in *Objets d'Art: Mélanges en l'honneur de Daniel Alcouffe* (Dijon, 2004): 243–50.

35. González-Palacios, "Arredi e ornamenti a Palazzo Caetani," p. 196, note 36.

The tables by Freddi show a similarity to the work of Landucci. Both of these artisans, whose workshops were nearby one another (Landucci's in the Piazza SS. XII Apostoli), worked for the Caetani. The table in the Capitoline Museum (in Gonzáles-Palacios, *Il Tempio del Gustio…*, fig. 152), despite its high quality, has still not been documented.

PIRANESI AS DESIGNER

1. This article is based to a considerable degree on research I did in 1983–84, published in the exhibition catalogue *Herinneringen aan Italië. Kunst en toerisme in de 18de eeuw*, Den Bosch (Noordbrabants Museum), 1984, referred to hereafter as *Herinneringen*, particularly the introductory chapter, "Nederlanders op Grand Tour," pp. 11–33, and the catalogue entries devoted to Piranesi and his sons, nos. 80, 101, 183. For the references to the travel journals of Dutch grand tourists, see esp. the bibliography in Appendix I, pp. 257–58, in this catalogue. I also made grateful use of the numerous publications on Piranesi by John Wilton-Ely, particularly *The Mind and Art of Giovanni Battista Piranesi* (London: Thames and Hudson, 1978), and *Piranesi as Architect and Designer* (New Haven: Yale University Press, 1993). Quoted from *Herinneringen*, p. 27.

2. *Herinneringen*, p. 31.

3. Ibid.

4. For the Piranesi decorations in Biljoen Castle, see Fransje Kuyvenhoven & Heimerick Tromp, "Van Spaen in Arcadië," in: *Herinneringen*: 42–53.

5. For John Hope as a collector, see J. W. Niemeijer, "De kunstverzameling van John Hope (1737–1784)," in *Nederlands Kunsthistorisch Jaarboek* 32 (1980): 127–226.

6. *Herinneringen*, p. 32.

7. Jonathan Scott, *Piranesi* (New York: St. Martin's Press, 1975), p. 317.

8. *Herinneringen*, p. 167.

9. Scott, p. 242.

10. Ibid.

11. Alexis de Krüdener, *Voyage en Italie en 1786* (Paris: Fischbacher, 1983), p. 129. Citation translated from the French.

12. Scott, p. 341.

13. John Wilton-Ely, *Piranesi, Paestum & Soane* (London: Azimuth, 2002), p. 13.

14. Scott, p. 317, n. 18.

15. "C'est chez lui un marché continuel où l'on est fâché de voir sans cesse le talent doublement dégradé par une avidité à la fois âpre & mesquine." Quoted from Jonathan Scott, "Some sculptures from Hadrian'sVilla, Tivoli," in *Piranesi e la cultura antiquarian* (Rome, 1983): 339.

16. Scott, p. 226.

17. Letter from Vanvitelli to his brother, dated October 25, 1766; cited by Alvar González-Palacios, *Il tempi del gusto* (Vicenza: Neri Pozza, 2000): 105.

18. Quoted from John Brewer, *The Pleasures of the Imagination* (New York: Farrar, Straus & Giroux, 1997), p. 207.

DRAWING FROM PIRANESI

1. In 1960, I won the Rome Prize and spent two years in residence as a Fellow at the American Academy. I have been a Trustee of the Academy since 1981 and have returned to Rome many times. During my Fellowship in the 1960s, I made hundreds of drawings of buildings, experimenting with various media, from large ink washes to delicate pencil sketches on clay-coated paper, based on what I was trying to document. A selection of those drawings has recently been published in *Michael Graves, Images of a Grand Tour* by Brian M. Ambroziak (New York: Princeton Architectural Press, 2005).

2. This curious view also reminds us that the ancients had no problem making an adjectival addition, such as a rectilinear porch, to the more dominant object behind, the great rotunda. This device was used repeatedly at the time. In today's modernism, the collision of those two objects would be viewed as unwelcome.

3. It is interesting to note that Corot shows the Abruzzi Hills beyond. It would be hard to see the hills from the city, except possibly in December.

SELECTED BIBLIOGRAPHY

FOR A COMPLETE LIST OF PIRANESI'S PUBLISHED WORKS, SEE:

Focillon, Henri. *Giovanni-Battista Piranesi: Essai de catalogue raisonné de son oeuvre.* Paris: Librairie Renouard/Henri Laurens, 1918.

Accademia di Francia (Rome, Italy). *Piranèse et les Français, 1740–1790* (exhibition catalogue). Rome: Edizioni Dell'Elefante, 1976.

Avery Library, Lois Katz, and Jessica Berman. *Piranesi: Drawings and Etchings at the Avery Architectural Library, Columbia University, New York.* New York: Arthur M. Sackler Foundation, 1975.

Barry, Fabio. "Rinovare, anziché ristorare: Piranesi as Architect." In *The Rome of Piranesi*, edited by Mario Bevilacqua and Mario Gori Sassoli, 91–111. Rome: Museo del Corso, 2006.

Bassi, Elena. *Architettura del Sei e Settecento a Venezia.* Naples: Edizioni scientifiche italiane, 1962.

Battaglia, R. "Le 'Diverse maniere d'adornare I cammini…' di Giovanni Battista Piranesi. Gusto e cultura antiquarian." In *Saggi e memorie di Storia dell'arte* 19, 191–273. Florence: L. S. Olschki, 1994.

Bettagno, Alessandro. *Piranesi tra Venezia e l'Europa.* Civiltà veneziana, 29. Florence: L. S. Olschki, 1983.

Bettagno, Alessandro, and Rodolfo Pallucchini. *Disegni di Giambattista Piranesi.* Cataloghi di mostre, 41. Vicenza: Neri Pozza, 1978.

Bevilacqua, Mario. *Nolli vasi piranesi: imagine di Roma antica e moderna: rappresentare e conoscere la metropoli dei lumi.* Rome: Artenude, 2004.

Bevilacqua, Mario, Heather Hyde Minor, and Fabio Barry. *The Serpent and the Stylus: Essays on G. B. Piranesi.* Ann Arbor: University of Michigan Press, 2006.

Bevilacqua, Mario, and Mario Gori Sassoli. *La Roma di Piranesi: la città del Settecento nelle grandi vedute.* Rome: Artemide, 2006.

Bianconi, Giovanni Lodovico. "Elogio storico del cavaliere Giambattista Piranesi (1778)," 1802. In *Opere* 2: 133–34.

Bloomer, Jennifer. *Architecture and the Text: The (S)cripts of Joyce and Piranesi.* New Haven: Yale University Press, 1993.

Borsi, Franco, ed. *Giovanni Battista Piranesi. Il Campo Marzio dell'Antica Roma. I'inventario dei beni del 1778.* Rome, 1972.

Braham, Allan. *The Architecture of the French Enlightenment.* Berkeley: University of California Press, 1980.

British Museum. *Giovanni Battista Piranesi, His Predecessors and His Heritage* (exhibition catalogue). London: British Museum, 1968.

Brunel, Georges. *Piranèse et les Français: colloque tenu à la Villa Médicis, 12–14 mai 1976.* Rome: Edizioni dell'Elefante, 1978.

Calcografia nazionale (Italy) and Maurizio Calvesi. *Giovanni Battista e Francesco Piranesi.* [Mostra] 1967–68. 1967.

Calvesi, Maurizio. "Nota ai 'grotteschi' o capricci di Piranesi." In *Piranesi e la cultura antiquaria, gli antecedenti e il contesto: atti del convegno, 14–17 novembre 1979* (a cura di A. Lo Bianco), 135–40. Rome: Multigrafica, 1983.

Coen, Paolo. *Le magnificenze di Roma nelle incisioni di Giuseppe Vasi: un affascinante viaggio settecentesco dalle Mura Aureliane fino alle maestose ville patrizie, attraverso le antiche rovine, le basiliche e le più belle piazze della Città Eterna.* Quest'Italia, 235. Rome: Newton & Compton, 1996.

Contardi, B. "Piranesi in Campidoglio." In *700 disegnatore. Incisioni, progetti, caricature* (edited by E. Debenedetti), 161–81. Rome: Bonsignori, 1997.

Curl, James Stevens. *The Egyptian Revival: An Introductory Study of a Recurring Theme in the History of Taste.* London: G. Allen & Unwin, 1982.

Dal Co, Francesco. "G. B. Piranesi, 1720–1778. La malincolia del libertino." In *Storia dell'architettura italiana. Il Settecento*, vol. 2, edited by Giovanni Curcio and Elisabeth Kieven. Milan, 2000: pp. 580–613.

Dal Co, Francesco and Juan José. *Piranesi.* Barcelona: Mudito & Co., 2006.

Debenedetti, Elisa. *Giovanni Battista Piranesi: la raccolta di stampe della Biblioteca Fardelliana.* Trapani: Corrao, 1996.

Denison, Cara D., Myra Nan Rosenfeld, and Stephanie Wiles. *Exploring Rome: Piranesi and His Contemporaries.* New York: Pierpont Morgan Library, 1993.

Dixon, Susan M. "Giovanni Battista Piranesi's *Diverse maniere d'adornare i cammini* and Chimneypiece Design as a Vehicle of Polemic." In *Studies in the Decorative Arts* 1 (1983), no. 1: 76–98.

Ficacci, Luigi, Bradley Baker Dick, Verena Listl, Isabelle Baraton. *Giovanni Battista Piranesi: Selected Etchings.* New York: Taschen, 2001.

Fischer, M. "Die Umbaupläne des G. B. Piranesi für Chor von S. Giovanni in Laterano, Rom." In *Münchner Jahrbuch der Bildenden Kunst* 18 (1968): 207–26.

———. "Piranesi's Projekte für den Neubau des Chores von S. Giovanni in Laterano." In *Kunstochronik* 21 (1968), no. 12: 378 ff.

Fleming, John. *Robert Adam and His Circle, in Edinburgh & Rome.* London: J. Murray, 1962.

Furlan, C. "Matteo Lucchesi." In *Arte Veneta* 25 (1971): 292 ff.

Gasparri, C. "Una fontana ritrovata. Ancora su Piranesi a Villa Albani." In *Artisti e Mecenati: Dipinti, disegni, sculture e carteggi nella Roma curiale* (a cura di Elisa Debenedetti), 193-206. Rome: Bonsignori, 1996.

Ghersi, L. Finocchi. "Piranesi architetto. La formazione venezia e I progetti romani." In *Antonio Canova e il suo ambiente artistico fra Venezia, Roma e Parigi* (a cura di G. Pavanello), 193–208. Venice: Instituto Veneto di scienze lettere ed arti, 2000.

González-Palacios, Alvar. *Il tempio del gusto: Roma e il Regno delle Due Sicilie: le arti decorative in Italia fra classicismi e barocco.* Milan: Longanesi, 1984.

"Piranesi and Sir Roger Newdigate." In *The Burlington Magazine*, 114 (1972), no. 835: 716–19.

———. "Un orologio per i Rezzonico." In *Sculture romane del Settecento: la professione dello scultore* (edited by Elisa Debenedetti), 123–35. Rome: Bonsignori, 2001.

Gasparri, C. "Piranesi a Villa Albani." In *Committenze della famiglia Albani. Note sulla Villa Albani Torlonia* (a cura di Elisa Debenedetti), 211–23. Rome: Multigrafica, 1985.

Gavuzzo-Stewart, Silvia. *Nelle Carceri di G.B. Piranesi.* Italian perspectives 2. Leeds: Northern Universities Press, 1999.

Hind, Arthur M. *Giovanni Battista Piranesi: A Critical Study with a List of His Published Works and Detailed Catalogues of the Prisons and Views of Rome.* London: Phaidon, 1967.

Howard, Seymour. "An Antiquarian Handlist and the Beginnings of the Pio Clementino." In *Antiquity Restored. Essays on the Afterlife of the Antique*, 142–153, 274, n. 52. Vienna: IRSA, 1990.

Jatta, Barbara. *Piranesi e l'Aventino.* Milan: Electa, 1998.

Kantor-Kazovsky, Lola. *Piranesi as interpreter of Roman Architecture and the Origins of His Intellectual World.* Florence: L. S. Olschki, 2006.

Kaufmann, Edgar. "Piranesi, Algarotti and Lodoli. A controversy in 18th-century Venice." In *Gazette des Beaux-Arts* 46 (1955): 21–28.

Keller, Luzius. *Piranèse et les Romantiques français: Le mythe des escaliers en spirale.* Paris: José Corti, 1966.

Kennedy, J. "Life of the Chevalier Giovanni Battista Piranesi. 7 August 1831." In *Library of the Fine Arts or Repertory of Painting, Sculpture, Architecture and Engraving* 2, 8–13.

Kieven, Elisabeth, and Joseph Connors. *Von Bernini bis Piranesi: römische Architekturzeichnungen des Barock.* Stuttgart: Hatje, 1993.

Kimball, Fiske. "Piranesi, Algarotti and Lodoli." In *Essays in Honour of Hans Tietze.*

New York, 1958: 309–16.

Körte, Werner. "Giovanni Battista Piranesi als praktischer Architekt." In *Zeitschrift für Kunstgeschichte* 2 (1958): 16–33.

Laroque, D., and B. Saint Girons. "Piranèse et l'archéologie des Lumières." In *Hadrien, empereur et achitecte. La Villa Hadrien: tradition et modernité d'un paysage culturel, atti del Convegno Internazionale di Studi* (Paris, 1999, edited by M. Mosser & H. Lavagne). Geneva, 2002: 107–20.

Lewis, D. "Matteo Lucchesi." In *Bolletino dei Musei Civici Veneziani* 2 (1967): 17–48.

Lo Bianco, Anna. *Piranesi e la cultura antiquaria: gli antecedenti e il contesto : atti del convegno, 14–17 novembre 1979*. Rome: Multigrafica, 1985.

Lütgens, Annelie. *Giovanni Battista Piranesi: Bilder von Orten und Raümen*. Stuttgart: G. Hatje, 1994.

Maclaren, Sarah Fiona. *La magnificenza e il suo doppio: il pensiero estetico di Giovanni Battista Piranesi*. Collana Morfologie. Milan: Mimesis, 2005.

McCarthy, Michael. "Sir Roger Newdigate: Some Piranesian Drawings." In *The Burlington Magazine* 120 (1978), no. 907: 671–74.

——. "Thomas Pitt, Piranesi and Sir John Soane: English Architects in Italy in the 1770s." In *Apollo* 134 (1991): 380–86.

McCormick, Thomas J. *Charles-Louis Clérisseau and the Genesis of Neoclassicism*. New York: Architectural History Foundation, 1990.

MacDonald, William Lloyd. *Piranesi's Carceri: Sources of Invention*. Northampton: Smith College, 1979.

Marks, Richard, and Brian J. R. Blench. *The Warwick Vase*. Glasgow: Burrell Collection, 1979.

Mayor, A. Hyatt. *Giovanni Battista Piranesi*. New York: H. Bittner, 1952.

Mazzi, Giuliana, and Stefano Zaggia. *Architetto sia l'ingegniero che discorre: ingegneri, architetti e proti nell'età della Repubblica*. Venice: Marsilio, 2004.

Miller, Norbert. *Archäologie des Traums. Versuch über Giovanni Battista Piranesi*. Munich: Hanser Verlag, 1978.

Minor, Heather Hyde. "Rejecting Piranesi." In *The Burlington Magazine* 143 (2001), no. 1180: 412–19.

de Montaiglon, Anatole. *Correspondance des Directeurs de l'Académie de France à Rome*. Paris, 1901.

Murray, Peter. *Piranesi and the Grandeur of Ancient Rome (Walter Neurath Memorial Lectures)*, 3rd ed. London: Thames and Hudson, 1971.

Nyberg, Dorothea, and H. Mitchell, eds., *Giovanni Battista Piranesi, Drawings and Etchings at Columbia University*. New York, 1972.

Panza, Pierluigi. *Piranesi architetto*. Milan: Guerini studio, 1998.

Penny, Nicholas. *Piranesi*. London: Oresko, 1978.

Pietrangeli, Carlo. "La Sala Nuova di Don Abbondio Rezzonico." In *Capitolium* 38 (1963): 244–46.

——. 1954. "Sull'iconografia di G. B. Piranesi." In *Bolletino dei Musei Comunali di Roma* I (1954), nos. 3 and 4: 40-43.

Pinto, John A. "Forma Urbis Romae: Fragment and Fantasy." In *Architectural Studies in Memory of Richard Krautheimer*, edited by Cecil Striker. Mainz, 1994: pp. 143–46.

Piranesi, Giovanni Battista. *Piranesi (exhibition catalogue)*. Northampton: Smith College Museum of Art, 1961.

Pontrandolfo, A. "Paestum and Its Archaeological History." In *Paestum and the Doric Revival, 1750-1830: Essential Outlines of an Approach: New York, National Academy of Design: February 19–March 30, 1986*, 51–55. Florence: Centro Di, 1986.

Reudenbach, Bruno. *G. B. Piranesi, Architektur als Bild: der Wandel in der Architekturauffassung des achtzehnten Jahrhunderts*. München: Prestel-Verlag, 1979.

Resch, Raffaella, and Domenico Pertocoli. *Piranesi: antichità romane, vedute di Roma: opere della Fondazione Antonio Mazzota*. Milan: Mazzotta, 2000.

Rieder, William. "Piranesi at Gorhambury." In *The Burlington Magazine* 107 (1975): 582–91.

——. "Piranesi's *Diverse Maniere*." In *The Burlington Magazine* 115 (1973), no. 842: 308–17.

Rimondino, G. "Il carteggio tra Giovanni Bianchi e Tommaso Temanza in occasione della redazione dell'opera *Delle Antchità di Rimino*, 1735–42."

In T. Temanza, *Delle Antichità di Rimino* (edited by G. Rimondino), Venice: G. Pasquaili, 1997.

——. "Giovanni Battista Piranesi." In *The Glory of Venice: Art in the Eighteenth Century*, edited by Jan Martineau and Andrew Robison. New Haven: Yale University Press, 1994.

Robison, Andrew. *Piranesi—Early Architectural Fantasies: A Catalogue Raisonné of the Etchings*. Chicago: University of Chicago Press, 1997.

Rowan, A. "Weddeburn Castle, Berwickshire." In *Country Life* 46 (1974): 356.

Rykwert, Joseph. *The First Moderns: The Architects of the Eighteenth Century*. Cambridge, MA: MIT Press, 1980.

Sade, Maurice Lever, and Jean-Baptiste Tierce. *Voyage d'Italie, ou Dissertations critiques, historiques et philosophiques sur les villes de Florence, Rome, Naples, Lorette et les routes adjacentes à ces quatre villes*. Paris: Fayard, 1995.

Scott, Jonathan. *Piranesi*. London: Academy Editions, 1975.

——. "Another Chimney Piece by Piranesi." In Alessandro Bettagno, ed., *Piranesi tra Venezia e l'Europa*, 51–57. Proceedings, Fondazione Giorgio Cini, Venice, October 13–15, 1978. Florence: L. S. Olschki, 1983.

Sørensen, Bent. "An Unpublished Project by Piranesi for Clement XIII." In *The Burlington Magazine* 142 (2000), no. 1169: 497–501.

Stampfle, Felice. *Giovanni Battista Piranesi: Drawings in the Pierpont Morgan Library*. New York: Dover Publications in association with the Pierpont Morgan Library, 1978.

Stillman, Damie. "Chimney-Pieces for English Market: A Thriving Business in Late Eighteenth-century Rome." In *The Art Bulletin* 59 (1977), no. 1: 85–94.

——. "Robert Adam and Piranesi." In *Essays in the History of Architecture Presented to Rudolf Wittkower*, edited by Douglas Fraser, Howard Hibbard, and Milton J. Lewine, 197–206. London: Phaidon, 1967.

Strazzullo, F. *Le lettere di Luigi Vanvitelli, nella Biblioteca palatina di Caserta*. Galatina, 1976.

Tafuri, Manfredo. "Il complesso di S. Maria del Priorato sull'Aventino: Furor analiticus." In *Piranesi, Incisioni, rami, legature, architetture* (a cura di Alessandro Bettagno, 77–87. Vicenza: N. Pozza, 1978.

——. *The Sphere and the Labyrinth: Avant-gardes and Architecture from Piranesi to the 1970s*. Cambridge, MA: MIT Press, 1987.

Thomas, Hylton. *The Drawings of Piranesi*. London: Faber and Faber, 1954.

Vogt-Göknil, Ulya. *Giovanni Battista Piranesi: Carceri*. Zürich: Origo Verlag, 1958.

von Höper, Corinna. "Die 'Legende zum Bild'—Über das verhältnis von Schrift und Darstellung in den Radierungen Piranesis." In *Akten des internationalen Symposiums, Stuttgart, Staatsgalerie, June, 25–26, 1999* (edited by C. von Höper, J. Stoschek, E. Kieven), 2002: 9–20.

von Höper, Corinna, Jeannette Stoschek, and Elisabeth Kieven. *Giovanni Battista Piranesi: Die Wahrnehmung von Raum und Zeit*. Marburg: Jonas Verlag, 2002.

Volkmann, Hans. *Giovanni Baptista Piranesi, Architekt und Graphiker*. Berlin, 1965.

Wendorf, Richard. *Piranesi's Double Ruin. Boston Athenaeum Occasional Papers*, no. 2. Boston: Boston Athenaeum, 2001.

Wilton-Ely, John. "Antiquity Applied: Piranesi, Clérisseau and the Adam Brothers." In *Bulletin de l'Association des Historiens d'Art Italien* 2 (1996): 15–24.

——. "A bust of Piranesi by Nollekens." In *The Burlington Magazine* 118 (1976), no. 881: 593–95 .

——. *Giovanni Battista Piranesi: The Complete Etchings*, 2 vols. San Francisco: Alan Wofsy Fine Arts, 1994.

——. *Giovanni Battista Piranesi: Vision und Werk*. Munich: Hirmer, 1978.

——. "Ledoux et Piranèse: Spéculation et Communication." In *Claude Nicolas Ledoux et le livre d'architecture en français. Étienne Louis Boullée. L'utopie et la poésie de l'art, actes du Colloque International d'Histoire de l'Art, Paris, Bibliothèque Nationale de France, 3–4 décembre 2004* (edited by D. Rabreau and D. Massounie): 110–19. Paris: Monum, Editions du Patrimoine, 2006.

——. *The Mind and Art of Giovanni Battista Piranesi*. London: Thames and Hudson, 1988.

——. "Nature and Antiquity: Reflections on Piranesi as a Furniture Designer." In *Furniture History* 26 (1990): 191–97.

——. *Observations on the Letter of Monsieur Mariette: With Opinions on Architecture, and a Preface to a New Treatise on the Introduction and Progress of the Fine Arts in Europe in*

Ancient Times. Texts and documents. Los Angeles: Getty Research Institute, 2002. Introduction.

——. *Piranèse: Les vues de Rome: Les prisons.* Paris: Arts et Métiers Graphiques, 1979.

Piranèse as Architect and Designer. New York: Pierpont Morgan Library, 1993.

Piranèse: Catalogue. London: Arts Council of Great Britain, 1978.

Piranèse, Paestum & Soane. London: Azimuth, 2002.

——. "Piranesian Symbols on the Aventine." In *Apollo* 103 (1976): 214–27.

——. *The polemical Works.* Westmead: Gregg, 1972.

——. "Sognare il Sublime: l'influenza di Piranesi e della scuola sul Grand Tour." In *Grand Tour. Viaggi narrati e dipinti* (a cura di Caesare de Seta), 106–18. Naples: Electa Napoli, 2001.

——. "The Relationship between Giambattista Piranesi and Luigi Vanvitelli in 18th-century Architectural Theory and Practice." In *Vanvitelli e il '700 europeo: congresso internazionale di studi: atti,* 83–99. Naples: Istituto di storia dell'architettura, Università di Napoli, 1979.

Wilton-Ely, John, Augustino Roca De Amicis, and Giovanni Battista Piranesi. *Piranesi.* Milan: Electa, 1994.

Wilton-Ely, John, and Joseph Connors. *Piranesi architetto: Roma, 15 maggio–5 luglio 1992, American Academy in Rome.* Rome: Edizioni dell'Elefante, 1992.

Wittkower, Rudolf. "Piranesi's Parere su l'architettura." In *Journal of the Warburg Institute* 2 (1938.), no. 2: 147–58.

——. *Studies in the Italian Baroque.* Boulder: Westview Press, 1975.

Wittkower, Rudolf, Douglas Fraser, Howard Hibbard, and Milton J. Lewine. *Essays in the History of Architecture Presented to Rudolf Wittkower.* London: Phaidon, 1967.

Wolf, Norbert. *Giovanni Battista Piranesi, Der Römische Circus: die Arena als Weltsymbol.* Kunststück. Frankfurt: Fischer Taschenbuch Verlag, 1997.

SELECTED INDEX

Academy of the Arcadians, 18

Accademia Clementina, 207, 348

Accademia di San Luca, 34, 256, 329

Adam, James, 330

Adam, Robert, 23, 24, 27, 29, 36, 84,
    87, 97, 226, 265, 307, 310, 313, 329,
    330, 341, 342, 343, 349, 350, 351

Albacini, Carlo, 256

Albani, Cardinal Alessandro,
    and Villa, 26, 84, 85, 95, 262,
    265, 313, 329, 345, 351

Alberti, Leon Battista, 305

Alexander I, Czar, 227

Alexander Severus (Alessandro
    Severo), 128, 130, 306

Antonine Column, 223, 330

Aphrodite Anadyomene, relic of, 244

Artois, Comte (Count) d', 232, 342, 350

Ashmolean Museum, 81, 256, 330, 335,
    347, 355

Asprucci, Antonio, 226, 235

Bader, Herman, 244

Bagatelle, Pavilion of, 59, 232, 332,
    336, 342, 350

Bali de Breteuil, Ambassador
    of Malta, 222

Barberini, 229

Barnard, Edward, 79, 81, 227, 333

Barry, James, 64, 256, 342

Barthélémy, Jean-Jacques, Abbé
    (Voyage of the Young Anacharsis),
    134–36, 346

Bartoli, Pietro Santi, 210, 212, 213, 216,
    218, 349

Batoni, Pompeo, 232, 233, 350

Bélanger, François-Joseph, 56, 59, 63,
    230, 232, 342, 350

Benedict XIV, Pope, 34, 226, 328,
    348, 351

Bernini, Giovanni Lorenzo, 14, 67, 104

Bernis, Cardinal de, 244

Bianchini, Francesco, 127

Bianconi, Carlo, 242

Bibiena, Ferdinando, 32, 139, 205,
    206–09

Bibiena, Francesco, 207, 208, 348

Bibiena, Giuseppe (Architettura e
    prospettive, Bazajet), 139, 208, 328

Biljoen Castle, 244, 246–48, 350

Blondel, Jacques-François, 24

Boccapaduli, Marchesa Margherita
    Gentili, 220–22, 349, 350

Boncompagni Ludivisi, 224

Borghese, Prince Marcantonio,
    and Villa, 46, 226, 234, 235,
    238, 349, 350

Borromini, Francesco, 18, 26, 36, 37,
    39, 52, 64, 67, 90, 97, 104, 172, 173,
    175, 180, 185, 188, 190, 196, 199,
    201, 341, 348

Boschetti, B., 227, 350

Boschi, Giuseppe, 227, 350

Bracciolini, Poggio, 124

Braschi, Giovan Angelo, Duke of,
    Pope Puis VI, 233, 234, 330

British Regency, 65, 75, 79, 89, 229,
    328, 342

Brocklesby Park, Lincolnshire, 227

Brongniart, Théodore, 227

Brunelleschi, Filippo, 124, 132

Buffalino, 301

Burckhardt, Jacob, 124, 137

Burns, Howard, 125, 346

Buzard, Giovanni, 162

Byres, James, 255

Caecilia Metella, 130, 132, 244

Caetani, family and Palazzo, 226, 235,
    239, 349, 350

Caffè degli Inglesi, 60, 63, 227, 350

Callot, Jacques, 140

Campagnola, Domenico and Giulio,
    141

Camper, Adriaan Gillis, 242

Campidoglio (Capitoline Hill), 34, 58,
    73, 224, 271, 273, 277, 278, 330, 342

Campo Vaccino, 224, 262, 267

Camporese, Pietro, 234

Canaletto, Antonio, 14, 141, 204, 328

Canova, Antonio, 40, 230, 341, 348

Capitoline Museum, 226, 350

capriccio, 11, 14, 15, 18, 28, 63, 98, 142,
    159, 162, 169, 242, 340, 344, 351

Cardelli, Lorenzo, 225, 226, 256, 349

Cartoni, Filippo and Nicola, 224

Caserta, Duke of, 235, 352

Castel Gandolfo, 111

Castiglione, Giovanni Benedetto,
    15, 140, 151

Cavaceppi, Bartolomeo, 77, 79, 165,
    256, 257

Caylus, Comte de (Recueil d'antiquités
    égyptiennes, étrusques, grecques,
    romaines, et gauloises), 60, 123, 128

Challe, Charles Michel-Ange, 17, 340

Chambers, William, 23, 24, 25, 210,
    329, 341, 344

Chardin, Jean-Baptiste-Siméon
    (Le singe antiquaire), 122, 124

Charlemont, Lord, 25, 26, 97, 329,
    341, 344

Cicero, 97, 98

Clement XIV, Pope, 234, 237, 330

Clérisseau, Charles-Louis, 24, 222, 307,
    329, 341, 349, 351

Colonna, Francesco (Hypnerotomachia
    Poliphilii), 14, 125, 126

Colosseum, 14, 22, 255, 290, 291, 303

Connolly, Caroline, Duchess
    of Buckingham, 244

Contardi, Bruno, 224, 342, 348,
    349, 351

Cyriac of Ancona, 125, 126, 127, 346

David, Jacques-Louis, Sorrow
    of Andromache (Douleur
    d'Andromaque), 227, 228

Della Bella, Stefano, 140

Didascalo, 28, 103–05

Diderot, Denis (L'Encyclopédie, ou
    Dictionnaire raisonné des sciences, des
    arts et des métiers…), 123, 329, 346

Dixon, Susan, 127, 133, 342, 345, 346,
    351

Dugourc, Jean-Démosthène, 59, 232

Dürer, Albrecht, 141

Edison, Thomas, 123

Egypt and Egyptian style, 8, 11, 28,
    53, 54, 60–67, 76, 98, 100, 106–11,
    114–16, 128–21, 128, 157, 221, 252,
    312, 314, 315, 330, 344, 345, 346,
    349, 351

Elswout, 243–44

Emes, Rebecca, 79, 80, 227

Erlach, Johann Bernard Fischer von
    (Entwurff einer Historischen
    Architekur), 98, 99, 127, 157, 328,
    347, 349

Etruscan, 8, 11, 13, 26, 27, 28, 31, 42, 43,
    46, 49, 54, 59, 62, 66, 95, 101, 103,
    106, 110, 114–18, 121, 216, 313, 330,
    342, 344–46

European Enlightenment, 11, 14, 22,
    121, 328, 343, 344, 351

Fagel, Hendrik, the Elder, 242

Fagel, Hendrik, the Younger, 243

Feltrini, Rocco, 224

Flaubert, Gustave, 135

Focillon, Henri, 126, 233, 342, 345,
    346, 348, 349, 351

Foscarini, Marco, 14, 143, 328, 340

Franzoni, Francesco Antonio, 225,
    256, 349, 350

Freddi, Nicola, 235, 239, 350

French Academy in Rome, 15, 17, 23,
    172, 207, 210, 328, 329, 340, 341,
    342, 346, 352

Freud, Sigmund, 125, 346

Furietti, Cardinal, 226

Gibbon, Edward, 134, 330

Giobbe, Nicola, 15, 94, 143, 328, 344

Goethe, Johann Wolfgang von, 243

Graeco-Roman debate, 11, 26, 33, 61,
    103, 116, 329, 341, 344

Grafton, Anthony, 125, 346

Grand Tour, 14, 56, 63, 79, 143, 241–67,
    269, 328, 330, 340, 350, 353

Grandjacquet, Antonio Guglielmo,
    225, 256, 349

Greece and Greek style, 8, 13, 26–28,
    34, 54, 65, 66, 95–98, 100, 101,
    103, 106, 107, 110, 115, 116, 118,
    121, 208, 216, 284, 329, 330, 341,
    344, 346

Grespi, Giovanni, 234, 237, 350

Groenendaal, 252

Gualtieri Collection, 222

Guardi, Francesco, 169, 340

Guercino, 164, 165, 329, 347

Gustav III, King of Sweden, 84, 227,
    267, 343

Haarlem, 3, 8, 255, 306, 331, 337, 358,
    359, 360

Hadrian, Emperor, and Villa, 22, 78,
    79, 97, 114, 252, 255, 291, 293, 328,
    330, 340, 343, 350

Hamilton, Gavin, 79, 256, 330

Hamilton, Sir William, 59, 79, 216,
    244, 256, 330

Herculaneum, 17, 71, 328, 340

Hochepied, D. J. de, 262

Holland, Henry, 229

Hollis, Thomas, 63, 114

Hope, Henry, 255

Hope, John, 56, 57, 58, 250, 252, 253,
    255, 342, 350

Hope, Thomas, 65, 66, 67, 75–77, 229,
    250, 251, 252, 342, 343

Ingres, Jean-Auguste-Dominique, 227,
    229, 270, 273, 295, 296, 350

Iolli, Antonio, 208, 348

Jenkins, Thomas, 255, 256, 342

Johannes, Gerrit, Baron de
    Hochepied, 242, 258, 262

Juvarra, Filippo, 14, 32, 207, 216, 328,
    340, 349

Kantor-Kazovsky, Lola, 126, 134, 341,
    345, 346, 351

Koetter, Fred, 301

Koolhaas, Rem, 305

Krier, Leon, 297, 301

Krudemer, Baron de, 256

La Platière, Roland de, 259

Lady Lever Gallery, Port Sunlight, 252

Landucci, Antonio, 235, 238, 350

Latium, villas of, 97

Laugier, Marc-Antoine (*Essai sur L'Architecture*), 26–28, 31, 36, 95, 96, 341, 344

Lavallée-Poussin, Etienne, 222

Le Lorrain, Louis-Joseph, 17

Le Roy, Julien-David (*Les ruines des plus beaux monuments de la Grèce*), 26, 27, 95, 106, 107, 329, 341, 344, 345

Leeuw, Derk de, 244

Legrand, J.-G. (*Notice Historique sur la vie et les ouvrages de G. B. Piranèse*), 162, 165, 205, 221, 222, 223, 225, 259, 341, 347, 348, 349

Leto, Pomponio, 125

Ligorio, Pirro, 15, 42, 125–29, 346, 349

Longhena, Baldessare, 18, 37

Luchesi, Laura, 328

Lucchesi, Matteo, 13, 328, 340, 351, 352

Ludovisi, Ippolita Boncompagni, 224

Machy, Pierre-Antoine de, 213

Maffei, Scipione, 208, 340

Magistrato delle Acque, 13, 328, 340

Malta, Order of and Priory Church, 40, 41, 42, 44, 52, 111, 201, 223, 242, 329, 330, 342

Mantegna, Andrea, 14

Marcello, Benedetto, 207, 348

Marchis, Carlo Puri de, 224

Marieschi, Michele, 140

Mariette, Pierre-Jean, 28, 101, 329, 341, 344, 352

Mazzi, Vincenzo (*Capricci di carceri tea[trali]*), 213, 215, 349

Meerman, Johan, 241, 250, 255

Mengs, Anton Raphael, 253, 329

Mermion, Shackerly, 123

Metsu, Gabriel, 250

Minneapolis Institute of Arts, 71, 79, 223, 343, 349, 355

Momigliano, Arnaldo, 124, 134, 346

Monfereini, Augusta, 126

Montesquieu, baron de (Charles-Louis de Secondat), 103, 328, 345

Montfaucon, Bernard de, 60, 218, 349

Morgan Library & Museum, 8, 17, 20, 36, 40, 42, 46, 47, 48, 50, 58, 67, 73, 84, 175, 196, 331–39, 340, 341, 342, 346, 347, 348, 351, 352, 353, 359

Morison, Colin, 253

Museo Pio Clementino, 213, 222, 259, 330

Museo (Piranesi's salesroom), 77, 84, 213, 216, 227, 256, 330, 348, 351, 352

National Museum of Antiquities, Leiden, the Netherlands, 244, 250

Neoclassicism, 7, 11, 17, 37, 40, 67, 75, 85, 126, 221, 223, 232, 349, 350, 352

Newdigate, Sir Roger, and Caldelabrum, 81, 82, 216, 227, 256, 330, 343, 351, 352

Nietzsche, Friedrich Wilhelm, 137

Nollekens, Joseph, 77, 256, 329, 343, 352

Nolli, Giovanni Battista, 301–05, 328, 351

Orlandi, Orazio, 244

Osterley Park, 59, 62, 226, 313

Ovid, 106, 345

Paderni, Camillo, 17, 340

Paestum, 266, 267, 268, 280, 281, 330, 343, 352

Palazzo Senatorio, 58, 111, 224–26, 235, 277, 279, 330

Palladio, Andrea, 37, 94, 208, 210

Panini, Giovanni Paolo, 15, 172, 213, 284, 348

Pantheon, 14, 22, 244, 246, 282, 284, 286, 287

Pécheux, Laurent, 220, 221, 223, 349

Peiresc, Nicolas-Claude Fabri de, 123, 124

Percier, Charles, and Pierre-François-Léonard Fontaine (*Recueil des décorations intérieures*), 56, 58, 230, 349, 350

Perrault, Charles, 210

Perrault, Claude, 97, 349

Petitot, Ennemond-Alexandre, 216, 230

Petrarch, 124, 126

Phillips, Mark, 136, 346

Piazza di S. Pietro (St. Peter's), 36, 40, 282, 283, 330

Piazza di Spagna, 34, 60, 234, 328, 330

Piazza Navona, 14, 22, 303

Piranesi, Angelo (Giovanni Battista's father), 13, 328

Piranesi, Angelo (Giovanni Battista's brother), 14

Piranesi, Angelo Domenico (Giovanni Battista's son), 262, 265

Piranesi, Francesco (Giovanni Battista's son), 77, 84, 262, 264, 267, 329, 330, 343, 346, 351

Piranesi, Giovanni Battista

Antichità Romane, Le, 23–26, 92, 95–98, 100, 128–31, 210, 213, 282, 286, 306, 328, 329, 340, 344, 346, 352

Campo Marzio dell'Antica Roma, Il (Campus Martius), 27, 29, 31, 97, 115, 210, 300–05, 329, 341, 344, 345, 351

Carceri d'invenzione, 31–35, 78, 90, 126, 127, 162, 163, 281, 327, 329, 341, 347, 348, 351, 352

Della introduzione e del progresso delle belle arti in Europa ne' tempi antichi, 330

Della Magnificenza ed Architettura de'Romani, 26–28, 45, 46, 53, 95–97, 101, 299, 329, 341

Diverse maniere d'adornare i cammini…, 28, 43, 46, 49, 52–60, 63–66, 71–73, 75, 77, 109-15, 118, 120, 121, 221–24, 226, 232, 235, 253, 256, 310, 314, 330, 341, 343, 345, 346, 351, 352

Grotteschi, 18, 19, 31, 138, 151, 155–59, 169, 328, 340, 347, 351

Invenzioni capric di carceri, 18, 31, 95, 159, 329

Lettere di Giustificazione scritte a Milord Charlemont, 25, 329, 345

Opere varie, 18, 95, 100, 101, 329

Parere su l'architettura, 28, 33, 39, 46, 61, 103–11, 114, 116, 118, 329, 341, 343, 344, 345, 353

Prima parte di architetture e prospettive, 15, 18, 31, 94, 95, 126, 143, 144, 151, 156, 159, 205, 208, 209, 210, 216, 328, 329, 340, 344, 347, 348

Rovine del Castello del'Acqua Giulia, 133, 135, 136, 329

Trofei di Ottaviano Augusto, 91, 97, 329, 345

Vasi, candelabri, cippi, sarcofagi…, 77, 78, 79, 81, 82, 84, 213, 216, 222, 223, 227, 230, 233, 259, 262, 267, 316, 330, 342, 343, 349, 351

Varie Vedute di Roma Antica, e Moderna, 95

Vedute di Roma, 21, 31, 90, 241, 242, 244, 270, 273, 280, 284, 295, 308, 346, 351, 352

Pius VI, Pope, 171

Pius IX, Pope, 227

Polanzani, Francesco (Felice), 12, 13

Pompeii, 71, 262, 263, 328, 330

Poniatowski, Stanislas Augustus, King of Poland, 233, 330

Ponte Molle, 244, 245, 247

Porta Capena, 92, 97, 98, 344, 345

Portland Vase, 256

Poussin, Nicolas (*The Sacraments*), 221

Pyramid of Gaius Cestius, 244

Quirinal (Palazzo Quirinale), 34, 58, 111, 221, 223, 234, 330, 237, 238, 344, 359

Ramsey, Allan, 95, 344

Reiffenstein, Johann Friedrich von, 243

Rembrant van Rijn, 159, 161, 242, 250

Renaissance, 11, 15, 26, 32, 67, 140, 141, 159, 165, 305, 344, 346

Rezzonico, Carlo della Torre, Pope Clement XIII, 27, 28, 36, 40, 46, 58, 71, 77, 109, 172, 175, 180, 185, 188, 196, 223, 242, 329, 330, 341, 342, 345, 348, 352

Rezzonico, Don Abbondio, Senator, 34, 56, 58, 59, 73, 75, 223, 224, 330, 349, 352

Rezzonico, Giovanni Battista, Monsignor and Cardinal, 34, 36, 40, 53, 58, 109, 223, 329, 330, 341

Ricci, Marco, 14, 32, 140, 141, 328

Rienzo, Cola di, 126

Righetti, Francesco, 255, 349

Rijksmuseum, Amsterdam, 3, 5, 8, 54, 70, 71, 223, 252, 265, 337, 360

Ripa, Cesare (*Iconologia*), 234

Robert, Hubert, 165, 222, 329

Robison, Andrew, 119, 120, 165, 216, 306, 340, 341, 344–49, 352, 359

Rococo, 11, 17, 22, 37, 66, 67, 69, 71, 73, 75, 145, 147, 155, 216, 233

Romanticism, 13, 22, 34, 90, 126, 321, 344, 345, 348

Rome, 5, 7, 11, 14–20, 22–27, 31, 34, 36, 37, 40, 43, 44, 48, 49, 50, 52, 54, 60, 75, 84, 85, 94–98, 114, 121, 124, 125, 128, 130, 133, 143, 145, 151, 165, 169, 171–201, 207, 208, 210, 213, 219, 221–24, 226, 229, 230, 232, 235, 241–67, 269, 270, 273, 284, 286, 290, 296, 297, 301–05, 315, 323, 328–30, 340–53, 359

Romney, George, 262

Rosa, Salvator, 15, 140, 151, 169

Rowe, Colin, 301

S. Trinità dei Monti, 222, 328

Sallust (*Bellum Igurthinum*), 107, 345

Salvi, Nicola, 15, 328

San Giovanni in Laterano, 15, 28, 34–40, 46, 47, 52, 81, 111, 171–201, 276, 277, 308, 328, 329, 341, 348, 351

San Romualdo, 235

Santa Cecilia in Trastevere, 230

Santa Maria del Priorato, 28, 40–52, 81, 89, 201, 223, 310, 315, 329, 341, 342, 343, 352

Santa Maria della Salute, 18, 37, 341, 347

Scalfurotto, Giovanni, 31, 328

Scaliger, Joseph, 123

Serlio, Sebastiano (*I Quattro libri del l'architettura*), 97, 216, 345, 349

Servandoni, Giovanni Nicolo, 208, 348, 349

Seven United Provinces, Republic of, 241

Sèvres porcelain, 227, 350

Seznec, Jean, 125, 346

Sirletti, Giovanni, 252

Sixtus V, Pope, 171, 305

Smith, Benjamin, 227

Society of Antiquaries, London, 34, 106, 114, 329

Spanish Steps, 15, 111, 262, 328

Stockholm Royal Palace (Museum), 84, 227, 343

Storr, Paul, 227

Strada Novissima, 301

Tanaglia of Vitruvius, 132

Tatham, Charles Heathcote, 229

Temanza, Tommaso, 13, 348, 352

Temple of Jupiter Stator, 262

Temple of the Sybil, 244

Theater of Marcellus, 96, 213, 214

Theodore, Elector Karl, 233

Thomas, Hylton, 17, 340, 346, 352

Tiber River, 46, 303

Tiepolo, Giovanni Battista (*Scherzi di Fantasia, Vari Capricci*), 17, 31, 141, 143, 145, 150, 151, 152, 157, 159, 169, 328, 340, 347, 348

Toledo Museum, 227

Trajan Column, 223, 330

Trevi Fountain, 15, 328, 329

Ungers, Mathias, 305

Valadier, Luigi, 233, 234, 350

Valeriani, Giuseppe and brothers, 14,
205, 208, 209, 211, 328, 348

Vanvitelli, Luigi, 172, 259, 350, 352,
353

Vasari, Giorgio, 124, 347

Vasi, Giuseppe (*Le Magnificenze di
Roma*), 15, 143, 145, 159, 328, 340,
347, 351

Vatican, 58, 60, 229, 260, 328, 330, 341,
342, 359

Veduta, 14, 15, 17, 20–23, 26, 27, 129,
142, 143, 169, 244, 328, 329, 340

Venice, 11, 13, 14, 17, 18, 31, 141, 143, 145,
151, 205, 208, 223, 301, 328, 340,
346, 347, 351, 352

Venus Pudica, 253

Vermeer, Jan, 250

Via Appia (Appian Way), 97, 98, 128,
129, 316, 345

Vinci, Leonardo da, 162, 165, 169, 347

Vitruvius, 23, 26, 96, 97, 130, 132, 205,
207, 208, 210, 346, 348

Vosmaer, Aernout, 255, 256, 262, 263,
264, 359

Wagner, Joseph, 17, 328

Wales, Frederick, Prince of, 25, 229

Walpole, Horatio, 219, 349

Walter, Edward, 267

Warwick Vase, 78, 79, 227, 256, 258,
330, 343, 350, 352

Watteau, Jean-Antoine, 169

Wedgwood, Josiah, 213

Welgelegen, 255

Willem, Johan Frederik, Baron van
Spaen, 243, 244, 250, 350

William V, Prince of Orange, 255

Wilton-Ely, John, 4, 9, 10–91, 126, 180,
216, 256, 340 341–53, 359

Winckelmann, Johann Joachim
(*Gedanken über die Nachaghmung der
griechischen Wercke…*), 26, 28, 36,
37, 40, 66, 85, 89, 95, 134, 253,
329, 340, 341, 344, 348

Wolf, Norbert (*Der Römische Circus*),
126, 346, 353

Wyndham, Joseph, 165

Zanetti, Girolamo, 208, 348

Zucchi, Carlo, 14, 328

Compiled by Claire Kenny
and Chul R. Kim

DESIGN FOR A CHIMNEYPIECE
AND CHAIR, n.d.
Pen and brown ink over black
chalk on off-white laid paper

ACKNOWLEDGMENTS

Sarah E. Lawrence and Cooper-Hewitt, National Design Museum would like to thank the following individuals and organizations, listed in no particular order, for their invaluable help and cooperation during the preparation of the *Piranesi as Designer* exhibition and book.

Piranesi as Designer Honorary Advisory Committee:
Esme Usdan, Chair
Barry Bergdoll
Veronica Bulgari
Giovanna d'Andrea
Massimo Ferragamo
Susan Gutfreund
Evelyn Kraus

At Cooper-Hewitt: Communications and Marketing: William Berry, Jennifer Northrop, Laurie Olivieri; Conservation: Lucy Commoner and staff; Development/External Affairs: Caroline Baumann, Bruce Lineker, Anne Shisler-Hughes; Education: Shamus Adams, Caroline Payson, and staff; Exhibitions: Matthew O'Connor, Mathew Weaver; Finance: Chris Jeannopoulos; Image Rights and Reproductions: Jill Bloomer, Annie Chambers; Library: Stephen Van Dyk and staff; Shop: Gregory Krum and staff

Parsons The New School for Design: Amy Azzarito, Claire Kenny

Rijksmuseum, Amsterdam, the Netherlands: Ronald de Leeuw, Director General of the Rijksmuseum and Guest Curator, Hanneke Asselbergs, Reinier Baarsen, Angie Barth, Iskander Breebaart, Charlotte Caspers, Flore Diekstra, Paul van Duin, Anne van Grevenstein, Mischa Janknegt, Elles Kamphuis, Kris Schiermeier, Siebe Tettero, Elsbeth Geldhof

Teylers Museum, Haarlem, the Netherlands: Marjan Scharloo, Director, Hans Gramberg, Celeste Langedijk, Marijke Naber, Fred Pelt, Frank van der Velden

Tsang Seymour Design: Patrick Seymour, Michael Brenner, Susan Brzozowski, Thomas Ryun

Leven Betts Studio: Stella Betts, David Leven, Lucas Echeveste

Lighting Design: Mary Ann Hoag

Peter Krueger Foundation
Connie and Harvey Krueger
Lynne Richards
Artur Ramon Navarro
Cara Denison
Geoffrey Beard
John Pinto
William Rieder
James Lomax
Adam White
Joseph Connors
Robin Middleton
Andrew Robison
Matthew Rutenberg

For more information on the Museum and the exhibition, visit Cooper-Hewitt's Web site, www.cooperhewitt.org.

PHOTOGRAPHIC CREDITS

Cooper-Hewit, National Design Museum is grateful to the organizations and individuals listed below, in no particular order, for their permission to reproduce images in this book. Every effort has been made to trace and contact the copyright holders of the images reproduced; any errors or omissions shall be corrected in subsequent editions. Further information on the images in this publication are provided in the List of Illustrations.

Rijksmuseum, Amsterdam, the Netherlands
Teylers Museum, Haarlem, the Netherlands
The Pierpont Morgan Library, New York
Avery Architectural and Fine Arts Library, Columbia University
John Wilton-Ely
Smithsonian Institution Libraries, Cooper-Hewitt, National Design Museum
Smithsonian Institution Libraries, Dibner Library of the History of Science
    and Technology
Minneapolis Institute of Arts
Arthur Ross Foundation
Sir John Soane's Museum, London
Robison Collection
Michael Graves
Venturi, Scott Brown and Associates, Inc.
Robert A. M. Stern Architects, LLP
Daniel Libeskind
Eisenman Architects
Kunstbibliothek, Berlin
RIBA Library Drawings and Archives Collections
A. C. Cooper
Art Resource, NY
Museo di Roma, Palazzo Braschi
National Gallery of Scotland
Biblioteca Comunale dell'Archiginnasio, Bologna
National Trust for Places of Historic Interest or Natural Beauty
Powerhouse Museum
Victoria and Albert Museum
Gahlin Collection
Royal Pavilion, Library & Museum, Brighton & Hove
Los Angles County Museum of Art

Leeds Art Galleries, Lotherton Hall
Musée des Beaux-Arts, Chartres, France
National Gallery of Art, Washington, D.C.
British Museum, London
Courtauld Institute of Art Gallery, London
CCA
Bildarchiv Preussischer Kulturbesitz/Art Resource, NY/Kunsthalle, Hamburg
Musée du Louvre, Paris
Ashmolean Museum, Oxford
Department of Printing and Graphic Arts, Houghton Library,
    Harvard College Library
Museo Capitolini, Rome
National Gallery of Victoria, Melbourne, Australia
London, Kenwood House
Palazzo del Quirinale
Palazzo Caetani
Istituto Nazionale per la Grafica per gentile concessione
    del Ministero per i Beni e le Attività Culturali
Leiden, Rijksmuseum van Oudheden
London, Marylebone Cricket Club
Vosmaer heirs
Leiden, University Library
Vatican Museums
Fondation Le Corbusier
Artists Rights Society
National Gallery, London
Bibliothèque Nationale de France
J. H. Aronson

MILLER, fig. 1: © Réunion des Musées Nationaux/Art Resource, NY
ROSAND, fig. 18: © Bildarchiv Preussischer Kulturbesitz/Art Resource,
    NY/Kunsthalle, Hamburg
ROSAND, fig. 21: © Musée du Louvre, Paris/Art Resource, NY
GONZALEZ-PALACIOS, fig. 3: © Musée du Louvre, Paris, 1969-1/Art Resource, NY

All photos of works from the Smithsonian Institution and
Smithsonian Institution Libraries are by Matt Flynn, © Smithsonian Institution.

Piranesi as Designer
© 2007 Smithsonian Institution

Published by
Cooper-Hewitt, National Design Museum
Smithsonian Institution
2 East 91st Street
New York, NY 10128, USA
www.cooperhewitt.org

Published on the occasion of the exhibition
Piranesi as Designer
at Cooper-Hewitt, National Design Museum, Smithsonian Institution,
September 14, 2007–January 20, 2008.

Piranesi as Designer is also on view at
The Teylers Museum, Haarlem, the Netherlands,
February 9–May 18, 2008.

Piranesi as Designer is sponsored by Eli Wilner & Company.

The exhibition is made possible in part by The Polonsky Foundation, the Arthur Ross
Foundation, Elise Jaffe + Jeffrey Brown, The Italian Cultural Institute, and Mr. and
Mrs. Frederic A. Sharf. Additional support is provided by The Cowles Charitable Trust.

This publication is made possible in part by The Andrew W. Mellon Foundation.
Additional support is provided by Furthermore: a program of the J. M. Kaplan Fund and
The Felicia Fund.

Distributed to the trade worldwide by Assouline Publishing
601 West 26th Street, 18th floor
New York, NY 10001, USA
www.assouline.com

First edition: September 2007

ISBN: 0-910503-96-6 (HC)

ISBN: 0-910503-95-8 (PB)

Library of Congress CIP data available from the publisher.

Museum Editor: Chul R. Kim, Head of Publications

Image Editors: Floramae McCarron-Cates, Jill Bloomer, Annie Chambers

Design: Tsang Seymour Design, Inc.

Printed in China by Oceanic Graphic Printing.

COVER:
Giovanni Battista Piranesi (Italian, 1720–1778)
PIER TABLE DESIGNED FOR CARDINAL GIOVANNI BATTISTA REZZONICO, ca. 1768
Oak, lime wood, marble, gilt
Courtesy of the Rijksmuseum, Amsterdam, the Netherlands